Transforming the Organization

A Social-Technical Approach

HOWARD W. ODEN

Q

QUORUM BOOKS
Westport, Connecticut • London

Library of Congress Cataloging-in-Publication Data

Oden, Howard W.
  Transforming the organization : a social-technical approach /
Howard W. Oden.
    p. cm.
  Includes bibliographical references and index.
  ISBN 1–56720–226–8 (alk. paper)
  1. Organizational change. I. Title.
HD58.8.O3386 1999
658.4'06—dc21   99–27827

British Library Cataloguing in Publication Data is available.

Library of Congress Catalog Card Number: 99–27827
ISBN: 1–56720–226–8

JK First published in 1999

Quorum Books, 88 Post Road West, Westport, CT 06881
An imprint of Greenwood Publishing Group, Inc.
www.quorumbooks.com

Printed in the United States of America

The paper used in this book complies with the
Permanent Paper Standard issued by the National
Information Standards Organization (Z39.48–1984).

10 9 8 7 6 5 4 3 2 1

Contents

Preface and Introduction ix
    Purpose of the Book ix
    Content of the Book ix
    Features of the Book xiii

I. Initiating Transformation **1**

1. Introducing the Transformation Process 3
    The Situation Facing Today's Organizations 3
    Required Response of Future Organizations 7
    The Nature of Transformational Change 10
    Social-Technical Systems Approach to Transformation 14
    Implementing Transformational Change 17

2. Transformational Leadership 19
    Introduction 19
    Top-Level Preparations and Diagnosis 20
    Planning for Transformation 28
    Implementing Change 33
    Evaluate and Consolidate 38

3. Strategic Planning for Transformation 43
    Introduction 43

Define the Business and Develop the Mission   47
Conduct External Analysis: Develop Value Propositions   49
Conduct Internal Analysis: Develop Competencies   55
Assess External and Internal Analysis: Match Value Propositions and Competencies   61
Develop, Evaluate, and Select Strategies   64
Implement Strategic Plans   65
Evaluate Results   65

4. Transforming the Organizational Culture   67
    Introduction   67
    Cultural Planning   71

5. Organizing and Planning for Transformation   89
    Introduction   89
    Organization Plan   90
    Developing an Action Plan   99
    Executing the Plan   105

II. **Technically Redesigning the Organization**   **109**

6. Introduction to Technical Redesign   111
    The Need for Process Redesign   111
    The Evolution of Process Redesign   114
    The Nature of Process Redesign   116
    Process Mapping and Process Redesign   119
    The IDEF0 Functional Modeling Method   122
    The IDEF3 Process Description Capture Method   128

7. Broad Technical Redesign of the Enterprise   133
    Introduction   133
    Collect and Analyze Information on the Existing Processes of the Enterprise   134
    Collect and Analyze Information on Future Enterprise Processes   136
    Diagnose Future Needs and Develop Enterprise Concept   140
    Select Processes for Improvement   145
    Allocate Process to Project Team for Implementation   151

8. Detailed Technical Redesign of Work Processes   155
    Introduction   155
    Jump Start the Project Redesign Team   156
    Document and Analyze Existing Process   157
    Determine Needs, Outputs, and Applications   159
    Creative Process Redesign   160
    Develop Process Architecture   164
    Conduct Detailed Analysis and Redesign   169
    Synthesize and Document Improved Process   176

9. Information Redesign of Processes   179
    Introduction   179
    The Information Technology Development Process   180
    Design Teams and Information Technology   191
    Information Modeling Methods   193

III. Socially Redesigning the Organization   **201**

10. Introduction to Social Redesign   203
    The Nature of Social Change   203
    Implementing Cultural Change   204
    The Role of Communication in Social Change   215
    Other Change Methods   219

11. Broad Social Redesign of the Organization   223
    Introduction   223
    Document the Existing Organization Structure   223
    Analyze the Existing Organization Structure   226
    Diagnose Future Organization Needs   228
    Develop the Future Organization Concept   234
    Diagnose Human Resource Requirements   241

12. Detailed Social Redesign of the Organization   245
    Introduction   245
    Preparing for the Team-Based Organization   245
    Designing Work Teams   249
    The Networked Organization   253
    Education and Training   258
    Toward Continuous Individual Learning   260
    The Learning Organization   262

13. Redesigning Human Resource Processes   267
    Introduction   267
    A New Role for Human Resources   268
    Recruiting and Selecting Personnel   271
    Performance Measurement and Assessment   274
    Recognition and Reward System   279
    Career Paths and Development   284

IV. Completing the Transformation   **289**

14. Evaluating and Incorporating Redesigned Systems   291
    Diagnose Performance of Redesigned Prototype   291
    Prepare for Incorporation   296
    Update Design of Existing Enterprise System   300
    Incorporate Redesigned Process   304
    Follow-Up Actions   307

15. Integrating the Transformation   309
    Introduction   309
    Integration Through Enlightened Direction Setting   313
    The Integrated Social-Technical Approach   317
    Integration Through Technology   320
    Integration Through Teams   321

Selected Bibliography   327
Index   337

Preface and Introduction

PURPOSE OF THE BOOK

As we approach the 21st century, the pace of change accelerates to an even faster rate. The size and complexity of necessary changes are increasing while the window of opportunity for making the necessary modifications becomes narrower. With changes becoming so fast and so complex, organizations cannot hope to cope by incremental changes. They must undergo a complete and radical change in strategy, culture, structure, and processes. This level of change is called *transformation*.

Since transformations are long and complex efforts, organizations must have some guidance that will enable them to accomplish their transformations effectively and efficiently. Such a book of guidance does not currently exist. Several books on the market purport to provide such a guide, but they simply are not adequate. *The purpose of this book is to fulfill this urgent need.*

CONTENT OF THE BOOK

To achieve this purpose, the book is divided into four parts. Part I covers the action that must be performed prior to initiating transformation. Part II provides guidance in performing the technical aspects of transformation. Part III discusses the social or behavioral aspects of transformation. Part IV delineates what actions are required to complete and integrate all the efforts in the transformation.

Figure I-1 provides a graphical description of the book's contents. A chapter-by-chapter narrative description follows.

Figure I-1
Organization Transformation Process

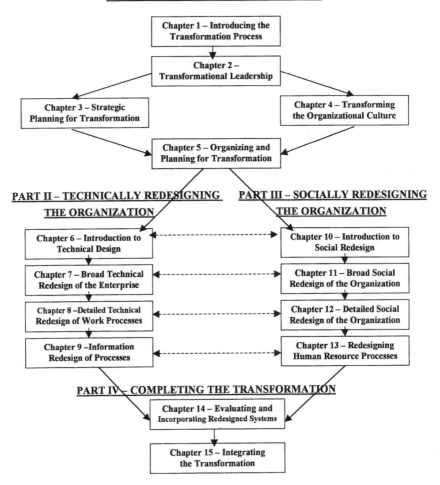

PART I – INITIATING TRANSFORMATION

Chapter 1 – Introducing the
Transformation Process

Chapter 2 –
Transformational Leadership

Chapter 3 – Strategic
Planning for Transformation

Chapter 4 – Transforming
the Organizational Culture

Chapter 5 – Organizing and
Planning for Transformation

**PART II – TECHNICALLY REDESIGNING
THE ORGANIZATION**

**PART III – SOCIALLY REDESIGNING
THE ORGANIZATION**

Chapter 6 – Introduction to
Technical Design

Chapter 10 – Introduction to
Social Redesign

Chapter 7 – Broad Technical
Redesign of the Enterprise

Chapter 11 – Broad Social
Redesign of the Organization

Chapter 8 –Detailed Technical
Redesign of Work Processes

Chapter 12 – Detailed Social
Redesign of the Organization

Chapter 9 –Information
Redesign of Processes

Chapter 13 – Redesigning
Human Resource Processes

PART IV – COMPLETING THE TRANSFORMATION

Chapter 14 – Evaluating and
Incorporating Redesigned Systems

Chapter 15 – Integrating
the Transformation

Part I: Initiating Transformation

Part I covers those preparatory actions that an organization should take before initiating a transformation effort. If the required leadership, organization, and planning (including strategic and cultural planning) are not performed before the transformation is initiated, the transformation is doomed to failure.

Chapter 1, "Introducing the Transformation Process," describes the need for the transformation process, what it is, and the overall guidelines for accomplishing it.

Chapter 2, "Transformational Leadership," outlines the actions that top-level leadership must take to ensure the transformation is accomplished effectively. Especially they must obtain commitment of the entire organization, develop a guiding coalition, and develop and communicate a vision to guide the transformation.

Chapter 3, "Strategic Planning for Transformation," develops the mission and strategic intent which technically guide the efforts of the transformation. Strategic planning also develops and matches value propositions and core competencies that guide detailed process redesign.

Chapter 4, "Transforming the Organizational Culture," develops the company's ideology—its creed, core values, and guiding principles—that will guide the social aspects of the transformation. The cultural plans to achieve the ideology are developed in this chapter, while implementation methods are discussed in Chapter 10.

Chapter 5, "Organizing and Planning for Transformation," outlines the organizing and planning that must be accomplished prior to initiating transformation. Specifically, an organization plan and an action plan must be developed with methods for executing both specified.

Part II: Technically Redesigning the Organization

Part II covers the technical or engineering aspects of the transformation. In it we first develop a process map of the organization as the basis for improving the processes. We diagnose both the existing and the future organization to determine how processes should be improved. Information technology (IT) will play a big part in process improvement.

Chapter 6, "Introduction to Technical Redesign," utilizes the procedure for Business Process Reengineering (BPR) to provide the foundation for our process redesign procedures. We also look at Process Mapping, which is an indispensable, but sometimes overused, tool for process redesign.

Chapter 7, "Broad Technical Redesign of the Enterprise," looks at both the existing and the future total organization (enterprise) to determine which processes should be improved and how they should be improved. The final action of the chapter is to select the processes that will be redesigned and allocate them to redesign teams for prosecution.

Chapter 8, "Detailed Technical Redesign of Work Processes," outlines the actions the redesign teams take to redesign their assigned processes. They develop detailed "As Is" and "To Be" process maps to provide the basis for their redesign. Improvement will be accomplished through technical analysis and creative synthesis procedures.

Chapter 9, "Information Redesign of Processes," describes how information technology helps improve organizational processes. It looks at the information technology development process and the IDEF1 modeling method.

Part III: Socially Redesigning the Organization

Part III covers the social or behavioral aspects of the transformation. In it we will look at the various organizational change methods available, conduct a broad design of the total organization and then perform a detailed design based upon work teams and networking. We complete our social design by designing the supporting human resources processes for the improved organization.

Chapter 10, "Introduction to Social Redesign," looks at various methods of implementing social change, particularly cultural change. The role of high-level leaders, kick-off conferences, and cascading are delineated. The importance of communications and employee empowerment in social change is discussed.

Chapter 11, "Broad Social Redesign of the Organization," discusses the redesign of the overall structure of the organization. Various possible overall organization structures are presented, and guidelines are provided for selecting the best structure for a particular organization.

Chapter 12, "Detailed Social Redesign of the Organization," looks in detail at the design of work teams that conduct the normal work of the organization. The process of networking these teams and transitioning the company into a learning organization is then discussed.

Chapter 13, "Redesigning Human Resource Processes," indicates that critical supporting Human Resources (HR) processes must be redesigned if the transformation is to be successful. Among these HR processes are a more active role for HR, recruiting and selecting personnel, performance measurement and assessment, and recognition and reward.

Part IV: Completing the Transformation

Now comes the difficult part. Incorporating the redesigned processes into the existing system is the most difficult part of transformation. It has both technical and behavioral difficulties, with the behavioral problems being the more difficult. We also discuss how better integration can be achieved to provide better results.

Chapter 14, "Evaluating and Incorporating Redesigned Systems," discusses first how the redesigned prototype should be evaluated to determine if it is ready for incorporation into the parent system. Once selected for incorporation, considerable planning and preparation must be accomplished before it can be incorporated.

Chapter 15, "Integrating the Transformation," discusses several methods of integrating the transformation by (1) integrating strategic and cultural planning, (2) integrating the social and technical approach, (3) integrating through technology, and (4) integrating design teams and work teams.

FEATURES OF THE BOOK

The following specific benefits (which are not provided by any other book) will be provided by this book:

- *Provides a clear goal for the transformation.* The form of the enterprise required to succeed in the 21st century is clearly outlined in Chapter 1. This provides the reader with a clear idea of what should be accomplished in the transformation.
- *Provides an excellent description of transformational leadership.* Without strong leadership, the transformation process is going nowhere. Getting the transformation process started is nearly impossible without a strong high-level leadership.
- *Provides a simple but powerful model of the transformation process.* By laying out the transformation process in a matrix format with the types of redesign (Work redesign, IT redesign, and Social redesign) on the horizontal axis and the stages of design (Diagnose System, Broad System Design, Diagnose Process, and Detailed Process Design) on the vertical axis, a clear and very useful picture of the transformation process is obtained.
- *Provides the necessary concepts and advice to actually conduct a transformation.* By understanding the concepts in the model and developing and following the plan, the success of a transformation is assured. Although other books purport to do this, they fail on many counts.
- *Importance of changing culture is stressed.* Changing the culture of an enterprise is a long and difficult task. However, if the culture is not changed, it is doubtful that anything else will change. For a successful transformation, culture change must be a visible and important part of the process.
- *Integrates technical and social approach to transformation.* This book recognizes that technical- and social-oriented people in most organizations have very different views on transformation, and it provides the concepts and procedures needed to integrate these two very different approaches.
- *Book is concrete and specific.* Rather than speaking in generalities about what you could do, this book lays out specific actions that you should do. In some instances these "should do" actions may have to be modified slightly to fit your actual situation. If so, concrete guidance for modification is provided.
- *Shows how to fully utilize the two most important enablers for transformation.* The two most important elements for enabling change are empowered employees and information technology. When these two enablers are led with a proactive strategy and culture, they can move mountains.
- *Utilizes experience from Total Quality Management (TQM) and Business Process Reengineering (BPR).* The extensive experience gained in transformation from TQM and BPR is fully utilized. Although the process of total change associated with these two programs was not called transformation at the time, the principles and techniques are very similar.
- *Educates the reader in the technique of process mapping.* Most books only talk about process mapping, but they do not show the reader how to do it. We show the reader how to perform process mapping. A person really doesn't understand process mapping until they have done it.

PART I

Initiating Transformation

CHAPTER 1

Introducing the Transformation Process

THE SITUATION FACING TODAY'S ORGANIZATIONS

Today's organizations are being bombarded from every side by pressures for change, be the pressures social or political, economic or technological. The results are manifested in various ways. New competitors enter the marketplace and sweep away established customer bases. Technology changes the rules about how business can be undertaken. Legislation demands changes in the way in which products and services are delivered. Deregulation throws up whole new trading blocks and industry sectors. Behind it all, the expectations of customers grow as they become ever more knowledgeable and demanding.

Without consciously intending to render the mass-production system obsolete, producers and consumers have fundamentally altered the processes by means of which goods and services are currently being defined, created, distributed, and consumed. The terms used to describe markets, products, business processes, and operating metrics have not changed, but what these terms mean is no longer the same. As commercial competition changes dramatically, the conduct of business changes correspondingly. Signs of this alteration abound, in the form of marketplace forces that are "pulling" responses from growing numbers of companies threatened by these forces.[1] The primary forces effecting organizations of today are listed and discussed below:

- Societal turbulence
- Market fragmentation
- Production to order in arbitrary lot sizes

- Shrinking product lifetimes
- Convergence of physical products and services
- Global production networks
- Simultaneous intercompany cooperation and competition
- Information technology and the informated organization
- Education of the workforce
- Workplace diversity and mobility
- Total quality management movement
- The business process reengineering movement

Societal Turbulence

Massive societal changes are taking place throughout the globe. Eastern Europe has overthrown the yoke of Communism and is now in the midst of further upheavals with ethnic warfare and economic problems. Japan, once an economic powerhouse, is undergoing profound economic challenges. The once flourishing economies of Asia are now undergoing difficult times. The specter of AIDS is affecting the availability of an educated, professional workforce in Africa and other countries. By the year 2000, more than 50 percent of all people will live in cities of a million inhabitants. There will be 21 megacities of more than 10 million where poverty, chaos, and danger will be the daily staple of life.

Market Fragmentation

Markets of all kinds are fragmenting at what seems like an accelerating pace. Magazines, beer, soft drinks, and snack foods; radio stations and cable TV channels; audio and video equipment; cameras, fax machines and copiers, printers, scanners; appliances, clothing, and financial, shopping, and business services all come in a bewildering array of choices aimed at constantly proliferating market niches. Personal computers are available in a very wide range of desktop varieties, but there are also portable computers ranging from laptops to notebooks, subnotebooks, and palmtops, which themselves come in a number of distinct varieties.

Production to Order in Arbitrary Lot Sizes

It is already possible for each of the many products made on a high-volume production line to be made differently from each of the others with little or no increase in production costs. This capability has revolutionary marketing consequences. Individualized production increases competition in existing markets, opens new markets, and creates competitive advantages by offering to mass-market customers individualized goods and services at as close to mass-production prices as a company chooses to price them.

Shrinking Product Lifetimes

The decreasing lifetimes of products, increasing proliferation of models, and accelerating pace of the introduction of new or improved models are among the most brutal facts of contemporary competition. Sony's Walkman line seems to change models daily. On a recent visit to one store in Tokyo's Akihabara electronics district, more than 400 Walkman-size products, offering some combination of AM, FM, cassette tape, and/or recording capabilities, were on display. Perhaps even more astonishing, the lifetime of mainframe computers has recently been halved, with significantly higher-performance models being introduced every two years rather than every four.

Convergence of Physical Products and Services

The traditional distinction between goods and services—reflected, for example, in the different rates at which the revenues generated by their creation and consumption are taxed—and between the kinds of companies and personnel that produce them is vanishing. This distinction is being replaced by markets for "fusion products," physical products the value of which lies overwhelmingly, if not exclusively, in the information and/or services to which the physical product provides access. A direct result of this convergence is that hardware companies are acquiring the capability to create both information and services or are working increasingly closely with information and service companies in order to create fusion products.

Sega and Nintendo game machines, for example, are sold at cost—at best. The machines are merely platforms for selling games, which have generated all the profits these companies have earned. The machines are therefore developed in collaboration with game developers, the technology driven by the requirements of games that will excite buyers.

Global Production Networks

No markets anywhere (for profitable products, at least) are domestic anymore, and no sizable producer can be a domestic producer only. The addition of high-capacity information and communication systems to existing global transportation systems opens every market to any producer for whom the economics is attractive. Furthermore, it is increasingly easy to integrate design, production, marketing, and distribution resources distributed around the world into a coherent "virtual" production facility.

As a result, every company has the potential for linking some portion of its capabilities with complementary capabilities of other companies regardless of their location. If a company whose strength is design recognizes an opportunity in a distant market but lacks local production facilities or distribution or marketing channels, the company no longer faces an obstacle to entering that market.

Simultaneous Intercompany Competition and Cooperation

To a degree unprecedented in American business history, companies are entering into partnerships, joint ventures, and collaborations of every imaginable kind, including the formation of virtual companies. Some of these relationships aim at creating economies of scale by merging similar capabilities in order to avoid the costs of adding capacity. Some aim at joint development of new "back-office" capabilities, and some cooperating companies work on the development of new generic technologies, even as they plan to compete with one another for end users. Some companies aim at achieving vertical integration or at creating economies of scope by synthesizing physically distributed complementary capabilities within or among enterprises. This is, of course, the essence of a virtual organization structure. What is particularly striking in all these forms of joint venture is the increasing frequency of participation of direct competitors.

Information Technology and the Informated Organization

We have entered an era of ever-increasing technological advancement—with new technologies such as optoelectronics, cyberspace, information highways, digital video, informating, local area networks, groupware, virtual reality, and electronic classrooms. The power of computer technology has progressed from mainframe to desktop to briefcase portable to user's hand. More and more of a company's operations are being totally automated. The impact on organizational work and on learning has been overwhelming.

Education of the Workforce

As levels of education rise, professionalism and quality of work life become dominant considerations. In 50 years, we will all be "professionals," whether we are doctors, lawyers, engineers, or file clerks—a position that may then be labeled "technical-information retriever." This does not mean everyone will be well educated or that all work will be professional work. On the contrary, much person-to-person routine, low-discretion work will still prevail. But the workforce will be different, and people's aspirations will have evolved. Managing an "expert" workforce will require recognition of different human aspirations within a new work culture of professionalism.

Workplace Diversity and Mobility

The global workforce is becoming ever more diverse and mobile. Hispanics and Asians will represent over 25 percent of the total U.S. workforce by the year 2000. Already, in California, Texas, and Florida, nearly half the workforce is Black, Hispanic, or Asian.

Total Quality Management (TQM) Movement

The ability to attract and retain customers by meeting their needs with quality products and quality service has become a pivotal issue for all organizations. In a global economy, quality standards are set not in the boardroom, but in the worldwide marketplace. Customers now have many choices, and quality is of high importance. Most organizations have established Total Quality Management (TQM) programs. Competitive advantage comes from the continuous, incremental innovation and refinement of a variety of ideas that spread throughout the organization.

The Business Process Reengineering (BPR) Movement

Business Process Reengineering is the radical redesign of broad, cross-functional business processes with the objective of order-of-magnitude performance gains, often with the aid of information technology. BPR is more difficult to implement than TQM but can be more productive—if done right. Many organizations have attempted BPR—not all have been successful.

REQUIRED RESPONSE OF FUTURE ORGANIZATIONS

How will organizations have to change to be successful in the 21st century? In other words, what is the desired output of the transformation process we are discussing in this book? Under 20th-century industrialization, bureaucracy was the preferred form of organization. The factory was designed to produce standardized products; the bureaucracy, to produce standardized decisions. Most major corporations developed in an industrial society, based on a bureaucratic model of machine-like division of function, routine activity, permanence, and a very long vertical hierarchy. It was a world of mass markets, uniform goods and services, and long production runs.

The Growing Recognition of the Need for Radical Change

There is growing recognition that yesterday's hierarchical bureaucracies do not work in today's knowledge society. The hierarchical structure where everyone has a superior and everyone has an inferior is demeaning to the human spirit—no matter how well it served us during the industrial period. The authoritarian organization has a stultifying effect on initiative and innovation. People feel they cannot change their environment and thus never seek the information that might change it. The top-down authoritarian management style is yielding to a networking style of management, where people learn from one another horizontally, where everyone is a resource for everyone else, and where each person gets support and assistance from many different directions.

As more companies realize that the key resource of business is not capital, personnel, or facilities but rather knowledge, information, and ideas, many new ways of viewing the organization begin to emerge. Everywhere companies are restructuring, creating integrated organizations, global networks, and leaner corporate centers. Organizations are becoming more fluid, ever shifting in size, shape, and arrangement. Many of these changes, in one form or another, have led to the path of *federalism* as the way to manage increasingly complex organizations in the increasingly rapidly changing environment.

Change, it seems, is everywhere. In our organizations, we are changing the way we produce our goods and modifying the way we deliver our services. Our governments change polices and legislation that alter the way society operates, removing monopolies, opening new markets, and creating new opportunities. In our working life, the nature of the job itself is changing, the prospect of a long-term career replaced by short-term contracts and demands for new skills and abilities. And beneath it all, rapid advances in information technology change the rules about how we communicate and with whom we are able to communicate.

The good news is that within our organizations a realization of the need for change at last seems to be aflame. We are waking up to the pressures around us and the opportunities before us. There is a recognition that out-of-date structures, systems, and processes must be overturned if we are to move forward and stay in business. The world is changing, and we are at last beginning to wake up and shake up our slumbering organizations and enterprises.

The bad news is that the attitude toward change deep within these organizations and enterprises is not always a positive one. Change has a checkered history, with previous initiatives leaving some ugly scars behind. Many people harbor a reluctance to face any more upheaval, and change is a dirty word, avoided or berated. Talk of change in the canteen or the coffee lounge draws raised eyebrows and groans of "not again." It conjures up visions of consultants and redundancies and of management making promises that are never delivered.

Changing Our Approach to Change

Against this background we have to modify our whole mindset about change.[2] Although there is an awareness of the need for change, there is also resistance to it. Management may believe that they are pursuing productive change programs, but the feeling on the shop floor and with the customer is one of constant, uncoordinated change and upheaval. In this environment we need to rethink the way the whole change process is managed. The biggest shift in that thinking is that *we have to live continuously with change.* Change is no longer an irregular outing, an inconvenient upheaval to be undertaken once every ten years. Change is something we have to learn to live with day in and day out, to structure and to manage. Change is here to stay, and the winners will be the ones who cope with it each and every day.

The problem is that our organizations and enterprises as they currently stand are just not built for continuous change. Change is not natural to them. They are actually built on the very premises that oppose change—stability, conformity, and consistency. We have to create organizations that are actually good at changing. The organizations we create now cannot be expected to remain the same for the next 20—or fifteen or even ten—years. As we tackle the long, laborious change programs that eradicate the burdens of the past 30 years, new organizations are created.

These new organizations have to come with a capability to reshape, reorient, and reorganize continuously, to respond to the opportunities and pressures and challenges—some call it chaos—that surround us. *They have to be equipped to change constantly,* albeit on a smaller scale in response to the new opportunities, rather than heading for one massive upheaval every five or ten years. It will be the companies that are equipped with flexible processes—and the people and IT systems that underpin them—that capitalize on the new markets that form and seize the opportunities that emerge. *The change task is, therefore, not just about transformation to cope with the current situation: It is about creating processes equipped to cope with as yet unknown opportunities, markets, competition, and legislation.* The challenge is to create organizations that can cope with any kind of change any time in the 21st century.

Transforming an organization with only present business conditions and current organizational considerations in mind might create a new organization capable of short-term success but will certainly fail to position the organization for longer-term market dominance or excellence. To avoid this mistake and to position the organization for long-term success, organizational leaders and employees must continually seek to create and take advantage of opportunities constantly occurring in the marketplace.

According to Hamel and Prahalad, who examined in detail the need for organizations not only to transform themselves but also to transform the industries they compete in:

Competition for the future is competition to create and dominate emerging opportunities—to stake out new competitive space. Creating the future is more challenging than playing catch up, in that you have to create your own road map. The goal is not simply to benchmark a competitor's products and processes and imitate its methods, but to develop an independent point of view about tomorrow's opportunities and how to exploit them.[3]

THE NATURE OF TRANSFORMATIONAL CHANGE

Types of Organizational Change

Given the urgent need for change, let's take a look at the types of change available. Basically, there are two broad ways to categorize large-scale change. The first is on the basis of scope, or the breadth of change. The second is on the basis of the timing in the industry change cycle. Let's consider each category separately, and then merge them to create a full picture of the possible types of organizational change.

The Scope of Change

Incremental, or Continuous, Change. Incremental changes involve subsystem adjustments needed to keep an organization on its chosen path. These changes are not necessarily small; they can involve large commitments of time, people, and money. But they are part of an orderly flow, and each step builds upon previous ones. Incremental change goes on all the time—or at least it ought to. This is the kind of change embodied in the quality management term *kaizen*, or step-by-step continuous improvement. Incremental change can have a major impact on large numbers of people, but that doesn't mean it has fundamentally altered the company's strategy, structures, and operating environment.

Radical, or Discontinuous, Change. Complex, wide-ranging changes brought on by fundamental shifts in the external environment are *radical*, or *discontinuous*, changes. As in statistics, discontinuity suggests the appearance of some factor that disrupts a normal progression. Typically, discontinuous changes require dramatic changes in strategy and abrupt departures from traditional work, structures, job requirements, and cultures, which in turn necessitate a complete overhaul of the organization. Radical change means people have to *unlearn* years, even decades, of

Figure 1-1
Four Types of Organizational Change

	Incremental	Radical
Proactive	*Tuning*	*Conversion*
Reactive	*Adaptation*	*Reclamation*

procedures, rituals, beliefs, work habits, and ways of dealing with customers, suppliers, and coworkers—all of which, in their view, have been working just fine.

The Timing of Change

Proactive, or Anticipatory, Change. Proactive changes are any systematically planned changes intended to take advantage of expected situations. They are made early in the disequilibrium cycle and often before a period of industry upheaval has even begun. They are made in the absence of any imminent threat from the environment. In a sense, AT&T's voluntary breakup was a proactive change. Bob Allen and a small group of senior advisors began making serious plans for the breakup in the spring and summer of 1995. The decision wasn't announced to the world until September 1995. By the time the bill landed on President Clinton's desk early in 1996, the breakup was already in progress.

Reactive Change. Reactive changes are those in response to unexpected environmental events or pressures. These changes generally arise either in response to some strategic initiative by a competitor or, in more dire situations, when the organization has its back to the wall. Typically, these changes come toward the tail end of periods of industry upheaval.

Four Responses to Change

We've discussed the four dimensions of change. Now let's combine them to create a matrix (see Figure 1-1) that identifies the four basic types of change that organizations can make. On the vertical axis of the matrix, change is characterized as proactive or reactive. The horizontal axis deals with the scope of a particular change, either incremental or radical. We will briefly discuss each of the four types of change: tuning, adaptation, conversion, and reclamation.

Tuning. This is the most common, least intense, and least risky type of change. Other names for it include preventive maintenance and the Japanese concept of *kaizen* (continuous improvement). The key to effective tuning is to actively anticipate and avoid problems rather than passively waiting for things to go wrong before taking action. For example, DuPont tuned its marketing efforts by developing an Adopt-a-Customer program. The program "encourages blue-collar workers to visit a customer once a month, learn his needs, and be his representative on the factory floor." This is a refreshing alternative to the traditional practice of waiting for customer complaints and only then trying to figure out how to fix them.

Adaptation. Like tuning, adaptation involves incremental changes. But this time, the changes are in *reaction* to external problems, events, or pressures. Corrective maintenance and problem solving are examples of adaptive change. For example, after Ford had great success with its aerodynamic styling, General Motors and Chrysler followed suit. In turn, Ford and GM broadened their product lines to compete with Chrysler's trend-setting minivans.

Conversion. This type of change is proactive and radical in scope. The development of new products and the development of new markets are conversion-type changes. Fast-food companies, for example, are creatively reaching out to the masses. The food may be the same, but the dining location certainly is not. In the past PepsiCo, which owns Pizza Hut and Kentucky Fried Chicken in addition to Taco Bell, has led the way in off-beat sites, such as mobile carts in airports. But now McDonald's runs restaurants inside Wal-Mart and Sears stores, and it is negotiating to open more such eateries in Home Depots. It takes a real conversion to end up with hamburgers next to the hammers and housewares.

Reclamation. Competitive pressures normally trigger this most intense and risky type of organizational change. In such a situation the organization is literally reclaimed from death. A prime example is Germany's Daimler-Benz, maker of the Mercedes Benz. CEO Helmut Werner, in response to severe competition in the costly luxury car market, has decided to make Mercedes Benz an "exclusive, full-line manufacturer" offering high-quality vehicles of all shapes and sizes. Werner is pushing Mercedes to expand into two fast-growing segments classified in the United States as light trucks: minivans and four-wheel-drive sport-utility vehicles.

Whenever possible a conversion type of change is preferred to a reclamation type. The basic difference is that conversion is initiated *before* the improved performance is needed, while the reclamation is initiated *after* the improved performance is needed.

The Characteristics of Transformational Change

In **transformation**, we will primarily be implementing conversion-type changes. In certain circumstances, where radical change is not needed, tuning may be appropriate. Although the end goal of both the incremental and radical approaches is to do things better, faster, and cheaper, there are some differences in how each approach operates. Radical process improvement assumes that everything currently being done is suspect and starts with a blank sheet of paper. Radical process improvement typically aims for:

- Widespread, radical change
- Improvements of 100 percent or more
- Revolution, not evolution, in current ways of doing business

An example of a radical process improvement project occurs when a company decides to combine the sales and order-processing departments and create a totally new way of generating and accepting customer orders.

Incremental process improvement is typically thought of as an approach that aims for:

- Incremental change
- Improvements of 25 percent or more
- Evolution of the current way of doing business

An example of a process improvement project occurs when a company decides to streamline the order entry process. Because of these differences in the amount of "payoff" or improvement promised between radical process improvement and incremental process improvement, it is usual to find that high-level people within the company want radical process improvements to be implemented. The high-level people want large amounts of improvements, but because they are so far removed from the day-to-day detail, they often drastically underestimate what it will take to successfully complete a radical improvement project.

Transformation is characterized by certain features that clearly differentiate it from other types of change. First it involves *radical and discontinuous* change to the shape, structure, and nature of the organization, rather than incremental adjustments and fine-tuning of the current situation. One example of a radical change would be when a firm changes from being production-driven to being customer-driven. Another would be a merger of two organizations. In both instances, the shape of the organization can be expected to change radically. An organization transforming from a production orientation to a customer orientation will need to drastically decentralize and delegate authority. In a merger, entirely new and different working relationships will be created.

A second characteristic of transformation is that the change *is caused by forces external* to the organization rather than forces inside the organization. A typical example would be when an organization changes from a functional to a divisional structure in response to market forces or industry pressures. Presently, globalization is one of the most powerful external forces for organizational transformation.

A third distinguishing feature of transformation is that change is *deep and pervasive*, rather than shallow and contained. The change affects all parts of the organization and involves many levels. Decentralization, downsizing, and the geographic relocation of functions and activities exemplify changes that transform structured relationships deeply and pervasively.

Finally, transformation requires significantly different, even entirely *new sets of actions* by the members of the organization, rather than more or less of existing behavior patterns. Examples are changes to the norms and core values of an organization that are brought about through acquisition, deregulation, and reorganization.

SOCIAL-TECHNICAL SYSTEMS APPROACH TO TRANSFORMATION

The Systems Approach

Classical analysts assume that the whole is equal to the sum of its parts and can be explained in terms of its parts. Systems theorists, in contrast, study organizations by putting things together and assume that the whole is greater than the sum of its parts. The difference is analytic versus systems thinking. According to one expert, "Analytic thinking is, so to speak, outside-in thinking; systems thinking is inside-out." Neither negates the value of the other, but by systems thinking we can gain understanding that we cannot obtain through analysis, particularly of collective phenomena.

Systems can be either closed or open. A **closed system** is not interactive with the outside environment and thus is not influenced by what is happening in that environment. On the other hand, an **open system**, such as an organization, tends to be in a dynamic relationship with its environment, receiving various inputs, transforming them in some way, and producing outputs. Receiving inputs in the form of material, energy, and information, along with feedback regarding outputs, allows the open system to offset the process of decline. Moreover, the open system adapts to its environment by changing the process of its internal components or structure as the need arises. All organizations are open systems because organizational survival depends on interaction with the surrounding environment.

The concept of the organization as a system is not new, since many successful business people have used the approach now called the systems concept. For example, many of the builders of great corporations, such as Theodore Vail of AT&T and Alfred Sloan of General Motors, had the ability to view the business as an integrated whole or system. They were able to identify strengths and weaknesses and to see how those factors were critical to success. This approach was the basis of their genius for organizing their companies and developing their management capabilities.

Because of the influence of the systems approach, managers now have a greater appreciation for the importance of seeing the whole picture.

Open-systems thinking does not permit the manager to become preoccupied with one aspect of organizational management while ignoring other internal and external realities. The manager of a business, for instance, must consider resource availability, technological developments, and market trends when producing and selling a product or service.

A system can be divided into its component subsystems for more detailed analysis as long as the relationships between subsystems are retained and considered. One subsystem cannot be analyzed completely independently of the other subsystems. Such analysis would be erroneous; a subsystem without its relations with the other subsystems is not a complete subsystem. Since subsystems are interdependent, they should work together to optimize the larger system. The better aligned the subsystems are, the higher the performance of the enterprise will be.

The Social-Technical Approach

For the purpose of studying transformation we will divide the organizational system into two subsystems: the social system and the technical system. We do this because this is the way that most organizations are actually structured and managed, whether they admit it or not. In most organizations there is a definite dividing line between technical people and behavioral people. We could hide our heads in the sand and refuse to admit that this is true, but this would only make it more difficult to integrate the two groups.

As indicated in Figure 1-2, the transformation process proceeds down two paths, the technical redesign path and the social redesign path. Although these two paths are very different, *they are not independent.* There must be constant communication and exchange of information between the two paths. For the transformation to be effective, these two paths must be highly integrated.

We have utilized the social-technical approach at the job level for some time. However the social-technical approach has been little discussed at the organizational level. The technical activities and the social activities of an organization have long followed their own paths, with their own procedures and own cultures. In this book, we will integrate these two paths in order to develop a total social-technical systems approach to organizational transformation.

Rationale for the Social-Technical Systems Approach

We have drawn the social and technical paths separately because this split and the resulting conflict are real in most organizations. This conflict, and failure to resolve it, is one of the main reasons that many transformations fail. We recognize that such a schism exists and will devise means to resolve it. The way to integrate the two paths is to admit that both

Figure 1-2
The Organization Transformation Process

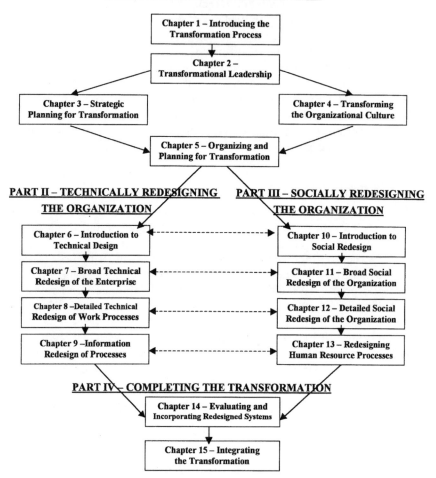

paths exist and then to take concrete steps to bring them together. Hiding our heads in the sand, trying to downplay and smooth over the differences and hoping they will go away, is not an effective approach.

Two factors—technology and people—are the keys to transforming business processes. Neither, alone, is the driver of transformation. Applying technology without social redesign is merely automation. Applying social change without technical reengineering is merely a reorganization or a total quality management effort. Only transformation, the holistic total-systems combination of the technical and social aspects of processes, will produce significant breakthroughs in performance.

The experiences of the Total Quality Management (TQM) and Business Process Engineering (BPR) programs bear out the need for a total social-technical approach to radical change. Many organizations completed the BPR effort in fine style until they tried to implement their proposed changes and ran into many behavioral snags and resistance. On the other hand, many companies completed TQM programs with great increases in employee morale, but when they looked at their productivity, there was very little improvement.

Many transformation projects make the mistake of "technocentricism." They say things like "We're doing great in transformation; we've installed image processing and client/server equipment." Certainly technology is a key *enabler* of transformation. But technology is not transformation. Transformation changes the business processes—the way the work is done. Applying technology to current processes has been rightly called "paving the cow path." Perhaps one reason that many practitioners fall into the error of technocentricism is that technical change is easier to implement than social change. In most cases the choice between technical alternatives is fairly clear cut. And there is usually an objective way of determining whether the solution is working or not.

By contrast, the social side of processes is far more imprecise and problematic. It involves not only all the eccentricities of organizations but also the infinite variety of individual personalities. That is why we have found, in providing advisory services on the management issues that arise when technology is applied to business, that the human issues are inevitably more difficult than the technical ones. Far more BPR projects (or other improvement programs, for that matter) have failed because of inadequate attention to the social issues than because of technical issues.

IMPLEMENTING TRANSFORMATIONAL CHANGE

As the true size of the transformation change task becomes clear, it can be a daunting prospect. To change successfully, new ways of working need to be devised—new ways that focus on the customer and make the best of people and technological capabilities in combination. To provide these new ways of working, changes have to be made to the very infrastructure of the business—the people and systems, the procedures and management. The number of variables in play and the number of components under modification at any one time present a massive challenge to the organization; and if the changes need to take place on a cross-enterprise scale, their extent may seem just too vast to tackle.

But this seemingly hopeless situation can be conquered. Complexity can be controlled, order can be restored, and the many components required to put together a new organization can be integrated successfully. The answer lies in *planning*. Major transformation cannot progress without a plan, a blueprint that sets out the new ways of working and how the components within it fit together to achieve strategic objectives: a plan that shows how customer needs are met and can identify the points of value; a plan of how IT is used in close integration with people, rather than as an add-on; a plan of processes, so that they work *because* of the component parts rather than in spite of them; a plan that works across the organization to meet customer needs.

Planning is fundamental to transformational change because it provides a means of:

- Actively deciding and selecting how the enterprise will work.
- Documenting the requirements to make them tangible, visible, and manageable rather than just a set of high-level wish lists.
- Specifying the actual changes that have to be carried out to make the new plan a reality.
- Managing and controlling the multitude of changes that have to be carried out so that risk can be minimized.
- Understanding what the impact of the changes and proposed changes will be on the existing business operations.

Transformational change initiation involves a fairly global perspective on strategic and cultural change, but it can be implemented by employing the basic tool of planning, which is available to almost every manager, not just the CEO and the senior team. No vision for change at the corporate level can succeed unless managers throughout the corporation fully understand and "buy into" its overall concepts and *plan* to achieve these concepts. At each level, managers must translate the overall vision into a consistent plan within their own areas of responsibility. Successful managers are neither bystanders nor victims; they stretch themselves to comprehend, embrace, and advance the principles developed for the organization as a whole.

Because of the importance of planning, Part I of this book, especially Chapter 5, is devoted to discussing the planning and preparation that must take place before the transformation effort is initiated.

NOTES

1. Steven L. Goldman, Roger N. Nagel, and Kenneth Preiss, *Agile Competitors and Virtual Organizations* (Van Nostrand Reinhold, 1995), p. 9.

2. Colin Bainbridge, *Designing for Change: A Practical Guide to Business Transformation* (Wiley, 1996), p. 4.

3. Gary Hamel and C. K. Prahalad, *Competing for the Future* (Harvard Business School Press, 1996), p. 22.

CHAPTER 2

Transformational Leadership

INTRODUCTION

When we speak of leadership, or high-level leadership, we are referring to the executives at the top of an enterprise including the president or general manager as well as the heads of major functions (marketing, operations, engineering, finance, human resources, etc.), plus other people reporting directly to the president. In the traditional company of the past, leaders primarily exercised command authority. Managers were technical experts who defined the jobs of their employees. In many cases, they literally wrote out job descriptions for them. Most of the time, the employees had no idea how their efforts fit into the bigger picture.

In a company being transformed, the role of the leader is dramatically different. Transformational leaders' success will hinge largely on their ability first to plan and then to empower other people to implement the plans. A transforming organization must be led by a leader who develops and aligns the organization with a vision, develops and maintains trust, ensures that coordinating and communicating occur, and encourages creativity and learning. What truly makes an organization transformational and keeps it that way, though, is *transformative intent*. Only the leader can infuse the organization with this intent and keep it burning brightly no matter what the circumstances.

As we will see in the paragraphs that follow, the leader is essential in getting the transformation started. Following are some of the actions that should be undertaken by top-level leadership.

TOP-LEVEL PREPARATIONS AND DIAGNOSIS

Heighten Commitment to Change

Creating Dissatisfaction with the Current State

To get to a desired future state, we must first create dissatisfaction with the current state. Change runs directly counter to our normal desire for stability. People are not going to buy into change until they have become thoroughly convinced that standing pat is not an acceptable option. They might smell smoke, but they are not going to leap from the burning house until the flames are licking at their heels.

Few among us are adventurous enough to step over the precipice without a fairly good reason. A critical step in motivating change is to help people understand why it's in their best interests to let go. The goal is to "unfreeze" people from their inertia and to persuade them at least to consider the necessity of change and the possibilities that lie ahead. The leadership must forcefully communicate the undesirability of the status quo, in such a way that a critical mass of members will want to change.

It's important at this stage to present specific information about the shifts in the business environment that led management to decide that change was absolutely necessary. It's useful to emphasize the discrepancies between people's perceptions and the realities of the current situation. It is particularly persuasive to point out the consequences of not changing, including the prospects for full-blown disaster. Sometimes, rather than having managers present this scenario, it's more effective to involve lower-level employees.

Creating a Sense of Urgency

Commitment to change is heightened by making everyone aware of the need for change. People can recognize the need but not recognize the urgency of the need—that we should do something **now** to satisfy that need. Establishing a sense of urgency is crucial to gaining needed co-operation.[1] With complacency high, transformations usually go nowhere because few people are interested in working on the change problem. With urgency low, it's difficult to put together a group with enough power and credibility to guide the effort or to convince key individuals to spend the time necessary to create and communicate a change vision. In those rare circumstances in which a committed group does exist inside a canyon of complacency, its members may be able to identify the general direction for change, to reorganize, and to make substantive changes. But sooner or later, no matter how hard they push, no matter how much they threaten, if many others don't feel the same sense of urgency, the momentum for change will probably die far short of the finish line. People will find a thousand ingenious ways to withhold cooperation from a process that they sincerely think is unnecessary or wrongheaded.

Increasing the Commitment to Change

Increasing the commitment to change demands that you remove sources of complacency or minimize their impact: for instance, eliminating such signs of excess as a big corporate air force; setting higher standards both formally in the planning process and informally in day-to-day interaction; changing internal measurement systems that focus on the wrong indexes; vastly increasing the amount of external performance feedback everyone gets; rewarding both honest talk in meetings and people who are willing to confront problems; and stopping baseless "happy talk" from the top.

When confronted with an organization that needs renewal, all competent managers take some of these revolutionary actions. But they often do not go nearly far enough. A panel of customers is brought to the annual management meeting, but no way is found to bring customer complaints to everyone's attention on a weekly or even daily basis. One or two relatively frank discussions of problems are initiated at the executive board level, but the company newspaper is allowed to be full of happy talk.

Heightening the commitment to change usually demands bold or even risky actions that we normally associate with entreprenuerial leadership. A few modest activities, like the customer panel at the annual management meeting, usually fail in the face of the overwhelmingly powerful forces fueling complacency. Bold means cleaning up the balance sheet and creating a huge loss for the quarter. Or selling corporate headquarters and moving into a building that looks more like a battle command center. Or telling all your businesses that they have 24 months to become first or second in their markets, with the penalty for failure being divestiture or closure. Or basing 50 percent of the pay for the top ten officers on tough product-quality targets for the whole organization. Or hiring consultants to gather and then force discussion of honest information at meetings, even though you know that such a strategy will upset some people greatly.

The Role of Crises

Visible crises can be enormously helpful in catching people's attention and heightening commitment to change. Conducting business as usual is difficult if the building seems to be on fire. But in an increasingly fast-moving world, waiting for a fire to break out is a dubious strategy. Leadership needs to create an appropriate crisis to get people's attention.

Some firms have successfully initiated transformation when they were making record profits. They did so by relentlessly bombarding employees with information about problems (profits up but market share down), potential problems (a new competitor is showing signs of becoming more aggressive), or potential opportunities (through technology or new markets). They did so by setting vastly ambitious goals that disrupted the status quo. They did so by aggressively removing signs of excess, happy talk, misleading information systems, and more. Catching people's attention during good times is far from easy, but it is possible. Following are some specific methods for heightening the commitment to change.

1. Create a crisis by allowing a financial loss, exposing managers to major weaknesses vis-à-vis competitors, or allowing errors to blow up instead of being corrected at the last minute.

2. Eliminate obvious examples of excess (e.g., company-owned country club facilities, a large air force, gourmet executive dining rooms).

3. Set revenue, income, productivity, customer satisfaction, and cycle-time targets so high that they can't be reached by conducting business as usual.

4. Stop measuring sub-unit performance only according to narrow functional goals. Insist that more people be held accountable for broader measures of business performance.

5. Send more data about customer satisfaction and financial performance to more employees, especially information that demonstrates weaknesses vis-à-vis the competition.

6. Insist that people talk regularly to unsatisfied customers, unhappy suppliers, and disgruntled shareholders.

7. Use consultants and other means to force more relevant data and honest discussion into management meetings.

8. Put more honest discussions of the firm's problems in company newspapers and senior management speeches. Stop senior management "happy talk."

9. Bombard people with information on future opportunities, on the wonderful rewards for capitalizing on those opportunities, and on the organization's current inability to pursue those opportunities.

Achieving Commitment for Transformation

Transformation is conceived in the individual human mind and is eventually transferred to the mind of the corporation as a whole. It is the result of a choice, an act of will, made first by one, then by a few, then by many, and finally by the critical mass needed to make radical change happen. Unlike mere change, which can occur by default, *transformation* is the result of an enduring, organization-wide commitment to achieve a common set of goals.

Achieving commitment is required to muster the mental energy needed to perform the transformation process. It involves expanding the realm of motivation and commitment from the level of the individual to the team, and finally to the entire organization. Creating a totally committed enterprise involves working from the leadership level down and from the grass roots level up.

When commitment efforts fail, it is usually because leaders fail to engage all paths in the process. Many companies rely almost solely on the "top-down" path, putting their trust in executive workshops and team building. Such efforts fail due to lack of interest at the bottom. Others focus just on mustering the troops from the bottom up, sending task force upon task force to tackle "total quality" or to reengineer processes independently of each other. Typically these efforts produce mixed and conflicting results or generate impossibly ambitious recommendations that, lacking guidance and obstacle-removing support from the top, never get off the ground. The key to successful commitment is to create a groundswell, which is guided by middle managers, who are directed and coached by senior managers, who are led by the CEO. It is neither a top-down nor a bottom-up process, but both simultaneously, working for and with the middle. The result is a controlled but inexorable stampede of motivation, commitment, and action, with the CEO riding at the head of the herd.

Developing an Executive Steering Board

Why Do We Need an Executive Steering Board?

Because major change is so difficult to accomplish, a powerful force is required to sustain the process. No one individual, not even a monarch-like CEO, is ever able to develop the right vision, communicate it to large numbers of people, eliminate all the key obstacles, generate short-term wins, lead and manage dozens of change projects, and anchor new approaches deep in the organization's culture. Weak committees are even worse. A strong Executive Steering Board is always needed—one with the right composition, level of trust, and shared objectives. Building such a team is always an essential part of the early stages of transformation.

Today's business environment clearly demands a new process for decision making. In a rapidly moving world, strong individuals and weak committees rarely have all the information needed to make good non-routine decisions. Nor do they seem to have the credibility or the time required to convince others to make the personal sacrifices called for in implementing changes. Only teams with the right composition and sufficient trust among members can be highly effective under these new circumstances. This applies equally well to guiding a change coalition on the factory floor, in the new-product development process, or at the very top of an organization during a major transformation effort. An Executive Steering Board that operates as an effective team can process more information, more quickly. It can also speed the implementation of new approaches because powerful people are truly informed and committed to key decisions.

The CEO's choice of leaders and of methods for selecting these leaders sets the tone and direction of the company's future. The CEO acts as a role model and induces the senior leadership team to do the same. Senior leadership, in turn, encourages key qualities of transformational leadership at lower levels of management, and so forth, creating a top-down, cascading migration of responsibility, motivation, and commitment, down and throughout the organization. Few people are born to lead this kind of effort; most grow into their role.

Desired Characteristics of Board Members

The first step in putting together the kind of team that can direct a change effort is to find the right membership. Four key characteristics are essential in guiding efforts to form a coalition. They are:

- *Position power.* Are enough key players on the board, especially the main line managers, so that those left out cannot easily block progress?
- *Expertise.* Are the various points of view—in terms of discipline, work experience, nationality, and the like—relevant to the task at hand adequately represented so that informed, intelligent decisions will be made?
- *Credibility.* Does the board have enough people with good reputations in the firm so that its pronouncements will be taken seriously by other employees?
- *Leadership.* Does the board include enough proven leaders to be able to drive the change process?

This last concern, about leadership, is particularly important. You need both management and leadership skills on the Executive Steering Board, and they must work in tandem, teamwork style. The former keeps the whole process under control, while the latter drives the change.

Forming the Executive Steering Board

In many traditional organizations, department heads get their instructions and do their best to carry them out, but do so in isolation, without regard for what the other departments are doing or how they fit into the larger system. Such situations are examples of dedicated people working at cross purposes—the worst possible approach for organizations trying to compete in the global marketplace or accomplish transformational change.

It is possible to correct such situations without changing the organization at all. You simply change the roles of department heads so that they become team players with the other department heads and the leader. When it comes to implementing transformation, the most successful organizations are those in which the CEO's staff serve as the Executive Board. The difference in how corporate staffs and Executive Boards operate are subtle and may seem minor at first, but they are very important differences:

- In traditional organizations, decisions are typically compartmentalized and made by the leader and the appropriate staff member. In transforming organizations, the entire Executive Board becomes involved in all decisions, regardless of to which department they apply.
- In traditional organizations, instructions have to be tailored to the appropriate department. In transforming organizations, a single objective can be set for the departments to achieve together.
- In traditional organizations, it is difficult to involve more than one department in a project, because of turf problems and parochial tendencies. In transforming organizations, all the department heads share responsibility, resulting in greater cooperation.
- In traditional organizations, it is often unclear how a project relates to the vision, goals, and objectives of the organization. In transforming organizations, the relationship becomes clear through Executive Board dialogue and the corresponding communication within and among departments.

As members of the Executive Board, staff members must function as a team under the leadership of the top executive, focusing on what is good for the entire organization rather than what is best for their individual departments. In many instances, the Executive Board will include a facilitator as an ex-officio member. The facilitator's role is to keep discussion flowing, keep members on track, bring special training to bear on problem solving, and generally use his or her expertise to ensure that the Executive Board functions as a team.

Educating the Executive Steering Board

With the Executive Board about to undertake its leadership role in implementing the transformation, the Board needs a strong foundation in the fundamentals of transformation. This training must include the entire Executive Board, full time, for the duration of the training. Training is best done off site, so that there are no interruptions or disturbances, and in relaxed, casual surroundings that promote attention and interaction. Training for the Executive Board typically takes three or four days. The primary purposes of the Executive Board training are as follows:

- *To provide training in team building.* The goal of team building is to enable team members to work together toward a common objective, complementing each other with their skills, experience, and offsetting strengths and weaknesses.
- *To develop a strong foundation of knowledge.* Since the Executive Board will guide the entire organization in the implementation of transformation, it is important that Executive Board members be well versed in the fundamentals of transformation.
- *To give Executive Board members credibility.* As the implementation of transformation means organization-wide change, it is critical that Executive Board

members have credibility. Members who can speak the language and apply the principles of transformation will have credibility.

- *To convert the holdouts and skeptics.* Some of the Executive Board members may not be sold on the transformation concept at the outset. Training in the fundamentals of transformation is a way to convert them, or at least to eliminate any outward hostility due to misconceptions about transformation.
- *To equip the Executive Board members to lead implementation.* At the conclusion of the training, the Executive Board should be well equipped to begin its work leading the organization in the implementation of transformation.

Building a Critical Mass of Support for Change by Winning Over the Key Power Groups

The organization, as a political system, is filled with groups, cliques, coalitions, and special interests, each competing for power, position, status, and resources. Some will favor the impending change, some will oppose it, and some won't care one way or the other. The political challenge facing the Executive Board is to build a critical mass of support for change—not necessarily a numerical majority, but an influential group whose support can ultimately be leveraged to win widespread acceptance.

The first step is to identify the crucial power relationships within the organization and to determine which groups and individuals have the most to gain or lose from the impending change. One method we strongly recommend is to actually construct a stakeholder map, illustrating not only who is likely to take which position but also people's relationships to one another and their patterns of influence. These diagrams can be extremely useful in anticipating successive waves of reaction to change beyond the obvious initial responses.

The next step is to think about specific approaches to building support. The first—and by far the most crucial—is participation. The single most common flaw we see in failed change efforts is an absence of appropriate participation by people who are expected to become major stakeholders in the future state. All too often, managers develop a new design behind closed doors, either alone or with the assistance of one or two consultants or trusted advisers, and then present their executive teams and the organization with a complete, finalized package. The predictable responses are skepticism, resentment, and resistance.[2]

Enterprise Assessment and Diagnosis

Once high-level management commitment has been obtained, it is tempting to immediately begin developing plans for immediately implementing the transformation. However, such planning is premature.[3] We first need to determine what that current situation is, and in particular the status of the commitment for change, so that we can ascertain the direction and magnitude of the required change. We first need to do an organizational assessment (or diagnosis, as it is sometimes called) that has several objectives:

- To explore all aspects of organizational functioning in order to identify the values, beliefs, and assumptions currently held by the organization's employees.
- To identify major opportunities for transformation.
- To identify possible barriers to transformation.
- To promote the transformation program.

A broad-based assessment project usually employs one or more of the following data-gathering techniques:

Personal and Confidential Interviews with a Cross-section of Employees. The personal interviewer can probe personal experiences, explore critical issues in depth, and obtain useful anecdotes. The confidential one-on-one nature of the personal interview ensures a greater degree of openness than can be obtained in a group setting. The drawback of this approach is that it is costly and time-consuming to interview a large number of employees.

Group Interviews. The major benefit of the group interview is that a larger number of employees can be involved in a cost- and time-effective manner. The trade-offs are that confidentiality concerns may inhibit some participants and that issues cannot generally be explored in as much detail as in the individual interview.

Written Surveys. The written survey is clearly the most cost-effective way to involve very large numbers of people in the assessment process. If input from an organization of several hundred or more people is desired, a written survey is perhaps the only practical technique. A survey provides quantifiable data to support (or contradict) the conclusions that have been reached through some other format. On the down side, a survey requires some interpretation and does not permit an in-depth evaluation of the issues.

It is generally advisable to employ a combination (if not all) of these techniques in the assessment process. Group interviews might be used, for example, to allow for the active participation of a sizable number of employees and to identify the major cultural values, beliefs, and issues. More detailed information on the issues could be obtained through individual interviews, and a written survey would provide quantitative support for the conclusions reached.

PLANNING FOR TRANSFORMATION

Developing an Enterprise Vision

Why Vision Is Essential

Vision refers to a picture of the future with some implicit or explicit commentary on why people should strive to create that future. Companies need mental focus, a sense of purpose. That is the function of the *vision*. A vision provides a shared mental framework that gives form to that future. A vision is a picture of the company's ultimate purpose, the corporate equivalent of a golfer envisioning the perfect golf game. It is an aspiration representing the convergence of the analytical, emotional, and political elements of the corporate mind. Analytically, it is based on a dispassionate diagnosis of the company's competitive situation vis-à-vis its customers and cost structure. Emotionally and politically, it is the banner that captures the imagination of the entire firm, and around which people will rally. In a transformation process, a good vision serves several important purposes as indicated below:

- *Inspiration.* A vision can energize people by legitimizing the organization's existence and satisfying a basic human need: the need to be important, to make a difference, to feel useful, and to be part of a worthwhile enterprise.

- *Clarity of direction.* With clarity of direction, inappropriate projects can be identified and terminated, even if they have political support. One simple question: "Is this in line with the vision?" can help eliminate hours, days, or even months of tortuous discussion.

- *Motivational force.* The changes required by transformation very often involve pain to many employees. A good vision helps to overcome this natural reluctance to do what is (often painfully) necessary by providing a promise of things to come that will make the pain worthwhile.

- *Focus.* A vision can channel the energy of the organization, preventing employees from dissipating their energy in a variety of unrelated directions. By focusing individuals' attention on what is most important to the organization, a vision helps people uncover and eliminate a myriad of unproductive activities.

- *Integration.* A vision is also an integrating force in organizations, a mechanism for coordinating the efforts of groups with divergent interests. A vision can lift people out of their petty private preoccupations and unify them in pursuit of objectives worthy of their best efforts.

- *Unobtrusive control.* A vision may provide an effective, yet unobtrusive, form of control. A vision may help to ensure that people will make decisions that are consistent with the organization's overall needs. Since managers cannot be everywhere at once, many decisions are made without their knowledge. A vision provides employees with a compass that points their feet in the right direction.

The Nature of an Effective Vision

A company's vision is, in essence, the firm's "ambition in life," a central motive designed not only to capture the imagination of the entire organization but also to extend boundaries within the realm of the possible. *Stretch* is the sine qua non of vision.

There are many classic examples of vision: AT&T's aim for universal telephone service; Coca-Cola's drive to put its product "within arm's reach of anyone in the world"; Pepsi's commitment to "defeat Coke;" or Toyota's design to "beat Benz." Some intents may be financially oriented, such as the vow of Eastman Chemicals, formerly part of the Kodak empire, to grow from a $3 billion company to a $20 billion company by the year 2000. Other companies may choose a more subjective customer orientation such as the British Airways vow to become the world's favorite airline, made at a time when it was clearly one of the world's least favorite.

Whatever its focus, an effective vision directs a company beyond the pale, forcing it to banish limits on what it thinks it can accomplish. It is ambitious enough to require strenuous and prolonged effort, but realistic enough to be a source of focus and motivation. Good vision statements do have a number of characteristics in common, which are delineated below:

- *Imaginable*. Conveys a picture of what the future will look like.
- *Desirable*. Appeals to the long-term interests of employees, customers, stockholders, and others who have a stake in the enterprise.
- *Feasible*. Comprises realistic, attainable goals.
- *Focused*. Is clear enough to provide guidance in decision making.
- *Flexible*. Is general enough to allow individual initiative and alternative responses in light of changing conditions.
- *Communicable*. Is easy to communicate; can be successfully explained within five minutes.
- *Bold*. There's no getting away from it: Good vision requires guts and nerve.
- *Broad*. A vision should encompass the existing business, as a whole, plus realistic extensions.
- *Future oriented*. A vision brings the future to the present. The idea is to start five to ten years from now, and work backward.

Creating the Vision

Just as people are limited by their view of themselves, so are companies. Developing a vision is the CEO's chance to *stretch* the company's view of itself, to extend the boundaries of the company's industry, to trash the orthodox rules of engagement. This is the heart of CEO territory, where individuals make their mark on the corporate annals. Collective processes rally people around a vision, but the intent itself is the child of the leader's creativity, carefully nurtured and cultivated over time.

For the CEO, creating the vision is more art than science. Except in rare cases, vision is discovered gradually, after repeated experimentation, not through sudden insight. While the intent takes form, balancing constituencies can be like playing a game of chess in which the rules change with every move. Embedded in the corporate culture, many "values" may not be values at all, but may instead be sapping corporate energy and impeding the change process. And changing embedded values is never easy.

Creating a vision is of critical importance. Striving for precision in the creative process, however, can be a fatal mistake. That precision comes later, with the strategic planning (Chapter 3) and cultural planning (Chapter 4). Because it lies in both the strategic and the cultural realms, creating a vision belies detailed programming.

In fact, the leader's task is not so much to articulate a vision as it is to give it life. It's as if, as many sculptors believe, the vision is already there, buried within the stone or the company, awaiting the hand of the sculptor or leader to bring it out. It usually begins as a "dumb vision," a hypothesis in the CEO's mind, not as a lightning bolt of inspiration. Then, with fanfare, he or she launches experiments to test the intent, to see if it captures and motivates the hearts and minds of the people. After repeated stops and starts, the intent seems to reveal itself.

Once adopted, the vision becomes the rallying point for leadership. It is up to the leadership team members to align themselves around the corporate ambition and become its role models. It is never easy. Sometimes it is impossible, given the existing leadership structure. At British Airways, for example, Sir Colin Marshall found it necessary to replace the vast majority of his leadership team. He brought in new people from within and outside the company. Many knew little about airlines but had the marketing skills and, more important, the conviction needed to drive British Airways toward its vision. If senior people who lack faith in the vision are left in their positions, they will surely make infidels of others.

Testing and Improving the Vision before Implementing

One of the better methods of testing the vision is through employee *focus groups*. The focus group approach involves leading a group of employees, from various divisions and levels in the company, through an open, in-depth discussion of the proposed vision. Members of each group session are chosen from a list of volunteers, so that each group represents a valid cross-section of the company's employees. A session is usually conducted as a casual roundtable discussion with eight to twelve participants. The setting should be relaxed and casual to encourage a free and uninhibited flow of ideas.

Figure 2-1
Relationship of Vision to Other Company Plans

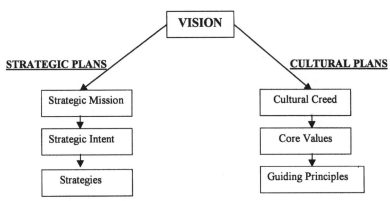

The focus group meetings should have a threefold purpose. First, to determine if all employees *understand* the vision. Second, to determine if all employees *accept* and are willing to carry out the vision. And third, to determine if there are any recommendations for *improvement.*

Relationship of Vision to Other Company Plans

The vision is the highest-level statement of purpose or plan in an organization. As such, it provides guidance to all other strategic and cultural plans of the company, as shown in Figure 2-1. In Chapters 4 and 5, the subordinate strategic and cultural plans will be developed to support and amplify the vision.

Communicating the Vision

A great vision can serve a useful purpose even if it is understood by only a few people. But the real power of a vision is unleashed only when most of those involved in an enterprise or activity have a common understanding of its goals and direction. The shared sense of a desired future can help motivate and coordinate the kinds of action that create transformations.

The development of a transformational vision often requires those on the Executive Steering Board to spend a few hundred hours collecting information, digesting it, considering alternatives, and eventually making choices. The characteristics that should be considered in arriving at a communication program for the vision are listed below and will be discussed in the remainder of this section.

- *Use simple language.* All jargon and technobabble must be eliminated.
- *Metaphor, analogy, and example.* A verbal picture is worth a thousand words.

- *Multiple forums.* Big meetings and small, memos and newspapers, formal and informal interaction—all are effective for spreading the word.
- *Repetition.* Ideas sink in deeply only after they have been heard many times.
- *Communicate by example.* Behavior from important people that is inconsistent with the vision overwhelms other forms of communication.
- *Two-way communication.* Two-way communication is always more powerful than one-way communication.

Keep It Simple

The challenge of simple and direct communication is that it requires great clarity of thought plus more than a little courage. Remember the old saw: If I had more time, I'd write you a shorter letter. It's much harder to be clear and concise than overcomplicated and wordy. Simple also means no bamboozling. Technobabble is a shield. If the ideas are dumb, others will recognize them as dumb. Dropping the armor makes us more vulnerable in the short term, which is why we are often reluctant to do so.

Use Metaphor, Analogy, and Example

Well-chosen words can make a message memorable, even if it has to compete with hundreds of other communications for people's attention. Really good advertising people are skilled at this sort of word/image selection. Those of us with degrees in engineering, economics, physical science, or finance are often not. Nevertheless, anyone can draw on the expertise of others. And most people, at least in my experience, can with practice become better at finding imaginative ways to get across their ideas.

Use Many Different Forums

The vision is usually communicated most effectively when many different vehicles are used: large group meetings, memos, newspapers, posters, informal one-on-one talks. When the same message comes at people from six different directions, it stands a better chance of being heard and remembered, on both intellectual and emotional levels. Channel A helps answer some of the questions people have, channel B addresses others, and so on.

From the top, using vehicles such as *town meetings*, the CEO takes a highly visible role, making it clear that he or she is personally driving the effort. The emphasis here is on width rather than depth. Interaction is the key. At lower levels of the organization, people actively involved in transformation projects play a key communications role. They are most effective when temporarily relieved of their former duties to become full-time *change agents*. Generally these are high performers, people who are well respected and to whom people listen. When 100 or more of the most talented people in the firm indicate their dedication to the transformation effort, people at all levels start to take notice.

Repeat, Repeat, Repeat

The most carefully crafted messages rarely sink deeply into the recipient's consciousness after only one pronouncement. Our minds are too cluttered, and any communication has to fight hundreds of other ideas for attention. In addition, a single airing will not address all the questions we have. As a result, effective information transferral almost always relies on repetition.

Communicate by Example

In most instances, the most powerful way to communicate a new direction is through behavior. When high-level leadership all live the change vision, employees will usually grasp it better than if there had been a hundred stories in the company newsletter. When they see high-level leadership acting out the vision, a whole set of troublesome questions about credibility and game playing tends to evaporate.

Telling people one thing and then behaving differently is the surest way to sabotage the communication of a change vision. Nothing undermines the communication of change vision more than behavior on the part of key players that seems inconsistent with the vision.

Interactive Two-Way Communication

Two-way interactive discussions are an essential method of helping people answer all the questions they may have during the transformation effort. Communications that are clear, simple, often repeated, from multiple sources, and modeled by executive behavior are very effective. However, most human beings, especially well-educated ones, buy into something only after they have had an opportunity to think about it. Thinking typically includes asking questions, discussing, and challenging.

IMPLEMENTING CHANGE

Developing Top-Level Organization

Once the commitment to the transformation effort has been made, senior management faces a difficult question: How will the effort be managed? In this era of concern about bloated administrative staffs, the answer often is, "We'll manage it through the existing management structure."

But further consideration typically raises more difficult questions. Who will build organizational awareness about transformation? Who will seek to build commitment at all levels of management? Who will explore and

Figure 2-2
Overall Organization for Transformation

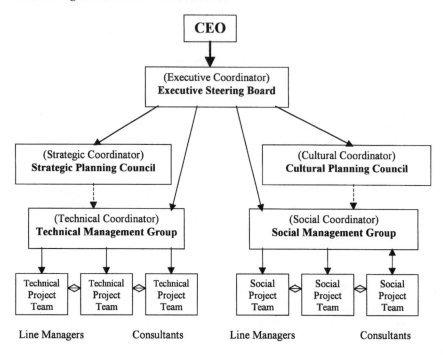

analyze the wide variety of improvement techniques available? Who will perform the strategic analysis to guide the effort? Who will conduct the cultural study to determine what kind of organization we want to be? Who will serve as a clearinghouse for information?

These tasks could, of course, be parceled out to various managers within the existing structure. But who will ensure that all of these activities are carried out in a planned, coordinated fashion? Who will ensure that the awareness-building, measurement, and employee involvement efforts will be integrated, consistent, and mutually reinforcing? Creating a transformation is a major undertaking and is both a *technical and social redesign* effort, which must be managed if it is to succeed.

To accomplish the required management and coordination, we suggest the following organization that will operate in parallel with the existing organization.

Figure 2-2 is intended to portray the functions that must be handled by the transformation organization rather than to indicate the exact configuration of the organization. The situation facing the organization will greatly influence the exact structure. For example, if a company has a group that regularly performs strategic planning, that group can be put under the control of the Executive Board rather than forming a separate Strategic Planning Council. The same is true of cultural planning, although that is much less likely. Also, Figure 2-2 is intended for a fairly large organization. A very small organization could have all these functions as subgroups in the Executive Steering Board. However the transformation organization is configured, it should contain all the functions shown in Figure 2-2, namely, executive steering, strategic planning, cultural planning, managing technical change, and managing social change.

The functions of the Executive Steering Board were discussed earlier in this chapter. The Strategic Planning Council will be discussed in Chapter 3, and the Cultural Planning Council will be discussed in Chapter 4. The Technical Management Group and the Social Management Groups will be discussed in Chapter 5.

Role of High-Level Leaders

Actions Speak Louder than Words

High-level leaders must realize that actions are much more convincing than words. Management should be clear on the actions that reflect the company's vision and demonstrate them personally. For example, if you want to encourage decentralized decision making, you should find a way to delegate high-visibility decisions currently being made. Above all, live the vision consistently; your people study your every move. If they catch you following the vision today and then not following it tomorrow, they will resist following it. Not only must the message be consistent, it must be omnipresent. Act out the vision; take every opportunity to drive home the message. Leaders live the vision by making all their actions and behaviors consistent with it and by creating a sense of urgency and passion for its attainment.

High-Level Leaders Involve Everyone in Implementation

High-level leaders must learn to let others take responsibility (and credit) for implementing the company's vision; they should check their egos at the door and be less of a guru/hero and more of a facilitator/coach. Following are some concrete suggestions for involving others in implementing the company's vision:

- Encourage others to take responsibility for executing the vision in their area. Get each person to set goals and action plans and then follow up with them.
- Set up regular multiple communications channels where supervisors discuss the new vision with their people.
- Refer questions and comments about the new vision to supervisors, rather than answering them directly.

- Lionize others; constantly communicate about the heroic actions of others in multiple mediums.
- Talk about "the team" and "our vision" and "our results." The leader's language has a dramatic empowering impact.
- Avoid answering all questions/problems/difficulties. "I don't know," is a legitimate answer. Employees will respect you for not giving glib, and often incorrect, answers just for the sake of answering.

Consider Transformation as a Campaign

One should think of transformation in terms of a campaign to be waged simultaneously on a variety of fronts.[4] Not only the content and planning are important; it also is important how you go about winning people over. You have to use a range of tactics, all aimed at winning broad support for a common vision. More work should be done on how to think about managing transformation in terms of a long, arduous political campaign. Companies make numerous errors because they fail to invest enough time and money in planning the campaign aspects of transformation. They make the assumption that once they have the mission, values, strategies, and some tactics, their work is done; all they have to do is to implement them. They are wrong.

The reality is that there are two distinct elements of the campaign. To be sure, you are waging a campaign for people's hearts and minds. But you also are trying to win for the enterprise as a whole. Within the context of your own values and beliefs about how people should be treated, you must be willing to do what it takes to win. You must plan for dealing with pockets of organized resistance.

Implementation Process Must Be Well Organized and Methodical

Transformational change may be radical, but the implementation process must be well organized and methodical. You have to cement each building block of change in place before moving on to the next. If you set out to do everything at once, you will get very little done, and what is accomplished will be done poorly. You must ascertain where your organization is in relation to where it wants to go and determine what capacities must be added or enhanced before you can get there. There is no way around it: You must accomplish the basics before you are ready to move on. Second, you need to formulate a plan for putting the building blocks in place in the proper sequence. Planning is a rational process of deciding how you are going to progress from point A to point B in order to move to point C.

Also, the timing of change is critical. The real art of change implementation lies in careful pacing. Pacing means moving simultaneously in a variety of areas and keeping each area progressing so that the combined cadence does not tear the organization apart.

Generating Short-Term Wins

The Role of Short-Term Wins

Early short-term wins will keep questionable efforts from collapsing. Many programs fail because they lose the necessary support in the early stages. Early wins will prevent this. Short-term wins will help transformation in six other ways:

1. *They provide the effort needed for reinforcement.* They show people that sacrifices are paying off, that they are getting stronger. They provide evidence that sacrifices are worth it. Wins greatly help justify the short-term costs involved.
2. *They reward change agents with a pat on the back.* For those performing the change, those little wins offer an opportunity to relax for a few minutes and celebrate. Constant tension for long periods of time is not healthy for people. The little celebration following a win can be good for the body and spirit. After a lot of hard work, positive feedback builds morale and motivation.
3. *They help fine-tune vision and strategies.* The process of producing short-term wins can help an Executive Steering Board test its vision against concrete conditions. What is learned in these tests can be extremely valuable. Without the effort to produce short-term wins, such problems can become apparent far too late in the game. Short-term wins give the Executive Steering Board concrete data on the viability of their ideas.
4. *They undermine cynics and self-serving resisters.* Quick performance improvements are the best way to undermine the efforts of cynics and major-league resisters. As a general rule, the more cynics and resisters, the more important are short-term wins. Clear improvements in performance make it difficult for people to block needed change.
5. *They keep bosses on board.* They provide those higher in the hierarchy with evidence that the transformation is on track. Visible results help retain the essential support of bosses from middle management all the way up to the board of directors. If those hierarchically above a transformation effort lose faith, the effort's in deep trouble.
6. *They help build necessary momentum.* Fence sitters are transformed into supporters, reluctant supporters into active participants, and so on. This momentum is critical because, as we will see in later chapters, the energy needed to accomplish late tasks is much greater.

The Role of Management in Short-Term Wins

Systematically targeting objectives and budgeting for them, creating plans to achieve those objectives, organizing for implementation, and then controlling the process to keep it on track—this is the essence of management. With that in mind, one can easily see that the need to create short-term wins in a successful change effort demonstrates an important principle: Transformation is not a process involving leadership alone; good management is also essential. A balance of the two is required.

Because leaders are so central to any major change effort, we sometimes conclude that transformation equals leadership. Certainly without strong and capable leadership from many people, restructurings, turnarounds, and cultural changes do not happen well or at all. But more is involved. Restructuring usually calls for financial expertise, reengineering for technical knowledge, acquisitions for strategic insight. And the process in all major change projects must be managed to keep the operation from lurching out of control or off a cliff.

EVALUATE AND CONSOLIDATE

Establish a Measurement System

Developing the Measurement System

To determine if a company is making progress in achieving its vision, it must have a viable measurement system. Many companies articulate inspiring visions and sets of values, but their actions are measured by an entirely different set of standards. They do not intend to be devious or dishonest. Rather, they simply lack the integrated set of goals and measures—the enterprise measurement system—needed to translate vision and values into actions that will move the company in the right direction.

To build such a measurement system, a company starts by translating the vision of the company into a high-level set of goals and measures that act as the standard for all other measurements.[5] The company needs to take a high-level view of itself, asking: "What should the company look like from a customer perspective, a financial (shareholder) perspective, an internal operations perspective, and an innovation and learning perspective?" Within each of these domains, a set of strategic goals is established with corresponding measurement targets attached. Ideally, if these strategic targets are reached, the vision of the firm is attained.

There is an inherent logic in the structure of the measurement system. In general, learning and innovation targets drive operational measures; operational achievements generate positive customer results; and, ultimately, positive customer results translate into improved financial performance. Early on, leaders focus on defining the cause-effect relationships across high-level targets, preparing the logic for deeper probes into the corporate body. Later the logic will be expanded to cover the entire measurement system.

Using the Cause and Effect Feature of the Measurement System

The real value of the measurement system lies less in the process of goal-setting than in providing a theory of cause and effect—provided by the logic that links operations, culture, and customers to financial performance and, ultimately, to strategy and the vision. Most companies lack a theory of cause and effect, and the measurement system provides them with a way to build one, with the top-level goals as a starting point. The company's leaders first form hypotheses or "what if" experiments and then define the path of cause and effect to test their validity. Once they have hit on a viable system of cause and effect, they can take action with reasonable certainty that the outcome will be desirable.

In this measurement system, all actions, even small localized initiatives directed by their own goals and measures, can be linked through a chain of cause and effect to their impact on the targets and measures established at the top. Thus, the goals and measures leaders adopt at the outset create the motivating force and the integrating framework for the activities of the entire organization. The leader's role here is to develop the top-level measurement system, thus providing the basic template for the entire transformation effort.

Leadership sets the stage for action by identifying the cause-effect relationships across the high-level targets. If the targets are correctly formulated, then there is an intrinsic flow within the measurement system. Learning and innovation targets drive operational and process goals; achieving operational and process goals leads to positive customer indicators; and ultimately, high scores on customer goals translate into favorable financial results.

The logic that translates "back room" indicators into "front room" financial results is one of the keys to healthy corporate life. It provides the conceptual architecture needed to build a hierarchy of cause-effect pathways down and throughout the corporation, making it possible, for example, to trace the financial impact of reducing the order fulfillment time from 30 days to three.

Building this web of linkages typically proves to be an extremely valuable exercise for leadership. It gives each member of the leadership team an opportunity to describe his or her own mental model of how the business works, while learning from the views of colleagues. It establishes a common framework for thinking about and planning the complexities of the transformation process.

Consolidate Gains

Transformations often take a long time, especially in big organizations. Many forces can stall the process far short of the finish line: turnover of key change agents, comeback of change resisters, sheer exhaustion on the part of leaders, and bad luck. Under these circumstances, short-term wins are essential to keep momentum going, but the celebration of those wins can be lethal if urgency is lost.[6] With complacency up, the opposition forces can sweep back in with remarkable force and speed.

Irrational and political resistance to change never fully dissipates. Even if you are successful during the early stages of transformation, you usually do not win over the self-centered manager who is appalled when reorganization approaches his area, or the narrowly focused engineer who cannot fathom why you want to spend so much time worrying about customers, or the old-time executive who thinks empowering employees is ridiculous. You can drive these resisters underground or into submission; but rather than changing or leaving, they will sit tight waiting for an opportunity for a comeback.

If not handled correctly, celebrations of short-term wins can provide them an opportunity for a comeback. After an emotional celebration, the resisters will try to convince us that we have made significant accomplishments, but the sacrifices were great, and we all deserve a breather. At this time our people are weary and prone to rationalize that a little rest and relaxation will not hurt.

However, experience has shown that *if you let up before the transformation is completed, critical momentum can be lost and regression may follow*. Until changed practices attain a new equilibrium and have been incorporated into the culture, they can be very fragile. Many months of work can be undone with remarkable speed. Once regression has begun, rebuilding momentum can be a daunting task.

Because changing anything of significance in highly interdependent systems (such as a business enterprise) often means changing nearly everything, business transformation can become a prolonged effort. Somewhere during the transformation effort, people begin to raise questions about the need for all the interdependence. All organizations have some unnecessary interdependencies that are the product of history rather than reason. Clearing up these unneeded interdependencies will mean additional near-term work but will make the overall transformation much easier.

To provide some benchmarks from which to assess the success of your transformation, the characteristics of a successful transformation at its midpoint are listed here:

- *More change, not less.* The Executive Steering Board uses the credibility afforded by short-term wins to tackle additional and bigger change projects.

- *Reduction of unnecessary interdependencies.* To make change easier in both the short term and the long term, managers identify unnecessary interdependencies and eliminate them.

- *Leadership from senior management.* Senior people focus on maintaining clarity of shared purpose for the overall effort and keeping urgency levels up.
- *Project management and leadership from below.* Lower ranks in the hierarchy both provide leadership for specific projects and manage those projects.
- *More help.* Additional people are brought in, promoted, and developed to help with all the changes.

NOTES

1. John P. Kotter, *Leading Change* (Harvard Business School Press, 1996), p. 36.

2. David A. Nadler, *Competing by Design: The Power of Organizational Architecture* (Oxford University Press, 1997), p. 62.

3. Howard W. Oden, *Managing Corporate Culture, Innovation, and Intrapreneurship* (Quorum, 1997), p. 54.

4. Donald C. Hambrick, Michael L. Tushmand, and David A. Nadler, *Navigating Change: How CEOs, Top Teams and Boards Steer Transformation* (Harvard Business School Press, 1997), p. 303.

5. Francis J. Gouillart and James H. Kelly, *Transforming the Organization: Reframing, Restructuring, Revitalizing, and Renewing* (McGraw-Hill, 1995), p. 70.

6. Kotter, *Leading Change*, p. 132.

CHAPTER 3

Strategic Planning
for Transformation

INTRODUCTION

An organization's *strategy* consists of the pattern of moves and approaches devised by management to produce successful organization performance in the *external* environment. In simpler terms, strategy is the enterprise's external game plan. If an organization is to succeed in transformation, it is imperative that its external game plan be optimized.

Strategic planning involves the total organization in that it specifies the organization's relation to its environment in terms of mission and strategies. The development of the strategic plan involves taking information from the environment and the organization and deciding on the organization's long-range course of action. To formulate a unique strategy that adds value to a desired segment of the market, you must examine the existing competencies of the organization, the current market conditions, who your customers are, and the competition. In addition, you must factor in educated predictions about the future needs of customers.

Lessons Learned from the Past

Are there important lessons to be learned from the companies that have survived over many generations?[1] What can they tell us about strategy in the 21st century? The first lesson is that behavioral context is all-important. Strategy must incorporate a sense of organizational purpose. For a firm to survive from one generation to the next, it must look beyond the narrow economic model that pervaded management thinking throughout the 20th century. Those strategy makers who see their roles as agents of economic opportunity may well satisfy their shareholder masters in the short term, but they will do so at the expense of longer-term survival. However, those who see their companies as both social and economic entities with a sense of long-term destiny and community spirit will likely pass a different and more worthwhile strategic test. Employees who feel a strong sense of belonging and identify closely with a given set of values are more likely to respond positively to alliances and webs, where each firm remains independent, than to mergers or takeovers, where clashes of cultures and values are inevitable. That is why so few mergers and takeovers are successful.

We take this first lesson to heart and establish a completely new avenue of planning called *Cultural Planning* (see Figure 2–1). Cultural planning includes the social and behavioral aspects of planning that were absent in past strategic planning.

The second lesson is that good strategy evolves continuously as the competitive environment changes. This lesson rings true particularly when major changes in technology reshape the environment. Otherwise today's success will turn into tomorrow's failure in the same way today's core competencies can turn into tomorrow's core rigidities.

The third lesson is that managers must keep learning by asking searching questions of the business—its products, markets, and operating models. Drucker's advice is to practice what he calls "abandonment." Every three years an organization should challenge every product, every service, every policy, every distribution channel with the question, If we were not in it already, would we be going into it now? This tests basic assumptions and forces managers to ask, Why didn't this work, even though it looked so promising when we went into it five years ago? Is it because we made a mistake? Is it because we did the wrong things? Or is it because the right things didn't work?

The Changing Nature of Strategy in the 21st Century

In recent years, Gary Hamel and C. K. Prahalad have taken corporate strategy into new dimensions.[2] Instead of the business school case studies that typically deal with *known* competitive factors (e.g., Coca-Cola versus Pepsi-Cola), they have stressed that building future prosperity—both for companies and for countries—is about imagining *unknown* business opportunities. It is about shaping the structure of future industries; it recognizes that competition for core competence leadership precedes competition for product leadership; and it recognizes that competition often takes place within and between coalitions of companies, and not only between individual businesses. They stress that getting *better* is not enough. Getting *different* is what matters. Figure 3-1 shows the three approaches to the quest for competitiveness.

Figure 3-1
The Quest for Competitiveness: Three Approaches

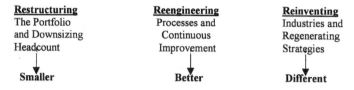

Restructuring	Reengineering	Reinventing
The Portfolio	Processes and	Industries and
and Downsizing	Continuous	Regenerating
Headcount	Improvement	Strategies
↓	↓	↓
Smaller	**Better**	**Different**

In support of their views, Hamel and Prahalad cite the example of Xerox, which received many plaudits for its efforts at quality, team-based management, and benchmarking but failed miserably in the acid test of creating new businesses. Although Xerox pioneered icon-based computing, laser printing, and the laptop computer, Hamel and Prahalad suggest that "Xerox has probably left more money on the table, in the form of under-exploited innovation, than any other company in history."

Gary Hamel sees 21st century strategy as nothing less than revolution. He suggests that if you look at any industry you will see three kinds of companies: the rule makers who built the industry (IBM, CBS, United Airlines, Merrill Lynch, Sears, Coca-Cola), the rule takers who follow the leaders (Fujitsu, ABC, U.S. Air, Smith Barney, J. C. Penney), and the revolutionaries who rewrite the rules (IEEA, The Body Shop, Charles Schwab, Dell Computer, Swatch, Southwest Airlines). In Hamel's view,

Never has the world been more hospitable to revolutionaries and more hostile to industry incumbents. The fortifications that protected the industrial oligarchy are crumbling under the weight of deregulation, technological upheaval, globilization, and social change. But it's not just the forces of change that are overturning old industrial structures—it's the actions of companies that harness those forces for the cause of revolution.[3]

Hamel poses and addresses the crucial question, "What if your company is more of a rule maker than a revolutionary?" You can either surrender the future to revolutionary challengers or revolutionize the way your company operates. There are no alternatives.

The Role of the Strategic Planning Council

The Strategic Planning process is developed and controlled by the Strategic Planning Council. The council consists of decision makers from all levels (corporate, business, and functional) in the corporation. Because strategic decisions have such a tremendous impact on a firm and because they require large commitments of company resources, they can only be made by top managers.

If this is so, what does the Strategic Council do? Its role consists primarily of gathering and organizing data and information needed for strategic planning and then coordinating the process of reviewing and approving the strategic plans developed in various parts of the company. Its contribution is facilitating and coordinating the strategic planning efforts, helping managers at all levels identify the strategic issues that ought to be addressed, providing information, helping with the analysis of industry and competitive conditions if asked, and generating information on the company's strategic performance. But it should not be charged with making strategic decisions, preparing detailed strategic plans (for someone else to implement), or making strategic action recommendations that usurp the strategy-making responsibilities of managers in charge of major operating units.

In summary, the role of the Strategic Planning Council can be stated as follows:

1. Developing a framework for strategic planning and providing the data base
2. Identifying and evaluating new product and market opportunities
3. Monitoring, reviewing, and revising the strategic plan
4. Forecasting economic conditions and trends
5. Developing contingency plans and alternate scenarios
6. Predicting the uncertain future.

As we mentioned on page 34, the functions of the Strategic Planning Council can be performed by a number of organizational structures. For a large organization, a newly formed council reporting to the Executive Steering Board as shown in Figure 2–2 would be appropriate. If the company already has a highly competent strategic planning unit, by all means use it. Don't create another one. For smaller organizations, the Strategic Planning Council may be a subgroup within the Executive Steering Board.

Outline of the Strategic Planning Process

In the remainder of this chapter we will discuss the strategic planning process following the outline provided here:

- Define the Business and Develop the Mission
- Conduct External Analysis: Develop Value Propositions
- Conduct Internal Analysis: Develop Competencies and Capabilities
- Assess External and Internal Analysis: Match Value Propositions and Competencies
- Develop, Evaluate, and Select Strategies

- Implement Strategies
- Evaluate Results

After defining the business and mission, we will conduct an analysis of the external environment, the internal environment, and an assessment of these two analyses. In the external analysis, we want to perform a study of our environment, especially our industry, our competitors, and particularly our customers. We will discuss the development and use of value propositions for our customers.

In our internal analysis we will examine the internal strengths and weaknesses of the company. We will especially identify and develop the resources, capabilities, and competencies needed to support the value propositions and our mission. In the assessment that follows, we will try to match value propositions with competencies so that we can develop viable strategies that will give us a competitive advantage. We will end the chapter with a discussion of the implementation and evaluation of the strategies developed.

DEFINE THE BUSINESS AND DEVELOP THE MISSION

Define the Mission Statement

The organization's mission statement specifies the organization's basic purpose, its reason for being. It should be a long-run concept of what the organization is trying to become—-the unique aim that differentiates it from similar organizations. The mission should provide direction and significance to all members of the organization, regardless of their level. The mission statement should take into account the organization's history, core competencies, and environment. While an organization may be able to do many things, it should seek to do what it can do best. Core competencies are those things that an organization does well—-so well that they offer an advantage over similar organizations. The organization's environment dictates the opportunities, constraints, and threats that must be identified before a mission statement is developed.

To be most useful, the mission statement should focus on markets rather than products and should be achievable and specific. The customers or clients of an organization are critical in determining its mission. Also, the mission should have an external rather than an internal focus. In other words, the mission statement should focus on the broad class of needs that the organization is seeking to satisfy (external focus), not on the physical product or service that the organization is offering (internal focus). While the mission statement should stretch the organization toward more effective performance, it should at the same time be realistic and achievable. It should provide guidance for the future, but should not lead the organization into unrealistic ventures far beyond its competencies. The mission statement must be sufficiently specific and detailed that it will be interpreted in the same manner by all who read it. Vaguely worded or ambiguous mission statements may do more harm than good.

What is the relationship between the mission statement and the vision statement we developed in Chapter 2? A vision statement differs from a mission statement in that the vision statement does not attempt to be as detailed or all-encompassing. Rather, it is a simple one-sentence guide or motto that everyone can remember, relate to, and visualize. It primarily serves an inspirational, motivational, or integrational purpose. Ford's motto, "Quality Is Job One," is an example of a short, simple, but effective vision statement. The organization's mission statement, strategic intent, and strategies should be developed to support and flesh out the vision statement.

When an organization has formulated its vision and mission, it knows where it wants to go and how it wants to proceed. The next task is to develop a grand design to get there. This grand design comprises the organization's long-range plans or strategies. Organizational strategies are the broad approaches the organization takes to achieve its mission.

Define the Strategic Intent

Strategic intent steers the firm's internal resources, capabilities, and core competencies to accomplish the firm's goals in the competitive environment. Concerned with winning competitive battles and obtaining global leadership, strategic intent implies a significant stretch of an organization's resources, capabilities, and core competencies. For example, when established effectively, a strategic intent can cause people to perform in ways they never imagined would be possible. Strategic intent exists when all employees and levels of a firm are committed to the pursuit of a specific (and significant) performance criterion. Some argue that strategic intent provides employees with the only goal worthy of personal effort and commitment—to unseat the best or remain the best, worldwide. Strategic intent has been formed effectively when people believe fervently in their product and industry and when they are focused totally on their firm's ability to outdo its competitors.

The rules for a useful strategic intent are that it be clearly understood, communicated, believed by the employees, and seen as feasible; that it provide consistency to the work done by the enterprise; and that it be *stable* for at least a few years at a time. The strategic intent must not change at the drop of a hat, although it will change periodically—as paradigms change.

Relationship between Mission and Strategic Intent

The mission is a statement of a firm's unique purpose and the scope of its operations in product and market terms. A strategic mission is *externally focused* and provides general descriptions of the products a firm intends to produce and the markets it will serve. On the other hand, the strategic intent is *internally focused*. It is concerned with identifying and developing the resources, capabilities, and core competencies on which a firm can base its strategic actions. Strategic intent reflects what a firm is capable of doing as a result of its core competencies and the unique ways they can be used to exploit a competitive advantage.

The strategic intent will be used primarily to guide internal employees in developing the competencies and capabilities that will be needed to achieve the firm's mission. It is normally somewhat more detailed and specific than the mission.

CONDUCT EXTERNAL ANALYSIS: DEVELOP VALUE PROPOSITIONS

In the external analysis, we want to perform a study of our environment, especially our industry and particularly our customers and our competitors in the industry. From this study we want to identify two types of information. First, we want to identify the opportunities and threats in the environment. We want to particularly identify opportunities for which we can develop value propositions. A second type of information needed is data suitable for benchmarking. In benchmarking, one takes the best in the business as a challenging but reasonable goal for oneself. By doing so, we know that we are not deluding ourselves by working toward goals that are too low.

Focusing on the Customer

Transformation implies growth, and focusing on customers is a good place to start, for providing the benefits customers seek—often new, as yet undiscovered benefits—is what leads to business growth. Market research is to the corporation what the *senses* are to the human body, connecting the corporate mind and body to its environment.

Rubbermaid has shown how identifying customer needs and quickly designing products around those needs can revitalize a company even in an industry as prosaic as rubber goods. Johnson and Johnson is another company that has sustained its customer-driven creativity over the years.

A key reason that firms must be able to satisfy customers' needs is that in the final analysis, returns earned from relationships with customers are the lifeblood of all organizations. The challenge of identifying and determining how to satisfy the needs of what some business analysts believe are increasingly sophisticated, knowledgeable, and fickle customers is difficult. Moreover, it is only through total satisfaction of their needs that customers develop the type of firm-specific loyalty companies seek.

Failing to observe and listen to customers carefully and with an open imagination creates an unintended bias toward reducing service levels, streamlining product lines, and driving product designs to uniformity. An even stronger bias, again unintended, is created to reduce costs. This is further reinforced, because when you don't know your customers intimately, it's hard to build a convincing case for improvement based on growth. Instead of building multiple processes around customer segments and the benefits they seek, companies trapped in commoditization drive each other toward a single, generic process producing like benefits. In the systematic application of market-blind methods, the corporation goes out in style, looking better and better until the very bitter end.

Strategically competitive organizations in the latter part of the 1990s and into the 21st century should (1) think continuously about who their customers are, (2) maintain close and frequent contacts with their customers, (3) determine how to use their core competencies in ways that competitors cannot imitate, and (4) design their strategies to allow them to satisfy customers' current, anticipated, and even unanticipated needs.

Determining Which, What, and How to Satisfy Customers

Determining **Which Customers** *to Serve*

Customers can be divided into groups based on differences in their needs. Any identifiable human or organizational characteristic can be used to subdivide a large potential market into segments that differ from one another in specified characteristics. Common characteristics on which customers' needs will vary include (1) demographic variables (e.g., age, gender, income, occupation, race, nationality, and social class), (2) geographic segmentation (regions, countries, states, counties, cities, and towns), (3) lifestyle (a set of values or tastes exhibited by a group of customers, especially as reflected in consumption patterns), (4) individual personality traits, (5) consumption patterns (e.g., usage rate and brand use), (6) industry structural characteristics, and (7) organizational size.

Determining **What Needs** *to Satisfy for Customers*

As a firm decides whom it will serve, it must simultaneously identify the needs of the chosen customer group that its goods or services can satisfy. Top-level managers play a critical role in efforts to recognize and understand customers' needs. Their capacity to gain valuable insights from listening to and studying customers influences product, technology, and distribution decisions.

An additional competitive advantage accrues to firms capable of anticipating and then satisfying needs that were unknown to target customers. Firms able to do this provide customers with unexpected value—that is, a product performance capability or characteristic they did not request, yet do value. Moreover anticipating customers' needs yields opportunities for firms to shape the industry's future and gain an early competitive advantage.

Determining **How** *to Satisfy Customers' Needs*

Firms use their *core competencies* to implement value-creating strategies to satisfy customers' needs. One of the strategic imperatives at IBM is to move quickly to convert the firm's technological competence into commercial products that customers value. This topic will be discussed in more detail in the following section on competencies.

Developing Value Propositions

What Are Value Propositions?

Companies exist to create value for customers. To create value, they provide customers with benefits, that is, things customers perceive as making their lives better. Those benefits are delivered at a price that allows the company to be profitable. A value proposition is *a description of the benefits offered and of the price charged.* The name of the game is to maximize the (conceptual) spread in the customer's mind between the benefits provided and the price charged.

A product or service is a benefit only if the customer perceives it as such. A benefit induces a positive emotional end state, or at the minimum a change in the customer's state of mind toward a problem he or she has. Identifying a benefit involves imagining the customer's life in a simple "before and after" video. Before, the customer is struggling with his daily lot, trying to resolve some irking issues. After using the value proposition (product), the customer has resolved several issues and is a happier person. Benefits are the magic wands that produce the happiness.

In the simplest competitive terms, the company with the best value proposition wins. Contrary to the popular belief that companies can win only if they are either low-cost providers or fully differentiated competitors, there can be as many value propositions as there are creative combinations of benefits and prices. This allows for an enormous range of strategic flexibility and business growth, with room for many winners. The key, again, is to have an "out-of-company" experience, to look from the outside through the eyes of the customer, while retaining the unique context of the company's genetic makeup. In practice, this requires detailed knowledge of and close relationships with customers. In market terms the company with the most intimate knowledge of its customer's problems and desires will own the customer relationship, and the company that owns the customer relationship wins.

Every business is characterized by value propositions—a description of what *benefits* it intends to provide its customers, and at what price. Customers judge the value propositions of several competitors and pick the one that provides the best combination of benefits offered and price charged. A benefit represents an emotional end state. It may be defined as one or more products and/or services that help the customer solve an irking issue that causes the customer to *perceive* his or her life as somehow better. The best way to identify benefits is to spend a day in the life of one's customer and to imagine what the company can do to solve some of the problems that the customer faces.

Developing Value Propositions

Three rules are helpful when developing a value proposition.[4] First, creativity requires that you pick customers as far down the value chain as is practical. The immediate customer often screens companies from more creative downstream plays. Second, working on one customer at a time allows insight development that no group approach can provide. Intimacy is the key to market focus, and there is no such thing as intimacy with a large population. Third, creative value propositions come from companies that never abdicate to their customers the task of defining their own value propositions. They listen to their customers, but don't rely on them to tell them what to do. These three simple rules are amplified in the following paragraphs.

1. *Choose the Right Customers, Through the Entire Value Chain.* This is no trivial matter, for often there is an infinite range of customers to select from. First, there's the issue of which stage of the value chain to focus on. Generally speaking, the most creative plays are those farthest away from the company's immediate business. Conversely, the further one ventures from one's immediate business, the more difficult it becomes to identify what the company can actually do to have an impact that far down the chain. The further the company ventures away from its immediate customers, the higher is the potential return, but also higher is the risk of striking out.

Once the stage of the value chain has been chosen, typically there are multiple possible customers at each step. Which should the company focus on? Experience is the best counselor. The size of the potential segment clearly is an important consideration. The complexity of the application is also critical. The more complex the environment in which the product or service is used, the better the chance to create a truly original value proposition.

2. *Take One Customer at a Time.* Becoming market-focused requires a great deal of patience. Identifying the benefits a customer will respond to requires an intimacy that, by definition, can be created only one customer at a time. While the economic pressure for shortcuts is always there, no group approach can succeed in matters of market focus. Segmentation is the key, and segmentation needs to be based on benefits, which are the result of intimacy.

3. *Don't Rely on Customers to Do Your Job.* It's important to listen to customers. But it's equally important not to let your customers define your strategy for you. Customers can give you ideas, but they don't know your business as well as you do—if they did, they would have moved into your territory a long time ago! Their counsel is always helpful when they are talking about their own business and the utilization they make of your products. But when they try to do *your* job, they often become naive or idealistic.

All companies have value propositions, whether they know it or not. They may be mixed and contradictory, but they are there nonetheless. To operate without clearly defined value propositions is like walking through a jungle in a sensory-deprivation suit; you may make it through, but only if you are lucky. Therefore, in addition to defining the high-level strategy, the role of leaders is to require each line of business to develop a set of value propositions. Ideally, the sum total of a company's value propositions forms an integrated set, supporting the corporation's ultimate mission.

Designing a Value Delivery System

A value delivery system is the unique set of capabilities required to create and deliver the benefits of the value proposition to the target customer segment. It represents a cross-section of company systems, brought to bear in a carefully crafted set of processes and learning loops. For example, the selection of the value proposition is a representation of the mission. Building the value delivery system requires creating the products and services, building needed physical infrastructure and organization, and designing information technology.

In bringing all the systems to bear, however, none is more important than the work processes. The benefits offered by the value proposition will materialize only if the processes and learning loops within the company are flexible and expandable, creating new paths to reach the newly set goals. Putting the concept into practice carries sweeping implications for the other systems. Benefits-based segmentation typically implies the need to reorganize marketing and sales, change the manufacturing strategy, make corresponding changes in physical infrastructure, and so forth. Ideally, all systems are designed around the benefits the company intends to provide. When all systems have been aligned with the business's set of value propositions, the company has created a *value delivery system.*

The need to align all systems around the value proposition of the firm produces a formidable logistical challenge. Every work-related decision is linked to the set of benefits the company intends to provide. To keep all systems aligned, the natural tendency of company systems to run in different directions must be overcome. The role of the CEO and other top leaders is to guide and orchestrate the realignment effort to create the new value delivery system.

The value proposition acts as the design standard. Without it, each design step would be dictated by functional knowledge, with no common context for alignment. If, for example, every step were entrusted to functional specialists, each, acting on his or her own best judgment, would unavoidably step out of alignment. Even if each were striving to contribute in good faith to the overall strategy, the system would have a tendency to work itself out of alignment, because each of us behaves according to his or her own version of the ultimate goal.

Segmenting the Customer Base by Benefits

In a perfect world a company would have a separate value proposition for each and every customer, but typically that's not a practical approach. Consequently, corporations need to build aggregations of customers, or *customer segments*. Homogeneous expectations of benefits and prices (i.e., similar value propositions) constitute the standard for grouping customers together.

Often, companies mistakenly group customers into demographically based units, such as industry, region, age group, product, or service. Unfortunately, these traditional ways of divvying up the customer base make it difficult, if not impossible, to effectively deliver the benefits offered by a value proposition.

Following a benefits-based segmentation strategy offers many advantages. In addition to providing focus and direction for the high-level strategy, it changes the standard of customer satisfaction from "selling products and services" to "making the customer's life better." The former tends to lock companies within their existing portfolio of products and services. The latter encourages creative thinking about how to recombine capabilities, products, and services to make customers' lives easier. It is the difference between stagnation and growth. The leader's role here is to sell the corporation on the merits of benefits-based segmentation.

Inventing New Businesses

Growth also comes by starting new businesses from scratch. This requires the cross-fertilization of capabilities that are often scattered throughout a firm's business portfolio and the creative assembling of them to develop new offerings. In many cases the capabilities of other firms are required, spawning alliances, partnerships, mergers, or acquisitions.

As we explore the inventing of new businesses, we see how the entire DuPont empire is built on a few hard-to-manipulate catalysts. We see how Sears used its customer knowledge as a launch pad for its Discover credit card and, more broadly, for its "socks and stocks" strategy. We see how BT (British Telecom) and MCI wed their competencies and gave birth to a new enterprise.

CONDUCT INTERNAL ANALYSIS: DEVELOP COMPETENCIES

In the internal analysis, managers examine the strengths and weaknesses of their companies. A strength is something an organization is good at or a characteristic the organization has that gives it a competitive advantage. A resource, a capability, a competence, or anything else that gives the company a market advantage can be a strength. A weakness is something an organization lacks or does poorly, or a condition that puts it at a disadvantage.

Importance of Internal Analysis

The demands of the new competitive landscape make it necessary for top-level managers to rethink the concept of the corporation. Although corporations are difficult to change, earning strategic competitiveness in the 1990s and into the 21st century requires the development and use of a different managerial mind-set. Most top-level managers recognize the need to change their mind-sets, but many hesitate to do so. In the words of a European CEO of a major U.S. company, "It is more reassuring for all of us to stay as we are, even though we know the result will be certain failure, than to jump into a new way of working when we cannot be sure it will succeed."

Critical to the managerial mind-set required is the view that a firm is a *bundle* of resources, capabilities, and core competencies that can be used to create an exclusive market position. This view suggests that individual firms possess at least some resources and capabilities that other companies do not have, at least not in the same combination. Resources are the source of capabilities, some of which lead to the development of a firm's core competencies.

By exploiting their core competencies and meeting the demanding standards of global competition, firms create value for their customers. Value entails the performance characteristics and attributes provided by companies in the form of goods or services for which customers are willing to pay. Ultimately, customer value is the source of a firm's potential to earn average or above-average returns. Value is provided to customers by a product's low cost, by its highly differentiated features, or by a combination of low cost and high differentiation, as compared to competitors' offerings. Core competencies, then, are actually a value-creating system through which a company seeks strategic competitiveness and above-average returns. In the new competitive landscape, managers need to determine if their firm's core competencies continue to create value for customers.

Resources, Capabilities, and Competencies

Our attention now turns to a description of resources, capabilities, and competencies—characteristics that are the foundation of competitive advantage.

Resources

Resources are inputs into a firm's production process such as capital equipment, the skills of individual employees, patents, finance, and talented managers. Broad in scope, resources cover a spectrum of individual, social, and organizational phenomena. Individually, resources typically do not yield a competitive advantage. A professional football team may benefit from employing the league's most talented running back. However, it is only when the running back integrates his running style with the blocking schemes of the offensive linemen and the team's offensive strategy that a competitive advantage may develop.

Capabilities

Capability is the capacity for a set of resources to integratively perform a task or activity. *Capabilities* are unique combinations of the firm's information-based resources and are what the firm is able to do as a result of teams of resources working together. Capabilities represent the firm's capacity to deploy resources that have been purposely *integrated* to achieve a desired end state. The glue that binds an organization together, capabilities emerge over time through complex interactions between and among tangible and intangible resources. They are based on developing, carrying, and exchanging information and knowledge through the firm's human capital. Thus, the firm's knowledge base is embedded in and reflected by its capabilities and is a key source of advantage in the new competitive landscape. Because a knowledge base is grounded in organizational actions that may not be explicitly understood by all employees, the firm's capabilities become stronger and more strategically valuable through repetition and practice.

The primary base for the firm's capabilities is the skills and knowledge of its employees. As such, the value of human capital in the development and use of capabilities and, ultimately, core competencies cannot be overstated. Microsoft, for example, believes that its best asset is the "intellectual horsepower" of its employees. To assure continued development of this capability and the core competence that follows, the firm strives continuously to hire people who are more talented than the current set of employees.

Some believe that the knowledge possessed by the firm's human capital is among the most significant of an organization's capabilities and may ultimately be at the root of all competitive advantages. In the words of a business analyst, companies have come to understand that one of the strongest competitive advantages is extensive knowledge. Some even view knowledge as the sum of everything everybody in a company knows that gives the firm a competitive edge in the marketplace. Moreover, the *rate* at which firms acquire new knowledge and develop the skills necessary to apply it in the marketplace is a key source of competitive advantage.

Competencies

Competencies are capabilities that are valuable, rare, costly to imitate, and non-substitutable and comprise a source of competitive advantage. As the sources of competitive advantage for a firm, core competencies distinguish a company competitively and reflect its personality. Core competencies emerge over time through an organizational process of accumulating and learning how to deploy different resources and capabilities. As a capacity to take action, core competencies are the essence of what makes an organization unique in its ability to provide value to customers over a long period of time.

However, not all of a firm's resources and capabilities are competencies—that is, assets that have competitive value and the potential to serve as a source of competitive advantage. In fact, some resources and capabilities may result in incompetence because they represent competitive areas in which the firm is weak compared to competitors. Thus, some resources or capabilities may stifle or prevent the development of a competence. Firms with insufficient financial capital, for example, may be unable to purchase facilities or hire the skilled workers required to manufacture products that yield customer value. In this situation, financial capital (a tangible resource) would be a weakness. Armed with in-depth understandings of their firm's resources and capabilities, strategic managers are challenged to find external environmental opportunities that can be exploited through the firm's capabilities while avoiding competition in areas of weakness.

Core Competencies

A *core competency* is a related set of skills, capabilities, and technologies that makes a company uniquely adept in an area or field that has applications across businesses and industries. Managers use four specific criteria to determine which of their firm's resources and capabilities are core competencies. If they satisfy the four criteria of sustainable competitive advantage, (Valuable, Rare, Costly to Imitate, and Non-substitutable), the capabilities are considered *core* competencies for the firms possessing them. Core competencies differ for every organization, but the realities of the new competitive landscape may demand that every organization seek to develop innovation as a core competency.

Core competencies—capabilities that are valuable, rare, costly to imitate, and non-substitutable—are a source of competitive advantage. Capabilities failing to satisfy these criteria are not core competencies. Every core competency is a capability, but every capability is not a core competency. A sustained competitive advantage is achieved only when competitors have tried, without success, to duplicate the benefits of a firm's strategy or when competitors lack the confidence to attempt imitation. However, for some period of time, a firm may earn a competitive advantage through the use of capabilities that, for example, are valuable and rare but can be imitated. In such an instance, the length of time a firm can expect to retain its competitive advantage is a function of how quickly competitors can successfully imitate a good, service, or process. It is only through the combination of conditions represented by all four criteria that a firm's capabilities have the potential to create a sustained competitive advantage.

An attractive attribute of a firm's core competencies is that, unlike physical assets, they tend to become more valuable through additional use. A key reason is that they are largely knowledge based. Sharing knowledge across people, jobs, and organizational functions often results in an expansion of that knowledge in competitively relevant ways.

Recent Emphasis on Core Competencies

The concept of core competencies has been taking the business world by storm.[5] According to Gary Hamel and C. K. Prahalad, the originators of the concept, a corporation's strength rests on its portfolio, not of businesses, but of core competencies. New businesses, they say, are spawned by leveraging core competencies in new business segments, by taking what you do well *across* businesses and creatively applying it in new, unexplored industries.

They define core competencies as the collective learning in organizations, especially understanding how to coordinate diverse production skills and integrate multiple streams of technologies. They further identify a core competency as having three critical elements. It provides potential access to a wide variety of markets, it makes a significant contribution to the values that customers appreciate in the bundle of goods and services provided, and it is difficult for competitors to imitate. These criteria apply to non-technical competencies as well as to the more common view of technical competence.

A core competency is a related set of skills, capabilities, and technologies that makes a company uniquely adept in an area or field that has applications across businesses and industries. Honda's core competence in engine design and manufacturing, for example, is what enabled it to expand from the motorcycle business to automobiles and trucks, to lawn mowers and power equipment, and to industrial compressors. Canon leveraged its optical and mechanical expertise to expand from the camera market into copiers, now competing side-by-side with the once dominant Xerox. A focus on core competencies is one of the driving forces behind the emergence of Japan as a major industrial power. In fact, it is the underlying principle that has spawned most large industries.

Consider, for example, what propelled the rise of DuPont as a major power in the chemical industry. It was their unique mastery of certain catalysts such as hydrogen cyanide and hydrogen fluoride. These are among the most toxic and difficult chemicals to handle, yet they drive key chemical processes and represent the foundation of DuPont's chemical empire, the inner sanctum of the firm, the roots of its chemical tree. The public knows about and buys Nylon, Lycra, Coriano, and Kevlar, but few would want to handle cyanide in their garage. Thus process catalysis is one of DuPont's core competencies.

It is core competencies that provide the connectors across businesses and industries. A corporation's strategic architecture can be viewed as a tree, with competencies as the roots and businesses as the fruits; the trunk represents core systems shared across businesses, and the branches the business-specific system. In DuPont's case, for example, process catalysis would be the root of the tree, while Lycra and Nylon would be its fruits.

The historical approach to managing businesses is tantamount to injecting water into the fruits instead of watering the roots and letting businesses draw the sap. The first approach may create a deceptively juicy-looking fruit in the short term, but the yield is likely to drop a year later. If by chance a bolt of lightning should strike, the once hallowed tree may reveal its hollow core. By contrast, the company that focuses on core competencies nurtures a healthy trunk and limbs, making it a prime candidate for the experimental grafting of new branches to grow exotic fruits, rich in nutritional content.

The Ephemeral Nature of Core Competencies

The ephemeral nature of core competence indicates that the required core competencies change over time and that those appropriate for playing yesterday's game just might be a serious drawback for today's—and even more so for tomorrow's. For example, IBM has great competence in design, manufacture, marketing, and after-sales service for mainframe computers, which may be nothing more than an albatross keeping it from responding to the latest discontinuities and expectation changes. Core competencies need to evolve—to meet the current discontinuities and changes in expectations, to develop the appropriate responses, and to enable whatever change in mission is necessary.

For many companies, competencies in pushing products out the door (design, building, selling, servicing, financing) today hinder their ability to achieve a true customer focus. In some cases, there is just too much unlearning required. Might General Motors' long history of applying the latest technology, for example, have kept it from adopting the simplicity dictates of Japanese manufacturing? An outsider's view suggests GM has seriously underestimated the paradigm shift required to move from the "mass production" stage to "continuous improvement."

Evidence and company experiences show that the value of core competencies, as sources of competitive advantage, should never be taken for granted. Moreover, the ability of any particular core competency to provide competitive advantage on a permanent basis should not be assumed. It must be remembered that all core capabilities simultaneously have the potential to be core rigidities. All capabilities then, are both strengths and weaknesses. They are strengths because they are the source of competitive advantage and, hence, strategic competitiveness; they are weaknesses because if emphasized when no longer competitively relevant, they can be the seeds of organizational inertia.

Finding Core Competencies

The quest to discover core competencies has disappointed many a company. More often than not, such attempts yield a fairly trivial model of the firm's strategic architecture, providing neither the insights nor the actions that were hoped for. One problem is that the process can be quite boring, involving long lists of technologies and capabilities to which are applied many tests. The attempt to generate exciting ideas dies because of lack of interest. What's the key? How do you unleash the power of core competencies?

It is predominantly a behavioral, not an analytical problem: The answer lies in the approach. Create interdivisional *projects* rather than interdivisional *reflection*. Get people excited and talking to each other, and the insights and actions often will jump to the surface. The essence of the approach is "design as you go—strategy in action." Pick a couple of initiatives requiring the cross-fertilization of capabilities across multiple businesses and run with them. Let people discover for themselves the value of sharing knowledge and information across organizational boundaries.

ASSESS EXTERNAL AND INTERNAL ANALYSIS: MATCH VALUE PROPOSITIONS AND COMPETENCIES

Formulation of a successful strategic plan requires managers to have an accurate and complete understanding of the external environment and the internal capabilities of the organization. In this stage we are going to assess the results of our internal and external analysis and try to match up value propositions with core competencies to create a viable strategy for the company. A company will achieve strategic success by integrating and increasing strengths and opportunities and by reducing weaknesses and threats.

Matching Value Propositions and Competencies

The organization must learn to think of itself not as producing goods and services, but as buying customers—doing the things that will make people want to do business with it. Many 20th-century companies have become highly proficient at designing and delivering products and services with high quality and reasonable prices. They have learned to compete aggressively, offer their customers good value for the money, and become lean and efficient, but still they have failed to keep their customers. Over the past 25 years, customers have become more demanding. At one time they considered only price and quality; now they want products and services with fast delivery, wide variety, state-of-the-art technology, low cost, high quality, convenience of purchase, and excellent service. Firms have responded by instigating improvement initiatives in all these areas. While 20th-century managers have been thinking about improving products and services to compete more aggressively in their markets, 21st-century managers have been thinking about *which* customers to serve and how to improve the value of the products and services they offer them.

Twenty-first-century managers, in other words, match customers to their *value proposition* and, with the power of strong competencies and processes behind them, continue to distance themselves from the competition. Whereas strategy is about foresight and ideas leading to a set of competencies, the value proposition is about translating those ideas into a set of deliverable promises to the customer.

Figure 3-2
Types of Customer Values

	Product Leadership	Operational Excellence	Customer Intimacy
Values	*State-of-the-art products	*Low costs, high quality	*Customization
	*Speed to market	*Excellent service	*Deep, long-term relationships
Examples	Microsoft	Direct Line	Saturn
	Hewlett-Packard	Wal-Mart	Staples
	3M	Dell	British Airways

Choosing the Right Value Proposition

Twenty-first-century managers must think like their customers. They must decide which market niche to attack, build a platform of competencies to undertake the assault, and with the backing of imaginative information systems ensure that they deliver more value than the competition. They should believe in three important principles: first, that different customers buy different kinds of value; second, that as value standards rise, so do customer expectations, which means they can stay ahead only by moving ahead; and third, that having an unrivaled level of a particular value requires a superior operating system dedicated to delivering it.

They understand that they cannot be all things to all people. Rather than trying to compete on all aspects of product and service delivery, they choose one of three propositions on which to compete: *product leadership, operational excellence,* or *customer intimacy.*[6] The one chosen defines the company in the eyes of the customer. This is not to say that the other propositions should be sacrificed. Companies must at least meet industry standards in all areas. But in their chosen specialties they must exceed customer expectations and build their operating models around this formula.

Customers fall broadly into three categories (see Figure 3-2). One set of customers is interested in the latest state-of-the-art products. Their choices are usually driven by a taste for fashion or a desire for a particular technology. Thus companies pursuing this market segment compete primarily on *product leadership.* The launch of Windows 98, for example, introduced a must-have product for many personal computer users. Microsoft's relationship with its customers is defined by its technical leadership position in the market. Customers see the company as innovative, regularly bringing out new high-quality products, and they like to be associated with it. Nike shoes, Hewlett-Packard printers, and Sony Walkman products all fall into this category.

A second set of customers is more interested in buying products and services on the basis of low price and convenience. These customers still demand high quality, but they are not prepared to pay premium prices or go out of their way to make a purchase. They typically buy on mail order, through membership warehouse clubs, and quality chain stores. They might buy their basics from Wal-Mart, their computers from Dell, and their insurance from Direct Line. Companies that define their customer value in this way compete on the basis of *operational excellence*. They must constantly increase speed and convenience and reduce costs in all their operations.

The third set of customers is interested in getting exactly what they want, even if they have to pay a higher price or wait a bit longer to get it. Such customers buy from suppliers that they can identify with their own special needs. Thus British Airways has dedicated its business to the needs of the executive traveler, and the Staples office supplies chain has identified itself with the small business customer. Customers see these companies as being responsive to their needs, and they repay this responsiveness with loyalty. Thus British Airways and Staples pursue a policy of *customer intimacy*—that is, they become specifically identified with the special needs of a particular niche market and satisfy it over a long period.

In each case, once the value proposition has been chosen, managers must ensure that the whole company is dedicated to its pursuit and improvement and that the appropriate systems are put in place to support it.

Developing the Core Competency to Achieve the Value Proposition

Now that we have identified the value propositions that the firm will pursue, we must also identify and develop the core competencies needed to achieve them. Core competencies are not something you will find hanging on a tree. They must be identified and painstakingly built up over a long period of time. At this point all we can do is identify where we should be building our core competencies.

The process improvement methodology that we will pursue in Part II will enable us to optimize the design of the company's processes that are needed to achieve the core competency. Identifying the value proposition and the core competency that will achieve it will provide much needed guidance to the process improvement effort of Part II.

There is nothing especially novel about defining a company's customer relationship in terms of delivering value. Marketing departments have been doing this for years. What will be different for 21st-century companies is the way they define value and then build their corporate competencies to support their value proposition.

Core competencies must be identified and developed, but core competencies alone do not determine profitability. They must be matched with winning products and services. Whereas core competencies are the springboard, the chosen value proposition and its accompanying operating model enable a company to align its processes and systems and ensure that its management culture and performance measures fulfill its promises to the customer.

DEVELOP, EVALUATE, AND SELECT STRATEGIES

The Nature of Strategy

Corporate strategies are the broad approaches the organization takes to achieve its mission. They should answer the following basic questions: (1) how do we respond to new opportunities in the environment, lessen the impact of environmental threats, and strengthen the mix of the organization's activities by doing more of some things and less of others; (2) how do we compete with other organizations for customer groups and customer needs through allocation of existing or new products and services; and (3) how do we assign resources among the various subunits of the organization? Each strategy should state one or more objectives and course/s of action to achieve these objectives.

We want to develop as many feasible alternative strategies as possible. The more we can develop, the greater the probability that we have developed the best ones. The results of the internal/external analysis assessment, ideas from other corporations gleaned through our external analysis, and any other source of ideas should be used. The following criteria may be used in evaluating alternative strategies: (1) the strategy should exploit a value proposition using core competencies, (2) the strategy and its component programs should have consistent goals and policies, and (3) it should be capable of producing the intended results. A corporation must select the strategies that are best suited to their capabilities. New capabilities that require investment in facilities or human resources cannot be built up quickly.

Relationship of Strategy with Mission and Strategic Intent

Strategy describes the set of action programs taken—either to implement a change effort or to implement a true transformation. At the same time, the strategy must be consistent with and clearly support the defined mission and strategic intent. If not, implementation of the actions will be difficult, belief in the mission and strategic intent will erode, and the organization will become confused. We all have a tendency to focus on action. Do it now, and worry about why tomorrow. As long as the result is not dysfunctional, this pragmatic impulse may be all right, but if the actions actually are leading to a transformation, it is important to step back and look at the implications. A transformation implies a change in mission and strategic intent. If we are changing the strategy drastically and not changing the mission and strategic intent, there will be much confusion in the organization.

IMPLEMENT STRATEGIC PLANS

As soon as a strategy has been determined, it should be implemented, or incorporated into the daily operations of the organization by means of appropriate organizational plans. The most sophisticated and creative strategy will not benefit the organization unless it is carried out effectively.

Define and Communicate the New Strategic Direction

Organizational transformations are undertaken to generate dramatic improvements in business performance and customer satisfaction. By defining and communicating the new strategic direction and specific organizational improvement goals, leaders of a transformation can help employees focus their efforts and energy on the key areas of the business that will determine future success.

A change program with too many initiatives confuses participants and inevitably drains energy and resources away from the handful of goals that supersede all others. By focusing the organization on a few specific stretch goals, employees can then track progress and evaluate whether each activity they perform helps the company move closer to its overall goals.

When Rockwell International's Tactical Systems Division went about its transformation, the company set clear performance improvement goals that everyone in the organization understood. Despite the intense competition in the rapidly declining defense industry, the company could excel by (1) doing things right the first time, (2) eliminating waste, and (3) removing non–value-added costs at all stages.

When the organization specifies clear performance improvement goals, employees will align their activities and measures with the overall goals of the company. Only when employees clearly understand the key business objectives can they brainstorm ways in which they can impact these important areas. If, for example, employees and managers understand that one of their company's key business objectives is to grow market share, they can increase the time spent on new product development or budget more resources for advertising and promotion. Without this knowledge, these employees and managers would be operating in the dark about how to prioritize activities and allocate resources.

EVALUATE RESULTS

As implementation proceeds, managers must check the progress at periodic or critical stages. Two questions should be asked at this point: (1)

is the strategy being implemented as planned? and (2) is the strategy achieving the intended results?

One absolutely critical part of strategic planning is the measurement of performance. If transformation is to occur, inevitably new measures will be required and old ones discarded. How else is a transformation process to be evaluated? If quality is a key part of the mission, quality needs to be measured, good quality practices need to be rewarded, and any measures that run counter to improved quality need to be eliminated systematically (and very publicly). Some typical old measures that need to be removed are measures that focus on volume at the expense of quality or financial measures that are now considered "passengers," rather than drivers.

NOTES

1. Jeremy Hope and Tony Hope, *Competing in the Third Wave* (Harvard Business School Press, 1997), p. 44.

2. Gary Hamel and C. K. Prahalad, *Competing for the Future* (Harvard Business School Press, 1996), p. 16.

3. Hope and Hope, *Competing in the Third Wave*, p. 30.

4. Francis J. Gouillart and James H. Kelly, *Transforming the Organization: Reframing, Restructuring, Revitalizing, and Renewing* (McGraw-Hill, 1995), p. 181.

5. Ibid.

6. Hope and Hope, *Competing in the Third Wave*, p. 48.

CHAPTER 4

Transforming the Organizational Culture

INTRODUCTION

The Essence of Organizational Culture

Close observation of an organization reveals a pattern of ceremonies, conventions about how to dress, use of jargon, ways of acknowledging status, mutually agreed-upon standards for doing various jobs, and frequently recited stories about how the organization came into being and how it has dealt with various crises. Further observation, and a little thinking, would convince one that all of these features of the organization actually are only surface manifestations—*artifacts*, if you will—of an underlying core of fundamental *beliefs* that are shared by the organization's members. These shared beliefs are about what is true, right, appropriate, proper, necessary, desirable, and unthinkable for the organization and about how one ought to act in the context of that organization. *The core beliefs and their artifacts are called the organization's culture.*

Because it is shared and because it lies at the heart of what they do and think, the organization's culture provides its members with a common viewpoint that binds them together as a group. It helps them understand the activities of others in the organization, and it guides their own activities within and on behalf of the organization. Because the shared beliefs include values about what is desirable and undesirable—how things should and should not be—they dictate the kinds of activities that are legitimate and the kinds that are illegitimate. Thus the culture not only places constraints upon activities of the organization and its members (cultural prohibitions), it also prescribes what the organization and its members must

Figure 4-1
Observable and Hidden Levels of Culture

OBSERVABLE LEVEL	Behaviors and Artifacts	Includes anecdotes, art, ceremonies, heroes, habits, communications, jargon, language, management practices, myths, norms, physical arrangements,
Readily observable, but hard to interpret		rituals, stories, symbols, and traditions
HIDDEN LEVEL	Values, Beliefs, and Assumptions	Includes assumptions, beliefs, cognitive processes, commitment, consensus, ethic, feelings, ideologies, mind-set, philosophy, principles, purpose, thinking,
Not directly observable—can be inferred from how people justify what they do.		sentiments, understanding, values, vision

do (cultural imperatives). In short, the culture guides the activities of the organization and its members.

Every organization has its own culture. Organizational culture is similar to an individual's personality—an intangible yet ever-present theme that provides meaning, direction, and the basis for action. Much as personality influences the behavior of an individual, shared values and beliefs within a company influences the pattern of activities, opinions, and actions within the firm. A company's culture influences how employees and managers approach problems, serve customers, deal with suppliers, react to competitors, and otherwise conduct activities now and in the future. Culture is the essence of what is important to the organization. As such, it prescribes and proscribes activities, and it defines the "dos and don'ts" that govern the behavior of its members.

We have found it helpful to think of organizational culture as having two levels, as shown in Figure 4-1: The upper level is outwardly observable, but the lower level is hidden in peoples' minds and is more difficult to know and change. The upper, observable level includes observable phenomena such as artifacts, patterns of behavior, speech, formal laws, technical know-how, and the use and production of physical objects and products. The deeper, hidden level, located in the minds of the members of the organization includes the mental frameworks, ideas, beliefs, values, attitudes, assumptions, and ways of perceiving the environment. It contains the internal processes through which behavior is learned and the implicit (often unstated) rules through which behavior is governed.

Each level of culture has a natural tendency to influence the other. This is perhaps most obvious in terms of shared values influencing a group's behavior—a commitment to customers, for example, influencing how quickly individuals tend to respond to customer complaints. But causality can flow in the other direction too—behavior and practices can influence values. When employees who have never had any contact with the marketplace begin to interact with customers and their problems and needs, they often begin to value the interests of customers more.

The hidden aspect of the culture is the more important part of the culture; it is the part that truly influences peoples' behavior. If managers focus only on the observable aspect of culture, they will not fully understand the human behavior they are trying to manage, which is controlled by employees' values and beliefs, the hidden aspect of culture. The hidden level of culture can usually be inferred by observing the behavior of organizational members, since the two cultural levels reflect and reinforce one another. Each person inherently desires the two levels to be consistent and will instinctively try to modify his or her behavior and/or thoughts to make them consistent.

Why Is Culture Important?

Culture is important because it pervades and influences all activities in an organization. It establishes the conditions for judging internal effectiveness. It determines whether performance is effective or ineffective, and what "effective" and "ineffective" mean in the organization. It sets the expectations and priorities—what's important around here—and conditions for reward and punishment. People who adhere to these expectations and priorities get promoted and advance; those who don't adhere, don't advance. Too much noncompliance typically leads to termination.

The many reasons cited for the failure of organizational behavior change efforts can be reduced to one sentence: *The culture of the organization remained unchanged.* Any attempt to introduce management practices or organizational behavior changes that are radically different from the existing culture will almost certainly fail if these changes are incompatible with the existing culture. The culture—that sum of values, beliefs, and assumptions that is the core of any organization—must support the new initiatives if these behavioral changes are to take hold. Without a change in the culture of the company, no new set of skills or work processes will bring about the kind of reform that is needed.

An organizational culture supports organizational strategy by providing a base of continuity around which a proactive company can evolve, experiment, and change. By being clear about what are its core values and beliefs (and therefore relatively fixed), a company can more easily seek strategic change and movement in all that is not core. A 21st-century company does not seek a mere balance between the culture and strategy; it seeks to develop both to their highest level at the same time, all the time.

An organization's culture provides order and structure for activity. It provides people with an internal way of life and, in so doing, plays the same role for people that a society's culture plays. It tells people which activities are in bounds and which are out of bounds. It establishes ground rules for people, determining what is right and what is wrong. Over time,

Figure 4-2
Performance of High-Performance and Low-Performance Cultures

Increase over Eleven Years	High-Performance Cultures	Low-Performance Cultures
Revenue growth	682%	166%
Employment growth	282%	36%
Stock price growth	901%	74%
Net income growth	56%	1%

a culture establishes communication patterns—the kind of language people use with one another and the assumptions upon which they consistently operate. It establishes membership criteria: who is included and who is excluded.

Culture determines the nature and use of power within an organization. It fixes power at the top of an organization, disperses power throughout, or some of both. It sets the pattern for how people and functions relate to one another. It emphasizes territory or it does not. Culture lets people know how close they can get to one another and determines whether or not teaming is important and expected. Culture also provides the framework for addressing, managing, and resolving conflicts in the organization.

A five-year study by Kotter and Heskett of 207 U.S. companies in 22 industries found that the financially successful companies focused first on fulfilling customer and employee needs and only secondarily on profits.[1] This research indicates that when companies focus on all key stakeholders and when they expect leadership from all employee levels, they outperform their competitors by wide margins. As Figure 4-2 shows, the performance gap between representatives of the high-performance and low-performance cultures is enormous.

The Nature of Culture Transformation

We have looked at the nature of culture. Now, let's look at a subject of even more interest to us, "What is the nature of *changing* culture?"

Times Have Changed. During less turbulent competitive times, the articulation of new strategies, structures, and infrastructure was thought to be sufficient to achieve desired cultural changes. People believed that if these formal elements of design were put in place and persistently applied, they would eventually induce changes in the slower-moving, more subjective cultural elements. The problem with this view of strategy implementation is that it presumed that very little change was needed in people, culture, and competencies. Today's global competitive environment requires strategic and cultural *transformation*, not incremental nudgings and coaxings. A more profound and direct intervention into the cultural elements of the organization is vital to the success of corporate transformations. Shared values and beliefs that endured through good and bad times, along with the style and behavior of its leaders, must be critically examined for their alignment with the new vision and strategies. Those found wanting must be changed immediately.

It Is a Massive Task. Changing business processes is one thing—changing management culture is quite another. To abandon a strong 20th-century culture and replace it by an empowered 21st-century culture is a huge learning challenge. You are being asked not to change things, but to change the very ways of changing. Culture is made up of the values, attitudes, and beliefs of people. It is held in the hearts and minds of individuals, not in some corporate pigeonhole where it can be unlocked and realigned overnight. The employees harbor their own idiosyncrasies, agendas, abilities, and individual preferences, and some also have the desire and ability to wield power and influence over those around them. Add to this the fact that many organizations have cultures developed over several decades with constantly reinforced norms and behaviors, and the true size of the task begins to emerge. An organization's culture is made up of hundreds of thousands of different elements and dozens more interconnected subcultures and informal networks.

There's No Such Thing as a Fresh Start. In most organizations the waters have already been muddied by previous change initiatives. The past few years alone have brought JIT, CIM, TQM, BPR, downsizing, and many others. Each project, whether integrated or discrete, has its own particular impact on the existing organization. As change projects forge on, employees tend to have a much more realistic (and usually cynical) view of such initiatives than their managers or directors. They remember the problems as well as the successes, the staff who were made redundant as well as the ones who were given new opportunities. No culture change initiative can start without the burdens of what has gone on previously.

Culture Must Support Vision and Mission. Cultural change is very difficult to effect in organizations, particularly in mature organizations. An existing strong culture can often resist a weak change effort. However, if the vision and mission is to be achieved they must be supported by an appropriate corporate culture. To be successful, our plans for change must be firmly focused on developing a culture that is aligned with the firm's intended vision and strategy. Trying to implement a cultural change that is counter to the vision and strategy is almost certain to fail. It is the leader's responsibility, once strategy is chosen, to bring the corporate culture into close alignment with strategy and keep it there.

CULTURAL PLANNING

Introduction to Cultural Planning

Instructions for performing cultural planning will be provided in this chapter. Guidance for implementing these cultural plans will be provided in Chapter 10.

Process of Cultural Planning

We will adhere to the following outline in discussing the cultural planning process:

1. Conduct External Analysis
2. Conduct Internal Analysis
3. Develop Company Ideology—Purposes, Core Values, and Principles
4. Develop Cultural Improvement Plans

As shown in the outline, the first stage in cultural planning is to perform the **External Analysis** that primarily looks at the organization's vision and mission and the supporting strategic plans to determine what type of organizational culture is needed to support the organization's vision and strategy. The strategy is presumed to be matched with the external environment. Certain parts of the *Strategic* External Environmental Analysis, such as the stakeholder analysis, may be studied, but it is not anticipated that a separate external environmental study will be conducted by cultural planning, since it should be available from strategic planning. The primary external concern of cultural planners is to match the culture to the strategy and vision.

The second stage is to conduct the **Internal Analysis**, which compares the current culture with the culture that best supports the firm's vision and mission and determines how the culture must change. It also assesses the organization's capability to make the required change. We need to determine the areas where the current culture is most divergent from the desired culture—these will be the focus of our improvement plans.

After conducting the Current Assessment, External Analysis and Internal Analysis, cultural planners are ready for the third stage, to **Develop Company Ideology: Purposes, Core Values, and Principles**.

The fourth stage is to develop **Cultural Improvement Plans** that will outline the stages for going from our current culture to our desired culture. Actions to implement these cultural improvement plans will be discussed in Chapter 10.

Outputs of Cultural Planning

At this point, we will briefly define the outputs of cultural planning. They will be described in more detail later in the chapter.

The **Cultural Creed** states what a company intends that its *internal* (cultural) environment should be or should become on a *continuing* basis. A creed is a picture of a preferred future state, a description of what the organization would be like some years from now. The creed provides an image of what the organization intends to be in the future, to provide the guidance for designing and managing the cultural changes that will be necessary to achieve those intentions. By providing a few broad concepts rather than a multitude of specific details, the creed can be easily remembered, allowing many levels of the organization to make decisions without the necessity of consulting with their superiors.

Core Values are the organization's essential and enduring tenets—a small set of general values, not to be compromised for financial gain or short-term expediency and not to be confused with specific cultural or operating practices that are included in the guiding principles. Excellent companies tend to have only a few core values, usually between three and six. Indeed, we should expect this, for only a few values can be truly *core*—values so fundamental and deeply held that they will never change or be compromised.

Guiding Principles describe *how* the creed and core values will be achieved. They establish the professional standards for the work done inside the organization. They specify the relationship between people in the organization—on all levels. In short, they outline how all members of the organization will behave to achieve the vision, mission, creed, and core values.

The **Company's Ideology**. Ideology is the core assumptions, beliefs, values, and principles of a culture. A culture consists of a large number of artifacts, rituals, ceremonies, symbols, anecdotes, and so on that are of little concern to us. When we are discussing the meaningful central core of the culture, we will use the term *ideology*. The term *culture* will be reserved for the total culture. A working definition of ideology that many companies have found to be very effective and useful is made up of the integrative sum of the three elements, as indicated in the following equation.

IDEOLOGY = CREED + CORE VALUES + GUIDING PRINCIPLES

Cultural Improvement Plans. These are specific time-phased plans for improving the company's culture in a logical and systematic manner in order to achieve the culture specified by the creed, core values, and guiding principles.

The Role of the Cultural Planning Council

The Cultural Planning Council, under the leadership of the Cultural Coordinator, is responsible for developing statements of creed, core values, guiding principles, and cultural improvement plans. The CEO and other high-level managers should be included as ex-officio members of the council, particularly for early deliberations to determine the creed and core values of the firm. The more the CEO participates, the better. Because of the interest and participation of the CEO and high-level managers, the function of the Cultural Council is very often performed by the Executive Steering Board in small and medium-sized companies.

The corporate creed and core values do not come down from the mountaintop engraved in stone. Rather they are shaped, crafted, and developed in cooperation with those who will live them. Necessary inputs for developing the creed, core values, and guiding principles of the organization are the vision statement from the company's leadership and the mission statement from the strategic planning effort. If either of these statements is missing, the Cultural Planning Council should take steps to ensure it is prepared before proceeding. The vision, mission, and creed should definitely be consistent and supportive, but they should not be exactly alike since they serve different purposes.

Conduct External Analysis

As we mentioned in the introduction, in this stage we will primarily look at the company's vision, mission, and supporting plans to determine the requirements for cultural improvement.

Influence of the Leader's Vision on Cultural Planning

At the heart of the every culture lies the vision of the leader. This vision includes the broader sense of who we are, why we are doing this work, why it's important, the promises we have made to customers, and the code of conduct governing how we operate with each other. Developing the vision, though, is not enough. The leader must be able to inspire others with the vision so that others want to say yes to it. In articulating the broader sense of vision, the new leader must be able to touch the hearts of the employees. The first person the new leader must convert to his or her vision is himself. If he is not sold on the company's vision, it will be next to impossible for him to effectively convert his employees.

As innovative companies move into the 21st century they will be operating with a culture of greater employee autonomy and self-direction. Teams will be less controlled by management and will exercise more autonomy in completing tasks from start to finish. It will be the leader's job to ensure that the team's efforts are bound together by a shared commitment to the vision, mission, and creed. Paradoxically *more* leadership will be required—not less. A unique reciprocal relationship should evolve between leadership and the front line. As the front line takes on greater tactical and operational authority, leaders should become ever more responsible for being the source and interpreter of the vision.

The single most visible factor that distinguishes major cultural changes that succeed from those that fail is competent leadership at the top. In all ten of the cases Kotter and Heskett studied, major change began after an individual who already had a track record for leadership was appointed to head the organization.[2] Each of these individuals had previously shown the capacity to do more than manage well. In their new jobs, they did this again, albeit on a grander scale. Each new leader created a team that established a new vision and set courses of action for achieving that vision. Each new leader succeeded in persuading important groups and individuals in the firm to commit themselves to that new direction and then energized the personnel sufficiently to make it happen, despite all obstacles. Ultimately hundreds (or even thousands) of people helped make all the changes in strategies, products, structures, policies, personnel, and eventually culture. But often, just one or two people seem to have been essential in getting the process started.

The necessity for three characteristics in the high-level leader—effective leadership, outsider's perspective, and insider's resources—helps explain why major cultural change does not happen more often in large organizations. It requires an effective leader on top. He or she must have both an outsider's openness to new ideas and an insider's power base. This leader must create a perceived need for change even if most people believe all is well. He must create and communicate effectively a new vision and set of strategies and then behave accordingly on a daily basis. He must motivate an increasingly large group of people to help with this leadership effort. These people must find hundreds or thousands of opportunities to influence behavior. The resulting action on the part of a growing group of people must produce positive results, or the whole effort loses credibility.

Influence of Mission and External Environment on Cultural Planning

There is no such thing as generically good culture; there is no one culture that works well everywhere. Instead, a culture is good only if it "fits" its context, which includes the company's vision, mission, strategies, and external environment. Only those cultures that are matched to their context will be associated with excellent performance. The better the fit, the better the performance; the poorer the fit, the poorer the performance.

For example, a culture characterized by rapid decision making and no bureaucratic behavior will enhance performance in the highly competitive deal-making environment of a mergers-and-acquisitions advisory firm but might hurt performance in a traditional life insurance company. Likewise, a culture in which managers place a very high value on excellent technology might help a computer manufacturer but would be inappropriate for a symphony orchestra. A culture favoring seat-of-the-pants decision making might be fine in a small firm but detrimental in a large one. A culture in which people value stable and tall hierarchical structures might work well in a slow-moving environment but be totally inappropriate in a very fast-moving and competitive industry.

A concrete example would be Swissair, an international airline with a culture in which managers have emphasized customer service, on-time performance, good equipment, conservative financing, and a feeling of kinship among employees not unlike that found in the traditionally close Swiss family. In an industry with excess capacity, meeting customers' needs is important to long-term economic performance, and Swissair's culture has helped its performance greatly.

Only cultures that can help organizations anticipate and *adapt* to environmental change will be associated with superior performance over long periods of time. Looking at cultures that are not very adaptive provides insight into what would constitute an adaptive culture. Nonadaptive cultures are usually very bureaucratic. People are reactive, risk averse, and not very creative. Information does not flow quickly and easily throughout the organization. A widespread emphasis on control dampens motivation and enthusiasm.

An adaptive culture entails a risk-taking, trusting, and proactive approach to organizational as well as individual life. Members actively support one another's efforts to identify all problems and implement workable solutions. There is a shared feeling of confidence: the members believe, without a doubt, that they can effectively manage whatever new problems and opportunities will come their way. There is widespread enthusiasm, a spirit of doing whatever it takes to achieve organizational success. The members are receptive to change and innovation.

Analyze Corporate Strategy and External Culture

Our culture must be consistent with and support the corporate mission, objectives, and strategies. To accomplish this, we must analyze our corporate strategy and determine the implications for our corporate culture. A detailed analysis of the company's actual mission, objectives, and strategies will enable us to deduce the general nature of the culture that would best support the corporate strategy.

Business organizations are immersed in cultures much larger than their own—those of the region and nation of which they are a part. In improving their corporate culture, they must keep these larger cultures in mind, since these larger cultures have considerable influence over the people they employ. What is our national and regional culture, and how is it changing? How might these changes affect what our corporate culture is or should be?

We should also look for trends that might affect these cultures—primarily social and political trends. *Social* trends include long-term changes in cultural attitudes, values, and behaviors, such as permissiveness, conservatism, family structure, entertainment leisure time patterns, health and environmental consciousness, educational achievement, cultural diversity, and so on. *Political* trends concern political party changes (especially at the national level), shifts from liberal to conservative views (or vice versa), and any other major change in political views.

Conduct Internal Analysis

Identify and Assess the Current Culture

Once high-level management commitment has been obtained and the implementation organization has been established, it is tempting to immediately begin developing the planned culture and the plans for implementation. However, such planning is premature. We first need to determine what that current culture is so that we ascertain the direction and magnitude of the required change.[3] We first need to do an organizational assessment that has several objectives:

- To explore all aspects of organizational functioning in order to identify the values, beliefs, and assumptions currently held by the organization's employees.
- To identify major opportunities for cultural improvement.
- To identify possible barriers to a cultural change program.
- To promote cultural change.

A broad-based assessment project usually employs one or more of the following data-gathering techniques:

Personal and Confidential Interviews with a Cross-section of Employees. The interviewer can probe personal experiences, explore critical issues in depth, and obtain useful anecdotes. In addition, the confidential, one-on-one nature of the process ensures a greater degree of openness than can be obtained in a group setting. The drawback of the personal interview approach is that it is costly and time-consuming to interview a large number of employees.

Group Interviews. The major benefit of the group interview is that a larger number of employees can be involved in a cost- and time-effective manner. The trade-offs are that confidentiality concerns may inhibit some participants, and issues cannot generally be explored in as much detail as in the individual interview.

Written Surveys. The written survey is clearly the most cost-effective way to involve very large numbers of people in the assessment process. If input from an organization of several hundred or more people is desired, a written survey is perhaps the only practical technique. A survey provides quantifiable data to support (or contradict) the conclusions that have been reached through some other format. On the down side, a survey requires some interpretation and does not permit an in-depth evaluation of the issues.

It is generally advisable to employ a combination of these techniques in the assessment process. Group interviews might be used, for example, to allow for the active participation of a sizable number of employees and to identify the major cultural values, beliefs, and issues. More detailed information on the issues could be obtained through individual interviews, and a written survey would provide quantitative support for the conclusions reached.

Conducting a Written Internal Assessment

As discussed earlier, the most practical approach for performing a company assessment is to conduct a written survey. The information obtained will be useful later in the transformation as well as now. The advantages of using internal staff to conduct the survey are that they know their company from the inside, and they are cheaper. However, employees may get treated like "prophets in their own country," that is, be ignored when they present their report, and they may well be blind to important factors that they have simply come to live with. Outside consultants have the advantage of being able to tell it as they see it with no worry about damaging their promotion prospects. Their experience and expertise in the subject can be useful, and they tend to be listened to more readily by senior management. However, they can be expensive. If feasible, a combination of inside and outside people is recommended.

Conducting a comprehensive survey needs to be a team job, and the survey team should be carefully chosen. Normally it should consist of a diagonal slice of people who know the business from various levels and areas. In addition, a balance of skills and personalities in the team is important. Preferably it should be a mix of practicality and intellect, long-service people and newcomers, an "ideas" person, a "worker/organizer," and at least one member with enough organizational clout and authority to carry weight with top management. If members of top management want to be members of the team, so much the better.

Do not get bogged down in an endless task of "culture analysis." Get in, get it done, and proceed to more productive pursuits. You don't have time to sit around and sift through the sands of your history, trying to figure out the intricate details of who you are and how you became that way. It's a seductive task, but you simply do not have time for it. In many cases the organization's very survival depends on speed. Competitive advantage will come from being faster than the next guy. In this situation, do not burn up precious time and waste resources looking backward.

Develop Company Ideology—Purpose, Core Values, and Principles

Clarifying the Meaning of Company Ideology

In the introduction we briefly defined a company's ideology and its elements. Before developing them, we should have a better understanding of the their meaning, which we will attend to in this section.

Company Ideology. It's important to understand that company ideology is an *internal* element, largely independent of the external environment. To use an analogy, the founders of the United States didn't instill the ideology of freedom and equality because the environment dictated it, nor did they expect the country to ever abandon those basic ideals in response to environmental conditions. They envisioned freedom and equality as timeless ideals independent of the environment—ideals to always work toward, providing guidance and inspiration to all future generations. The same holds true in excellent companies.

Robert W. Johnson, Jr. didn't write his credo because of a conceptual theory that linked credos with profits or because he read it in a book somewhere. He wrote the credo because the company embodied deeply held beliefs that he wanted to preserve. George Merck II deeply *believed* that medicine is for the patient, and he wanted every Merck person to share that belief. Thomas J. Watson, Jr. described IBM's core values as "bone deep" in his father: "As far as he was concerned, those values were the rules of life—to be preserved at all costs, to be commended to others, and to be followed conscientiously in one's business life."

David Packard and Bill Hewlett didn't "plan" the HP Way or HP's "way of business"; they simply held deep convictions about the way a business should be built and took tangible steps to articulate and disseminate these convictions so they could be preserved and acted upon. And they held these beliefs *independent of* the current management fashions of the day.

Hewlett-Packard, Merck, Johnson, and Watson didn't sit down and ask, "What business values would maximize our wealth?" or "What philosophy would look nice printed on glossy paper?" or "What beliefs would please the financial community?" No! They articulated what was inside them—what was in their gut, what was bone deep. It was as natural to them as breathing. It's not what they believed as much as how deeply they believed it (and how consistently their organizations lived it). Again, the key word is *authenticity*. No artificial flavors. No added sweeteners. Just 100 percent genuine authenticity.

We strongly encourage you *not* to fall into the trap of using the ideology from other companies as a source for ideology in your own organization. Company ideology does *not* come from mimicking the values of other companies—even highly successful companies. It does *not* come from following the dictates of outsiders; it does *not* come from reading management books; and it does *not* come from a sterile intellectual exercise of "calculating" what values would be most pragmatic, most popular, or most profitable. When articulating and codifying core ideology, the key step is to capture what is authentically believed, not what other companies set as their values or what the outside world thinks the ideology should be.

The **Cultural Creed** indicates what a company intends that its *internal* (cultural) environment should be or should become on a *continuing* basis. A creed is a concept of a preferred future state, a description of what the organization should be like some years in the future. The creed provides an image of what the organization intends to be in the future, to provide the guidance for designing and managing the cultural changes that will be necessary to achieve those intentions. It provides the organization's fundamental reasons for existence beyond just making money—a perpetual guiding star on the horizon, not to be confused with specific goals or business strategies. Excellent companies get at creed by asking questions such as the following: Why are we here? Although we must make money to stay here, what is our *real* reason for being here?

The creed need not be wholly unique. It's entirely possible that two companies could have a very similar creed, just as it's entirely possible that two companies can both share a rock-solid belief in a value like integrity. The primary role of creed is to guide and inspire, not necessarily to differentiate. For example, many companies could share HP's creed of making a contribution to society via electronic equipment for the advancement of science and the welfare of humanity. The question is, would they hold it as deeply and live it as consistently as HP? As with core values, the key is authenticity, not uniqueness. When properly conceived, the creed is broad, fundamental, and enduring.

Although the company's creed and ideology usually trace their roots to specific individuals, a highly successful company *institutionalizes* them— weaving them into the very fabric of the organization. These elements do not exist solely as a prevailing ethos or creed. A highly successful company does not simply have some vague set of intentions or passionate zeal. To be sure, a highly visionary company does have these, but it also has concrete, tangible mechanisms to *preserve the company ideology* while *stimulating progress*.

Walt Disney didn't leave ideology up to chance; he created Disney University and required every single employee to attend "Disney Traditions" seminars. Hewlett-Packard didn't just talk about the HP Way; it instituted a religious promote-from-within policy and translated its philosophy into the categories used for employee reviews and promotions, making it nearly impossible for anyone to become a senior executive without fitting tightly into the HP Way. Marriott didn't just talk about its core values; it instituted rigorous employee screening mechanisms, indoctrination processes, and elaborate customer feedback loops. Nordstrom didn't just philosophize about fanatical customer service; it created a cult of service reinforced by tangible rewards and penalties—"Nordies" who serve the customer well become well-paid heroes, and those who treat customers poorly get spit right out of the company.

A company's *creed* is usually not as concrete and measurable as its *mission*, but is somewhat more specific than the company's *vision*. It is not a specific objective or strategy. Rather, it tends to be a broad statement that inspires, integrates, and controls an organization. One of the roles of the creed is to promote and protect organizational values. A creed enables people in the organization to know the general purpose or role of their organization and the reasons why they should be proud of their organization.

Core Values are the organization's essential and enduring tenets—a small set of general values, not to be compromised for financial gain or short-term expediency and not to be confused with specific cultural or operating practices, which are included in the guiding principles. Excellent companies tend to have only a few core values, usually between three and six. Indeed, we should expect this, for only a few values can be truly *core*—values so fundamental and deeply held that they will not change or be compromised.

In most cases, a core value can be boiled down to a piercing simplicity that provides substantial guidance. Notice how Sam Walton captured the essence of Wal-Mart's number-one value: "[We put] the customer ahead of everything else.... If you're not serving the customer, or supporting the folks who do, then we don't need you." Notice how James Gamble simply and elegantly stated P&G's core value of product quality and honest business: "When you cannot make pure goods of full weight, go do something else that is honest, even if it is breaking stone." Notice how John Young, former HP chief executive, captured the simplicity of the HP Way: "The HP Way basically means respect and concern for the individual; it says, 'Do unto others as you would have them do unto you.' That's really what it's all about." The core value can be stated a number of different ways, yet it remains simple, clear, straightforward, and powerful.

In an excellent company, the core values need no rationale or external justification. Nor do they sway with the trends and fads of the day or even shift in response to changing market conditions. Collins and Porras found that none of the many companies they studied had more than six core values, and most had less.[4] This is to be expected, since only a few values can be truly core.

This finding has important implications for articulating core values in your own organization. If you list more than five or six values, you might not be capturing those that are truly core. If you have a statement of corporate values or are in the process of creating one, you might ask yourself, "Which of these values would we strive to live to for a hundred years regardless of changes in the external environment—even if the environment ceased to reward us for having these values, or perhaps even penalized us? Conversely, which values would we be willing to change or discard if the environment no longer favored them?" These questions can help you identify which values are authentically core.

Guiding Principles. The most successful companies worldwide are values-driven. That means a bedrock of common, positive values underlies the thinking and the creativity of everyone in these organizations. However, not all of these values can or should be considered core values. Those values not considered core values we will call principles. The principles provide the more detailed guidelines that will enable us to *achieve* our desired culture. Most of a company's principles will fall in the following areas.

First, the principles establish the professional standards for the work done inside the organization. Without clear standards, the organization may suffer inconsistent efforts because people do not know to what level they should strive. The principles establish a clear level of quality and excellence that every employee can understand and aspire to maintain.

Second, the desired relationships among all people at all levels in the organization need to be defined. If ignored, these relationships will emerge by themselves and will often be counterproductive. If consciously defined and nurtured, they will add vital strength and creativity to the organization.

The principles are especially important as top-down hierarchies give way to self-managed teams. As you unleash authority to the front line, the values and principles are often all people have left (and all they need, if done correctly) to show them *how* to achieve the organization's vision, mission, and creed. Many successful companies have adopted principles covering the following topics:

Strong Customer Focus. Every company and every person are part of a long chain (actually many long chains) of customers and suppliers. Each company and person is a customer to its suppliers and a supplier to its customers. All understand and appreciate both near-term and long-term customer needs and expectations.

Emphasis on Innovation and Achievement. All employees at all levels of the organization welcome new ideas and are extremely active in generating new approaches and new ways of doing things. There is a willingness to take risks and an eagerness to break new ground.

Emphasis on Total Quality Management. Both managers and workers are deeply involved in a continuous integrated effort to improve the quality of the firm's goods and services at every level. Continuously improving quality will maximize the customers' total satisfaction and minimize the firm's total costs.

Flexible and Adaptable Learning Organizations. Most work will be horizontal (process) knowledge work performed by multidisciplinary teams. Rather than satisfying their immediate supervisor (vertical relationship), team members concentrate on satisfying the needs of the next person in the process (horizontal relationship). The composition and life of the project teams will be dynamic.

High Levels of Collaboration, Teamwork, and Trust. The building of trust is emphasized. Politics, infighting, and departmental jealousies are minimized. Leaders work hard to earn their peoples' trust and to create conditions in which trust can flourish. There is widespread enthusiasm, a spirit of doing whatever it takes to achieve organizational success.

Emphasis on Employee Empowerment. The objective of empowerment is to tap the creative and intellectual energy of everybody in the company—not just those in the executive suite—and to provide everyone with the responsibility and resources to display real leadership within their own individual sphere of competence.

Emphasis on Human Resources. Human resources—not financial and physical capital—are the organization's competitive edge, and innovative organizations maximize the output of highly educated workers. Human resources management (HRM) evolves from a support function to a leadership function in the innovative organization.

Continuous Learning, Change, and Improvement. Everything, at all levels, at all times, should be improving. People, processes, management practices, everything should improve continually; the best is never good enough. Everyone, including all managers and employees, takes responsibility for continuous improvement.

Open Information, Communication, and Decision-Making Systems. Survival in today's competitive business world makes the sharing of information throughout an innovative organization absolutely critical. A supply of accurate, consistent, and timely information across all functional areas facilitates a better organizational response to rapidly changing customer needs.

Emphasis on Process Management. Process management involves aligning and coordinating all the operations necessary to deliver a product to a customer. It can be used to manage those critical processes that cut across the whole enterprise, such as new product development, quality, cost control, delivery, and the like.

Thinking and Decision Making Close to Doing. People think, decide, and do. Implementers help to develop strategy. Strategists stay close to what people do on the front lines. Specialists know the total business, and people everywhere do much of their own staff work.

Enhanced Quality of Work Life. People today seek work that is fulfill-ing, meaningful, and psychologically rewarding. Knowledge workers want a creative corporate environment that energizes them both mentally and physically. Keeping top-notch employees requires maintaining a top-notch quality of work life.

High Performance and Productivity. Employees in 21st-century organi-zations are achievement oriented and develop a high work ethic of pro-fessionalism. Knowledge workers use technology, such as automation and information technology, to become more productive. Their sense of time is different, and they are not confined by the nine-to-five syndrome.

Respect for the Individual. In order for people to collaborate from a position of strength and equality, they need a high level of self-esteem and a work environment that actively seeks to enhance and support the build-ing of self-esteem. People feel valued when they can work in an environ-ment free from fear, where can they make mistakes, learn, and grow.

Ownership and Alignment. When the workforce has a true sense of own-ership of the workplace, the job, and the enterprise, there is greater like-lihood they will take good care of it. When they feel alienated or not part of the business, their work becomes just a job, and they tend to do just enough to get a paycheck.

Is There an Ideal Ideology?

Is there a "right" ideology for being an excellent company? Are there any common elements or prevalent patterns across the ideologies in the excellent companies? Collins and Porras compiled the ideologies of nu-merous excellent companies and found that, although certain themes show up in a number of the excellent companies (such as contribution, integrity, respect for the individual employee, service to the customer, being on the creative or leading edge, or responsibility to the community), *no single item shows up consistently across all the excellent companies.*[5]

- Some companies, such as Johnson & Johnson and Wal-Mart, made their *custom-ers* central to their ideology; others, such as Sony and Ford, did not.
- Some companies, such as HP and Marriott, made concern for their *employees* central to their ideologies; others, such as Nordstrom and Disney, did not.
- Some companies, such as Ford and Disney, made their *products or services* cen-tral to their core ideology; others, such as IBM and Citicorp, did not.
- Some companies, such as Sony and Boeing, made audacious *risk taking* central to their ideology; others, such as HP and Nordstrom, did not.
- Some companies, such as Motorola and 3M, made *innovation* central to their ideology; others, such as P&G and American Express, did not.

In short, they did not find any specific ideological content essential to being an excellent company. Their research indicates that the *authenticy*

of the ideology and the extent to which a company attains consistent alignment with the ideology counts more than the *content* of the ideology.

Although there is no one specific value that should be included in a
company's ideology, a company's ideology should cover the following
three *types* of values:

- *Basic ground rules.* How people relate to one another fairly, ethically, and constructively in the workplace, their everyday rules of the road, are necessary for
any organization to be successful in any circumstance. These values are long-
held; they are deeply embedded in the culture and style of an organization and
can serve as anchors while everyone is attempting to navigate the stormy sea of
transformation.

- *Strategically aligned values.* These are uniquely aligned with the vision and mission and are the primary initiatives in the early stages of transformation. For
example, individual autonomy and initiative at the business-unit level may be
highly instrumental in achieving rapid business turnaround from the brink of
financial disaster, while an emphasis on sharing and leveraging across business
units and individual efforts might be more important during a transformation
phase focusing on rapid growth in revenues or market share.

- *Adaptiveness values.* These are the core values and principles that promote *adaptiveness* to cope with changing competitive conditions and appear to be needed
to cope with fundamental change over the long haul.

Testing and Improving the Ideology before Implementing

One of the better methods of testing the creed, core values, and guiding
principles is through employee *focus groups.* The focus group approach
involves leading a group of employees, from various disciplines and levels
in the company through an open, in-depth discussion of the proposed
creed, core values, and guiding principles. Members of each group session
are chosen from a list of volunteers, so that each group represents a valid
cross-section of the company's employees. A session is usually conducted
as a casual roundtable discussion with eight to twelve participants. The
setting should be relaxed and casual to encourage a free and uninhibited
flow of ideas.

The focus group meetings should have a threefold purpose. First, to
determine if all employees *understand* the creed, values, and principles.
Second, to determine if all employees *accept* and are willing to carry out
the creed, values, and principles. Third, to determine if there are any recommendations for *improvement.*

Develop Cultural Improvement Plans (CIPs)

Cultural Improvement Plans (CIPs) are to the cultural program as strategies are to the strategic program; they are the action plans that actually

get things done, that actually improve the culture. Whereas the company's ideology, including the creed, core values, and guiding principles, are continuing plans, the CIPs are one-time plans. As a result they are somewhat more specific and goal oriented.

An important aspect of successful culture change is that it needs to be tackled from many angles. The task is so large that every tool in the toolkit needs to be brought to bear, and every trick of the trade applied. More important, every other aspect of the process-led change program needs to be brought to bear to make the change happen.

In our experience, organizations that achieve real culture change focus *not on the culture but on those things that shape culture.* Successful transformations do not rely on lists of new, improved values and principles—that exercise is more likely to lead to cynicism than to valid cultural change. On the other hand, if you focus on the forces that shape culture, you avoid setting up a target for the opposition and the cynics. There are many targets, and none of them has "culture change" written all over it. Each target focuses on a specific, practical concern that any loyal executive will regard as workable.

Planning Approaches for Developing Cultural Improvement Plans

Following our own advice, we will now describe a number of areas where CIPs can be developed that focus on things that shape culture:

Develop a Plan for Leadership Action. The actions of the organization's leaders are extremely important since they communicate their beliefs, values, and assumptions. When the CEO abandons the executive dining room to eat in the cafeteria, spends significant time with customers, and walks the shop floor to talk with line workers, he or she is communicating powerfully. Such actions far outweigh any number of memos and newsletters from headquarters. The Cultural Planning Council should recommend a number of leadership actions.

Develop Plans for Communicating and Educating. First you must communicate the desired new culture to the organization. Explain to people what your objectives are for the culture. What, in concrete terms, do you want to change? This has to be reinforced by showing them how the new culture will benefit them.

Then we must explain why change is necessary. While an awareness of the overall change program should provide the main context, tailored education specific to the cultural impacts needs to be provided. Information about the general pressures for change, such as the increasing demands of the customer and the new challenges of the marketplace, has to be provided. Time spent in identifying opinion leaders and nurturing their behavior change will ultimately speed the culture change process by virtue of the people they in turn influence.

Develop Plans to Remodel the Reward System. What you reward is what you get. To get what they want, key leaders must sit down and take a long hard look at the reward systems. Ask yourself, "Who gets ahead around here, how, and for what reasons?" Be honest with your assessment, and be honest about the extent to which the culture of your organization is inviting people to act more intelligently about the way they work and whether it reinforces them for it.

Develop Plans for Updating the Company's Policies and Procedures. An organization's policies, methods, procedures, rules, and regulations can imprison people or they can empower them. In most organizations, especially larger ones, there tends to be a dense underbrush of rules and regulations that hinders creative action. It is true that all organizations need methods and procedures that promote efficiency and effective use of resources. But they also need a way of rethinking their methods and keeping them flexible. Take a hard look at your policies and procedures manual. These manuals tend to be too large, too verbose, too detailed, and too preoccupied with legislating things that are better left to common sense.

Develop Plans for Updating Performance Measures. Performance measures play an enormous role in determining an organization's culture. You may want to clarify the kinds of behavior you consider effective on the part of your managers and make their advancement contingent on that kind of behavior. Do the measures reinforce or unknowingly undermine *today's* culture and strategy?

Develop Plans for Improving People Practices. People practices include many, many things. Staffing: Are the right people hired with the right skills? Training and development: Are opportunities provided, mentorships established, and so on? Promotions: Do the best people get promoted? Is promotion a function of time in job or merit? Disciplinary measures: Does the punishment fit the crime? Are the rules clear?

Develop Plans to Support the Culture Change. Ensure money is budgeted where needed to carry out the culture change. An excellent plan is worthless if there is no money to carry it out. Also, do not expect people to change their behavior in line with a new culture if they are not equipped to do so. Cultural change has to be supported by any new skills, knowledge, and capabilities required to work and to behave differently.

NOTES

1. John P. Kotter and James L. Heskett, *Corporate Culture and Performance* (Free Press, 1992), p. 78.

2. Ibid., pp. 84–92.

3. Howard W. Oden, *Managing Corporate Culture, Innovation, and Intrapreneurship* (Quorum, 1997), p. 55.

4. James C. Collins and Jerry I. Porras, *Built to Last* (HarperBusiness, 1994), p. 74.

5. Ibid., p. 67.

CHAPTER 5

Organizing and Planning for Transformation

INTRODUCTION

This chapter deals with the organization and planning that leads up to the launch of the transformation process. This phase starts when a compelling reason for change has crystallized and top management has decided to act. This phase may be considered complete when top management has fully committed itself to a major transformation, has completed development of the first detailed plan for change, and has begun execution of that plan.

What brings about significant and lasting change is strong leadership, commitment, trust, and a transformation plan that works. Your plan will work if it considers the whole organization from the beginning rather than from pieces to be assembled at the end. It should outline a change management plan that stresses communication and develops a road map so that employees can understand how the company plans to attain its new vision. The plan should emphasize the need to tap into the potential of all employees and detail the role employees should play in designing the future organization.

With employees and management co-leading the transformation, your plan should move to the redesign of the company's social and technical systems. This stage is completed when the new processes are aligned and linked to form a network of capabilities that create a competitive advantage. With the new processes in place, the transformation plan details the steps needed to install natural work teams as the means by which work will be accomplished. Along with the establishment of the work teams, the plan focuses on the need to rebuild the rest of the organizational structure—middle and senior management positions.

Figure 5-1
Overall Organization for Transformation

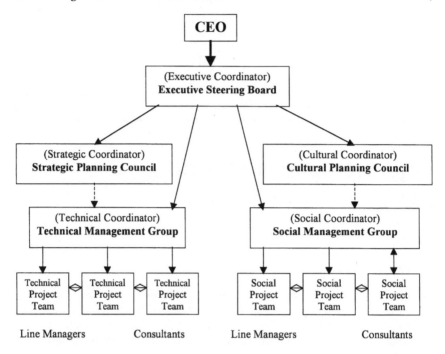

At this point your head is probably spinning at the number of things to consider for the initial plan. Don't be dismayed. Start small and simple, with manageable tasks that you can achieve. These will provide learning opportunities and some early successes and will build the confidence to tackle more ambitious tasks.

Your initial plan is just that—a first attempt at organized, systematic improvement. No one ever got started on this type of major change without some stumbles and setbacks. You should expect to make some mid-course corrections. Your initial plan should address only those high-priority issues that you believe you can tackle with the time and resources available. Follow-on versions of the plan can be more detailed and complete.

ORGANIZATION PLAN

Introduction

The overall organization plan for the transformation, shown in Figure 5-1, was introduced in Chapter 2. The Executive Steering Board, the Strategic Planning Council, and the Cultural Planning Council were discussed in chapters 2, 3, and 4 respectively. They will be briefly discussed here for completeness and to provide the basis for discussing the Management Groups and the Project Teams.

Top-Level Transformation Organization

In the following paragraphs we will discuss the purpose, composition, operation, and functions of the top five organizations shown in Figure 5-1. The coordinators of the top five groups serve as the leaders of their respective groups. They normally serve full-time while most of the other members will be part-time.

As we discussed in Chapter 2, all the functions for the organizations in Figure 5-1 must be performed, but the organization structure that performs them does not have to be the same as shown in Figure 5-1. For example, in a small company all the functions for the top five organizations could be performed by one organization, the Executive Steering Board. There could be many other combinations.

Executive Steering Board

The purpose of the Executive Steering Board is to provide overall direction and guidance to the transformation effort. It is the primary planning and decision-making body in the company regarding transformation. Because transformation change is so long and difficult to accomplish, a powerful force is needed to sustain the process. The Executive Steering Board fulfills this need. It can speed the implementation of new approaches because powerful people are truly informed and committed to transformation. The steering board is made up of five to ten top executives who have high position power, expertise, credibility, and leadership. The board, which typically meets monthly, establishes policy, sets goals for the effort, reviews progress, and provides the authority to modify organizational systems to support and reinforce transformation improvement.

The primary functions of the Executive Steering Board are:

- Provide overall direction and guidance
- Develop overall business vision
- Champion the change effort
- Select members for the four top groups in the organization
- Monitor results

Strategic Planning Council

The Strategic Planning process is controlled by the Strategic Planning Council. The council consists of decision-makers from all levels (corporate, business, and functional) in the corporation. Because strategic decisions have such a tremendous impact on a firm and because they require large commitments of company resources, they can only be made by top managers. The role of the Strategic Council consists primarily of gathering and organizing data and information needed for strategic planning and then coordinating the process of reviewing and approving the strategic plans developed in various parts of the company. Their contribution comes in their facilitating and coordinating the strategic planning efforts, helping managers at all levels identify the strategic issues that ought to be addressed, providing information, helping with the analysis of industry and competitive conditions if asked, and generating information on the company's strategic performance.

The primary functions of the Strategic Planning Council are:

- Work with the Executive Steering Board to finalize company's vision
- Develop the company's mission
- Identify and design plans for developing the company's value proposition
- Identify and design plans for developing the company's core competencies
- Develop strategies for achieving the company's mission

Cultural Planning Council

The Cultural Planning Council, under the leadership of the Cultural Coordinator, is responsible for developing statements of creed, core values, guiding principles, and cultural improvement plans. The CEO and other high-level managers should be included as ex-officio members of the council, particularly for early deliberations to determine the creed and core values of the firm. The more the CEO participates, the better. Necessary inputs for developing the creed, core values and guiding principles of the organization are the vision statement from the company's leadership and the mission statement from the strategic planning effort.

The primary functions of the Cultural Planning Council are:

- Work with Executive Steering Board to finalize company's vision
- Develop Cultural Creed
- Develop Core Values
- Develop Guiding Principles
- Develop Cultural Improvement Plans
- Assess Current Culture
- Coordinate plans to implement cultural change

Technical Management Group

Members of the technical management group are selected and chartered by the Executive Steering Board. Since most tasks are cross-functional and interorganizational, the technical group should represent all of the functional disciplines involved. The group members must not only provide information about their respective areas and how they are involved in the process, but they must also represent their areas. This means that they must present the viewpoints, priorities, and interests of their constituencies. This requirement leads to two characteristics useful in selecting group members: knowledge and stature. The group member must not only know about his or her own department, he or she must be perceived as someone who will represent the department interests in a balanced and nonpartisan way.

The primary functions of the Technical Management Group are:

- Conduct process design of the company
- Perform "as-is" analysis
- Develop "to-be" model
- Develop a process map of the firm
- Develop implementation plan
- Coordinate Technical Process Design
- Select processes to be redesigned
- Select teams to perform redesign

Social Management Group

Since the Social Management Group must perform two distinct types of tasks, it must have members with broad interests and outlooks. During the early part of transformation, they will be redesigning the organization of the company in parallel with the technical redesign of work processes. During the latter part of transformation, they will be supervising the redesign and improvement of selected social processes.

The primary functions of the Social Management Group are:

- Conduct organizational design of the company
- Determine social projects to be pursued
- Implement planned cultural change
- Coordinate Social Redesign: (1) select social processes to be redesigned and (2) select social project teams to perform the design

Technical Project Team

Once a process is selected for redesign, a *Technical Project Team* is selected by the Technical Management Group that is sufficiently expert in the process to perform the detailed analysis of the process. *Project Teams* are cross-functional and are pulled together to perform the redesign of assigned process and to develop the recommendations for change. They reengineer the process, develop process measurements and targets, and finally develop improvement plans.

The primary functions of the Technical Project Teams are:

• Collect data and document assigned work process
• Diagnose assigned work process
• Determine possible ways to improve work process
• Select optimum design for improving work process
• Implement and test design for improving work process

Social Project Team

The Social Project Team performs essentially the same functions in the social or behavioral area as the Technical Project team does in the technical or work area. They are expected to collect data on the assigned social process, diagnose this data, develop some proposals for improving the process, evaluate these proposals, and select one as the basis for the redesign of the process.

The primary functions of the Social Project Teams are:

• Collect data and document assigned social process
• Diagnose assigned social process
• Determine possible ways to improve social process
• Select optimum design for improving social process
• Implement and test design for improving social process

Line Management

Members of *line management* contribute resources to teams and work to implement short-term improvements. They also provide input to teams as internal customers. They participate selectively in executive workshops, and in the end they are responsible for implementing the reengineered processes.

Any changes in processes will have a large impact on line managers, who will necessarily feel challenged by and possibly ill at ease with what is going on around them. Successful change requires the participation of those who will be affected. The key is to take the steps necessary to involve them and to communicate constantly as the transformation effort moves along.

Consultants and Facilitators

Few transformations are completed without the assistance of a consultant or team of consultants who are skilled in change management and organizational redesign. When consultants are assisting clients during a transformation effort, the responsibilities of each partner must be clearly defined. The role of consultants (internal or external) is to *facilitate* a transformation process, *not own it*. The vision and changes must belong to the client, not the consultants. If the project teams feel that the transformation is being done to them, as opposed to their transforming the company, the teams will lose interest and will fail to implement, or will even fight, the changes that the consultants recommend. On the other hand, if they know the consultants are there to assist them in creating the vision, planning the transformation, and implementing the changes—if the employees themselves become the instrument in changing the culture— the organizational transformation has a much higher chance for success.

Rationale for the Transformation Organization

Having both social and technical aspects, as well as cultural and strategic aspects, in the organization chart emphasizes to all concerned that transformation is both a social and technical undertaking and that neither aspect can afford to be slighted. In the past, *business process reengineering* (BPR) efforts tended to ignore the social aspects of change and thus encountered serious behavioral problems in implementing proposed changes. Similarly, *total quality management* (TQM) efforts concentrated on social changes, paying little attention to possible technical changes, with the result that in many situations little real performance improvement was made.

We divide the total transformation effort into two parts to ensure that both are adequately covered and to make the total program more effective and efficient. The two programs utilize vastly different procedures and require vastly different talents of the people involved. We could try to train socially oriented people to do technical tasks and technically oriented people to perform social tasks, but such an approach would require considerable time and effort that we simply do not have in transformation. As will be discussed later, the social project teams and the technical project teams will be integrated through networks.

The Role of Project Teams in Transformation

Managers and consultants working in isolation cannot transform the company and expect employees to put the new design to work and make it happen. *The employees whose work will be affected must effect the changes*.[1] No one knows more about the work than those employees who are doing it every day. These are the true experts, and their total involvement in all aspects of the transformation is essential.

While independence is a virtue for these teams, *connectedness* is the goal. The role of leadership is to forge points of connectivity by redefining roles and responsibilities, driving communications, rewarding achievements, and allowing penalty-free failures. As more and more teams start succeeding and as leaders start building connectors between teams, networks start to emerge. Those networks then become the very core of the renewed organization and the basis of the future organizational structure.

Composition of the Project Team

The *full* project team is composed of two components: the core project team and the virtual project team.[2] The *core* project team consists of three to ten members who are assigned *full-time*. The *virtual* project team consists of an unlimited number of people who contribute to the project on a *part-time* or *as-needed* basis. The core team is the permanent nucleus of the team, while the virtual team is the ever-changing outer layer.

Members of the Core Team

An ideal core team would be staffed with ten or fewer members, with three being perhaps the minimum. The team should have at least one representative each from the user (U), information technology (IT), and human resources (HR) areas. The User members are primarily responsible for obtaining input data from the existing process and testing the redesigned process. The IT members are primarily responsible for applying information technology to the process to make it more productive. The HR members are primarily responsible for developing human jobs for the process and for providing recommended improvements in organization. Full-time participation and a small size for the core team are crucial to building a level of commitment that will get the development completed quickly and effectively. Part-time players lack the concentration and commitment needed to be effective.

Members of the Virtual Team

Members of the virtual team include all those personnel outside the core team that work for or contribute to the project on a part-time basis. Most of the members of the virtual team are in the functional departments of the parent organization, primarily marketing, engineering, production, procurement, finance, personnel, accounting, and legal. However, there may be some members from outside the parent organization, such as suppliers, customers, government personnel, and others.

Because project teams are small, many employees who would like to be members are left out. When the number of people who desire to be project team members exceeds the available slots, it is crucial that you enable individuals who are not selected for project teams to participate in other ways. Never make anyone feel as if his or her participation is unwanted or that his or her contribution will not add value to the process.

This is where the virtual teams come to the rescue. Although virtual team members do not work full time for the project, they continuously report to and receive information from the project office for coordination and motivation purposes. By including them in all general meetings and keeping them updated on schedules and other information, they are made to feel that they are definitely an important part of the team.

Responsibilities and Qualifications of Core Team Members

The more of the following criteria that the members of a core team can satisfy, the more effective the core team will be.[3]

- There are ten or fewer members on the core team.
- Members are assigned to the core team full time.
- Members volunteer to serve on the core team.
- Members stay on the core team until the project is completed.
- Members report solely to the core team leader.
- The key functions involved in the project are represented on the core team.
- Members are located within conversational distance of each other.

In reality, it is rare to have all team members meet all these criteria, but the more they can meet the better.

Managing the Project Team

Managing the Team's Work. Molding the *team's work* into effective *teamwork* is not an accident; nor does it come easily or automatically. Management of the team is a major and continuing task. The integration of persons from functions critical to successful process improvement into an effective team is the most fundamental requirement for success. Technical skills must match the technical task to be done. With highly skilled people in each area, the team can function effectively with only a few people. Evaluation methods used to assess the performance of team members must not divide the team or demoralize them; for this reason team-based performance measures are used increasingly.

Project or redesign teams need to feel empowered. When they share a sense of ownership and have a charter and a vision to guide them through the change process, they will work much harder because the design of the new process becomes their design. If the Management Group "runs the show" instead of guiding it or if external consultants take over instead of assisting, this will diminish the role of the project teams. Teams that do not have any ownership and that serve only to make a few minor recommendations to the Technical Management Group will not get seriously involved in the redesign effort. On the other hand, those teams that are empowered to recommend how the future organization should be redesigned will become more involved. They will make better decisions, as well as develop better solutions.

Managing the Team Culture. Team members come from different organizational subcultures that may be based on functions, divisions, or geography. Members of each subculture bring their own behaviors, values, beliefs, and ways of thinking to the team and usually assume that their language, styles, and meanings are shared. When these undiscovered differences are not worked through, people leave meetings and conversations assuming they understand and have been understood. When they discover otherwise, confusion and anger often result, much time may have been lost, and other damage may have resulted.

A team environment must be developed in which all team members feel free to air their differences in perceptions and understanding. They should be encouraged to talk about any and all problems that endanger the project's success and to take actions to assure success. Communications must occur so that all team members share the same vision for the new product and become motivated toward its success. Team members must be proud to be a member of the project team and must take ownership of all the tasks to be accomplished and all the problems to be solved.

Assembling the Project Team

Appointing the Team Leader. Of all the decisions that the Management Group makes in managing the project, none is more crucial than the choice of the project team leader. A strong leader will be able to overcome many shortcomings of imperfect management decisions, but a mediocre one will be stymied even by small obstacles. It is important to pick a leader carefully and announce the choice publicly. Everyone should know exactly who is responsible for successful completion of the project.

Experience has shown that better results are obtained by selecting project leaders who have a proven capability for planning and visioning, strong leadership skills, and experience in project management and have well-rounded technical capabilities. A person satisfying these qualifications combined with high energy and resourcefulness will make an outstanding project leader.

Recruiting Members. How companies go through the process of selecting team members varies from company to company. In most cases, the Management Group educates employees about the transformation effort and describes the various roles and responsibilities that must be filled by the project team. Once this is accomplished, employees and managers are asked to add their name to a list of potential candidates if they are interested in working on the team. The Management Groups take this information and make their selections, in private, and then recruit additional individuals who they feel would make a significant contribution to the team.

Members should be recruited to enable the core team to handle all the functions required by the project. The only way to obtain the required level of commitment to the project is for all participants to make a conscious decision to be fully involved—they must volunteer. However, if a desired member does not initially volunteer, the benefits of being on the team must be explained. The recruiter must identify each prospect's motivations and present the virtues of team membership forcefully but honestly.

Establishing and organizing project teams is an involved process. Since project teams are challenged with the task of recommending fundamental and substantial change company wide, the most respected and brightest managers and employees, specialists and experts, and frontline workers must become active participants on these teams. Companies that fail to put the most qualified and respected individuals on these teams clearly demonstrate that they view the transformation as less than the number-one priority for the company. These companies also jeopardize the outcome, because "the best and the brightest" in the company do not become involved in planning and implementing the changes that will directly affect the company's long-term performance.

DEVELOPING AN ACTION PLAN

Introduction

In addition to determining appropriate transformation management organization, an action or activity plan must be prepared before launching the transformation effort. Once the desired transformation objectives (vision, mission, and creed) have been clarified and the present state of affairs made clear, an explicit plan specifying activities to be undertaken and critical incidents or events that must occur to get from here to there must be made. For example, the transformation plan for a major structural change would incorporate a timetable of events, such as when first moves will take place, when meetings will be held to clarify new roles, what information will be communicated to whom on what day, and when the new structure will start to operate.

In essence, the transformation plan is the roadmap for the transformation effort. An effective transformation plan has the following characteristics:

1. It is purposeful: The activities are clearly linked to the change goals and priorities.

2. It is task-specific: The types of activities involved are clearly identified rather than broadly generalized.

3. It is *integrated*: The *discrete* activities are linked.

4. It is temporal: It is time-sequenced.

5. It is adaptable: There are contingency plans and ways of adapting to unexpected forces.

6. It is agreed to by the top of the organization.

7. It is cost-effective in terms of the investment of both time and people.

The Enterprise Transformation Plan

Content and Structure of the Plan

The content and structure of the enterprise transformation plan should basically follow the content and structure of this book. In other words there should be provisions for the pre-initiation actions described in Part I, the technical redesign procedures described in Part II, the social redesign efforts described in Part III, and the completion activities described in Part IV. The emphasis and degree of detail would be dependent upon the needs of a particular company. Instead of belaboring the obvious, we will spend more time on *how* planning is accomplished in the next section.

Developing the Plan

When the Executive Steering Board has successfully digested the assessment results and decided to go for transformation, the stage is set for some thorough and detailed planning work. Here are some suggestions to bear in mind as you begin to devise your planning process.

The planning effort should be led by the Executive Steering Board. This does not mean they will do all the planning. Far from it. But they should establish the goals and objectives, assign tasks to various activities, and review and approve the final product.

The planning must involve the two Planning Councils and the two Management Groups. The parts they play will be dependent upon the Executive Steering Board, but they should play some part. The CEO, or another manager, may take the lead by developing a draft plan, but he must not aim for something so polished and complete that there is no room for the Executive Steering Board, the Planning Councils, or the Management Groups to contribute. They need to understand and agree with the logic, take part in decisions where choices exist, and work out the details in areas where they will be personally responsible.

The draft plan should offer alternatives and should leave blanks where input from others is desirable, to ensure that others can contribute and take ownership. The initial plan should even include some controversial ideas that will ensure challenge and debate.

A plan that your colleagues own, even though it may be slightly flawed, is infinitely better than one that you consider perfect but they feel belongs to you. Owned plans get implemented; disowned ones do not.

Ownership lies in the assignment of the tasks as well as the development of the plan. Every member of the top-level organization should end up with a well-defined piece of the action that they are personally responsible for implementing.

Link the improvement plan to the organization's objectives—the vision, mission, and creed. This plan is only a means to an end. If the organization could get there by some other easier way, you would not be doing all this work. If the improvement plan will not help the organization reach these goals, it serves no purpose.

Work toward integrating the transformation planning process and the overall strategic and cultural planning process into a single combined activity. If this is not possible at first, at least ensure that the transformation plan gets built into the overall business plan and that transformation objectives are assigned in the same way as other objectives.

Thrash out the necessary compromises during the planning stage, rather than produce a plan that is not doable. The transformation plan will consume significant time, effort, and money. If you overload people or don't properly budget, the transformation plan will probably be the loser during implementation. You cannot stop the business while you are transforming it.

Use the assessment findings. The assessment process is also a well from which management can draw ideas and set priorities for improvement year after year. The initial assessment, if properly done, will provide extensive input to the plan and greatly simplify the team's task.

Build on existing initiatives. It is important to recognize the value of what has already been done, and to build on this. If you fail to do so, the new plan may be rejected as an emotional reflex by the very people who should be its strongest supporters—those who have already made attempts to create change for the better.

Do not antagonize your resistors. Rather, help educate those who do not yet understand the value of transforming the workplace, who have yet to tap into the potential of all employees. You will be confronted with many people who doubt your plans and resist your every move. Be patient, stay focused, and do not lose hope. Your perseverance and dedication will pay off as your organization succeeds.

Key Success Factors

Here is a final test of the transformation plan.[4] As a minimum the following elements should be included:

- Top management involvement and leadership

- Informed commitment to a long-term effort

- Buy-in of other key stakeholders (for example, unions, board, regulators, champions of previous initiatives)

- A plan developed and owned by those who will implement it

- Coverage of both technical and cultural issues

- A clear, practical vision of the future desired state, with measurable objectives linked to the key goals of the organization

- An adequate infrastructure for deployment of responsibilities and for guidance and support

- Education—both targeted (for early results) and universal (for widespread involvement)

- Planned opportunities for individual pride, participation, and fun

Project Team Action Plan

Most companies undergoing a transformation use project or redesign teams as a means to design the future state of the organization, both socially and technically. They do so because project teams bring together people with a diverse set of ideas, experiences, and backgrounds. By forming a small team that is a diverse sample of the organization, companies are able to redesign at a fast pace, yet are still able to think through how proposed changes will affect or benefit the company as a whole.

Although the roles and responsibilities of project teams will vary slightly from company to company and from social projects to technical projects, most project teams take part in a set of common activities during the transformation effort. This project team action plan will be used by the technical projects, as described on page 160 and by the social projects on page 215. In the following paragraphs we outline a six-stage process that most redesign teams will follow.

Stage 1: Formulate the Project

During this initial stage the social (or technical) management group will survey the projects that could be pursued and select those that appear most fruitful. They will develop charters for those tasks selected for prosecution. A charter will provide the purpose of the project, a brief description of work to be accomplished, the authority and resources available, interfaces with other projects and systems, and a rough time schedule. The responsible management group will then select a team leader for the project and recruit members for the project team.

Stage 2: Charter, Training, and System Identification

During this stage, project team members undergo extensive training in the different aspects of redesign. A combination of classroom education, readings, guest lectures, and individual instruction with a consultant or change expert, prior to any redesign team work, goes a long way toward preparing these team members for the challenges that lie ahead. They must develop the problem-solving tools and the interpersonal communication skills needed in order to be effective team members and decision makers. If team members do not have these skills, failure is virtually assured.

Next, team members need to understand and agree upon the meaning of the charter that was prepared by the Management Group to launch the project. The charter provides the basis for the team's plan. After training and charter clarification, team members must identify, study, and understand the system of which their process is a part. All members must understand the total system to understand how design changes to their process will interact with the rest of the organization. In other words, team members must learn to view the organization as a whole system.

Stage 3: Current State Data Collection and Research

Teams redesigning a core process must collect and analyze information so that the current state of the process is understood in detail. In Stage 1 we were interested in a general overview of the organization. In this stage, team members need to meet and interview key players involved in their process to learn all there is to know about their area of the business. Almost always the key players will be those individuals or teams that are closest to the process. By talking with these experts and observing their work, transformation team members can learn about the specifics of the process under redesign and can actually see how each component comes together to form the current process.

Stage 4: Process Mapping and Analysis of Current State

The goal in mapping the current state is to define how the process works today. Although information gathered during the research and data collection stage may motivate team members to discuss how different improvements would increase the performance of the process or improve customer relations, the process flow map must define the current reality.

The purpose of the *process flow map* is to visually present the current process such that everyone understands how we do business today. Only by clearly understanding the present can we hope to identify opportunities for change.

Process mapping has been used extensively in improving technical work processes, but it has been used very little in improving social processes. It is as applicable to social processes as to technical processes and should be used much more aggressively in redesigning social processes.

Stage 5: Benchmarking

In Stage 5 members shift from examining the way their process or processes work and turn their attention to how other companies with similar processes perform. The intent is not to copy from these companies, but to compare notes about such issues as customer service, cost, cycle time, and so on. You can apply the lessons learned from benchmarking when redesigning processes and systems. This information is invaluable when trying to create a competitive advantage.

Stage 6: Developing and Implementing an Integration Plan

After the project team completes the design stage, their focus switches to developing a plan to integrate the new system with the old. Heretofore we have been concerned with integrating the parts of the new system. Now we are faced with a new integration problem: integrating the new with the old. We must identify the process owners who will be responsible for leading the integration effort in their area. Then they create separate plans for each process and link them together through a master or macro-level plan that takes into consideration the whole organization.

Perspectives on Transformation Planning

The Management Control Dilemma: The Balance between Control and Empowerment

Managers in aspiring 21st-century companies are faced with a difficult dilemma.[5] On the one hand they want to devolve more decision-making power to frontline managers to give them more flexibility. On the other hand they are afraid to relax the tried and tested budgetary control systems that have served the company well for many years. Executives want to encourage enterprise and risk taking, yet they don't want unpleasant surprises. They want to invest in quality and longer-term improvement programs, but they don't want to sacrifice this year's results. They are keen to give divisional managers more autonomy, yet their executive information systems give them instant feedback on detailed variations from the original plan and thus encourage interference. They want to encourage cross-division and cross-company knowledge sharing and support, yet they don't want to change the product- and service-based strategic targets and financial plans for each Strategic Business Unit. And although they are not sure whether incentive plans really work, they are afraid to make changes lest they upset the performance apple cart.

Decentralization can only work well if two conditions are fulfilled: *first,* the center must be able to determine whether the business is on track with its strategy. Unless the center knows when to intervene, decentralization becomes abdication of responsibility. *Second*, the business heads must know what will be counted as good performance. Without clear goals, the whole concept of decentralized responsibility suffers, since the conditions under which a business head can expect to operate free from central intervention are ill defined.

Sometimes It Is Better to Experiment Than to Plan

Many company cultures do not place a particularly high value on experimentation that might fail. If they are to transform themselves into new organizations, they must change those beliefs. For too long, the requirements for excruciating planning and guaranteed results have been used as a crutch for not trying anything new. We must take that crutch away from people. Innovation and change must be encouraged at every turn.

Some people adapt to the new approach better than others. Some feel liberated by it and seize the opportunity to experiment. Others are uneasy and confused. Obviously, my sympathies were with people who wanted to take chances. Discontinuous change demands that we become more willing to try, to fail, and to learn from our mistakes. We continue to figure out both how to learn more quickly and how to transfer that learning from one part of the organization to another. And there is no doubt our risk profile is higher than ever before. But the long-term risks of failing to adopt a culture of experimentation far outweigh the short-term instability.

EXECUTING THE PLAN

Introduction

A typical strategy is to set up a few initial cross-functional teams, with the aim of securing early benefits and developing some experience and expertise in process improvement or problem-solving methods. These early wins help to sustain the mandate for the process and provide some insurance against setbacks in other areas.

A process that cycles slowly—such as designing a complete new product—takes much longer to demonstrate tangible results. If you need to work within such a setting, you might look for some troublesome sub-processes that are frequently repeated, such as reporting and correcting design problems or the design of sub-components.

The first teams usually tackle systemic issues that are critical to survival (for example, because they are important to customers) or have a high payback. These issues are typically chronic process problems that have proven, in the past, to be unsolvable using traditional management methods. Criteria for selecting early improvement projects are listed here:

- It is not too ambitious (not world hunger).
- A real desire to tackle this issue (and, hence, energy and commitment to do some work).
- There is potential for real, tangible benefits (and, hence, early wins).
- The process repeats frequently (preferably).
- The process is established (not brand-new or just being created).

Project Management Procedures

Recognize That Each Project Is Different

The key to successfully using the project management concepts is to realize that each project is indeed different. The project activity process is used to build the roadmap for that project to follow. The resulting activities for any specific project may be dramatically different, depending on the nature of the project.

Recognize the Need for Integration within and among Teams

The integration of persons from functions critical to successful project completion (including hardware and software engineering, manufacturing, marketing, human resources, etc.) into an effective team is the most fundamental requirement for success. Skills must match the task to be done. With highly skilled people in each area, the team can function effectively with the least number of people. Obviously, selecting an effective leader is also critical to the success of the project.

In transformation, the integration of the efforts of the various project teams is critical to the success of the endeavor. Adequate communications (both technical and human) and managerial support must be provided to make this integration possible.

Manage the Teamwork

Effective teamwork is not an accident, nor does it come automatically. Management of the team is a major (and continuing) task. Communications must occur so that all team members share the same vision, mission, and creed and become motivated toward their achievement. Evaluation methods used to assess the performance of team members must not divide the team or demoralize them; for this reason, team-based success measures are increasingly used. Leaders (managerial, technical, or otherwise) must act like coaches for the whole project and not be divisive. The team leader must create an environment where team members feel free to talk about *all* problems that potentially endanger the project's success and to take actions to assure success.

The term "ownership of the problems by the team" really does have meaning to those who have had the good fortune to be part of a successful, integrated team. Team members who feel this ownership assume responsibility for problems and solve them, rather than expecting someone else to solve them or blaming others. The team's leaders must understand ownership and its benefits and adapt their leadership styles to promote it.

Keep Score and Adapt

Transformation efforts inevitably experience surprises along the way, no matter how simple the project. The surprises may arise from technical, marketing, or people problems. In a technical project, one subsystem in a product may unexpectedly generate electrical emissions that confound information being received from a microprocessor in another area. Or in a social project, we may find that one group in the organization is vehemently opposed to our proposed change in the organization.

To minimize the number of surprises, superior teams must keep tabs on their project's performance. *Nonetheless, there will still be surprises.* Teams that keep good tabs on their results and the systems and people affected by them will get earlier and clearer warnings of impending problems than those who do not. Thus, they can solve or adapt to them sooner and at less difficulty and expense.

Good teamwork and problem ownership by the team enable problems to be discussed and solved without having to lay blame. In this positive environment, the team's major challenge is to find an acceptable solution to the problem quickly. Often, friendly competition may arise in seeing who can solve the problem first—a far cry from the delaying tactics and finger-pointing which often occurs in contentious functional organizations.

NOTES

1. Christopher W. Head, *Beyond Transformation* (Productivity Press, 1997), p. 73.

2. Howard W. Oden, *Managing Corporate Culture, Innovation, and Intrapreneurship* (Quorum, 1997), p. 163.

3. Ibid., p. 164.

4. David W. Hutton, *The Change Agent's Handbook* (ASQC Press, 1994), p. 161.

5. Jeremy Hope and Tony Hope, *Competing in the Third Wave: The Ten Key Management Issues of the Information Age* (Harvard Business School Press, 1997), p. 154.

PART II

Technically Redesigning
the Organization

CHAPTER 6

Introduction to Technical Redesign

THE NEED FOR PROCESS REDESIGN

Introduction

Definitions

Before discussing the need for process redesign, let us understand the basic terms we will be using. A **function** is a grouping of similar activities with similar inputs and outputs that can be performed by people with similar skills using similar equipment. In a business organization, three of the primary functions are marketing, engineering, and production. **Processes** are sets of work activities that are logically related and executed to create a business outcome such as producing a product, delivering a service, negotiating a contract, or processing an order. They occur when an individual or group takes input from support and supply groups and adds value— creating outputs to be consumed by customers.

The difference between a process and a function is important and should be clearly understood. A *process* is a sequence of operations that produces a useful product for a customer. Not only does it produce an identifiable product, but it produces a product that has value to a customer. A *function* is a grouping of similar operations with an output, but the output normally is not an identifiable product, and normally has little immediate value to a customer. Functions must usually be sequenced in a process to produce a product of value to a customer.

In this section we will describe, discuss, and compare *process* organizations and *functional* organizations. The terms lateral, cross-functional, and horizontal have all been used for *process*, but we will use the term

Figure 6-1
Flow Chart of a Basic Process

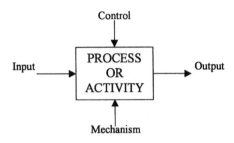

process since it provides a better indication of the real meaning. Similarly, the terms vertical, hierarchical, and traditional have been used for *functional*. Again we elected to use the term *functional*, since it is the more meaningful term. With these terms it is easy to remember that *process organization and management are designed to manage processes, while functional organization and management are designed to manage functions.*

Basics of Process Redesign

A process in its simplest form can be thought of as a transformation, a series of steps or activities that act on inputs and convert them into outputs, as shown in Figure 6-1.

The activities of the process are undertaken by mechanisms that operate under the regulation of controls. Inputs and outputs may be physical or virtual and include objects of all types, incorporating everything from people to information. Examples of typical processes include placing an order, paying an invoice, and developing a new product.

When Michael Hammer introduced the world to processes, he forced the corporate world to start thinking about design, and in particular about design around processes.[1] The structure and organization of most enterprises do not effectively support their existing processes. Strong functional organizations disrupt the flow across departmental boundaries and inhibit the speed and quality of service provided. The essence of redesign is looking at the way these processes or transformations of the business are carried out within an entire organization and consider how they could be restructured, simplified, and rearranged—or redesigned—to be more effective.

Process redesign introduces a new way of thinking about enterprises and organizations. It forces those in the corporate management to focus again on external requirements rather than on their management structures and functions and to consider how the organization can best be structured, equipped, and managed to meet the customer needs. In doing so, process redesign appeared to promise a way out of the corporate quagmire, a means at last for organizations to shed the complex procedural and organizational baggage of the past decades.

Process is a powerful means of designing, organizing, and managing a business. But making a process view of the world understandable to all those who will be tasked with developing and implementing it and who will subsequently staff and manage it often proves to be a major stumbling block. Although the basic concepts of process (working across functions, focusing on the customer, etc.) are relatively easy to grasp, nurturing a sufficiently detailed understanding of redesign process in the organization so that it becomes the means of "doing and managing" is fraught with difficulty. The process is all too often vague and conceptual, and ideas are in danger of being lost during implementation or proving impossible to translate into a new infrastructure.

We will endeavor to provide a guide for process redesign that is so simple, straightforward, and detailed, that everyone can easily understand and follow it.

Background

Most business organizations are currently organized as functional organizations. A functional organization has departments such as marketing, engineering, production, and human resources, with strong boundaries between departments. Employees look to their bosses for direction and authorization for actions; they are loyal to their own disciplines, and little communication occurs across functional boundaries. For example, in many traditional companies, marketing managers do not understand the problems of the production manager, production managers do not talk to engineers, and there is little coordination between the human resources department and all the other functional areas.

In the process organization, the hierarchy is reduced, departmental boundaries are eliminated, and the organization is run by multidisciplinary process teams. The idea is to manage *across* functional areas rather than managing *down* the functional structure. A large process organization might have only three or four layers of management between the CEO and the members of a team. The focus in these organizations is the customer, not the interests of the functional areas.

The only way that a company can become truly customer-focused is to employ process organization and management so that all processes are aimed at satisfying the customer. It is difficult to serve external customers well when the company is organized to serve internal functional managers. *The move from functional to process organization is an essential part of the transformation process.*

A process organization has a common overriding purpose: to produce a product for the customer. This purpose is the key to weaving a *process* horizontally across the firm so that all parts work in unison and not at cross-purposes. *Process management and organization* is a *horizontal* technique and structure that operates across vertical functional boundaries to achieve corporate-wide goals and objectives. It provides an approach to implementing important boundary spanning solutions to meet organization-wide needs.

The Need for Process Organization

In the process organization, the stress on process, or how to align all the operations of the company to best produce a product for the customer, is far different from the emphasis of the functional organization. In a functional organization, each function is primarily interested in maximizing the output of its function rather than maximizing the total output of the entire process. For example, marketing tries to maximize revenues, engineering tries to produce the best designs, and manufacturing tries to build products most efficiently with little regard to the other functions or the total process. Process management, on the other hand, is horizontal. It focuses on how marketing, engineering, and manufacturing and other functions can work together to best satisfy a customer requirement.

Without process organization, performance, in the eyes of the customer or shareholder, is sub-optimized because specialized functional departments plan and execute policy insulated from one another. One department's activities may work at cross-purposes with those of another department. Without process organization, major processes such as new product development, quality, cost, and delivery are rarely optimized.

In a functional organization, there are many company problems that cannot be effectively solved by any one vertical division or department or simply by issuing top-down executive orders. One example is the meeting of customer expectations in regard to quality or warranty management. In a functional organization there is no single department solely responsible, and certainly no single department is a "quality or warranty assurance department." Only by coordinating all pertinent departments through process management can the customer's needs be adequately satisfied.

THE EVOLUTION OF PROCESS REDESIGN

In the last fifteen years, five major methodologies for improving business organizations have evolved: Just-in-Time (JIT), Total Quality Management (TQM), Continuous Process Improvement (CPI), Computer-Integrated Manufacturing (CIM), and Business Process Reengineering (BPR). They are briefly described hereafter.

• JIT is an approach to manufacturing based on two concepts: (1) the planned elimination of all waste and (2) continuous improvement in productivity.[2] JIT encompasses all manufacturing activities required to produce a final product.

- TQM is a people-focused total management approach that aims to increase customer satisfaction at continually lower cost. It works horizontally across functions and departments, involving all employees, top to bottom, and extends backward and forward to include the supply chain and the customer chain.[3]
- CPI is a general approach that evolved from JIT and TQM that can be used in any application to make incremental improvements in any process.[4]
- CIM is the integration of the total manufacturing enterprise through the use of integrated systems and data communication coupled with new managerial philosophies that improve organizational and personnel efficiency.[5]
- CPR is the radical redesign of broad, cross-functional business processes with the objective of order-of-magnitude performance gains, often with the aid of information technology.[6]

We refer to all of these methodologies as "process improvement methodologies." The first three—JIT, TQM, and CPI—are often referred to as "*incremental* or *continuous* methodologies," since they tend to improve the existing system without major redesign. The last two methodologies, CIM and BPR, are often referred to as "*radical*, or *breakthrough* improvement methodologies," since they change the basic design of the system in the process of improving it.

Whereas incremental process improvement initiatives are often continuous in frequency, the goal being ongoing and simultaneous improvement across multiple processes, radical process improvement is generally a discrete initiative. Incremental process improvement can begin soon after changes in a process are identified, and incremental benefits can be achieved within months. Because of the magnitude of organizational change involved, radical improvement often takes a much longer time. We know of no large organization that has fully identified and implemented a major reengineering in less than two years.

Although the end goal of both the incremental and radical approaches is to do things better, faster, and cheaper, there are some differences in how each approach operates. Radical process improvement assumes that everything currently being done is suspect and starts with a blank sheet of paper. Radical process improvement typically aims for:

- Widespread, radical change
- Improvements of 100 percent or more
- Revolution, not evolution, in current ways of doing business

An example of a *radical* process improvement project is: The company decides to combine the sales and order processing departments and create a totally new way of generating and accepting customer orders.

Incremental process improvement is typically thought of as an approach that aims for:

Figure 6-2
Differences between Incremental and Radical Improvement

	Incremental Improvement	Radical Improvement
Level of Change	Incremental	Radical
Starting Point	Existing process	Clean slate
Frequency of Change	One-time/continuous	One-time
Required Length	Short	Long
Participation	Bottom-up	Top-down
Typical Scope	Narrow, within functions	Broad, cross-functional
Risk	Moderate	High
Primary Enabler	Measurement Info. Technology	Behavioral Info. Technology
Type of Change	Technical	Technical/Behavioral

- Incremental change
- Improvements of 25 percent or more
- Evolution in current way of doing business

An example of an *incremental* process improvement project is: The company decides to streamline the order-entry process.

Other important differences between incremental and radical process improvement are summarized in Figure 6-2.[7]

The process redesign approach described in the next section uses the best features of both the incremental and the radical improvement processes.

THE NATURE OF PROCESS REDESIGN

Underlying Concepts

For the purposes of understanding and designing processes, it is useful to divide processes into two types: value-adding and non–value-adding processes. A *value-adding process or activity* is an essential work effort, that is, it contributes to the production of an output valued by a customer. A non–value-adding process is a *nonessential* work effort, that is, it does not contribute to producing a useful output. In designing processes, we want to optimize the effectiveness of value-adding activities and reduce, or eliminate if possible, all non–value-adding activities.

Value-adding processes are divided into two types: core value-adding processes and non-core value-adding processes. *Core* processes are required for the company to perform its mission and to continue to exist. *Non-core* processes should be performed, but if they were not, the company could continue to exist. The core processes are supported by the core competencies discussed in Chapter 3. The distinction between core and non-core value-adding processes is somewhat arbitrary. In practice, a company prioritizes their value-adding processes, and then designates the top five to fifteen processes as their core processes. These are the processes they will transform first.

Non–value-added processes and activities can be divided into three types: support, management, and superfluous. Support processes provide no product that is of value to the customer, but they are needed to enable the value-added processes to proceed. In most cases support processes are invisible to the customer. Management processes include actions that managers take to ensure that value-added processes happen correctly and on time. Superfluous non–value-adding processes provide absolutely no benefit to the customer or to a value-adding process; they provide only a cost to the producer. Such activities as repeated counting of the product, inventorying the product, and excessive reporting provide no benefit to anyone and should be eliminated. *In summary, we should minimize support and management activities and eliminate superfluous activities.*

Clean-Sheet Approach

Process redesign requires using the clean-sheet approach. The first step is for project teams to form a detailed picture of all the components that impact the current process by documenting the process flow. Once project teams have a clear picture of the current process, they can start with a clean sheet of paper and redesign completely new processes. Realistically there are always constraints with regard to resources (time, capital, people, equipment), meaning that project teams cannot throw out everything current and start from scratch. Clearly the most important job of the redesign team is to "think outside the box" during the initial design stages and create processes that will align and link to create a system that exceeds customer expectations. This means they must have the authority to look beyond current processes, jobs, and business functions.

Just as we should not ask redesign teams to preserve current processes, we should not constrain them by forcing them to preserve certain jobs or titles that individuals had prior to launching the transformation effort. If some positions are off-limits, then the transition teams cannot start with a clean sheet of paper. If we hamper our teams by holding them to current processes or jobs, then we can expect our performance improvements to be less than optimum.

Major Decisions in Process Redesign

The goal of process improvement is to improve the performance of all processes, especially the core processes that serve customers. However, no organization just beginning process improvement has the resources to work on all processes at once. The organization may be able to focus on most of its core processes if there are only a few of them. If resources are scarce and/or the number of core processes are too high, leaders will need to prioritize the core processes and decide which ones to address. To select processes to study, consider:

- How central to our mission, strategies, and customer satisfaction is the process?
- How badly does the process need fixing?
- Is the scope of the process manageable?
- Are people and/or teams available who are interested and capable?

To take advantage of both the radical and incremental approaches, any process improvement project should start by taking the following steps:

- If the process is not needed, throw it out (radical improvement approach).
- If the process is core and value-adding, apply the radical improvement approach.
- If small incremental improvements are all that is needed, employ the incremental improvement approach.

Cautions in Process Redesign

Design for the Future

One thing organizations can count on is that technology will change. The state-of-the-art systems being implemented today could be outdated before they have had a chance to produce their expected returns on investment. Therefore, systems should be *designed for change* so that they can incorporate new technology as it comes on the market. Successful producers continually scan for new technological developments in their core business areas and assess their usefulness relative to their products. They are prepared to upgrade and alter their designs and implementation plans in light of the technical advances identified. Such an approach is especially important for long-term development efforts, so that new systems will not be obsolete by the time they are implemented. Clearly, this criterion is related to the previous one. If a system is relatively open, it is likely to be more compatible not only with contemporary systems but also with future open systems products.

Systems should be *modular* and *extensible*. Building in *modularity* means designing systems, tools, and applications as relatively self-contained sets of functions that are relatively independent of and yet compatible with other modules. If applications are designed as modules, users can pick and choose among them to address particular tasks. *Extensibility* refers to the ability to successfully add or upgrade modules—in other words, to incorporate new applications into a product and adapt it to changing needs.

Overemphasis on Processes

Focusing on the work processes, or horizontal work flows, is the key to achieving the cross-functional teamwork needed to provide superior customer value. Vertical flows of work, especially paperwork and reporting, should be minimized or eliminated unless they are key to providing customer value or sustaining the organization over the long term. However, the vertical flow of information and work between layers of management should not be ignored.

We must be careful not to go too far in eliminating vertical work flows and relationships. If we define the system entirely in terms of processes, or horizontal work flows, we are guilty of going to the opposite extreme— partitioning the system along horizontal lines and not paying any attention to how these processes needed to be integrated vertically. In the 21st century, managers must address how to integrate both the horizontal and vertical flows of work and information.

Overemphasis on Large Radical Improvements

Because of these differences in the amount of "payoff" or improvement promised between radical process improvement and incremental process improvement, it is usual to find that high-level people within the company want radical process improvements to be implemented. But because they are so far removed from the day-to-day detail, they normally drastically underestimate what it will take to successfully complete a radical improvement project. Sometimes this leads to a radical improvement project being half-implemented and then getting stuck.

PROCESS MAPPING AND PROCESS REDESIGN

Introduction

Process mapping visually presents the current version of the process so that everyone understands and agrees how we do business today. Only by clearly understanding the present can we hope to identify opportunities for improvement. Process mapping provides the tools and a proven methodology for identifying your current "as-is" business processes and can be used to provide a "to-be" roadmap for reengineering the firm's process.

At the outset we want to warn you that some companies have become so enamored with process mapping and spent so much time at it they never got around to doing any process redesign. This is unfortunate, since process redesign provides a real increase in productivity, while process mapping merely provides additional information at best. The difference between the two can be seen from the following definitions:

- *Process design* is the *creation* and description of how the business will carry out its core processes activities in the *future*. It defines how the business will look and helps to identify the changes to infrastructure that have to be made.
- *Process mapping* is the diagramming or modeling of the *existing* processes in the business, as they work *currently*.

Process design is creative and adds real value, when performed correctly. Process mapping, on the other hand, is concerned with documenting existing business operations. Process mapping should be performed *only when it contributes to process redesign*. Whatever use is made of process mapping, a close watch needs to be kept on the levels of detail that develop. Unmonitored, the activity can rapidly turn into a redundant intellectual exercise that attempts to squeeze every aspect of the existing enterprise into the model. The emphasis, as ever, should be on practicalities. If the mapping is not contributing directly to the progress of change, it should be set aside.

Now that we have issued our warning, we must emphasize that process mapping is a necessary and important part of the transformation process and should be pursued with vigor. One of the decisions we must make is selecting a process mapping techniques from the plethora of techniques available on the market. In order that our process mapping will be as effective as possible with as little effort as possible, it should satisfy the following criteria:

- It should be so simple that *everyone*, including top management, can understand and use it without extensive training.
- It should be able to express process operations in a natural and straightforward way.
- It should be concise and provide a straightforward means of locating details of interest easily and quickly.
- It should be able to communicate the process to a wide variety of different levels and types of business personnel.
- It should be well documented, highly standardized, and available to everyone in the public domain.

The Basics of IDEF

The IDEF mapping system developed by the U.S. Air Force comes closest to satisfying our criteria. In order to help reduce product and process development costs and cycle time, the U.S. Air Force sponsored process mapping efforts through its Integrated Computer Aided Manufacturing

(ICAM) Program. This ambitious program needed a common communication tool around which to plan, develop, and implement the process
subsystems. The IDEF (Integrated computer-aided manufacturing [Icam]
DEFinition) process mapping system was developed as the language for
this new architecture.

The IDEF mapping system consist of the following methods:

- IDEF0 Functional Modeling
- IDEF1 Information Modeling
- IDEF1X Data Modeling
- IDEF3 Process Description Capture
- IDEF4 Object-Oriented Design

IDEF contains three *descriptive* modeling methods than can graphically
characterize an organization:

1. IDEF0 is used to produce a *function* model that is a structured representation
   of the functions of a manufacturing system or environment and of the information and objects that interrelate those functions.
2. IDEF1 is used to produce an *information* model that represents the structure
   of information needed to support the functions of a manufacturing system or
   environment.
3. IDEF3 is used to produce a *dynamics* model that represents the time-varying
   behavior of functions, information, and resources of a manufacturing system or
   environment.

The second category of IDEF methods that have been developed are
focused on the *design* portion of the system development process. That is,
they encapsulate the best-known method for design with a particular technology (or class of technology). Currently there are two IDEF design
methods: IDEF1X (Data Modeling Method) and IDEF4 (Object-Oriented
Design Method). IDEF1X was developed to assist in the design of *relational* database design models. IDEF4 was developed to address the need
for a design method to assist in the production of quality designs for
object-oriented implementations. IDEF4, like IDEF1X, is intended to
serve the needs of the systems designers and programmer analysts who
are building and evolving large information systems.

The *descriptive* mapping methods, IDEF0 and IDEF3, are described in
this chapter and used in chapters 7 and 8 to describe and analyze the
existing organization and future organizations. We describe the IDEF0
method more completely since it is a basis for all the other methods and
we use it extensively. We defer discussion of the IDEF1, IDEF1X, and
IDEF4 methods until Chapter 9, where they are used. We do not attempt

to completely describe these mapping methods in this book. Rather, we provide sufficient information to understand their use in the book and then provide sources where additional information can be obtained.

The three descriptive methods are designed to work together. For instance, IDEF0 can be used to decompose the model to a level at which the relationships among activities can be determined using IDEF3. All IDEF3 boxes have a field for providing a reference to an activity in IDEF0. Similarly, the functional decomposition and the identification of model elements by IDEF0 are good starting points for the identification of entities in IDEF1. IDEF3 process descriptions can help users develop information models by focusing attention on the information to support the process. Also, by integrating a number of IDEF1 process view information models, IDEF3 can be used to construct scenarios that can simulate and predict human behavior.

THE IDEF0 FUNCTIONAL MODELING METHOD

The IDEF0 mapping system uses only two symbols for mapping: boxes and arrows. Thus, it is very easy for everyone, and especially top management, to understand the diagrams without extensive training. It can be drawn easily by hand or by a standard computer word-processing program. It takes no special equipment or training to prepare IDEF0 process maps. As shown in Figure 6-3, an IDEF0 process map is composed of a hierarchical series of diagrams that gradually display increasing levels of detail describing functions and their interfaces in the context of the overall process.

IDEF0 Process Map Organization

IDEF0 process maps are composed of three types of information: graphic diagrams, text, and glossary descriptions that are all cross-referenced to each other. The graphic diagram, the major component of an IDEF0 process map, contains boxes, arrows, box/arrow interconnections, and associated relationships. Boxes represent each major sub-process of a process. These sub-processes are broken down or decomposed into more detailed diagrams, as shown in Figure 6-3, until the subject is described at a level necessary to support the goals of a particular design team.

As indicated in Figure 6-4a, each side of the function box has a standard meaning in terms of box/arrow relationships. The side of the box with which an arrow interfaces reflects the arrow's role. Arrows entering the left side of the box are inputs. Inputs are transformed or consumed by the function to produce outputs. Arrows entering the box on the top are controls (or constraints). Controls specify the conditions required for the func-

Figure 6-3
IDEF0 Decomposition Structure

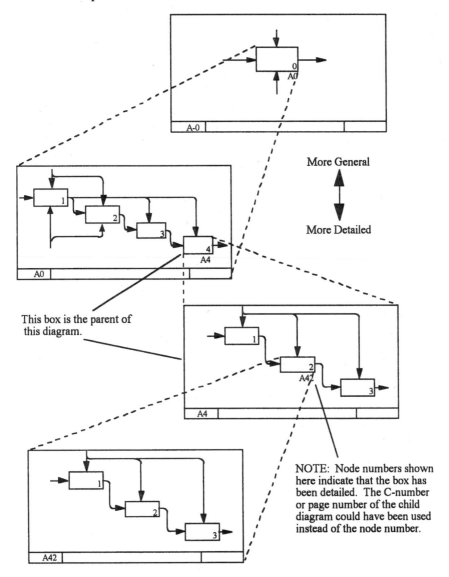

More General

⬆
⬇

More Detailed

This box is the parent of
this diagram.

NOTE: Node numbers shown
here indicate that the box has
been detailed. The C-number
or page number of the child
diagram could have been used
instead of the node number.

Figure 6-4a
Arrow Positions and Roles

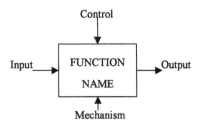

Figure 6-4b
An Example of an A0 Diagram

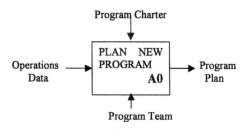

tion to product correct outputs. Arrows leaving the box on the right side are outputs. Outputs are the data or objects produced by the function. Arrows connected to the bottom side of the box represent mechanisms (or means). Upward-pointing arrows identify some of the means that support the execution of the function.

The top-level diagram is the enterprise process map and provides the most general description of the total process. This diagram is followed by a series of child diagrams providing more detail about the sub-processes. The IDEF0 process map starts by presenting the whole process as a single unit—a box with external arrow boundary conditions connecting it to functions and resources outside the whole process. The single box is called the "top box" of the mode, with node number A0. The arrows on this process diagram interface with process functions outside the process area to establish a focal point for your process map. An example A0 diagram is shown in Figure 6-4b.

One of the most important features of IDEF0 as a process mapping concept is that it gradually introduces greater and greater levels of detail through the process of decomposition. In this way, communication is enhanced by providing the reader with a well-bounded topic with a manageable amount of detail to learn from each process map diagram.

Figure 6-5
Node Index (Table of Contents) Showing Diagram Order

A0 Manufacture product
    A1 Plan for manufacture
        A11 Assume a structure and method of manufacture
        A12 Estimate requirements, time, cost to produce
        A13 Develop production plans
        A14 Develop support activities plans
    A2 Make and administer schedules and budgets
        A21 Develop master schedule
        A22 Develop coordinating schedule
        A23 Estimate costs and make budget
        A24 Monitor performance to schedule and budget
    A3 Plan production

How to Read an IDEF0 Process Map

A process map is made up of a collection of process diagrams and associated materials arranged in a hierarchical manner. An index (or table of contents) is created. Placing the diagrams in hierarchical order gives an overall view of the process and an access to any portion of the process map.

Reading is done top-down, considering each process diagram a center of process activity, bounded by its parent box. After the top-level diagrams are read, first-level diagrams are read, then second-level diagrams are read, and so on. If specific details about a process map are needed, the node index is used to descend through the levels to the required process diagram.

All diagrams are in "node index" order, meaning that all child diagrams relating to one box on a process map diagram are presented before the children of the next box. This places related process map diagrams together in the same order used in an ordinary table of contents, as shown in Figure 6-5.

Process maps provide an overview of the whole process or details of a particular process. To read a process map to obtain an overview, use the index to find all high-level diagrams. To read a process map for detail, use the index as shown in Figure 6-5 to find all process map diagrams detailing the process of interest.

Process Diagram Reading Steps

The primary information about a process is contained in the diagrams. The following reading sequence is recommended:

1. Scan the boxes of the process diagram to gain an impression of what is being described.
2. Refer back to the parent diagram and note the arrow connections to the parent box. Try to identify a "most important" input, control, and output.

Figure 6-6
Example of Main Path

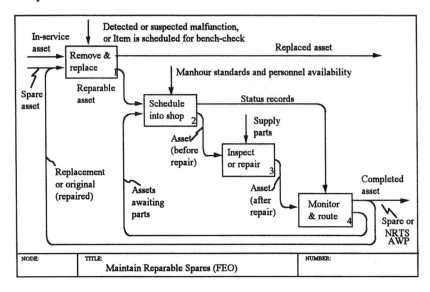

NODE:	TITLE: Maintain Reparable Spares (FEO)	NUMBER:

3. Consider the arrows of the current process diagram. Try to determine if there is a main path linking the "most important" input or control and the "most important" output.

4. Mentally walk through the process diagram, from upper left to lower right, using the main path as a guide. Note how other arrows interact with each box. Determine if there are secondary paths. Check the story being told by the process map diagram by considering how familiar situations are handled.

5. Finally, read the text and glossary, if provided.

This sequence ensures that the major features of each diagram receive attention. The text will call attention to anything that the process map author wishes to emphasize. The glossary will define the interpretation of the terminology used.

Each process diagram has a central theme, running from the most important incoming boundary arrow to the most important outgoing boundary arrow. This main path through the boxes and arrows outlines the primary function of the diagram, as shown in Figure 6-6. Other parts of the process diagram represent qualifying or alternative conditions that are secondary to the main path.

The system's operation can be mentally envisioned by pursuing the main path. Specific kinds of data inputs, the handling of errors, and possible alternative outputs lend detail to the story. This walk-through enhances your understanding of the process map.

Preparing an IDEF0 Process Map

Preparing an IDEF0 process map is a creative endeavor that varies with each author. Following is a procedure used by many authors.

1. *Determine the context, viewpoint, and purpose for the map.* Before beginning the map it is important to determine the map's orientation—its context, viewpoint, and purpose. While they may be refined as the map proceeds, they must remain clear and undistorted. The context basically states what is in the model and what is outside. The viewpoint describes from what perspective or slant the model is developed. Purpose embodies why the model is created, what the intent or goal of the model is.

2. *Create the A0 or Context Diagram.* Draw a single box containing the name of the function that encompasses the entire scope of the system being described. Use input, control, and output arrows entering and leaving the box to represent the interfaces of the system with its environment. This single-box diagram bounds the context for the entire model and forms the basis for further decomposition efforts.

3. *Create the topmost Decomposition Diagram.* Identify the major activities that enable you to go from the input to the output shown on the A0 diagram, and arrange them in sequential order. One should expect considerable trial and error in this step.

4. *Complete the Decomposition Task.* Continue breaking down the parent functions into child functions until no further breakdown is feasible. Take care that in each decomposition the child boxes cover the entire function in the parent box.

5. *Compile a list of model elements.* The *elements* are all those parts of the IDEF0 diagram except activities (i.e., inputs, outputs, controls, and mechanisms). (To confuse the user, these model elements are called *objects* in IDEF3 and *entities* in IDEF1 and IDEF1X.) The intent of this step is simply to develop a pool of elements through research and interviews that can be used in the next step. There will be a pool for each type of element (inputs, outputs, controls, and mechanisms).

6. *Using the arrow notation, place these model elements at appropriate places on the diagram.* This is the most detailed and time-consuming part of process mapping. But, if we are really going to describe the functions of an organization, these model elements must be properly identified and associated with the correct activity. There are a number of computerized applications that make this task somewhat less onerous.

Unless you are actually involved in the development of a model, the detail provided by applying the last two steps tends to be more confusing than helpful. For this reason most of the IDEF0 models we will use in this book will not include these steps. Also IDEF0 does not utilize sequence arrows between activities, since the sequence is indicated by the flow of the element arrows. Since we are not drawing the element arrows, we will borrow from IDEF3 and provide sequence arrows in our IDEF0 diagrams.

Additional Information on IDEF0

Because of space limitations, we could only provide a brief introduction to IDEF0. Readers desiring additional information may consult Hunt's book on *Process Mapping*[8] or the federal standard on IDEF0.[9]

THE IDEF3 PROCESS DESCRIPTION CAPTURE METHOD

Introduction

IDEF3, which is often used in conjunction with IDEF0, is described in this chapter. IDEF1, IDEF1X, and IDEF4, which are used for information analysis and design, are described in Chapter 9.

IDEF3 is designed to assist those engaged in capturing and analyzing the dynamics of an existing or proposed system. Guidelines and simple-to-use graphical language structures aid users in successfully capturing and organizing process information for multiple downstream uses. IDEF3 provides the ability to capture and structure *descriptions* of how a system works from multiple viewpoints, thereby enabling users to capture information conveyed by knowledgeable experts about the behavior of a system rather than directing user activity toward constructing engineering *models* to simulate system behavior. This feature is among the central characteristics distinguishing IDEF3 from alternative offerings.

Benefits previously realized through the application of IDEF3 can be measured in terms of cost savings, schedule gains, quality improvements, organic capability improvements, and lasting changes to organizational culture. IDEF3 has been used to:

• Identify obscure process links between organizations.
• Highlight redundant and/or non-value-added activities.
• Rapidly design new processes.
• Provide an implementation-independent specification for human-system inter-action.
• Speed the development and validation of simulation models.

IDEF3 mapping is similar to IDEF0 in that it consists only of boxes and lines. The boxes are similar to those used in IDEF0, although they are called "Unit of Behavior (UOB)" rather than "Activity." However, the role of the lines, or "links" as they are called in IDEF3, are quite different.

Figure 6-7a
Basic Precedence Link

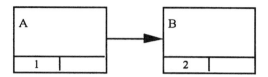

The Role of Links in IDEF3

Introducing Links

Links are the glue that connects UOB boxes to form representations of dynamic processes. Links are used primarily to denote significant relationships among UOBs. Examples of the types of relations that can be highlighted by IDEF3 links include temporal, logical, causal, natural, and conventional. However, in the vast majority of cases, users are most interested in indicating simple temporal precedence. Hence, a special class of links is devoted to expressing this relation. The *precedence link elaboration document* enables users to capture additional details about a particular precedence link. Links are drawn to start or terminate at any point on a UOB box or junction symbol. The symbols that represent each type are shown below:

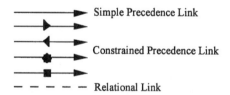

Simple Precedence Links

Precedence links express temporal precedence relations between instances of one UOB and those of another. They are the most widely used link and are denoted by a solid arrow, perhaps with an additional marker attached to the stem of the arrow, as indicated in Figure 6-7a. Precedence links connect UOB boxes, as illustrated in Figure 6-7a, with a simple precedence link. The lines that we have been using in our IDEF0 diagrams are essentially simple precedence links borrowed from IDEF3.

Box 1 (labeled "A"), at the "back" end of the link, is known as the *source* of the link, and box 2 (labeled "B"), at the "front" end of the link, is known as the *destination*. Considered as an IDEF3 schematic, box 1 is known as the (immediate) *predecessor* of box 2 in the schematic, and box 2 the (immediate) *successor* of box 1.

Figure 6-7b
Constrained Precedence Link

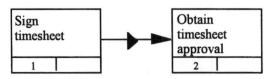

Figure 6-8
Further Examples of Constrained Precedence Links

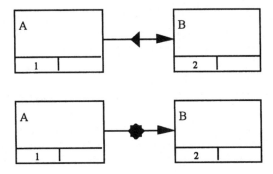

Constrained Precedence Links

Figure 6–7a, with a simple precedence link, says nothing about whether instances of either UOB can occur in the system being described without a corresponding instance of the other. For all Figure 6-7a says, an instance of A could occur without an instance of B; or an instance of B could occur before an instance of A. The semantics of the simple precedence link is thus rather permissive. Constrained precedence links add constraints beyond simple precedence.

The constrained precedence link shown in Figure 6-7b indicates that any instance of the source UOB must be followed by an instance of the destination UOB. This is what is meant by the "directionality" of the link; the constraint is in force only from "left to right." For example, an activation of the schematic in Figure 6-7b consists of an instance of "Sign timesheet" followed by an instance of "Obtain timesheet approval." Given the directionality of the link in Figure 6-7b, instances of "Obtain timesheet approval" alone are not prohibited by Figure 6-7b; such cases might occur, for example, when an employee quits before timesheets for a given pay period are turned in (in which case the subsequently approved timesheet was never signed).

Two additional constrained precedence links are used often. The precedence link in the top schematic of Figure 6-8 indicates that an occurrence of B must be preceded by an occurrence of A. The bottom schematic indicates both that any instance of A must be followed by an instance of B and that an instance of B must be preceded by an instance of A. These constraints add a *normative* component to the description of a system, that is, a component that expresses not just how the system has been observed to behave, but how it *ought* to behave. Constrained links are thus particularly useful when IDEF3 is used to *model* a system, not just to record beliefs and observations about its behavior.

Clearly, these three links do not exhaust the possible constraints that might hold between UOBs. But hopefully they will give the reader an idea of the kind of relationships that can be expressed in IDEF3, and how IDEF3 can be used for dynamic modeling and simulation.

NOTES

1. Michael Hammer and James Champy, *Reengineering the Corporation: A Manifesto for Business Revolution* (HarperBusiness, 1993).

2. William M. Boyst, "Just-in-Time: Driver for Continuous Improvement," in Thomas F. Wallace and Steven J. Bennett (eds.), *World Class Manufacturing* (Omneo, 1994), p. 267.

3. Greg Bounds et al., *Beyond Total Quality Management: Toward the Emerging Paradigm* (McGraw-Hill, 1994), p. 4.

4. Richard Y. Chang, *Continuous Process Improvement* (Richard Chang Associates, 1994), p. 7.

5. Warren L. Shrensker, *CIM: A Working Definition* (SME, 1990), p. 2.

6. Richard L. Nolan et al., *Reengineering the Organization* (Harvard Business School Press, 1995), p. 27.

7. Thomas H. Davenport, *Process Innovation* (Harvard Business School Press, 1993), p. 11.

8. V. Daniel Hunt, *Process Mapping* (Wiley, 1996).

9. National Institute of Standards and Technology, *Integration Definition for Function Modeling (IDEF0)*, FIPS PUB 183 (Secretary of Commerce, December 1993).

CHAPTER 7

Broad Technical Redesign of the Enterprise

INTRODUCTION

The purpose of this chapter is to identify the major processes in the company and decide which processes are to be redesigned. To accomplish this we will develop, understand, and diagnose a process flow model of our existing and planned future business. The key questions answered by this chapter include:

- What are the major business processes of our enterprise?
- What are our core, value-adding processes?
- What processes will be selected for redesign?

Bringing the very basics of the business to the surface paves the way for considering major process changes. The emphasis is on overview, rather than details. Looking at existing processes in detail or analyzing costs or constraints at low level should be avoided, because this tends to encourage solving existing problems rather than designing completely new ways of working.

The procedures in this chapter will be performed *only once* during the transformation program by the Technical Management Group. Following this, the Project Team (or teams) will redesign individual processes, following the guidance in chapters 8, 9, and 14. In other words, chapters 6 and 7 enable a company to decide which processes to transform in which sequence, while chapters 8, 9, and 14 provide guidance on how to transform the individual processes.

The Technical Management Group's understanding of their company's current processes will determine how much effort has to be put into this chapter. Most companies, and particularly those companies just beginning transformation programs, do not have a good understanding of their current processes. Traditionally, companies are organized around functions and/or products, and most of the company's resources, procedures, systems, practices, and finances are structured vertically. It is often very difficult for the people in a company to identify and understand their current processes, even the simplest ones. Lacking this understanding, a Technical Management Group may find it difficult to identify a company's processes and to select the most important ones to transform. The Social Management Group will serve as the design review activity for the efforts of the Technical Management Group.

COLLECT AND ANALYZE INFORMATION ON THE *EXISTING* PROCESSES OF THE ENTERPRISE

Identify Existing External Customers and Suppliers

This task identifies the *external* customers and suppliers, defines their needs and wants, and identifies the various interactions between the organization and its customers and suppliers. Each major process will have at least one external customer and supplier. Of the two, we should pay more attention to the customers, since they determine our sales, but every process must have both.

In compiling the list of customer/supplier needs and wants, the transformation team must be careful to distinguish between what a customer/supplier says and what they mean. When quoting a price on a product, they may be assuming certain quality and delivery conditions that are not acceptable to your company.

A second issue is knowing who the customer or supplier really is. Retailers and personal service companies, for example, deal directly with the ultimate users of their products and services. Many manufacturers, however, deal with resellers, who are not the ultimate users. The transformation team must understand and model this distinction.

Develop Enterprise Process Map

Before we can identify our core processes and select processes for redesign, we must have a good understanding of the current way of doing things. This is the purpose for developing the *enterprise process map*, which will be used as the reference point against which all recommendations for change will be made. In the enterprise process map we develop a flow chart of the company's total current processes, using the IDEF0 and IDEF3 procedures outlined in Chapter 6. We define each process and identify the activities of which it is composed. We identify the process inputs and outputs, as well as any additional stimuli that affect the activities.

By using techniques of process mapping described in Chapter 6, the Technical Management Group traces jobs through the factory from order entry to design specification, scheduling and purchasing materials, actual factory processing, and all the way to shipment to the customer. Here they ask the five questions, What? Where? When? How? Who?—followed by, Why? The Technical Management Group must understand the details of how their company makes its products. They must understand down to the level of who actually performs the various communications and control jobs. They have to create the base from which all improvements can be made. The input from the Social Management Groups after their comparison of the process map with the organization charts and manuals, as described on page 226, should be of considerable help.

The enterprise process map requires extensive information, which can be obtained by performing the following tasks:

- Interview the people who actually do the work.
- Observe the work being performed.
- Gather pertinent documents used in doing the work.
- Put the flow, the information and documents, in sequential order on the process map.
- Review the flow with the people interviewed.
- Correct mistakes, as required.

An example of a top-level enterprise process map is shown in Figure 7-1.

The process map was developed using the process mapping procedures outlined in Chapter 6. Specifically we followed the first four steps of IDEF0 on page 127 and the fifth step was taken from IDEF3 on page 128.

1. Determine the context, viewpoint, and purpose of the map.
2. Create the A0 or Context Diagram.
3. Create the topmost Decomposition Diagram.
4. Complete the Decomposition Task.
5. Determine the sequence of activities.

We did not use the last two steps of the IDEF0 procedure, as they would provide more detail than we need at this point in time. To conserve space, the full decomposition of the ABC Manufacturing Co. is not shown.

Figure 7-1
Enterprise Process Map for the ABC Manufacturing Co.

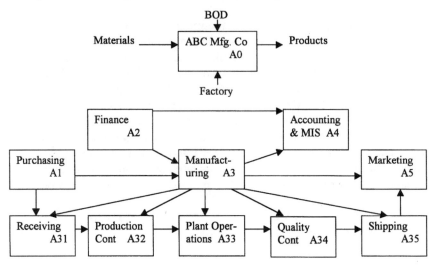

COLLECT AND ANALYZE INFORMATION ON *FUTURE* ENTERPRISE PROCESSES

The purpose of this section is to define in broad terms what the *future* enterprise will be like. As in the previous section, we will look at the entire enterprise in fairly general terms. The key questions regarding the *future enterprise* to be answered include:

- What are the primary processes, activities, and tasks that should be performed? In what order should they be performed?

- How should resources, information, and work flow through each selected process?

- Are there ways to achieve our business goals and address customer needs that seem impossible today but would, if they could be done, fundamentally change our business?

- Consider the boundaries between our processes and our business partners, that is, our customers, suppliers, strategic allies. How might we redefine these boundaries to improve overall performance?

- What are the specific improvement goals for our new processes? What are our concept and strategy for change? How can we communicate our concept to all employees?

The *enterprise concept* that is the goal and product of this stage is more than a vision and less than a design. It is an articulation of the purpose of transforming the process. A well-defined concept should have the following characteristics:

- It should be comprehensible by a management audience that understands the business.
- It should describe the primary features that distinguish the transformed enterprise from the current enterprise.
- The description should include both the behavioral aspects (e.g., organization, staffing, jobs) and the technical aspects (e.g., technology, systems, procedures) of the processes in the enterprise.
- It should state—at least qualitatively, and preferably quantitatively—how the performance of the transformed process will be improved.
- It should be motivational and inspirational. The stakeholders should feel that the concept is a goal worthy of aspiration.
- It should be apparent that the concept represents a break with the thinking and assumptions that led to the current enterprise.

Obtain Strategic Input

Corporate strategy must be the starting point for a transformation effort because strategic mission and strategic intent gives the company a consistent course for the future. Strategic planning activities often reveal the need for dramatic change and may even immediately pinpoint the processes that need transformation. Companies often put in a considerable effort early on to understand what drives competitive advantage in a particular industry. The company's strategy is derived by asking a series of questions:

- What is the product or service the company will offer?
- Where will that product or service be offered, in terms of segmentation?

These are the standard strategist's questions. But then, as the focus turns to processes, the strategic executives ask:

- What competencies are required to support the company's mission and strategic intent?
- What core and supporting processes are required to support the company's competencies?
- What are the key processes (both core business processes and key supporting processes) that support the product or service in the related market segments?

The company's strategy should also include objectives in specific competitive dimensions, such as:

- Better meeting customer needs (attractive product features, service, price/positioning).
- Superior economics (lower basic product/service costs, cost-to-serve advantage).
- Time (more timely delivery, faster new product development).

Instead of relying solely on traditional structured methods of competitive positioning, such as market segmentation and product positioning, our strategic assessment for transformation revisits customer and shareholder expectations, market dynamics, the role of information, and the core capabilities of the business. While significant process improvement can result from focusing on internal conditions, you can't catch or overtake the competition unless you know where you are relative to them—unless you engage in *competitive analysis*. Detailed knowledge of competitors' strengths and weaknesses can help identify where your company's competitive edge may lie.

To complete the picture, you also need to understand the dynamics of your industry and market. Companies get information on the competition and market in several ways. They survey their competitors' customers to get their perspectives on strengths and weaknesses. Trade associations, survey research firms, chambers of commerce, and advisory panels can also provide information.

Determine Future Customer Requirements

You cannot define future customer requirements unless you know who your future customers are. Thus, the first step in our diagnosis of future customer requirements is to identify the future customers. Existing customers are easy to identify, but identifying future customers is somewhat more difficult.

Identify Your Future Customers

First start with a list of current customers and brainstorm how they will change in the next ten years. Then look at your strategic plans, particularly product and service development plans, and predict what new customers will result. The final step is to look at the general social, demographic, environmental, and other trends to get a handle on how general trends will change the composition and needs of future customers.

Identify Your Customers' Future Requirement Areas

Now that you have identified your future customers, try to put yourself in their shoes and visualize what they might require. Are they primarily interested in saving money? Time? Or perhaps they'd like you to offer a wider variety of goods and services? Customer requirements typically fall into one of the areas listed below:

- Timeliness
- Cost
- Accuracy
- Functionality
- Responsiveness
- Follow-through
- Quantity
- Thoroughness
- Dimension
- Yield
- Price
- Availability

Develop Interview Survey Questions

Once you've predicted your customers' requirement areas, you can formulate interview/survey questions that will verify or correct your predictions. Devise questions that will help you gauge whether customer requirements are being met and the importance of a particular requirement. Make your questionnaire short, as your customers need to know that you consider their time valuable.

Interview/Survey Your Customer

The final step in defining key requirements for core future customers is to interview your customers. Whenever possible, interview your customer in a face-to-face meeting. Write down all feedback so that you and/or your team can review it later. When defining customer requirements, be sure to understand both needs and expectations.

Not just any customer will do for this survey. Most organizations perform their market research using the broad undifferentiated type of customer. Instead, we should focus on those customers who are on the leading edge, responding to a vision, and engaging in innovation and radical change. When you are looking for new requirements, their opinions are most important.[1]

Customer Requirements Feedback

After you have completed all of the customer interviews, you need to make sense of the data you have gathered. How well did you predict the customer requirements? Which requirement area is most important?

Which area needs the most work? Customer feedback is valuable information; use it to your advantage. It will take several weeks for the group members to gather all the survey data from external customers.

Gathering baseline customer performance data helps you see how effectively the process and the activities within the process function to meet the requirements of your customers. Your picture of the process may be quite different from the process itself. The data you gather will clear up any discrepancies.

DIAGNOSE FUTURE NEEDS AND DEVELOP ENTERPRISE CONCEPT

In this section we develop the "enterprise concept" and develop detailed concepts for each of the individual processes to be transformed. The individual process concepts must be sufficiently detailed and clear that the project team can pursue the transformation without confusion.

Develop Enterprise Concept

In this section we develop the future concept for the total enterprise. A concept provides a picture of what the enterprise will or could be like in the future. A concept is more specific than a vision but less specific than a design. The enterprise concept should be in accordance with and support the company's vision, mission, and creed. The Technical Management Group has the primary responsibility for developing the enterprise concept.

An enterprise concept consists of a process mapping of the firm's major processes supplemented by written description, an artist's rendering, a model or any other suitable presentation format that depicts the concept. The enterprise concept should be in sufficient detail to enable (1) top-level managers to understand and evaluate it, (2) customers to understand and comment on it, (3) engineers to visualize how technology might be applied to implement the concept, and (4) operating managers to determine how they would operate under the new concept.

It is not expected that the first enterprise concept document would be a final and full-blown document. Rather, we would anticipate that the enterprise concept document would be evolutionary and developed in a participatory manner. We are dealing with very general high-level ideas here, and the more minds we can bring to bear the better. The enterprise process map will serve as the primary communication aid during this and the following creative stage.

Extend Process Model Outside Company

Some of the greatest opportunities to improve both customer service and process efficiency come from integrating a company's processes more

Figure 7-2
Typical Customer-Supplier Chain

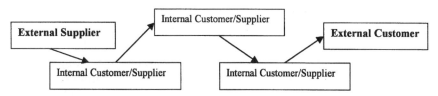

closely with those of its customers. Well-known examples of this include Procter & Gamble's integration of its outbound logistics with Wal-Mart's in-store inventory and Baxter Health Care's integration of its order processing with the supplies management processes of its hospital customers.

In order to uncover these opportunities, it is necessary to extend the boundaries of the process model to include its interfaces with customers' processes. For example, Fulfill Orders interfaces with the customers' purchasing at one end and with their accounts payable at the other end. This task also identifies internal and external suppliers and their interactions with the processes.

At this point, the process model begins to reveal that certain individuals and groups within the organization are both suppliers and customers. In this case, the process takes the form shown in Figure 7-2.

This very important and powerful insight will serve as a key enabler for transformation. It means that all of the tools, techniques, and perspectives that we bring to improve service to external customers can also be used to improve service to internal customers. In other words, by treating each participant in the process as the customer of the participants who supply him, the optimization of work flow and efficiency becomes synonymous with optimization of customer service. This is entirely consistent with the well-known observation that the best customer service is provided by those organizations in which the customer contact personnel are themselves well served.

Just as effective management of a process from the customer perspective requires measurement of *external* performance, so too does it require measurement of *internal* performance. The task therefore identifies additional measures of performance oriented toward the internal customers and incorporates these into the process model as well.

Improving Enterprise Concept through Creative Synthesis

A number of creative procedures have been developed to generate new ideas. These procedures can be utilized to develop ideas for the enterprise concept and ideas for the individual process concepts at the end of this chapter. We describe here two of the more popular and useful, brainstorming and checklists.

Brainstorming

Brainstorming is probably the best known and most widely used concept-generating technique. It is an unstructured process for generating—through spontaneous contributions by participants—all possible concepts for a new enterprise/process in a particular area. The technique can be used on an individual basis, but it is primarily a group process, providing organized concept generation. Because brainstorming is so well known, planning is often disregarded and groups just get together, often with disastrous results. For a good brainstorming session, a problem statement that is neither too broad (so as to diversify concepts too much) nor too narrow (so as to confine responses too much) should be carefully prepared. An enterprise process map with supporting material should be provided as the basis for brainstorming.

After the problem statement is prepared, group members are chosen to represent a wide variety of knowledge. Group members should have a general knowledge of the process area under discussion, but they need not be experts. Some companies exclude experts because they tend to crimp the creativity of others. A group leader should be selected that has the capability of both stimulating discussion and controlling behavior. Individuals with supervisor-subordinate relationships should not be in the same group.

Brainstorming is based on two principles and four rules. The two principles are:

- *Deferral of judgment.* Participants should be free to express any concept that comes to mind without having to worry about criticism from others in the group. The judicial mind weighs evidence, but it discourages the free flowing of concepts.

- *Quantity breeds quality.* According to associationist psychology, our thoughts are structured hierarchically; the most dominant are the habitual thoughts with which we are most comfortable. To have really new concepts we must break through these conventional concepts. We can do this by generating a large number of concepts.

These two principles lead to the following four rules for conducting a brainstorming session:

- *No criticism is allowed.* Negative judgments must be withheld until later. Even chuckles or raised eyebrows are banned.

- *Freewheeling is encouraged.* The wilder the concept, the better; it is easier to tame down than to think up.

- *Quantity is encouraged.* The greater the number of concepts, the more likely the best concept is in the group.

Figure 7-3
Osborn's General Checklist

• Put to other uses? New ways to use as is? Other uses if modified?
• Adapt? What else is like this? What other concepts does this suggest? Does past offer a parallel? What could I copy? Whom could I emulate?
• Modify? New twist? Change meaning, color, motion, odor, form, shape? Other changes?
• Magnify? What to add? More time? Greater frequency? Stronger? Larger? Thicker? Extra value? Plus ingredient? Duplicate? Multiply? Exaggerate?
• Minify? What to substitute? Smaller? Condensed? Miniature? Lower? Shorter? Lighter? Omit? Streamline? Split up? Understated?
• Substitute? Who else instead: What else instead? Other ingredient? Other material? Other process? Other power? Other place? Other approach? Other tone of voice?
• Rearrange? Interchange components? Other pattern? Other layout? Other sequence? Transpose cause and effect? Change pace? Change schedule?
• Reverse? Transpose positive and negative? How about opposites? Turn it backwards? Turn it upside down? Reverse roles? Change shoes? Turn tables? Turn other cheek?
• Combine? How about a blend, an alloy, an assortment, an ensemble? Combine units? Combine purposes? Combine appeals? Combine concepts?

• *Combinations and improvements are sought.* In addition to contributing concepts of their own, participants should suggest how concepts of others can be modified or improved to produce still another concept.

Using Checklists

The checklist method involves preparing a list of related questions that bring significant issues to the attention of the participants. Participants use the list to guide the direction but not necessarily the content of their concepts. The checklist primarily forces the user to concentrate in specific areas. Checklists may be specialized or generalized and may be of any length. Alex F. Osborn developed a general checklist using nine ways of changing an existing concept, as shown in Figure 7-3.[2]

If a more complete checklist is desired, Small's general checklist contains 112 questions in nine categories with examples for each.[3] These general checklists can be used to develop a more specific checklist that is exactly tailored to a company's requirements. *A company can develop their own unique check-off list that is especially tailored to developing their enterprise concept.*

Building Core Competencies

One of the most fruitful methods of improving an enterprise's concept is to concentrate on building up the core competencies of the enterprise. A core competency (discussed previously on page 58) is what an organization does particularly well. To qualify as a core competency, a corporate capability should provide the company with access to a wide variety of markets and customers, and it should be very difficult for competitors to imitate. It should also be capable of leverage across a variety of corporate units and product lines. Without the requisite core competencies, an otherwise perfectly aligned and arranged organization is incapable of achieving its enterprise concept.

Ideally, the organization-wide competencies needed to pursue a given enterprise concept should be identified during the development of the enterprise concept. However, as the transformation process proceeds, the need for new competencies often becomes apparent, as well as a need for changes in the dissemination of existing competencies. *Development and alignment of core competencies must be guided by direct intervention as part of the corporate transformation process.* As progress is made toward the enterprise concept, some hard-earned core competencies receive new investment and attention; others have to be painfully abandoned in order to release resources to support the enterprise concept. Some needed competencies are developed, and others are imported; all of them need to be leveraged throughout the enterprise.

By way of illustration, the core competencies of several leading corporations are listed here:

Black & Decker	Small electric motors
Canon	Optics, precision mechanics
GE	General management
Honda	Engines, power trains
Intel	Microprocessor technology
JVC	Videotape
Microsoft	Computer software expertise
Netscape	Web browser design
Sony	Miniaturization, videotape
Vickers	Fluid power, electric power, electronic controls

Their core competencies give these firms considerable competitive advantage because they tightly align with and provide broad support for the company's concept and strategic intent. Conversely, some core competencies may limit a company's ability to pursue a new visionary course to cope with or create a new competitive environment. Such was the case of Swiss watchmakers, who were so wedded to the mechanical technology of timekeeping that they missed the shift to digital electronics in the manufacture of watches during the late 1970s and early 1980s.

Benchmark Performance

Benchmarking compares both the performances of the organization's processes and the way those processes are conducted with those of relevant peer organizations to obtain concepts for improvement. The peer organizations may be within the same corporate family, or they may be comparable companies, industry leaders, or best-in-class performers. The task consists of identifying relevant peers, determining their process performance and the primary differences in their processes that account for the performance differences, and assessing the applicability of those process differences to our processes. The purpose of this task is to ask the important questions: Why do we do our process the way we do? Why do they do their process differently? Can we learn something from them?

The purpose of all this benchmarking activity is twofold: first, to provide additional insights into the idiosyncrasies of your own practices, and second, to get concepts on how to do them better. To accomplish this purpose it is not necessary to have precise numerical measures of relative performance. It is sufficient to know the relative performance in a general way. If company X appears to have a 15 percent better performance than our process, it does not matter if it is really 10 percent or 20 percent better.

SELECT PROCESSES FOR IMPROVEMENT

Identify Number of Processes for Transformation

Considerable controversy revolves around the number of processes appropriate to a given organization. The difficulty derives from the almost infinite divisibility of the processes. The "appropriate" number of processes in an entire organization has been pegged at from two to more than 50.

The level of process change desired is key to the number of processes identified. If the objective is incremental improvement, it is possible to work with many narrowly defined processes; both the rewards and risk of failure will be relatively low. But when the objective is radical process change, a process must be defined as broadly as possible. A key source of process benefit is improving hand-offs between functions, which can occur only when processes are broadly defined.

Most of the companies have identified 10 to 20 processes to be redesigned during the entire transformation effort. It is suggested that they focus on three or fewer processes during each round of transformation. The survey by Carr corroborated this advice by indicating that companies transforming one to three processes reported more satisfaction with their efforts than those redesigning more processes.[4] Fully 73 percent were transforming one to three processes. The largest percentage of companies (31 percent) were transforming two processes.

The appropriate number reflects a trade-off between managing process interdependence and ensuring that process scope is manageable. The fewer and broader the processes, the greater the possibility of innovation through transformation, and the greater the difficulties of understanding, measuring, and changing the process. Whatever the number of processes identified, their identification should be understood to be exploratory and iterative. As a process becomes the focus for a transformation or improvement effort, its boundaries and relative importance become much clearer. Most companies that have worked on their processes for a number of years have revised their original lists.

Screening Methods for Selecting Processes

In screening processes for redesign, we will primarily utilize qualitative methods to avoid the time and cost of collecting quantitative data. Screening methods should probably not be used to make the final selection since they do not adequately account for intangible factors and factors unique to the situation. However, they can be used to narrow down the field so that human decision making can be more effective.[5] There are several simple qualitative screening methods that can be employed. We describe two of the most popular of these: qualitative ranking, and weighted multifactor scoring matrix.

Qualitative Ranking of Process Ideas

The *qualitative ranking* method is the quickest, but probably the least accurate, method of screening. In this procedure, a small group of knowledgeable people are given a written list of numbered processes. The first phase of the procedure consists of making certain that each member of the group understands what each process on the list means. When everyone understands each process to their satisfaction, the ranking can commence. Each member of the group is asked to select the top ten processes for redesign from the list and to assign a score of ten to the top process and a score of one to the last process. The ballots are then collected and tabulated. The results of the tabulation are made available to all members followed by a discussion of the relative merits of the various processes. Another voting takes place, especially if there was no consensus on the first ballot. A number larger than ten could be used with a resultant small increase in accuracy, but the time required for voting and tabulating will be increased considerably.

One of the main deficiencies of the qualitative ranking is that each member of the group is using his or her own criteria or value system for determining which process is the most desirable for redesign. This deficiency

Figure 7-4
Weighted Multi-Criteria Matrix for Screening Processes

CRITERIA		Process A		Process B	
Output Criteria	Weight	Score	Weighted Score	Score	Weighted Score
Contributes to a competency	1.5	10	15.0	7	10.5
It is a core process	1.2	6	7.2	7	8.4
Supports a major product	.9	9	8.1	5	4.5
Large and profitable process	.6	6	3.6	8	4.8
Agrees with strategic plans	.5	9	5.4	7	3.5
Provides competitive advantage	.7	8	5.6	6	5.6
Supports other processes	.3	6	1.8	6	1.8
Required by law	.2	7	1.4	8	1.6
Input Criteria					
Cost to redesign	1.0	5	5.0	8	8.0
Time to redesign	.8	8	6.4	9	7.2
People and talent required	.6	8	4.8	8	4.8
Interference with other redesigns	.4	6	2.4	7	2.8
Total weighted scores	8.7		66.4		63.5
Normalized scores			7.63		7.30

can be corrected somewhat by providing, or having the group develop, a common list of criteria, similar to the one shown in Figure 7-4. The criteria list is used only as a reference to improve ranking. It is not used to score the processes. That is left to the next procedure, the weighted multi-criteria matrix.

The Weighted Multi-Criteria Matrix

In using the Weighted Multi-Criteria Matrix shown in Figure 7-4, the following sequence of steps is recommended:

Develop the Screening Criteria. The screening criteria must be carefully chosen, so that they are consistent with the company's vision, mission, and creed and will therefore select the processs of greatest benefit for the company. Normally the criteria and their weights are developed by a cross-functional group.

Determine the Weight of Each Screening Criterion. Normally it is best to *rank* the criteria first before assigning weights. A weight can then be assigned to the highest-ranking criteria and corresponding weights assigned to lesser criteria. Weights need not equal one, or some power of ten, since we can divide by the sum of the weights to obtain a "normalized score."

Determine the Scale for Each Criterion. A scale of "0 to 10" is usually appropriate for criteria that are subjectively measured. A more refined scale can be used for criteria that can be measured objectively.

Score Each Process against the Screening Criteria. This is where the real evaluation occurs. In most cases the scores are determined subjectively by the scorer. The scorer must be knowledgeable in the process area in order to be able to make an accurate evaluation. Normally, multiple scorers are utilized with their scores appropriately combined.

Calculate Weighted Scores by Multiplying Scores Times the Weight of the Criterion. This is nothing but arithmetic, which can best be done by a computer. More specifically, it can be done by a computer *spreadsheet.*

Calculate the Total Weighted Score for Each Process. More arithmetic can be done by the computer spreadsheet.

Compute Normalized Scores by Dividing Weighted Scores by the Sum of the Weights. The largest weighted score represents the process that best meets the criteria. Normalizing the scores converts the scores to values we are accustomed to viewing, but does not change the relative ranking of the processes.

Selecting the Method for Screening Processes

The method selected for screening process ideas depends primarily on the (1) number of processes to screen, (2) time and talent available for screening, and (3) desired confidence in the results. The ranking method provides the most rapid screening with the least talent, but the confidence level in the results is quite low. The multi-criteria matrix provides the most valid results, but it is considerably more time consuming than the ranking method. Many companies use a combination of methods, starting with the simple ranking method to reduce the number of processes down to 20 or less and then using the matrix method to prioritize the top 20 processes.

Evaluate the Potential Costs and Benefits of Each Alternative

The purpose of this task is to estimate the costs and benefits of the processes retained by the screening procedures outlined in the previous section, to provide the basis for deciding which processes to redesign. For the most part, this task uses standard cost-benefit analysis. Since most managers have performed these studies throughout their careers, we will assume that our readers are well acquainted with cost-benefit methods. The following discussion will be directed to considerations that we wish to highlight or that apply especially to transformation.

This task estimates the head count and expense dollars in each major activity of each process. It also estimates transaction volumes and frequencies. This information is used to compute estimated annual costs per activity and process and unit costs per transaction. A second purpose of this task is to estimate the performance of the pertinent processes. We are looking for processes where the performance per cost is currently low, but could be significantly improved with appropriate transformation.

A very important word in the preceding description is "estimate." Great precision is not needed at this time. The primary purpose of this task is to obtain a "first cut" of the productivity of each process in order to understand the relative resource intensity of each process. This understanding will be used in the following task to help determine the priorities for transforming various processes.

There are two different types of costs associated with each new process: the one-time cost of implementation and the continuing cost of operation afterward. The sum of the cost of implementation and the cost to redesign the process will be the investment that the company will make in the new process.

In transformation, it is often the intangibles that provide the most compelling reason to implement a new operational design. In the long run, improving product reliability and customer satisfaction will provide the highest benefit—certainly more than cutting a cost or eliminating positions from the payroll. For "bottom-line" managers this concept is foreign: accepting this category of benefit as valid represents a paradigm shift for these individuals.

Prioritize Processes

This task weights each process by its impact on the business goals and priorities and by the resources consumed. It considers these, as well as the time, cost, difficulty, and risk of transformation, in a multidimensional approach to setting priorities for transforming the processes.

Sometimes the members of the Executive Board and/or the Technical Group will know what processes the company has and which are most in need of transformation. In those cases, much of the work covered in this chapter can be eliminated. Other companies will start out pretty much in the dark as to what their processes are and which are most important to the business changes they seek. In that case, they will probably want to do a fairly full coverage of this chapter's work to ensure that they miss nothing important. Still other companies will find themselves in intermediate positions, with a partial understanding of the processes and a limited scope. In that case, they will want to do most of this task, but only for those processes for which they were not familiar.

This task is designed to enable the transformation team to develop recommended priorities for transformation, obtain executive concurrence, and move ahead. Development of priorities for transformation is a complex task, requiring multi-factor analysis and trade-off analysis. Ultimately, it requires sound business judgment. There is no algorithm guaranteed to produce the "right" answer, nor is one company's right answer the right answer for another company. The three major components of the analysis are:

1. *Strategic Impact*: the current and potential contribution of each process toward the company's business goals.
2. *Size*: the resources consumed or utilized by each process.
3. *Scope*: the time, cost, risk, and behavioral change implicit in transforming each process.

In order to assess the importance of transforming a process, the transformation team will have to identify the business opportunities that they foresee coming from the redesign of each process. It is helpful to divide the company's processes into the following five categories:

1. The most important strategic processes are *identity* processes. These processes define the organization to itself, to customers, and to investors. For example, on-time delivery is an identity process for Federal Express.
2. Next come *priority* processes. These directly and significantly affect everyday performance, producing the products that are of value to the customer.
3. Lower still on the strategic hierarchy are *background* processes. These are necessary for the business to survive in the long term.
4. Finally come *mandated* processes, carried out because of government or other regulations. Most accounting processes are mandated.
5. Last on the list come *superfluous* processes, which provide no value to anyone— they only incur cost for the producer. Such actions as counting products, moving products, and inspecting products do not provide value, but they do cost money.

All of a company's **core** business processes are either *identity* processes or *priority* processes. While it is desirable for a company to have an identity process, few do. In general, we want to redesign our core processes whenever possible since their redesign will have the greatest return. If we can, we want to *eliminate* rather than redesign *superfluous* processes. There's little to be gained in improving a process that provides no value.

Selecting Processes for Transformation

The approach used to select the processes for transformation will vary in each company. The differences will be related primarily to corporate culture: Each company will have different comfort levels with allowing staff to make decisions. Regardless of the selection approach, the selection will be related to benefit and cost. Select the processes with the greatest benefits for the least impact and smallest cost.

The selectors will change with respect to the scope of the effort. With large high-impact efforts, the senior officers on the Executive Board will have the final selection authority. For department-oriented change, process improvement, and often problem-resolution-oriented change, the Technical Management Group will probably make the final decision.

The selection review opens the alternative processes to comment and potentially to change. As line managers become more familiar with the design, they may notice opportunities for improvement that have been overlooked. These managers will provide a different perspective and offer a different background from which to evaluate the processes.

ALLOCATE PROCESS TO PROJECT TEAM FOR IMPLEMENTATION

Develop Individual Process Concept

In this task the Technical Management Group will develop a *process concept* for the process they have selected for redesign before allocating it to a Project Design Team for redesign. The process concept includes the *process objectives* and the *process attributes*. Process objectives include the overall process goal, specific type of improvement desired, numeric target for the innovation, and time frame in which the objectives are to be accomplished. Both general process functionality and change goals should be addressed by these objectives, creation of which begins with a "concept team" asking itself and key stakeholders, "What are we expected to achieve in this project?"

Process attributes, the descriptive, non-quantitative adjunct to process objectives, constitute a concept of process operation in a future state. They address both high-level process characteristics and specific enablers. Process attributes for an order-management process, for example, might specify that the process will employ automated credit checking, automated proposal generation, increased worker empowerment, and a financial structure resembling dealerships for customer-facing teams. Other attributes might specify that the process be performed by one person or team and that credit, shipping, and scheduling functions will be performed by the customer-facing individual. It is sometimes useful to categorize attributes as "technology," "people," "process outputs," and so forth.

Process objectives and process attributes are derived from multiple sources—among them, the enterprise concept, analyses of corporate strategy and concept, high-level overviews of the roles of technology and people (as both opportunities and constraints), customer interviews, benchmarking of the best processes in other companies, and a firm's performance objectives.

The Steering Board and the Technical Management Group should check the individual process concepts for consistency with the overall enterprise concept and to ensure they are understandable by the project team that will pursue them. This serves to synchronize executive thinking with team thinking. At a minimum, the process concept should describe:

- The new process's expected capabilities, as well as the expected performance improvements in time, quality, cost, and service.

- How the new process will support the strategy, respond to the customer, and respond to the competitive challenge.

Prepare a Project Plan

Prior to assigning a process to a project team for redesign, the Technical Management Group will prepare a Project Plan to guide the Project Team. The project plan must illustrate current status, expected needs, and projected results of the proposed process project. Every aspect of the development needs to be described—the organization, marketing, research and development, production, critical risks, finances, and milestones. A description of all of these facets of the proposed project is necessary to demonstrate a clear picture of what that project is, where it is projected to go, and how the company proposes it will get there. It is important that the project plan show a clear line of action in realistic terms, from the process concept to the commercial process.

Description of the Elements of a Project Plan

Executive Summary

The **executive summary** should be no longer than three pages and should be written only after the entire plan has been completed. In this way the salient features of each segment can be identified for inclusion in the summary. Since the summary is the first, and sometimes the only, part of a plan that is read, particularly by high-level management, it must present the essence of the entire plan.

Process Concept

The **process concept** indicates to the technical designer what the new process is expected to *do* (i.e., what *benefits* it should deliver to the customer). It should not specify how it should be built or what features it should have. The concept should be a *needs* document, not a *solutions* document. The process concept includes process objectives and process attributes.

Process objectives provide the overall process purpose, specific type of improvement desired, numeric target for process performance, and time frame in which the redesign is to be accomplished.

Process attributes provide a descriptive, non-quantitative amplification of the process objectives by providing a qualitative description of future process operations, particularly with respect to interfacing processes.

Project Definition

The **project definition** should outline the tentative schedule and budget for the project.

Organization and Management Plan

This section should outline the **organization and management plan** for the project development process. Most companies utilize the project team organization and management approach described in Chapter 5. At this time we should indicate what the organization will be when the process becomes fully operational and outline the timing and plan for shifting from redesign organization to an operational organization.

Risk Management Plan

In planning for project redesign we must make a number of forecasts or assumptions on which we base our planning. Although these assumptions are made by highly competent personnel using the latest and most accurate techniques, they are still predictions and are prone to error. These risky assumptions must be identified now so they can be monitored throughout the development, in order that timely corrective action can be taken if our initial assumptions prove to be incorrect.

Enterprise Concept and Enterprise Process Map

These two documents are primarily forwarded for information. The Technical Project Team will use them for reference throughout their redesign.

NOTES

1. David K. Carr, *Best Practices in Reengineering: What Works and What Doesn't in the Engineering Process* (McGraw-Hill, 1995), p. 106.

2. Alex F. Osborn, *Applied Imagination* (Charles Scribner's Sons, 1957), p. 318.

3. Marvin Small, *How to Make More Money* (Pocket Books, 1959).

4. Carr, *Best Practices in Reengineering*, p. 125.

5. Howard W. Oden, *Managing Corporate Culture, Innovation, and Intrapreneurship* (Quorum, 1997), p. 143.

CHAPTER 8

Detailed Technical Redesign of Work Processes

INTRODUCTION

In Chapter 7 the focus of attention was on the entire enterprise, with the Technical Management Group (TMG) responsible for selecting the processes that would be redesigned. In this chapter our focus is on the single process, with the Technical Project Team responsible for redesigning the process so that it will perform in the optimum manner.

The purpose of the technical redesign is to transform the technical aspects of the new process to achieve optimum performance. The technical design stage produces detailed process and information flows, detailed process architectures and human resource plans, job descriptions, and prototypes of the process and its key enablers. It (together with the social redesign in Chapter 12) produces designs for the interaction of behavioral and technical elements.

For best results, the detailed technical redesign in this chapter should be closely coordinated with the detailed social redesign in Chapter 12. The key questions that will be answered by this chapter include:

- What technical and social resources and technologies will we need in the redesigned process?
- What technical and social information will the redesigned process use?
- How will the technical and behavioral elements interact? (e.g., the human interface of the system)

With a project plan and a process concept available from Chapter 7, the technical redesign activity involves having a Technical Project Team follow the Project Action Plan (Chapter 5) and analyze the information available to synthesize a new process. There are techniques for facilitating the analysis and synthesis process, but the success or failure of the effort will turn on the particular people gathered together in the project team.

Technical and social redesign lies at the very heart of major change. In many ways, it is the most exciting, dramatic stage of business transformation. It provides the opportunity to free the business from the constraints and outdated practices of the past and consider new ways of working. In so doing, it catches the imagination of staff and managers alike, because it provides the opportunity to actually change the way business is done and thus to steal a lead on the competition. Through an innovative means of creating a product or delivering a service, new business can be won, more customers attracted, and better performance attained.

JUMP START THE PROJECT REDESIGN TEAM

The TMG should ensure that each technical project team gets off to a running start. The TMG should follow the detailed guidelines in Chapter 5 in selecting and assembling the core and virtual project teams. The project team should have the IT, HR, User, and General members needed to redesign the specific process. The technical redesign project officially starts when the TMG presents the team and team leader with the project plan. The most important part of the project plan is the process concept. The process concept tells the project team what the new process is expected to *do*, that is, what *benefits* it should deliver to the customer. It should specify what need the process is expected to satisfy, but it will provide little information on how the need is to be satisfied. That is the mission of the project team.

Team Must Understand Process Plan—Especially the Process Concept

The TMG should ensure that each member of the project team (including the virtual team as well as the core team) thoroughly understands the project plan and especially the process concept. If technical project members do not have a clear sense of the direction and the boundaries of their assignment, they will flounder, lose their energy, and fail to meet expectations. A key part of the TMG role is to ensure that each design team member understands the answers to the following questions:

- What is the driving issue and why are we redesigning this process? (Why are we here?)
- What are the specific project/process goals? (What constitutes success?)

- What is our role and that of others involved in the effort? (Why has each of us been selected? Who are the IT, HR, User, and General members?)
- What is the relationship between members of the core team and the virtual team?
- What are the deliverables? (New work flows? Benchmarking information? Action plans? Cost-benefit analysis?)
- What are the boundaries of the process we are to improve? (Where does it begin and end?)
- What, if any, are the constraints? (What is "off-limits"?)
- What is the deadline? What is the schedule? How much time are we expected to spend on this effort?
- What happens to our "regular jobs" while we're involved in this project?
- How will we be rewarded for our contribution? (What's in it for us?)[1]

Team Training and Preparations

When a project team of employees prepares to begin their first transformation project, they typically lack the skills necessary for success. They must develop the problem-solving tools and the interpersonal communication skills needed in order to be effective team members and decision makers. Additionally, the training should provide additional knowledge and skills to enable the project team to undertake its assigned task. If team members do not have these skills, failure is virtually assured. In a transformation organization, nothing is more important, more essential, or more critical to success than team training.

DOCUMENT AND ANALYZE EXISTING PROCESS

The project team needs to define and map out all the activities involved in their assigned process. They should use the enterprise process map developed by the TMG as the starting point but their chart will have to be much more detailed. For example, if the company is using IDEF,[2] the TMG would only use the first four steps of the IDEF0 procedure in Chapter 6, while all six steps should be utilized by the project team.

For use by the project team, an expanded version of the procedure for preparing an IDEF0 process map is provided below that supplements the basic procedure given in Chapter 5.

1. *Determine the Context, Viewpoint, and Purpose for the Map.* This should be provided by the TMG in the process concept section of the project plan. The context, viewpoint, and purpose of the process may change as time progresses and the project team should be alert to such changes, but they normally do not change before the project starts.

2. *Create the A0 or Context Diagram.* This should be available in the enterprise process map provided by the TMG in the project plan. However, the team should not take the TMG's diagram as gospel, but should endeavor to ensure that the top diagram for their process is correct.

3. *Create the Topmost Decomposition Diagram.* This may or may not be in the enterprise process map forwarded in the project plan, depending on the detail of the map. Even if it is there, its accuracy would be highly suspect and should be thoroughly reanalyzed by the project team.

4. *Complete the Decomposition Task.* The team will continue breaking down the parent functions into child functions until no further breakdown is feasible. Take care that in each decomposition the child boxes cover the entire function in the parent box. To obtain the clearest possible diagram, modify or re-draw the diagram several times until satisfied. Split (break up a box into two or more parts) and cluster (combine two or more parts into a single box) until you have a reasonable number of activities that are about the same size. While any layout is acceptable, it is recommended the boxes be laid out on the diagonal from upper left to lower right if possible.

5. *Compile a List of Model Elements.* The *elements* are all those parts of the IDEF0 diagram except activities (i.e. inputs, outputs, controls, and mechanisms). The intent of this step is simply to develop a pool of elements through research and interviews that can be used in the next step. There will be a pool for each type of element (inputs, outputs, controls, and mechanisms) and one for unknowns. Elements whose type is yet to be defined will be placed in the unknown pool. You can quickly move unknowns into other pools as needed. By creating pools you can gather all the elements you need before you start drawing your diagrams. One element can be attached to more than one activity. For example, the sales forecast can be both an input to marketing research and an output from sales. Pools facilitate group brainstorming sessions, in which several team members identify elements of the activity being modeled.

6. *Using the Arrow Notation, Place These Model Elements at Appropriate Places on the Diagram.* This is the most detailed and time-consuming part of process mapping. But, if we are really going to describe the functions of an organization, these model elements must be properly identified and associated with the correct activity. There are a number of computerized applications that make this somewhat less onerous. Recall that input data are transformed by the activity to produce the output. If an arrow contains both input and control data, show it as a control. If it is uncertain whether an arrow is a control or an input, make it a control. If it is unclear whether or not a particular data arrow is needed at all, leave it out unless it is the only control.

7. *Develop Supporting Material.* Each diagram in the map should normally be accompanied by a page of text. The text page should tell a brief concise story for each diagram. It should not duplicate the diagram, but rather should tell those things that are not obvious from looking at the diagram. The map should be accompanied by a glossary that explains the definitions the author gives to activities and elements.

Figure 8-1
Maintain Reparable Spares

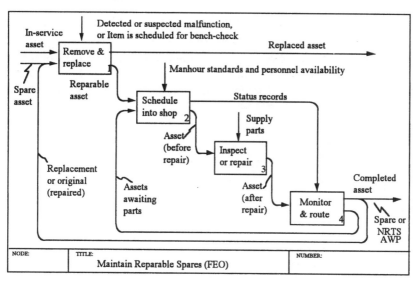

Maintain Reparable Spares (FEO)

A complete IDEF0 first-level decomposition diagram is shown in Figure 8-1.

DETERMINE NEEDS, OUTPUTS, AND APPLICATIONS

Determine Future Customer Requirements

In the broad redesign of Chapter 7, we dealt with all of a company's major processes, and it was necessary to understand all of the customer's needs and wants. In the individual process redesign in this chapter, we deal only with one or a few processes, so the team needs only to understand the customer's needs of the selected process.

Regardless of the process involved, the needs of the customer determine the outputs and applications of the process. In turn, the outputs of the process determine the structure (data model) and processing required. Also, the structure and processing determine the data base, data base management system, and application software. Thus, if we are going to redesign the process we must start by determining the needs of the customers.

You cannot define future customer requirements unless you know who your future customers are. Thus, the first step in our diagnosis of future customer requirements is to identify the future customers. Existing customers are easy to identify, but identifying future customers is somewhat more difficult. The most fruitful approach is to start with a list of current customers and brainstorm how they will change in the next ten years.

Identify Your Customers' Future Requirement Areas

Now that you have identified your future customers, try to put yourself in their shoes and visualize what they might require. Are they primarily interested in saving money? Time? Or perhaps they'd like you to offer a wider variety of goods and services? Customer requirements typically fall into one of the areas listed here:

- Timeliness
- Cost
- Accuracy
- Quantity
- Price
- Availability

Interview Your Customers

The final step in defining key requirements for core future customers is to interview your customers. Whenever possible, interview your customer in a face-to-face meeting. Write down all feedback so that you and/or your team can review it later. When defining customer requirements, be sure to understand both needs and expectations. You should jot down interview questions that will enable you to verify or correct your predictions. Devise questions that will help you gauge whether customer requirements are being met and the importance of a particular requirement.

Not just any customer will do for this survey. Instead we should focus on those customers who are on the leading edge, responding to a vision and engaging in innovation and radical change. When you are looking for new requirements, their opinions are most important.[3]

CREATIVE PROCESS REDESIGN

Fundamentals of Creative Process Redesign

The essence of redesign is about coming up with a new, more effective way of working: a way of working that focuses on the customer, takes advantage of new trends and technology, and removes the bottlenecks and constraints of existing methods. There really is no miracle cure. Redesign is merely about taking a clean sheet of paper and thinking things through so that the inner workings of the business can be reconsidered and more effective alternatives designed. It's as simple as that.

This is undertaken by throwing into the creative melting pot all of the variables—a knowledge about what the business is and how it interacts with customers and suppliers, an understanding of inputs and outputs, products and services, and a grasp of the capability of IT and HR trends taking place around us. From these variables, a search for a more effective way of transforming the inputs into outputs can begin. Process design has to consider how rules about doing business can be broken in pursuit of new ways of working. The phase is quite literally one of creativity and needs to be stimulated where necessary with more formal techniques such as lateral thinking and brainstorming.

Breaking the Rules

A key part of creative design is to consider whether the very funda- mentals of how the business and the key processes within it operate can be changed. How could the business be turned on its head to steal a lead on the competition? How could it be operated differently if the biggest constraint were removed? It is the willingness to pose such groundbreak- ing questions that paves the way for entirely new ways of doing business. This is the first stage of creative redesign. It needs to be far reaching, and it needs to be radical. The following questions help to point the way:

• What is the single biggest constraint, and how could it be removed?
• How could technology be used to change the rules?
• What tasks could you get your customers to do?
• What tasks could you get your suppliers to do?
• What alternatives are there to the main delivery channel?

From Ideas to Designs

The next stage is concerned with designing the business processes that will be at the heart of the transformed organization. These process designs pave the way for a new business infrastructure. Their shape and content will depend on the exact set of design principles and measures for the organization in question, but the key to a good process is one that is simple and straightforward, without delays or bottlenecks.

The essence of such design is about considering many alternatives and coming up with the most appropriate. Often there seems to be a belief, no doubt encouraged by the extravagant claims of the experts and "gu- rus," that there is some magical revelation about process design. Puzzled brows remain and, when faced with such a task, many people seem to be in search of some sort of Holy Grail of redesign. "But what do you actually do?" they ask.

The short answer is—*think*.[4] Toss ideas around, look at alternatives, be creative—but *think*. What is the most appropriate way to achieve the conversion of inputs to outputs, bearing in mind the technology at your disposal and the objectives reflected by design principles?

During the design activity, certain questions help to provoke the thought process:

- Which steps add the most/least value as far as the customer is concerned?
- Which steps have the highest costs associated with them?
- Where do the most errors occur, and how can they be eliminated?
- Where do the most delays occur?
- How can we build in and ensure quality rather than check for it at the end?
- What can be done elsewhere upstream and downstream to prevent errors?
- What is the simplest way?
- Is there something that could be fast-tracked or eliminated?
- Can IT or HR be harnessed in a different way?
- Can one or more activities be combined in parallel to speed up the process?

These questions may help to provoke the thoughts, but the design activity itself is really one of creativity, exploring various options until a suitable one is found. In many ways redesign is an art; certainly, it is a creative exercise, because it is about coming up with new, innovative ideas about how the business could be run. The new idea could achieve higher speeds, reduce costs, produce higher-quality products, or develop more satisfied customers. The key ingredients are brainpower and a willingness to try new ideas.

As the creative activity progresses, the ideas and outlines raised have to be gradually distilled and refined into the new business process designs. This is represented as a high-level architecture of the new processes showing how the work will be carried out and how the key transformations will occur in the business. The emphasis is on an outline at this stage, with the production of a detailed design coming later, but key assumptions and major new uses of technology have to be documented.

Iteration of Designs

The design itself should take place in any form that encourages a rapid and far-ranging exchange of ideas. Formal tools are less important than methods that allow rapid generation and rearrangement of options—scrawl on pieces of paper, move Post-it notes around on an office wall, role play the dream "customer contact" when every last little need from first desire to order delivery is completed during one transaction. The objective at this stage is to freewheel through ideas and capture the aspects of design that will allow the organization to develop a more effective process.

While the overall design itself is often best undertaken off-site, away from the demands and distractions of business, design must involve dialogue with both customers and representatives of the business. Throughout the design stage new designs and "straw men" have to be continually reviewed with representatives from the business, both at a management and a front-line or end user level. Both of these aspects of design reflect the need for iteration, with several different versions of design usually being produced on the route to the solution ultimately agreed upon.

Guidelines for Creative Design

Process design is more art and creative thinking than it is science.[5] It requires a combination of "out of the box" thinking with a willingness to knuckle down and squeeze the value out of outrageous ideas so that the real gem can be found. Technology helps in capturing decisions and requirements, but ultimately it is the thought processes that count. There are, however, as always, some guidelines that help the creative process along:

- *Nurture creativity.* Coming up with new ideas that challenge the way things are done is alien to staff in many organizations. An attitude of innovation and a desire to take a new view of the world has to be fostered, and formal training in techniques such as brainstorming and lateral thinking may be appropriate. External consultants or facilitators are often a worthwhile investment in this respect. But once people get over their initial cynicism for creativity, they love it.

- *Cross-fertilize.* Look around and steal other people's ideas. What have your competitors done? What has been successfully carried out in other industries? How are other organizations rebuilding their processes to exploit IT? As long as these sources are used to stimulate creative thinking, rather than as copycat material, they can be useful starting points to start the creative process.

- *Encourage freewheeling.* Generate lots of ideas. Often it is not the idea itself that is valuable, but the second or third idea it sparks off may prove useful. Ninety-nine out of a hundred ideas may be useless, the hundredth little less so—but it will spawn an idea that can be developed.

- *Work at it.* Be prepared to search long and hard before something valuable is unearthed. Generating a winning process design is like panning for gold, and you have to filter through a mass of debris before the nugget comes to light. It might take two weeks before anything of value surfaces, but then one five-minute brainstorm may provide the route forward.

- *Create the environment.* Those involved in design have to feel comfortable to contribute anything, however ridiculous or "wacko" it might seem at first sight.

Allowing this to happen needs the right environment, where outrageous thinking is positively encouraged and built upon rather than mocked.

In practice, it tends to be the early days of process design that are the most difficult to initiate. By their very nature, our organizations stifle creativity, innovation, and imagination. Staff and management alike are used to restriction and confinement, regulation and control. Once they are suitably equipped, encouraged, and enabled, the ideas tend to flow thick and fast.

The creative techniques of **brainstorming** and **checklists**, discussed in Chapter 7, are as applicable and useful here.

DEVELOP PROCESS ARCHITECTURE

Process architecture creates an overall process design in response to the process concept specified in the project plan. Sometimes called concept design, it defines functional and performance requirements, initial layout and packaging, boundaries and descriptions of major sub-processes, and priorities for optimization. Process architecture provide a structure for work on the sub-processes, just as a plot gives structure to a novel.

Process architecture is the top-level design of a process—the arrangement of the functional elements of a product into physical blocks. A process's architecture begins to emerge during the enterprise redesign of Chapter 7. This happens informally—in the sketches, function diagrams, and process maps of the enterprise. However, the final architectural decisions should be made only after the process concept has been selected (at the end of Chapter 7) and before the detailed design of the process begins in the latter part of this chapter. The purpose of the process architecture is to define the basic physical building blocks of the process in terms of what they do and what their interfaces are to the rest of the process. Architectural decisions allow the detailed design and test of these building blocks to be assigned to teams, individuals, and/or suppliers, during detailed process design, such that the development of different portions of the product can be carried out simultaneously.

Is Process Architecture Compatible with Organization Concept?

The process architecture determines how the organization can utilize the technology—what functions will be centralized or decentralized, and what the connections are between parts of the organization and the organization and its customers and suppliers. The interactive system must be carefully thought out. Serious problems occur when the process architecture and organizational structure are designed separately, as they often are. To ensure that this does not occur, each project team will provide a copy of its process architecture to the Social Management Group, who will check it against the organization concept before the project team proceeds with their detailed design.

The primary reason for conducting the technical design in two phases (process architecture and detailed design) was to permit this integration between the technical designers and the social designers. Providing such a check at the end of detailed design would not be appropriate. First, design changes at the detailed design level can be very expensive. Second, as the design at the end of detailed design is very detailed and technical, the Social Management Group would have a difficult time finding the big picture amongst all the technical details.

The systems architecture provides the highways of the organization and applications are the traffic. The highways and the traffic must be planned to accommodate each other. Because the process architecture will have profound implications for subsequent process development activities as well as for the manufacturing and marketing, it should be developed by a cross-functional team effort. The end result of this activity is an approximate geometric layout of the product, descriptions of the major modules, and documentation of the key interactions among the modules.

Structured, Top-Down Design

The rationale for performing design in a top-down fashion is quite straightforward. That is, by starting with a global overview of the new system, the analyst, in effect, constructs a comprehensive picture of what the new system must achieve. History has taught us that, when design begins at a very low level of detail (the bottom-up approach), frequently pieces are missing or the details do not fit neatly back into a wholistic system. By starting at the top, one creates a structure that ensures that sound interrelationships between systems components are built into the design at the outset.

Finally, note that structured design techniques help the project manager allocate technical resources and evaluate project status. By dissecting a complex system into its natural taxonomy of functions, the project manager can assign design responsibility to specific technical staff members for various logically contained design components. This approach minimizes wasteful job overlap. As design components are completed, the responsible person submits evidence of competition to the project manager in the form of a deliverable such as a completed chart, diagram, or narrative.

Process Breakdown

The first activity in product redesign is to break down the processes into their key sub-processes and confirm the mechanisms used to carry out each of these sub-processes. This forms the basis for controlling and coordinating the redesign of specific individual processes, covered in the detailed design section that follows.

So far, the design of the new business or enterprise has concentrated on the design of new processes. In so doing, the focus has been on producing a design that describes how the new process works—and, in particular, how the various people and technological capabilities within it are combined to produce the desired ways of working. The design has to be rich and comprehensive enough to describe the various components within it, so that they can be identified for construction.

The process design has been used to embrace any or all of the mechanisms that may be required to carry that process out. This is a key part of the process approach, but for the purposes of development, the requirements for these capabilities now need to be split up into their component areas. For example, all of the sub-processes that require IT support have to be identified so that the required support can be specified in more depth and developed. Similarly, all of the sub-processes within the process that require procedural support or the definition of other manual mechanisms can be identified.

Smoothing Process Flow

One approach to improving the efficiency of a process is to take action to *smooth the flow* of the process.[6] Smoothing the flow of a process can be achieved by engaging in four activities that use as their basis the process map. We will define each of these activities and indicate what is involved:

1. Eliminate buffers.
2. Search for and correct discontinuities.
3. Analyze flows for redundancies.
4. Maximize process throughput rate.
5. Identify bottlenecks and balance flow.
6. Construct an ideal flow.

Eliminate Buffers

Workers sometimes rely on backlogs or buffers (an in-process inventory or work-in-progress) as a kind of security blanket. Whether intentional or not, product or paperwork buffers cause logistical nightmares, create unnecessary work and communication problems, and stymie learning. With buffers there is the need for tracking systems to identify what is in each buffer. Time is spent detecting and correcting errors in the tracking system. Effort is then allocated to finding lost orders, expediting work, and communicating status to customers. Not only are buffers unnecessary, but they also create unneeded work and distractions. Buffers should be eliminated.

Search for and Correct Discontinuities

The process should be traceable from its input to its output. The trail should show that an input is received by someone and that someone does something with it. That demonstrates a direct linkage between an input and the subsequent action. Many times we find that there is a discontinuity and we cannot trace an action as a result of the input.

For each discontinuity, we want to find the root cause and correct it. We will find that the flowchart is not as thorough as we would hope. For all the un-traced activities we now have to determine if these are oversights by the makers of the flowchart or if they are really omissions from our system for conducting business. If it is the former, then we amend the flowchart. If it is the latter, then we have to be concerned with them.

With a corrected flowchart, one that truly represents how information flows or does not flow, we start to analyze why the discontinuities exist. These un-traced activities represent the ad hoc method of doing business to which most companies fall prey. For each un-traced activity, we ask the following questions: Where is the action train disrupted? Why? How can we correct the situation?

Analyze Flows for Redundancies

At this point we have eliminated discontinuities, and at least we can trace the process from start to finish. If we stopped here we would have a manufacturing system that is controllable for each and every activity; it is far from optimum. Now we have to critically evaluate each work sequence to see if it is really necessary.

Because of the inherent fallibility of manual systems, it was common to introduce redundancy into manual processes in order to maintain control. Double-entry bookkeeping, which was invented in the Middle Ages, is a good example. Many of these same control devices were carried over into automated systems. At first, when automated systems were fairly unreliable, these controls made good sense. Today, however, there is less need for them.

Each time that we introduce redundancy, we not only create the additional work to do the same thing twice, we create the additional work to make sure that the two are still the same. These kinds of controls are needed far less often today, yet they keep appearing in our business processes.

What is an unnecessary work sequence? This is a difficult question to answer directly. It will depend on the specific situation. But, in general, a work sequence can be considered unnecessary if it does not have a value-added outcome. Also, a work sequence may be considered unnecessary if, when we ask the question, "What will happen if I eliminate this work sequence?" The answer is, "Nothing will happen if this work sequence is not done." So all work sequences, even though they are traceable should be evaluated for:

- Do they add value to the process?
- What would happen if the work sequence were not included?

Maximize Process Throughput Rate

Rapid processing can have a liberating effect on employees. Increasing the speed of the process will not only increase its efficiency but will also improve quality. Defects are detected and corrected sooner when the process throughput rate is high. At AT&T the rapid throughput on the Orion Project gave the work team a feeling of accomplishment in finishing something quickly while improving product quality.

One of the biggest benefits comes from instantaneous feedback. An error detected in Task 2 can be communicated to Task 1 before additional defective units are processed. One worker told us, "I never knew it mattered to anyone how I did my job. Even if it did, they wouldn't know where to find me. Now I'm right next to the person who uses my output and I know within seconds if something is wrong."

Identify Bottlenecks and Balance the Flow through Them

Understanding bottlenecks and balancing the flow of work through them is one of the major contributions made by Ellyahu Goldratt. It makes no sense to pass more things (material, paperwork) through any operation than any subsequent operation can handle. In most business processes, bottlenecks are seldom fixed. They are constantly changing because of the mix of products/services, lot sizes, and the set-up times for each product or service. From a redesign perspective, the key to balancing work flows to the bottleneck is designing processes that make the bottleneck visible and then building in process flexibility in terms of communication and workers' capabilities.

Construct the Ideal Flow

With all the information and documentation gained from the previous activities, the team can now construct a streamlined flow that we call the "*ideal flow*." It will only have sequences that will be as direct as possible, and all forms of redundancy will be eliminated. Most important, there will be no ad hoc actions because all reasonably expected contingencies have been planned for. As a further protection against ad hoc actions, a procedure will be put in place to ensure that unplanned-for contingencies are routed to the appropriate managerial problem solvers and decision makers in a formal manner (examples: material review boards, structured problem analysis routines).

CONDUCT DETAILED ANALYSIS AND REDESIGN

Many organizations make the mistake of believing that the high-level design or process architecture is adequate to drive the change program along. They set off down the path of implementation in the mistaken belief that this is all that is required. Not surprisingly, the program stumbles and invariably falls back into the abyss between fond hopes and horrible results. Ultimately, the initiative flounders and becomes consigned to the list of "what might have been" projects.

To move forward from a high-level design to a detailed design that can support the creation and roll-out of a whole new business infrastructure, the design must be developed and "fleshed out" until it is substantial enough to act as a genuine design for change. The key actions within this stage are to continue the design of the process outlined in the process architecture down to a lower level of detail—down to the sub-processes.

Producing this detailed design is essentially concerned with further design activity and adding levels of detail. This involves the project team working through each sub-process identified in the process architecture. In short, it is about the project design team determining and documenting how it is going to work and who or what is going to do it. This involves making trade-offs between alternatives and describing and documenting the outcomes so that a detailed design can be produced.

Evaluate and Redesign Sub-processes in the Process

In the previous section, we looked at process redesign from the perspective of the process architecture. Here we make a more detailed investigation from the viewpoint of detailed design of the sub-processes within the overall process. Sub-processes can be formed in several ways. A *permanent sub-process* is a sequence of fraction of the process activities that are performed each time the process is performed. For example, the purchasing process always contains a sub-process of preparing and signing the purchase request. *Temporary sub-processes* are sequences of activities that are employed under differing circumstances, primarily because processes are not performed the same way under all situations. For example, in the fulfill-orders process, there are four potential sub-processes:

1. A *new customer* sub-process, which is performed when an order is received from a new customer.

2. A *change order* sub-process, which is performed when the order received is not new but rather modifies a previously received order.

3. A *credit risk* sub-process, which is performed when the customer's credit is insufficient to ship the order as requested.

4. A *consolidate orders* sub-process, which is performed when more than one order to the same customer ship-to address is in hand.

In dealing with sub-processes, we should begin by asking a very important question, "Is this sub-process really necessary?" Time and money can be spent improving a sub-process that we don't really even need. Some sub-processes may have come into being based on a requirement that no longer even exists. Completely eliminating sub-processes is the greatest time and money saver of all! Temporary sub-processes are more amenable to elimination than are permanent sub-processes.

If you have decided that the process is necessary, then review the non–value-added sub-processes currently included in the process. It would be nice if all you had to do was just stop doing the non–value-added steps. Unfortunately, if you eliminate the non–value-added steps without understanding why they are there, you could soon find yourself with a process that does not work at all. Take the time to understand the reason for the non–value-added steps. Understanding will make it easier for you to eliminate the non–value-added steps and design a process that produces a valued output.

There are a few main reasons why non–value-added sub-processes normally creep into existing processes. After all, when the process is first thought up, no one sits around and says, "Let's create a sub-process that wastes a lot of time and money." When you focus on your non–value-added sub-processes, you are probably looking at a sub-process that was put in place to minimize the impact of one or more of the following issues:

1. Backlogs of Work

2. Errors and Quality Issues

3. Hand-offs between People or Organizations

4. Physical Movement of People or Work

5. Changeover Times of Equipment or People

6. Changing Sub-processes to Processes[7]

If you can figure out how to eliminate or minimize these issues then you have a very good chance at eliminating the non–value-added steps that have crept into your process. Let's take a look at each one of these issues in more detail.

Backlogs of Work

Those backlogs of work stacking up everywhere mean long cycle times and poor work flow. Whenever you have a backlog, you normally have non–value-added sub-processes in your process flow that might include:

• Wait time or items in backlog
• Counting of items in backlog
• Report status of items in backlog
• Storing of items in backlog

To find out how deep of a hole you are in, you can create a measurement indicator of Days of Backlog. You can identify this measure for the entire process or just one step in the process. Your goal is to eliminate the backlog. If you eliminate the backlog, then you eliminate the non–value-added steps associated with the backlog.

Errors and Quality Issues

Error checking, scrap, rework, inspection, and control points all indicate a process that has quality problems. These problems waste time and lead to non–value-added activities. Non–value-added activities can be eliminated if we eliminate the source problem. You will want to focus on two measures to better understand your quality problems:

• The number of errors within a sub-process
• The number of items reworked to correct problems

Within each category there may be many causes. You need to collect information at the most basic level so you can discover the underlying problems that cause these errors. Fortunately, there are usually only one or two problems that create the majority of the errors. The trick is to identify the underlying problem.

Hand-offs between People or Organizations

Hand-offs occur when work passes from one person to another or from one organization to another. It could be from the stock clerk to the shipping clerk or from the purchasing organization to the accounts payable organization. Hand-offs add a great deal of complexity and usually a large number of non–value-added steps to your process. Go to your process flow and identify every time there is a hand-off.

It is important to pay attention to hand-offs because there is usually at least one wait with every hand-off in your process. These wait periods cause the work to move in batches that interrupt your continuous, balanced, synchronized flow. Also, depending upon the trust level between organizations (or individuals) there may be counts, sign-offs and status reports required before a hand-off can even occur.

After you have identified all the hand-offs in your process, you can create another indicator of the health of your process. Since processes vary in complexity and length, the total number of hand-offs is not necessarily significant. We want to look at the number of hand-offs per value-added sub-process. Strive for a ratio of less than one. You want to minimize the amount of hand-offs in your process. If your hand-off ratio is greater than one, take a look at where you can begin to eliminate hand-offs by:

• Cross training individuals to do more than one step in the process

• Combining organizations

• Transferring the total process into one organization

Physical Movement of People or Work

Every time there is a hand-off, work moves, or people move, or both move. Work or people may also move without a hand-off. If you do a task and then carry the work to another location to perform another task, the work has moved.

For example, you have a job as a cook in a restaurant. The food is stored in the freezer at one end of the kitchen, prepared at a station in the center of the room, and cooked at the opposite end. Many moves are involved in retrieving, preparing, and cooking the food. Movement is a non–value-added activity. Like hand-offs, movements usually result in at least one wait. That wait is another non–value-added activity. Other hidden non–value-added items could include:

• Equipment to move the work (forklifts, trucks, or carts)

• Space to be able to move the work through

• Wasted time in movement (different from wait time)

• A person being away from their desk or workstation

Usually it is easier to see the amount of movement tied to your process if you plot it on a process map. You will be amazed at the miles that your work or you travel. You probably have figured out by now that you can create yet another indicator of the health of your process. You can measure the number of movements in a process compared to the number of value-added tasks. If your process is movement heavy, then look for places to reduce the number of moves.

Changeover Times of Equipment or People

Usually when people think of changeovers they think of machine set-up time. While that is an example of one kind of changeover, there are many others that may be less obvious. Stopping in the middle of a copying job to add paper to the machine and holding your telephone order to get the terminal up and running to take your order are both examples of changeovers within a process.

Not all changeovers result in substantial time loss, but they all interrupt the flow of work. All of them are non–value-added activities! The longer the changeover time, the greater the impact to the work flow. When long changeovers are part of a process, you will find a degree of inflexibility in operations and larger backlogs of work in process. This is due to a desire for larger batch sizes so that there will be longer times between change-overs. To reduce changeover time consider some of the following:

• Have tools and supplies ready before beginning the job.

• Eliminate as many control points, inspection checks, and approvals as possible.

• Make sure the person doing the changeover has detailed instructions that describe easy-to-follow, sequential steps.

Changing Sub-processes to Processes

In a complex process if special cases (temporary sub-processes) are repeated often enough, it may be advantageous to establish a separate process for each special case. In other words, we *replace a single complex process with one or more simpler processes*. Sometimes we will determine that a single process should be split into two, by segmenting the process inputs and creating parallel flows.

Relocate and Retime Controls

This task seeks to reduce the number of non–value-added activities in the process by simplifying the control structure of the process. It accomplishes this by integrating controls into value-adding activities, by replacing error detection with error avoidance, and by moving error detection closer to the point of occurrence of the error. This task also reviews the logical relationships among activities in order to find opportunities to perform in parallel activities currently performed serially. Obviously this would increase the speed of the process.

When we use manual systems, we have largely serial processes, because all of the information necessary to process a transaction must move through the process with the transaction. Different people cannot work on the transaction at the same time because the "file" can be in only one place at one time. Organizations using such systems often have large, centralized filing departments that store and retrieve the files as needed. You can imagine the problems that arise when a transaction arrives that requires a file that was checked out to process an earlier transaction that is not yet completed!

Modularize and Decentralize

The purpose of this task is to define parts of the redesigned process in such a manner that they are used in more than one process. This partition of the process, if one exists, enables the process to be distributed in space (e.g., by decentralizing it). This concept is particularly applicable to the Information Technology aspects of the design. Object centered programming is essentially based on this principle.

The formal analysis of this task consists of determining the dependencies among the activities of the revised process and determining the interactions between activities. This analysis allows the clustering of activities by related changes and by time/space adjacency, so that modules can be defined.

The modules defined can be used to evaluate alternatives (e.g., centralized versus decentralized) and implementation alternatives. Analysis of these alternatives then leads to the selected deployment of each module in space, time, and organization.

Utilize Performance Enablers

After a process has been selected for redesign, the design team can begin to address how the primary "enablers" of business processes will enable a new way of working. Enablers are those entities that enable the designer to improve the performance of a process. Information technology and people are the primary enablers of change; however, they are also the primary constraints. The difficult task is to determine what opportunities for new IT and HR management approaches can be taken advantage of and what existing constraints must be accepted.

Using Information Technology Enablers

Information technology not only is important in implementing new processes but also makes possible entirely new process designs. Therefore, IT should be considered both before and after process design. When we understand how companies in many industries have used technology in innovative ways to improve their processes, we can better design new processes. Emphasis should be on the question, "What could we do if we had (some specific technologies) in our process?" Then, after a process design is envisioned, the focus should shift to IT implementation issues—supporting the new process with information from applications and databases.

It is possible, of course, to take enablement in redesign too far. IT and other enablers should never be employed for their own sake. To redesign a process solely to take advantage of imaging technology, as one insurance company did, is an example of such an excess. A process design should be enabled, not driven by, a particular change lever.

To focus only on information and associated technologies as vehicles for process change is to overlook other factors that are at least as powerful, namely, organization structure and human resource policy. In fact, information and IT are rarely sufficient to bring about process changes, most of which are enabled by a combination of IT and organization/human resource changes.

Use Organization Enablers, Too

Too many managers undertake carefully managed projects, employing tested methodologies and strict timetables, to build new systems to enable processes that, because the human aspects of change are managed as afterthoughts, lead to significant human resource problems. Too many systems fail to yield any real business benefit because of human problems in implementation. If redesign is to succeed, the human side cannot be left to manage itself. Organizational and human resource issues are more central than technology issues to the behavioral changes that must occur within a process.

Organizational enablers of redesign fall into two categories: structure and culture. Of the many kinds of structural changes that can facilitate new, process-oriented behaviors, one of the most powerful involves structuring process performance by teams.

Companies adopting teams are looking for cross-functional skills in single work units. Cross-functional skills facilitate functional interfaces and parallel design activities. New product development teams, for example, increasingly include representatives from all the functions involved in the development process. A second benefit is improved quality of work life. Most human beings seem to prefer jobs that include social interaction, and work teams provide opportunities for small talk, development of friendships, and empathic reactions from other employees.

Changes in organizational culture can also facilitate new process designs. Most recent shifts in organizational culture have been in the direction of greater empowerment and participation in decision making and more open, nonhierarchical communications. The resulting participative cultures, which have a structural side in flatter organizational hierarchies or broader spans of control, have been widely documented to lead to both higher productivity and greater employee satisfaction.

Beware of IT and HR Constraints

Just as information technology and human/organizational enablers can provide exciting opportunities for redesign, they can also impose considerable *constraints* on process designs. It is easy, but seldom realistic, to suggest that firms ignore existing systems and technology infrastructures, organizational barriers, and existing skill levels in designing a new process. Existing systems are often too expensive, complex, and embedded in an organization to simply assume them away. Organizational and human issues may be too imposing to change quickly. Instead of pretending to have a "clean sheet of paper," firms should acknowledge the constraints.

IT constraints are perhaps the most pervasive. Many firms, particularly in manufacturing industries, are beginning to employ integrated packages that support a broad array of processes from a single database. The most successful of such package vendors is currently SAP, a German firm that claims its package supports more than 800 processes. Because such an integrated package is difficult to modify substantially, its adoption is a major constraint on process design.

SYNTHESIZE AND DOCUMENT IMPROVED PROCESS

Process design is about coming up with a new, streamlined, possibly radical way of doing business. But the really hard part of this "redesign" is converting the design into reality: transforming the bold new ideas into the new infrastructure. The real secret of good design, once the innovative ideas have been thrashed out, is capturing it in a format that can be used to implement the new ideas. The real secret of design is producing a good detailed design.

The detailed process design has to be captured in such a way that it can act as the guide for all those involved in making the change. IT developers, HR specialists, trainers, and Process Owners all take their cue from the new design, with inherent demands on how it is captured. The most effective means is a combination of graphical and textual descriptions, which states in words and diagrams or pictures how particular "things"—be they physical entities (such as raw materials, goods or people) or information entities (such as requests or orders)—pass through the organization and are transformed.

The objective by the end of the detailed design stage is to arrive at a process description that can pave the way for change. It therefore has to describe and document the basis of the new ways of working and the key activities and their implications for building new capabilities. This has to be tested and reviewed within the business and finally approved before proceeding to implementation. The most appropriate means of capturing the design is a combination of graphical and textual representation, describing the main process steps and the interfaces between them, as shown in the following list:

- A process map documenting the steps of the process and who performs them
- A textual description of the activities or transformations that take place in each process step
- Detailed sub-process maps documenting the steps of each sub-process with a textual description of each activity and who performs them
- The external scope of the process defining interfaces and boundaries with customers, suppliers, and other external organizations
- The internal scope of the process, including any boundaries with other processes, departments, or parts of the organization
- Identification of the process owner
- Measures and mechanisms for monitoring process performance
- Procedures and vehicles for solving process problems and capitalizing on process opportunities
- Identification and description of the rules and controls on how the process operates
- Description of the role of people (the human element) within the process
- Description of the types of people, skills, and attitudes required
- Identification of any issues that could not be resolved in design and should be resolved in operation
- A glossary of terms and definitions used in the design

NOTES

1. Geary A. Rummler and A. P. Brache, *Improving Performance: How to Manage White Space on the Organization Chart* (Jossey-Bass, 1995), p. 128.

2. National Institute of Standards and Technology, *Integration Definition for Function Modeling (IDEF0)*, FIPS PUB 183 (Secretary of Commerce, December 1993).

3. David K. Carr, *Best Practices in Reengineering: What Works and What Doesn't in the Engineering Process* (McGraw-Hill, 1995), p. 106.

4. Colin Bainbridge, *Designing for Change: A Practical Guide to Business Transformation* (Wiley, 1996), p. 67.

5. Ibid., p. 71.

6. Kelvin F. Cross, John J. Feather, and Richard L. Lynch, *Corporate Renaissance: The Art of Reengineering* (Blackwell, 1994), p. 132.

7. Eileen Flannigan and Jon Scott, *Process Improvement* (Crisp, 1995), p. 56.

CHAPTER 9

Information Redesign
of Processes

INTRODUCTION

Although information technology (IT) is not the only technical resource involved in transformation, it overshadows all the others by such a great margin that we elected to devote this entire chapter to information technology. This chapter describes how IT is applied to process design. It covers the key stages of information collection, developing enterprise IT architecture, defining process information requirements, and developing detailed IT design for the individual processes.

Process-led change marks a significant shift in the role of IT. Rather than being the overriding driver behind change, as it usually is during traditional systems development, it becomes just one of several actors within the change program. IT no longer leads; it plays a supporting part. The design itself leads, and the IT development team has to look to the process design, not to a set of users or existing methods, for their requirements.

Traditionally IT produced a set of requirements based on an analysis of the existing business, defining to the nth level of detail a specification of the systems to be developed. This hefty tome was then signed off by both parties as the requirement for all of the development work that followed. Once documented, these requirements became set in stone, an exorbitant price and convoluted change control procedure usually being attached to any request for modifications. While this gave the IT department something to point to and say "you got what you asked for," it rarely ensured that the most appropriate solution was delivered.

Taking the process design rather than the existing business as the source of requirements calls for new ways of working. IT systems, therefore, have to be built to support the new process and not to solve the problems of the old one. This often proves to be a problem for IT departments whose methods are based around modeling an existing operation, rather than working afresh from a paper or conceptual design.

One fundamental principle is key above all others in IT development for transformation and must be followed religiously: *The process design drives the IT requirements*. The process design is about new ways of working and, as such, it is the only representation of these new ways. There is no existing manifestation of it for the business analysts and data modelers to copy, analyze, and pore over. There are no "users" already working that way who can be interviewed. So the process design itself must be the sole source of IT requirements.

This in turn demands some change to the way in which IT is developed. But it does not replace the IT development life cycle, it merely changes where the requirements come from.[1] The information requirements of the new process, rather than the existing business, drive the IT life cycle. Instead of looking at current operations and automating them, IT analysts and designers take their cue from the process design itself. This represents a major shift in the way requirements are obtained—but not in the way systems themselves are produced.

THE INFORMATION TECHNOLOGY DEVELOPMENT PROCESS

Before embarking on the path of IT development, a word about integration: Although IT is treated in a separate chapter, this does not imply that the IT development occurs in isolation. Transformation involves creating a new way of working that combines the appropriate mix of IT, people, and other capabilities in the optimum way. IT development must therefore integrate with other areas of development, in particular HR, and vice versa. IT staff need to understand the capabilities of the people who will be using the new systems and applications, just as HR staff, trainers, and managers must understand the nature of the new IT systems. This demands a new level of cooperation and dialogue between areas of the business that have traditionally been isolated.

Developing the New IT Capability

In developing the IT capability to support the new processes, the objective is to identify the information needed by the process and to define how that information is captured, transmitted, processed, and stored. From this it should be clear that process-led IT development is not radically different from traditional methods. It is still concerned with eliciting the

Figure 9-1
Comparison of Work and IT Development Procedures

	Work Development Procedure	IT Development Procedure
Diagnose System	Diagnose Existing and Future Enterprise *(pp. 134-140)* **Output = Process Map**	Diagnose Process Maps to Obtain Data Model *(pp. 180-182)* **Output = Data Model**
Broad System Design	Develop Enterprise Concept *(pp. 140-143)* **Output = Enterprise Concept**	Develop Enterprise IT Architecture *(pp. 182-183)* **Output = Enterprise IT Architecture**
Diagnose Process	Determine Customer Requirements for Process *(pp. 159-160)* **Output = Customer Requirements**	Define IT Requirements for Process *(pp. 184-185)* **Output = IT Requirements**
Detailed Process Design	Conduct Detailed Analysis and Redesign *(pp. 169-176)* **Output = Work Design**	Detailed IT Design of Individual Process *(pp. 185-191)* **Output = Information Design**

IT requirements so that those with the expertise can build the necessary programs, applications, databases, and interfaces.

The development of new IT capability follows the same four stages of development, shown in the right-hand column of Figure 9-1, as the basic work development procedure of chapters 7 and 8, shown in the left-hand column.

The IT development should be performed by a project team, as described in Chapter 5. *For best results it is recommended that the IT team and the basic technical team be integrated into one team responsible for both the basic work design and IT design of the process.* This approach will achieve better results with fewer people and less time. However, if an integrated project team is not feasible for some reason, it is recommended that the IT team work alongside and in parallel with the basic technical team.

In this book, the IT procedure is presented in a separate chapter to avoid complicating the basic work design procedure and to emphasize the new procedures for IT design under a process-led design approach. However, in practice, basic work design and IT design should always be performed together.

Collect Information for IT Design

As the design efforts progress, the Enterprise Process Map and the Individual Process Maps will reveal both requirements and opportunities for the use of information and technology at the enterprise and individual process levels. Analytical efforts can be conducted to determine the best ways to satisfy the requirements and to take advantage of the opportunities. The results will provide the basis for information technology support and also influence design of the business processes.

The process maps are the first place to look for points in the business processes where information and technology will be important. The enterprise level map may even identify processes that have names similar to those of the company's major information systems, suggesting that these processes or even the entire enterprise can be supported by a large automated system. However, the detailed individual-level process maps will provide much more reliable information on the nature of the information systems that will best support the work process. *Because technology can, and should, influence the design of work processes, the information technology analysis should be done at the same time as the Process Maps are being drawn, as part of the redesign effort.*

And remember, process maps and designs are not data models. While those closely involved with process design know this, some IT personnel jump to the wrong conclusion. Process maps and designs are developed using IDEF0 and IDEF3, or similar methods, and consist of boxes representing activities connected by labeled lines representing relationships between the activities. IT people have a tendency to treat such maps as data models, which they are not. To develop a data model, an IT person must apply IDEF1, or a similar method, to the IDEF0/IDEF3 process map. It takes considerable analysis by an IT person, as described in the latter part of this chapter, to go from the IDEF0 process map to an IDEF1 data model. Applying the IDEF1 method will result in a non-redundant collection of information in a form that can easily be translated into any data base management system. If the IT staff expect the IDEF0 map to provide the data required for IT development and if the full IT analysis is omitted, there will be serious consequences.

IDEF0 and IDEF3 are described in Chapter 6. IDEF1, IDEF1X, and IDEF4 are described at the end of this chapter.

Develop Enterprise IT Architecture

This stage outlines the procedures for determining the overall information technology requirements for the entire enterprise. It describes the technologies that will be required for collecting, validating, storing, processing, and communicating information and how they fit together. The result will be considered the IT architecture or framework and will be closely allied to the organization's IT strategy. As well as setting out the various technologies required to support the new processes in their entirety, the architecture helps to identify the individual development areas needed to build the new IT capability.

The enterprise concept, developed in Chapter 7, serves as the prime source for determining requirements. However, as the enterprise concept is concerned with all aspects of the process, those specific to IT must be sought out. This is achieved by working through each individual process to confirm the most appropriate use of IT to support that individual process and the whole enterprise. The task is undertaken jointly by the process design team and IT team members, such as chief analysts and designers. The exercise requires cooperation and iteration, with the process team clarifying the requirements of the process design and the IT staff advising on the most appropriate technology. "Most appropriate" depends on many peripheral issues, such as the cost of maintenance and compatibility with other parts of the organization. Given that some significant decisions may have to be made (such as the implications of re-skilling an existing IT development workforce if a switch from technology platforms is considered), this stage needs to be overseen by senior IT managers able to make decisions about existing and future IT strategy. The other key influence on the IT architecture may be any design principles that relate specifically to IT.

By the end of this stage, the core applications required to support the new processes will have been identified. The main databases and applications that will be required in each area are identified and form the basis for detailed specification and development. The actual applications required will depend on the industry in question and the processes being redesigned. Typically they will include a central customer information data base, usually complemented by a pricing or quoting package and accounting and administration applications by way of support. Beyond these, each industry will require its own packages, reflecting the nature of the business.

The definition of the enterprise IT architecture is an iterative exercise, which involves revisiting both process requirements and the organization's existing IT strategy before final decisions are reached. Where the process change is organization-wide, and a major change to the existing IT architecture is envisaged, the company's IT strategy may have to be revised, and board-level agreement and sign-off are likely to be required. Alternatively, if the change is taking place within the context of a wider organization, such as a multinational with an established IT strategy already in place, some constraints may exist.

The IT architecture needs to be confirmed at an early stage so that the necessary project areas for development can be established. Separate initiatives incorporating the sizing, sourcing, tendering, and procurement of the necessary equipment can then be started. It may be necessary to evaluate options from several different suppliers. So, for example, where a new call center capability is required, services may have to be sought from several different third-party suppliers where the capability cannot be built in-house.

Define Detailed IT Requirements of Individual Processes

This stage defines in detail the information requirements of each new process. This includes both the information (data) and its associated values, and the operations and transactions that will be performed upon it. This is a long and detailed phase, taking many weeks and probably months to complete. It is a critical stage in the development of the new IT capability and requires the highest-quality individuals assigned to it, be they process design teams or IT staff.

As with the enterprise IT architecture, the individual process design drives the requirements. The detailed requirements are elicited by a joint team of process designers and IT analysts working through the process concept to determine the information required and the transactions that will be performed on it. The procedure is the same as that used for enterprise architecture; the only difference is the amount of detail. The objective is to determine what must be done to support the process with IT, namely:

- What is the most appropriate information (about what, and in what form)
- What has to be done to that information
- How that information is accessed, transferred and stored
- What validation is required

Ultimately, every single item of information required to support the new processes has to be defined, along with the validation, format, and operations that will be performed on it. This includes the business rules that operate on processes, and their format or values.

The important point is that the information required is extracted from the overall context of the process design. Because the process concept describes the new ways of working in generic terms (rather than purely informational ones), it is possible to determine the information required to support these new ways of working. So, for example, a process step can contain the requirement, "Use the information from past transactions to check the customer's satisfaction with previous work carried out"; this analysis stage can then consider the most appropriate information to support such an action.

This stage encapsulates much of what is new about process-led IT design and development. First, IT staff have to use the process concept as their source of requirements rather than analyzing and modeling the existing business operations. Second, they have to work closely with the process designers and owners, working out the most appropriate solution where it is not yet clear. Thus, the activity is a recursive, discursive one, rather than merely a case of looking at the existing *modus operandi* and computerizing it. Finally, it has to be made clear that the process design does not equate to the set of user requirements traditionally produced. It represents a total business description for a set of new processes, which has to be further analyzed to determine the most appropriate information needs. The enterprise concept and the individual process concepts are guiding lights, not an IT specification or a statement of requirements. Although it represents a picture of the new ways of working, it still requires interpretation by the process designer and analysis by the IT team. A simple message has to be driven home to IT staff. It is a process design, not a data model.

Detailed IT Design of Individual Processes

When the basic technology and information points in the preliminary process design have been identified, the most important step takes place. The analyst suggests changes to the process that can be made by using new technology implementations. These changes should simplify the process, improve the quality of products or services, reduce the cost of the process, decrease delays in the process, or make some other measurable improvement.

Each of the areas that information technology can support provides a potential for improvements, but only an IT expert working with the design team can judge what available information technologies can do to help. The best places to look for improvements are where redundant information activities occur and where there are obvious delays resulting from information not being where it is needed.

To provide guidance for using information technology during detailed design, we divide the applications into five levels of business operations, in increasing order of ambition and complexity: (1) localized process improvements, (2) performing new tasks with IT, (3) technology-based integration of internal business operations, (4) developing business-to-business networks, and (5) redefining the entire business through IT.[2] The first two areas can be handled by a process design team. The third area can be undertaken by the Technical Management Team and/or a group of process design teams. The fourth and fifth areas require the input of top management: the CEO, the Executive Committee, or some group of top managers.

Localized Process Improvements

The most apparent and wide use of information technology rests in its ability to automate information-intensive (and formerly paper-intensive) transactions and services *within a single process*. These are the more traditional applications that tend to be locally or functionally based. Payroll, order entry, customer support, CAD/CAM, reservation, and JIT inventory systems are but a few examples here. Most companies use such systems, achieving remarkable increases in efficiency compared to days gone by.

Alignment of IT to business strategy requires that you know what effective uses of IT are. From that base, the best-run companies then decide what applications to implement, improve, or replace. It is best to start by identifying application strategies. So our first question is, What are the best application areas? It turns out that there are several areas that must be understood clearly to get at the answer. Following are some of the application areas where Information Technology can make a significant contribution. These area descriptions can be used by the redesign teams to locate areas for improvement in their process design studies.

Reducing Labor and Improving Productivity. Since the beginning of the century corporations in all industries have attempted to increase productivity through the use of automation. They have installed a vast array of technology to do the work of people. It is a process that has continued and, according to the experts on labor, economics, and technology, will accelerate. The intent is normally to displace human labor with equipment, much of which uses information technology.

What the most successful companies did was to increase the ease and quantity of communications horizontally through the use of IT (e.g., E-mail and groupware), use significant quantities of IT on the manufacturing floor (especially numeric control [NC], robotics, and data collection), and automate repetitive tasks. That allowed them to implement many of the new management practices of: Just-in-Time, Computer-Integrated Manufacturing, Agile Manufacturing, and lean production strategies, for example.

Speeding Up Work. Increasing your responsiveness and the speed with which you do everything—change, react, do work, and deliver goods and services, for example—make you more competitive and more profitable. While how much varies by industry, on average you could have a growth advantage of a factor of three over your competitors and an advantage on profit of a factor of two.

The rationale for the improvements is as follows. If you can reduce complexity—which is what has to happen frequently in order to speed up work—costs go down. Second, customers will pay a premium for getting what they want when they want it, in other words, sooner rather than later. And, there is the traditional first-entrant advantage. Time-based attitudes have been put on the short list of things executives worry about. Even with process reengineering projects, cycle time reduction is of major concern.

Improved Customer Service. Customer service is essential to differentiation between manufacturers, and competition is based on value-added services customized to individual customers. These may range from special packaging, labeling, and consolidated ordering and shipment of product to Electronic Data Interchange (EDI) transactions and Continuous Replenishment Planning (CRP). The information systems required to meet these demands require sophisticated order fulfillment systems, integrated logistics systems, and system integration across the organizational boundaries of manufacturers and distributors.

Quality. Information technology can facilitate a more rapid and objective analysis of production process problems, leading to improved product quality and reduced scrap. Other quality-related benefits include:

• Support for Continuous Improvement through better understanding and modeling of production processes.
• Support for quality assurance and regulatory compliance processes.

Reducing Cost of Process. Technology can assist in ways other than increasing speed and improving quality. Often it is possible for automation to reduce the cost of an effort by the automation simply being less expensive than labor. When applied to demand forecasting, warehouse management, Distribution Requirements Planning, Production Planning and Scheduling, and Material Requirements Planning, information systems can reduce product supply chain costs. Integrated logistics systems, along with Automated Storage and Retrieval Systems (ASRS), can significantly lower distribution costs.

Improved Yields and Efficiencies. The key to improving product yields and process efficiencies is assessing what happens during the production process and determining the appropriate response. In many plants, process control equipment aids in collecting data and can provide quick analyses and responses to steps in the process. Substantial cost savings are possible if cause-and-effect relationships between product quality and process variables are better understood. Understanding how the individual characteristics of a process affects product quality or production costs requires high volumes of data and appropriate information technology applications.

Flexibility. Computer control/robotics applications have dramatically lowered the economies of scale for manufacturing. Information technology makes it possible to achieve the production flexibility that delivers mass production efficiencies in lots of one. Thus, companies can economically manufacture products that meet the unique requirements of customers.

Time to Market. Information technology is making Concurrent Engineering possible by distributed multifunctional teams across computer networks. Product development design and manufacturing design do not have to be done sequentially. With the help of information technology, they can be done in parallel, cutting product development cycles by a factor of three or more. Technology can be used to do something more quickly than a person and can decrease the elapsed time on the critical path of a process.

Communicating. Technology can move data and information from one point in a process to another virtually instantly, and in a variety of forms. For a team-network organization to operate effectively, accurate and rapid communications are required.

Supporting Decision-Making. The data required to make business decisions can be gathered and used at a decision point in the process to help the staff make better decisions or, in some cases, to make them automatically. The data can be presented in convenient forms, in graphics, to make the decision process easier.

Monitoring and Controlling Process. Technology can compare what is being done to a set of standards, either as the process is being performed or afterward. Immediate problems that are reported can then be corrected and the monitoring function can test them again. Technology can directly control tasks in a business process. In general, this increases the quality of the output, since human error is eliminated and automated equipment can provide much finer measurement and manufacturing control than a person.

Storage and Retrieval. Technology can store information and retrieve it later very quickly and with as much organizational and search capability as may be required, but at increasing costs for increasing capabilities. Technology can perform functions in this area that cannot reasonably be expected of any workforce.

Performing New Tasks with Information Technology

This is where the design study starts being fun for the design team. It's where revolutions are started, where new ideas take root and spring to life. This is where radical change begins, where the "could be's" start becoming the "will be's." It is no longer enough to design a process, then overlay technology to simplify it. Now the team simultaneously looks at what technology can do and designs systems and processes accordingly.

There are four approaches that have been especially effective in developing technology to perform new tasks.

Look for an application using a recently arrived technology to offer new services useful to customers. The most obvious examples include use of ATMs to give customers greater access to banking services in the 1980s and the use of credit-card-sized modems and friendly networking software to make portable computers able to log into e-mail and Internet services in the 1990s.

Combine technologies in new ways before your competitors do. We are seeing this now in the trucking industry, where logistical systems are being reengineered using databases, PCs, mobile telecommunications, and EDI between manufacturers and distributors The intent here is to make inventory and warehouse management a thing of the past; your basic 18-wheeler becomes your Just-in-Time warehouse!

Experiment with various technologies within your organizations and watch what others are doing. The larger the IT organization, the easier it is for management to try using every major new technology that comes on the market, learning its strengths and weaknesses and then applying the other rules of the road listed above and below. But they also watch what other companies are doing both inside and outside their industries to see what their experiences are. Migrating over a new use into your industry often becomes a best practice.

Look for uses that are specific to your industry. New uses are most successful when they are industry specific. Using a better spreadsheet or word processor does not do the trick. The major improvements have always come from industry-specific applications.

Technology-Based Integration of Internal Business Operations

Common information is the central component of business process integration. Today's technology makes it possible to build an electronic "Main Street," where related business processes are linked through shared information on a common IT platform. This in turn requires the integration of organizational roles and responsibilities needed to use that shared information. Internal integration should be considered during the development of the Enterprise IT Architecture. Incorporating it later would be extremely disruptive and expensive. This area cannot be handled by a single process design team since the scope is too broad. It requires a coordinated group of design teams, or better yet, the Technical Management Group.

This electronic Main Street is a company's electronic equivalent of its physical infrastructure. As with physical infrastructure, designing and deploying a technology infrastructure is a highly strategic choice, involving many options and tradeoffs. It is the corporate leadership's job to set the high-level direction upon which a consistent set of policies can be built. And setting that direction involves not only looking at comparisons of the efficiency and effectiveness of internal options, but also taking an outward view to ensure that Main Street connects easily with the tributaries and highways that link the company with suppliers, customers, and other members of the supply chain.

While most leading companies take advantage of technology within processes, many companies are only now launching initiatives to link their processes through technology. They are attempting to build an electronic and digital infrastructure that will act as Main Street for inter-process transactions across the business. The idea is to have a common pool of data and information that is input once and then automatically flows to the point of need in every affected process. And as new information is generated within processes, it too must enter the pool and find its way to the processes it affects.

In principle, this sounds simple. In practice, it never is. Many corporations have been burned by the extravagant spending of their MIS depart-ments' internal application developments in recent years, so they have resolved to buy standard packages from outside vendors. SAP, originally developed in Germany, is perhaps the best recent example of such an application; MRP played the same role in the previous generation.

First, the arrival of a new, powerful, integrated software package often causes the reengineering river to reverse its natural flow. While the ap-plication should be tailored to the processes it is supposed to serve, many process owners, in practice, become intimidated by the software and start to fit their process to the technology. Second, process owners look for the same benefits in the same areas, usually the inventory, cycle time, and service areas. This is the stuff that disasters are made of, because the same software package is rolled from competitor to competitor, leveling the competitive floor. In the end, the software vendor ends up as sole bene-ficiary of the effort, having successfully led entire industries to competitive parity, by selling each member the same expensive weapon.

And yet if you *don't* integrate your processes through technology, one of your competitors will, and will then beat you. Successful CEOs subtly induce internal process integration through technology, for it is upon this logic that the detailed technological and organizational decisions will be made. The more advanced technology-based process redesign and business network integration are impossible without it.

Developing Business-to-Business Networks

Technology can be used to form links with other companies and cus-tomers that can be expanded or decoupled fast. Virtual organizations, partnerships, and other buzz phrases only become realities if multiple com-panies can find ways to work together. In practice, that usually means sharing information so that they coordinate and participate jointly in proj-ects. Having a tire manufacturing company deliver each day exactly the right number and types of tires needed by a Ford, GM, Toyota, or Nissan plant to put on the cars built the same day requires sharing databases, EDI, and common IT tools.

This is CEO and strategic management territory par excellence, because it involves both a vision and the creation of strategic alliances. It means working with other businesses to build new capabilities and to create new market discontinuities, building and supporting an infrastructure that al-lows controlled information and knowledge sharing. It involves linking one's own business's learning loops with those of other businesses. The benefits to be gained range from reduced costs to increased effectiveness, to doors being opened to entirely new businesses. It involves applying the principles of technology-enabled transformation to the supply chain as a whole.

Redefining the Entire Business Through Information Technology

Using technology to expand a business's scope or redefine it altogether is perhaps the CEO's greatest revitalization challenge. It can feel like being weaned a second time—altering or discarding the very capability that has nurtured the company for decades. Few leadership teams accept the challenge, fewer still have surmounted it. Accepting or meeting the challenge is no longer an option. Acceptance is a requirement for the survival of the business. The preferable course is for a corporation to *outmode itself* with innovative applications of technology, while leveraging that innovation to redefine its business.

Ultimately, technology can help corporations fundamentally change the nature of the game. This is what successful CEOs have done in numerous industries, as in the invention of home shopping, the birth of CNN and of cable stations and operators, and the advent of the video game industry and on-line information services.

DESIGN TEAMS AND INFORMATION TECHNOLOGY

Just as one could argue that user participation was one of the most important IT issues during the 1980s, the role of the information technology expert may become one of the most important issues of the 1990s and beyond. The issues are different, of course. No one has ever had to argue, for example, that information technology expertise is essential to systems development. But who provides this expertise, how they provide it and what their relationship should be with users and the corporate IT function are very much in dispute. Dramatic changes in the nature of the technology—including greater emphasis on personal computers and distributed architectures—have produced equally dramatic changes in where information technology experts are located and what roles they can play in the design process.

Sources of Expertise

Organizations today draw their information technology expertise from three different sources:

1. Their internal, team-based, "local" experts;

2. Their internal, centralized IT department; and

3. External vendors, contractors and consultants.[3]

Most large organizations employ all three individually or in combination, depending on the project, corporate culture, availability of resources, and the perceived quality of the sources on which they can draw.

Connecting the Redesign Team with the Internal IT Department

Regardless of which source of technical expertise the design team uses to develop the new system, the corporate information technology department may be responsible for maintaining and supporting it, or at least for integrating it into the organization's IT infrastructure. Therefore, this department should also be linked with the design team. Establishing a connection can sometimes be problematic when other sources of information technology expertise are used.

When local, team-based experts are the primary source of expertise, the source of the problem is the historically thorny relationship between internal information technology departments and the user teams they serve. The principal tensions arise from their frequently conflicting objectives. Business users want the tools that best fit their needs, while IT departments want systems that are compatible with each other and that serve the needs of many units. When the IT department prevails, users may feel that their needs have been compromised. When users prevail, the IT department may resent being asked to provide support for systems it had no role in purchasing or developing and with which it has little experience and expertise. In addition, each may undervalue the other's expertise and attribute too much significance to what they may lack—technological sophistication on the part of the user, and knowledge of the users' business and information needs by the IT department.

Most projects require both users and IT experts to develop applications that can meet business needs as well as be integrated into the IT infrastructure; the two sources of expertise must collaborate. Collaborations can take several forms. In one form, the IT consultant from the information services department (ISD) created a dotted-line relationship between ISD and the team member that served as the project team's IT expert. More important than the fact of the connection itself was the nature of that connection. The local expert, the systems consultant, and ISD established a complementary, noncompetitive, collaborative relationship in which the different kinds of expertise and responsibilities of the two individuals were acknowledged, respected, and used to good effect.

The underlying issue is somewhat different when an external contractor is used as the design team's principal source of IT expertise. The problem arises from what actually happens when systems development is "outsourced." In spite of what this expression implies, the work is rarely shipped out to offices, locations, or personnel outside the organization.

Instead, external participants often take up residence in the organization as if they themselves were at least part-time employees for the duration of the project. And as our story also suggests, the close proximity of external contractors can create significant tensions with corporate IT departments and personnel, especially if they have been passed over for the project because of perceived or actual inadequacies. These circumstances can make it difficult to forge collaborative links—and even more important to do so. In time, the external contractor will be gone, and the information technology department will end up supporting and maintaining the system. Clearly, the IT department needs to be involved, at least in collaboration with the external contractors.

Ultimately, the best solution, regardless of the source of project-specific IT expertise, is to add a representative from the internal IT department to the redesign team. In this capacity, corporate IT experts can help the team understand the implications of various design options on systems integration and identify the tradeoffs associated with each option. Their technical sophistication may also come in handy in the development of the applications themselves. Finally, with their broad-based knowledge of IT applications throughout the organization, they can fulfill an important internal "benchmarking" function for the project. By helping the redesign team identify and adapt systems and tools used successfully by others in the organization, the project can save considerable time, money, and aggravation.

INFORMATION MODELING METHODS

In Chapter 6 we discussed IDEF0 and IDEF3, which are primarily used for analysis and design of *work* processes. In the following paragraphs we will discuss three methods that are used for *information* analysis and design:

1. *IDEF1—Information Modeling Method* for analyzing an IDEF0/IDEF3 process map to determine the information required to support the process

2. *IDEF1X—Data Design System* for designing relational databases

3. *IDEF4—Object-Oriented Design System* for designing object-oriented databases

The IDEF1 Information Modeling Method

IDEF1 is primarily focused on determining the requirements for what *information* is or should be managed by an enterprise.[4] Rather than a design method, IDEF1 is an analysis method used to develop models to identify:

- What information is collected, stored, and managed by the enterprise.
- The rules governing the management of information.
- Logical relationships within the enterprise reflected in the information.
- Problems resulting from the lack of good information management.

The IDEF1 and IDEF1X are intended to be used together as follows:

1. Build an integrated information model using IDEF1.
2. Design database(s) from the information model using IDEF1X.
3. Implement and install the data base(s) and associated functional and procedural components.

Multiphase Development

Because the information modeling discipline involves an evolutionary process, the IDEF1 method is organized into phases with measurable results and specific products at each phase. A more exact definition is developed with each iteration. The objectives for each of the four phases are indicated here:

1. To define the Entity Classes that are readily apparent at this stage of the model development.
2. To define the Relation Classes that exist between the entity classes of which the model is comprised at this level.
3. To identify the Key Classes for each Entity Class of which the model is comprised at this time and to define each Attribute Class that is used in a Key Class.
4. To identify which Non-Key Attribute Classes should be associated with which entity classes in the model and to fully define each of these Non-Key Attribute Classes.

We want to re-emphasize that the process of developing an information model is iterative in nature, that is, the model evolves from one phase to another. It is not until the completion of Phase Four that the basic structural characteristics of the information model are complete.

Phase One: Define Entity Classes

Phase One serves the purpose of identifying and defining *entity classes* in the model. First, "entity classes" must be identified. An entity may be thought of as an object, either real (i.e., physical; something we could pick up and handle), or abstract (i.e., not within our physical grasp) that has properties. It is something about which specific characteristics or information are known. For example, a person is a physical entity. Each person has identifiable properties. These properties can be used to describe the person. One person (entity) that might be discussed is Jerry, the manager of production control. It is the properties known about the person—the name Jerry, the job position Manager of Production Control—that enable an exact identification of this entity. Conversely, the phoned-in complaint received this afternoon about the wrong product being delivered to one of our customers is a good example of the non-physical entity—the conceptual entity. The complaint exists, as an entity, whether it is represented on a complaint form or not. It has properties by which it is identifiable, such as the customer, its subject, the time received, and so on.

Phase Two: Define Relation Classes

Phase Two identifies the relationships that give meaning to associations between entities. It results in the construction of Entity Class Diagrams, appropriately displaying the syntax that communicates the meaning of the relationships represented as "relation classes" in the model. Relationship is an association between two entities. The entity known by the name Jerry is related to the entity known by the name Production Control in a way that may be defined as "manages." Some meaningful sense can be made out of the relationship between these two entities if we express them in sentence form: "Jerry manages Production Control."

It is not unusual for one entity to relate to many other entities. A good example of this is the relationship between the buyer, JoAnn, and the many purchase orders that she releases. JoAnn then has some relationship with Purchase Order 123, Purchase Order 457, Purchase Order 972, and so on. Each of these purchase order entities is a member of the Entity Class that can be called Purchase Order, just as JoAnn is a member of the Entity Class called Buyer. The entity JoAnn (a member of the Entity Class Buyer) has some relationship with many entities (members of the Entity Class called Purchase Order).

To successfully identify the relationships between entities and to build the diagrams that represent them, one must create a Relation Matrix. This matrix is the preliminary indicator that some relationship may in fact exist between two entity classes. An example of a Relation Matrix is shown in Figure 9-2.

From the Relation Matrix, the first set of model diagrams can be built. These diagrams are called the Entity Class Diagrams. An Entity Class Diagram focuses attention on a single Entity Class, which is called the subject. The subject Entity Class is approximately in the center of the diagram. Surrounding the subject Entity Class are other entity classes which share some relation class with the subject Entity Class. Other than the subject Entity Class, the only other entity classes which appear on an Entity Class Diagram are those which have a direct relation class linking them to the subject Entity Class. IDEF1 diagrams consist of some number

Figure 9-2
Relation Matrix

		Entity Class							
		1	**2**	**3**	**4**	**5**	**6**	**7**	**8**
	1		X			X			
	2	X			X	X			
Entity	**3**						X		
Class	**4**		X						
	5	X	X						
	6			X					
Only reflects that a	**7**								
relationship of some kind may exist	**8**								

of entity classes connected by lines and symbols to represent the relationships between entities being represented. The combination of lines and symbols represents the basic relation class syntax employed.

An example of an Entity Class Diagram is reflected in Figure 9-3. The title tells us that entity class number 32 is "Customer Representative." The entity class name is confirmed since it appears in the unnumbered box on the diagram. Abbreviations of titles are allowed in the boxes when space limitations make use of the formal title difficult. Another entity class, "Customer" E36, is linked to the entity class "Customer Representative" by the relation class "Employs."

The label on the relation class line is read from the "one" end to the "n" (or diamond) end. The relation class "Employs" used in Figure 9-3 says that:

• Any "customer" entity may employ zero customer representative entities or any positive integer of "customer representative" entities (usually expressed as 0, 1, or n).

• Each "customer representative" entity is employed by precisely one customer.

Phase Three: Identify Key Classes

The objective of Phase Three is to identify how members of one Entity Class are identified among members of the same Entity Class. This involves the identification of what are called "Key Classes." A Key Class is composed of some number of "Attribute Classes" by which each member of an Entity Class is uniquely identified. An attribute is what we call an individual property of an entity. An attribute has both a name and a value. A value alone, such as "123," has no meaning in and of itself until we associate it with a name, but as soon as we say "length in centimeters equals 123," the characters "123" now take on some meaning. In this example, "length in centimeters" is the name of the attribute and "123"

Figure 9-3
A Simple Entity Diagram

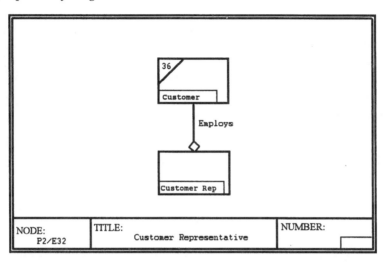

is the value of the attribute. It is by some combination of individual attributes that individual entities are described. Entities that are described as a group by the use of the same attribute names are represented as entity classes. Each member of that Entity Class is uniquely identified, one from the other, by some unique combination of values associated with the attribute names, which are themselves common to all members of the Entity Class. The attribute names common to all members of an Entity Class are referred to as Attribute Classes.

Phase Four: Identify Non-Key Attribute Classes

The primary activity in Phase Four involves assignment of all non-key attribute classes to their appropriate entity classes. The objective is the distribution of attribute classes throughout the model in such a way that all members of every Entity Class can be individually and appropriately described. With disciplined application of the "validity" tests to each Entity Class, the basic structural nature of the information in the enterprise is evolved.

Upon completion of Phase Four, the modeler will have produced a structurally sound information model. If all of the methodology rules have been applied correctly up to this point, each Entity Class will represent a non-redundant collection of information and each Entity Class pair sharing a relation class will convey some non-redundant meaning in the model. The information model is now in a form that will facilitate translation into any data base management system currently on the market.

Computerized IT Design Methods

The complexity and difficulty of IT design has been offset to a certain extent by the development of computerized design systems. The development of IDEF1X and IDEF4, as an extension of IDEF0 discussed in Chapter 6, is indicative of the type of design systems being developed. We will briefly describe these two systems to provide some background on the capability of these new design systems.

The IDEF1X Data Design System

IDEF1X is a method for designing relational databases with a syntax designed to support the semantic constructs necessary in developing a conceptual schema.[5] A conceptual schema is a single integrated definition of the enterprise data that is unbiased toward any single application and independent of its access and physical storage. IDEF1X is most useful for logical database design after the information requirements are known and the decision to implement a relational database has been made. Hence, the IDEF1X system perspective is focused on the actual data elements in a relational database.

A powerful feature of IDEF1X is its support for modeling logical data types through the use of a classification structure or generalization/specialization construct. This construct is an attempt to overlay models of the natural kinds of things that the data represents whereas the boxes, or entities, attempt to model types of data things. These categorization relationships represent mutually exclusive subsets of a generic entity or set. Subsets of the superset cannot have common instances. For example, a generic entity PERSON has two subsets representing all complete categories, namely, MALE and FEMALE. No instance of the MALE subset can be an instance of the FEMALE subset, and vice versa. The unique identifier attribute for each subset is the same attribute as that for a generic entity instance.

The IDEF4 Object-Oriented Design System

IDEF4 divides the object-oriented design activity into discrete, manageable chunks. Each sub-activity is supported by a graphical syntax that highlights the design decisions that must be made and their impact on other perspectives of the design. No single diagram shows all the information contained in the IDEF4 design model, thus limiting confusion and allowing rapid inspection of the desired information. Carefully designed overlap among diagram types serves to ensure compatibility between the different sub-models. The IDEF4 method allows the designer to easily make tradeoffs between class composition, class inheritance, functional decomposition, and polymorphism in a design. IDEF4 is more than a graphical syntax—the graphical syntax provides a convenient framework for navigating an evolving object-oriented design that is ultimately specified on class invariant data sheets and method set contracts.

Conceptually, an IDEF4 model consists of two sub-models, the class sub-model and the method sub-model. The two sub-models are linked through a dispatch mapping. These two structures capture all the information represented in a design model. Because of the size of the class and method sub-models, the IDEF4 object designer never sees these structures in their entirety. Instead, the designer makes use of the collection of smaller diagrams and data sheets that effectively capture the information represented in the class and method sub-models.

NOTES

1. Colin Bainbridge, *Designing for Change* (Wiley, 1996), p. 146.

2. Francis J. Gouillart and James H. Kelly, *Transforming the Organization: Reframing, Restructuring, Revitalizing, and Renewing* (McGraw-Hill, 1995), p. 216.

3. Don Mankin, Susan G. Cohen, and Tora K. Bikson, *Teams and Technology: Fulfilling the Promise of the New Organization* (Harvard Business School Press, 1996), p. 83.

4. Richard J. Mayer (ed.), *IDEF1 Modeling: A Reconstruction of the Original Air Force Report* (Knowledge Based Systems, Inc., 1992).

5. National Institute of Standards and Technology, *Integration Definition for Information Modeling (IDEF1X)*, FIPS PUB 184 (Secretary of Commerce, 1993).

PART III

Socially Redesigning the Organization

CHAPTER 10

Introduction to Social Redesign

THE NATURE OF SOCIAL CHANGE

In technical redesign, once requirements have been specified, modules can be designed, prototypes constructed, and ultimately new systems built. The challenges of information technology in technical development are immense, but with the right disciplines they can be surmounted. Once built, such systems will perform in a consistent and predictable manner.

Social redesign is not like that, unfortunately. Changing behavior and reshaping capabilities and organizations is an altogether more nebulous task. People do not conform rigorously and reliably to norms and expectations. They have preferences and idiosyncrasies, personal motivations and emotions; sometimes they just have bad days when they don't feel like cooperating. They stray from procedures, modify the way work is carried out, and amend their own jobs according to particular preferences or capabilities. Although the development of the human resource component still requires the same stages of change—design, develop, and deploy—the distinction between stages is much more blurred. Sometimes it is not even possible to distinguish the completion of one stage from the beginning of another.

There are two distinct aspects to social redesign. The first aspect pertains to the *tangible* outputs that have to be produced to support the new processes. Jobs have to be designed, organizational structures drawn up, reinforcing mechanisms (such as contracts and remuneration) put in place, and training programs conducted. These are the physical deliverables, which can be specified, managed from a project plan, and tested for conformance with certain quality standards. The second area covers the *in-*

tangible aspects of change, often referred to as cultural change. It includes the realignment of the attitudes and values of the people in the organization to fit the newly designed processes. It embraces a myriad of intangible activities, including the management of resistance to change and the building of commitment. It requires a sensitivity to the nuances and undercurrents running within organizations and must be backed up by constant monitoring and feedback activities.

Although these areas are separated for the purposes of explanation, they are inextricably linked in practice. With the people issues, more than any other part of change, this multidimensional approach is acutely important. Process-led change may be about specifying and then producing new capability, but that is only the first step. Successful change is not achieved by working out a set of deliverables to train and reorganize staff and then sitting back to tick off progress. There is a need to listen and to monitor, to watch and to sense, and then to fine-tune the approach accordingly. The intangible aspects of change are the ones that are unique to each and every organization, and the responses, too, have to be unique. We will cover the intangible aspects of social change in this chapter and in Chapter 13. The tangible aspects of change are covered in chapters 11 and 12.

Social design must be performed in parallel with technical design: The social and technical components of a process must be congruent if the process is to be effective. Chapter 6 both introduces the subject of process design and provides the methodology for technical design. This chapter provides the methodology for social design. Please remember that Social Design is performed concurrently with Technical Design and by the same people on the design team. Thus, technical and social issues should be addressed concurrently.

American companies are still likely to seek solutions to business problems by working on the technical side of the equation. As one manager put it, "The American corporate landscape is littered with the remains of technically sound programs that have been crushed by employee resistance to change."

Part of the reason for this is that many companies, as part their previous efforts to alter the business, have failed to build coherent, unified corporate culture with a unity of purpose. Often, these companies have a hierarchical structure that leaves people feeling powerless and defensive, at the whim of supervisors or senior managers.

IMPLEMENTING CULTURAL CHANGE

Introduction

In Chapter 5 we developed an ideology, or planned culture, consisting of a creed, core values, and guiding principles to guide the company in the 21st century. Now we come to the more difficult, and probably more important, task of implementing the planned culture. Our planning will be of no avail unless we can effectively implement it. Cultural change should be the first social change to be implemented since it pervades all other change efforts. However, it will probably be the last change completed, since changing culture is a long, drawn-out process.

In the following pages we will discuss three powerful approaches for implementing a 21st-century culture: (1) initial kick-off conferences, (2) periodic cascade efforts, and (3) as-needed task group efforts. Each of these methods has an important role to play in implementing a company's creed, values, and principles; all can be used in the same company at different times. The Initial Kickoff Conferences are used to initiate a new or major change in the creed, values, and principles; they enable a company to get a fast start on cultural improvement. The Periodic Cascade Efforts are less dramatic, but are highly efficient and effective for implementing cultural change over the long haul. The As-Needed Task Group approach can be used to implement cultural change wherever and whenever change is needed. It is a very effective and flexible tool for implementing specific changes.

The Role of High-Level Leaders in Implementing Culture

Getting Ready for Kick-off

Do not let the existing culture dictate your implementation approach for the new culture. You will have trouble creating a new culture if you insist on implementing it in ways that are consistent with the old one. Culture change moves at a slow crawl if the existing culture gets to call the shots on methodology. Remember, the old culture is designed to protect and perpetuate itself, not to bring about its own demise. From the very outset you must free yourself from the existing culture and conceive a plan of action that starts to liberate the organization from its past.

The kick-off should be dramatic enough to jar your organization from its past. High-level management must hit the organization with a change big enough to shatter the status quo and dislodge the old culture. Heavy duty intervention is required because the existing corporate culture has a very strong immune system. Unless you can overwhelm its defenses— weaken the culture somehow—it launches a fierce counteroffensive, and usually wins. Attempts at incrementally changing the culture are doomed to failure. Significant culture change should start to occur in months, not years. Start out fast and keep trying to pick up speed. There are many good reasons for a high-velocity approach to culture change. There are no valid arguments for going slowly.

Actions Speak Louder than Words

High-level management must realize that actions are much more convincing than words. Management should be clear on the actions that reflect the company's creed, values, and principles and demonstrate them personally.[1] For example, if you want to encourage decentralized decision making, you should find a way to delegate high-visibility decisions. Above all, live the creed, values, and principles consistently. Your people study your every move. If they catch you following the creed today and then not following it tomorrow, they will resist following it. Not only must the messages be consistent, they must be omnipresent. Act out your creed, values, and principles continuously. Take every opportunity to drive home the message. Leaders live the creed by making all their actions and behaviors consistent with it and by creating a sense of urgency and passion for its attainment.

High-Level Leaders Involve Everyone in Implementation

High-level leaders must learn to let others take responsibility (and credit) for implementing the company's creed, values, and principles; they should check their egos at the door and be less like a guru/hero and more like a facilitator/coach. Following are some concrete suggestions:

- Encourage others to take responsibility for executing the ideology in their area. Get each person to set goals and action plans and then follow up with them.
- Set up regular multiple communications channels where supervisors discuss the new ideology with their people.
- Refer questions and comments about the new ideology to supervisors, rather than answering them directly.
- Lionize others; constantly communicate about the hero actions of others in multiple mediums.
- Talk about "the team" and "our purpose" and "our results." The leader's language has a dramatic empowering impact.
- Avoid answering all questions/problems/difficulties. "I don't know" is a legitimate answer. Employees will respect you for not giving glib, and often incorrect, answers just for the sake of giving an answer.

Initial Kick-off Conferences

The implementation kick-off for cultural change involves a series of three high-powered conferences for high-level management, middle management, and all employees.[2] These three conferences, which can be scheduled within a three- to six-month time frame, constitute an intensive organization-wide intervention that constitutes a form of shock therapy. They are intended for kicking off either a new program or a major change in cultural improvement. They enable the organization to come out of the gate running, rather than having to wait several years for something to happen. The kick-off approach should *not* be used for a continuing or long-range change efforts. Other methods, described later in the chapter, are more appropriate for these situations. The Executive Coordinator with the advice and assistance of the Cultural Coordinator and Social Coordinator should plan and conduct these conferences.

High-Level Managers Conference

Members of the Executive Steering Board and selected other high-level leaders of the organization come together at an off-site location for a one- or two-day workshop to discuss and approve the company's creed, values, and principles (ideology). High-level leaders should return from the session with a clear sense of direction and a commitment to achieving their ideology.

Once the high-level management team is ready, it's time to begin to lay a foundation of trust among the front-line employees. The most important element in this foundation is credibility. The management team's actions must be consistent with their words. When the ideology is released, it proclaims that certain values are paramount in your organization. These values *must* be reflected in the actions of high-level management. Chief among these is creating a fear-free environment in which every employee is encouraged to participate in a spirit of equality and teamwork.

Nothing will sabotage the entire effort faster than for a manager to say one thing and do another. An obvious example of this is the manager who encourages participation and open communication, then does not listen to anything his or her subordinates have to say, or worse yet, punishes an employee for proposing an idea different from his or her own.

Middle Managers Conference

The most likely source of resistance to the "new thinking" will be middle managers and supervisors. A retreat, where fears and concerns can be expressed and answered, will pay rich dividends. Our approach for implementing a 21st-century culture must take into account the feelings of vulnerability on the part of middle managers. These middle managers can and will sabotage implementation if not given a chance to buy in. An implementation strategy that bypasses the middle managers is doomed to failure.

The change to a 21st-century culture requires a new mind-set, new behaviors, and a new skill-set for middle managers. We must convince middle managers to accept and embrace these new behaviors if we are to implement a 21st-century culture. A brief description of the shift that must take place at each of the three levels is provided in Figure 10-1.[3]

Change does not come easily to managers who have climbed the cor-

Figure 10-1
Mind-Set, Style, and Skills of Middle Managers: Old and New

The Old Mind-Set
  I am the boss.
  People are a liability.
  I must have the answers.
  You do as I say.

The New Mind-Set
  I am a coach.
  People are an asset.
  We need to find answers.
  How can I help you?

Old Behavior Style
  Acts as "lone ranger."
  Tightly controls information.
  Demands conformity.
  Maintains the status quo.

New Behavior Style
  Acts as team player.
  Shares information.
  Encourages diversity.
  Encourages innovation.

Old Skills
  Ability to set goals.
  Ability to speak well.
  Ability to develop self.
  Ability to solve problems.

New Skills
  Ability to follow shared purpose.
  Ability to listen.
  Ability to develop group.
  Ability to facilitate team problem solving.

porate ladder through sheer personal drive and a hands-on style that borders on benevolent dictatorship. It is difficult psychologically and philosophically for those managers to recognize that their role has shifted from being a director and order giver to becoming more an educator and motivator. One of the toughest things for them to learn is that empowerment of subordinates does not mean loss of responsibility. It's just that execution is different.

This new way of operating is not something that can be forced on middle managers. Managers must be given support as they move through the change process. The primary purpose of the Middle Managers Conference is to indicate to the middle managers that the company understands their difficult problem of change and will provide all support needed to make the change easier. We should also stress the very important part they are expected to play in achieving the new vision, creed, values, and principles.

All-Employee Conferences

After the high-level management and the middle management conferences have been completed, the organization is ready for the all-employee conferences. Included in the all-employee conferences are members from all levels and departments. Participants explore common ground, develop a shared understanding of the direction for the future, and identify ways of increasing the responsiveness of the organization to its mission and creed.

Ordinarily the all-employee conference lasts two days. Each conference should contain 75 to 150 participants; large organizations will require several conferences. Participation should be voluntary, except for management. The goal is to get a critical mass committed to the new direction.

Those who do not participate are given a complete briefing on what transpired at the conference. The data supplied to the conference participants provide a basis for the exploration of ways to improve the way the company operates. The data provided comes primarily from the cultural planning effort that generated the creed, core values, and guiding principles. By the end of the conference, each participant:

• Has a clear understanding of the company's direction for the future.
• Has a strong commitment to helping the company achieve its vision, mission, creed, core values, and guiding principles.

Planning and executing an all-employee conference is not something that can be reduced to a list of do's and don'ts. It is a highly dynamic event that needs to be skillfully managed. With effective management, it has the potential for generating extraordinary enthusiasm and commitment. The conference can become the defining moment as the organization moves from the old way of doing things to the innovative culture.

Every detail of the two-day conference should be planned. To the casual observer, the conference many seem like a spontaneous unstructured experience. However, the most creative and energizing learning experiences are usually the direct result of a scenario that has been carefully planned. Preplanning includes everything—the number and mix of people in breakout groups, guidelines for discussions, and the amount of time for reporting back to the conference.

While it does not have to resemble a religious revival meeting, a well-planned conference should generate excitement and enthusiasm. It should be fast paced to maintain the momentum. No activity should be scheduled to last more than one hour, presentations to the group should generally not exceed 15 minutes, and reports from break-out groups should be limited to less than five minutes.

The all-employee conferences generate openness and enthusiasm throughout the organization. It is important that arrangements be made to provide a detailed briefing for employees who did not attend one of the conferences. The major challenge at this stage is to get all employees to accept and embrace the company vision, creed, core values, and guiding principles and to maintain the momentum generated.

Cascading: A Periodic Approach to Cultural Change

The kick-off approach to implementation just discussed is intended as a one-time effort to initiate a cultural improvement effort. The approach described hereafter is an annual or periodic effort that extends over a number of years. Our message will be cascaded level by level throughout all departments until every man and woman in the organization understands and is committed to the ideology.

Overview of Cascading

The purpose of cascading is to discuss the company's vision, mission, creed, values, and principles with every employee in the company in an efficient and effective manner. Cascading involves each manager sitting down with his or her immediate team for a series of meetings. These meetings should enable everyone to understand and become committed to the company's vision, mission, creed, core values, and guiding principles.

Who Should Lead the Cascading Meetings?

Managers should lead these meetings themselves. Do not use an outside facilitator. It is important for team members to hear about the company's ideology directly from their leaders. Managers must understand and be committed to the company's vision, mission, creed, values, and principles in order to properly explain and support them.

The leader's purpose in these meetings is to promote discussion among team members. The leader should stay out of the discussions as much as possible after the initial explanation. Talk only as necessary to keep the team members talking. You do not want to give the impression that the vision, mission, creed, values, and particularly the principles are being rammed down their throats by management. Commitment will come only after they have voluntarily accepted them following open and frank discussions. That means you should explain, give examples, and discuss what they mean to you, but you should not engage in a long tirade about why they should be adopted.

The Cascading Process

Cascading is a top-down, bottom-up discussion process that proceeds through the organization one level at a time. The first series of discussions is between top managers and their next level of managers. At the end of each series of discussions, the organization's ideology (plus the ideology of higher levels) are passed down to the next level for discussion. Proposed changes and unanswered questions will go up until they are resolved or answered. Attendees at one series of discussions will become the leaders of the next series. In the following guide, we have suggested dividing the discussions into four meetings. The actual number and length of the meetings should be determined by the local situation.

- First Meeting. Leader explains and discusses the company's ideology. Team members ask questions and discuss for understanding.

- Second Meeting. Team members discuss ideology further for understanding and *commitment*, with the leader acting only as a facilitator and explainer.

- Third Meeting. Teams develop their own team-specific mission and ideology.

- Fourth Meeting. Teams plan action to achieve the company's and their own ideology.

Making the Cascading Process Successful

In the preceding guide, we divided the discussions into four types of meetings. We did not intend to imply that only four meetings would be required. It may take a greater number of meetings, particularly if the ideology is brand new. Do not try to rush the process. This is a major change for everybody in the company. It takes time for people to examine and absorb the ideology and decide how they feel about it.

The cascading process should be repeated whenever there is a change in the company's ideology, or annually if there are no changes. If there is a *major* change, the kick-off approach may be advisable. The annual cascading is primarily a review and can be accomplished much more rapidly than the initial cascading.

Social Project Team Efforts

Introduction

An *organization-wide* project team is one of the most effective tools for sustaining involvement and commitment after completing the kick-off conferences and the cascading meetings. This is particularly true if the *core* and *virtual* team concept, as discussed in Chapter 5, is utilized. The project teams take up where the kick-off conferences and the cascading meetings stop. It should be recognized that the information on project teams in Chapter 5 is as applicable to social project teams of this chapter as it is to technical project teams. Following are a few additional guidelines to keep in mind in establishing a social project team:

- Include representation from all major constituencies, including high-level management.

- The mandate for the task group should be stated in a clear written statement. The statement should originate with the CEO.

- The time frame for accomplishing the task must be clearly specified.

- Resources needed to accomplish the task must be provided. This will include time to hold meetings. Some groups will need the services of a trained facilitator.

Suggested Topics for Social Project Team Assignments

Some suggested subjects for project team study are described next. This list is not meant to be all-inclusive, but only indicative of the types of topics suitable for social project teams. Some of these topics are discussed in more detail in Chapter 13.

Cultural Assessment. We may want to get a handle on whether our cultural improvement program is succeeding or not. We can do this with a cultural assessment. The procedures for conducting a cultural assessment are provided on pages 77 and 78 of Chapter 4.

Customer/Supplier Study. Despite long involvement with particular customers, managers, and employees, companies will always learn something new from this study. The better you know your customers, the better you can serve their needs.

Competitive Benchmarking Study. This study compares the company's operations with those of other firms. Typically, the comparison is made with those firms believed to exhibit the most effective operations. Speed to market is a particularly useful benchmark.

Company Information Study. This study group, composed of representatives of all major employee groups, has the responsibility for developing systems and procedures for ensuring that all employees have access to all information on the business. They analyze current communication channels and develop recommendations.

Recruiting Personnel. How do we recruit personnel? How do other companies recruit personnel? How can we recruit personnel to ensure we have an adequate pool of highly qualified candidates?

Selecting and Hiring Personnel. What are our hiring procedures? How do other companies select and hire people? How can we change our selecting and hiring procedures to ensure we obtain the highest-quality people?

Performance Measurement and Appraisal. Are our performance measures in line with our vision, mission, and creed? Do they encourage the kind of performance we want? How can we change them to encourage higher performance?

Recognition and Reward. Do we adequately recognize and reward our employees? How do we compare with other companies? What can we do to improve our recognition and reward system?

Employee Involvement and Empowerment. Do our employees truly feel they are truly involved and empowered? If not, why not? How can we improve the involvement and empowerment of all employees?

Compensation. Do employees feel their compensation is fair and adequate? How does it compare with other companies? How can we improve our compensation system?

Training and Development. Do employees feel that their training and development opportunities are fair and adequate? How do we compare with other firms? How should our training and development program be improved?

Work/Job Design. Does our work/job design process result in good jobs? If not, why not? How can our job design process be improved?

Decision Making. How are decisions made in this company at the various levels? Is everyone involved in decision making that should be? How can we improve our decision-making ability?

Conflict. What are the causes of conflict in this company? How does the level of conflict in our company compare with other companies? How can conflict be reduced?

Most of these topics involve social processes, which are as amenable as technical processes to the process improvement approach described in chapters 5 and 6. Although this is a new way of thinking for socially oriented people, it is an extremely powerful approach for improvement that should not be ignored.

Summary of Implementation Efforts

Each of the three different methods has a specific role to play in implementing a company's creed, values, and principles. The Initial Kick-off Conferences are used to initiate a new or major change in the creed, values, and principles; they enable a company to get a fast start on cultural improvement. The Periodic Cascading Efforts are less dramatic, but they are highly efficient and effective for implementing cultural change over the long haul. The Project Team approach can be used to implement specific change wherever and whenever change is needed. It is a very effective and flexible tool for implementing specific changes.

Guidelines for Implementing Cultural Change

Implementation Efforts Immediately after Kick-off and Cascading

The kick-off conferences and the cascading meetings provide a dynamic and decisive beginning to cultural change. With kick-off and cascading completed, management has to prove that they mean what they say in the company ideology. Management should seize this opportunity to build trust and commitment for immediately translating the ideology into action. This period after cascading is a crucial test of the company's leadership, because building trust and commitment to the ideology is vital to the success of cultural change. Following are some guidelines for effective leadership immediately after the kick-off and cascading.

Provide a Living Example. The company ideology should be your guide to any and all actions you take. Follow it, and you build a strong foundation of trust. Deliberately go about your management duties with a style and manner that leaves no doubt about your acceptance and endorsement of the culture shift. You can make no stronger statement about your belief in the culture change than to embrace it—*embody it*—yourself.

Talk It Up. You get what you talk about. Airtime keeps the organization's attention on the vision, mission, creed, values, and principles. In the absence of regular conversations about the ideology, people will become absorbed by the details of their work and go back to business as usual.

Walk Around. Walking is an extension of talking. Walking around serves two purposes. First, it allows leaders to have weekly and/or daily discussions with employees. These discussions not only deepen the employees' understanding of the ideology, but the leader gets valuable information that can be obtained in no other way. Second, the employees see first-hand that the leaders are committed to the ideology.

Eliminate Fear. Continuous improvement is the cornerstone to success in cultural change. At the heart of continuous improvement is employee participation and commitment. Fear is lethal to both. It also destroys optimism, creativity, and trust. The single greatest fear factor in your company is a leader who continues to manage using authority and force. He or she is likely to be non-participative and punishing in disagreements. If nothing is done with this manager, you will lose everyone within his or her span of management.

Seize the Teachable Moments. Teachable moments are those incidents that provide an opportunity to talk about the ideology in a way that reinforces it. Sometimes a teachable moment follows something positive you have observed. At other times, it may follow an action that is inconsistent with the ideology.

Induce Pain and Provide a Reward. To help employees change, managers must orchestrate pain messages (what will happen if we don't change) throughout the organization as a way of gaining commitment to change. However, while management points out the grim situation, they should also point out how employees can positively impact their future. Let everyone see the opportunities in changing as well as the dangers in not changing.

Communicate the Message: "There Will Be No Turning Back." Everyone in the organization must believe that the innovative culture is not another passing fad, but an irreversible change in the way the organization will be managed. Any kind of second thoughts on the part of management will unfortunately telegraph the opposite message to employees. Let people know that they will be either the architects or the victims of change; there is no other choice.

Energize the Communication Effort. A tremendous amount of high quality communication is needed to sustain a culture change. Managers typically underestimate the effort that is required. They rely on the normal communication practices and patterns, failing to consider that those methods were never designed for times like this. Standard communication procedures simply will not cut it.

Achieve Concrete Results in a Hurry. The importance of quick wins cannot be overstated. Culture change needs to produce a tangible payoff in short order. It's crucial that you obtain early proof that the effort is well conceived and is, in fact, working. Just remember, concrete results talk louder than intangibles. Resistance to change always slows a bit when it looks like top management just might be right after all. Deliver concrete results in a hurry, and you buy some time for culture change to build momentum.

THE ROLE OF COMMUNICATION IN SOCIAL CHANGE

The Need for Communication

One of the most powerful tools that a company has in implementing change is communication. The one thing that every company can be certain of is that once a transformation program begins, everyone will know about it—instantly. Change occurs on the basis of available information. So the choice is not between communication and no communication. It is between unmanaged communication and managed communication. With unmanaged communication, the goals, procedures, and impact of the transformation will all be misunderstood. Rumors will abound. People's worst fears will run rampant. Productivity and morale will sink. And resistance, if not opposition, to change will harden. With managed communication, a company has at least a chance of circumventing these events.

To continue building mutual trust and to develop a new corporate culture, the organization must create a two-way communication flow of open and honest information between managers and employees—an open communication that permeates the entire organization. A two-way communication flow means that managers and subordinates alike express their opinions and actively listen to one another. This type of communication flow enables (and requires) everyone in the organization to make contributions, without regard to rank or title. This is especially important for a successful organizational transformation because it takes everyone's involvement and contribution to make the change process work.

A communication plan prepared by the Social Management Group and approved by the Executive Board should be one of the first orders of business for a company undergoing transformation. The primary purpose of the communication plan is to align all audiences with the company's ideology.

Initial Communication

The initial communication is critical, because it sets the tone and context for the entire program. The initial communication should be delivered as early in the program as possible and should contain the following elements:

1. Why the transformation program is needed
2. What the scope of the program is
3. What results management expects (Where the results include a change in competitive position, management may want to be circumspect.)
4. Who was and will be selected for the project teams and why
5. What will happen during the program and when
6. What involvement people will have in the effort
7. What can be told now about how transformation will affect all involved
8. When the rest of the story can be told

This communication is best delivered in two parts. Points 1 through 4 should be delivered by the Executive Steering Board to underline the importance of the message. Points 5 through 8 should be delivered by the members of the Social Management Group in order to give people a sense of who they are and their commitment to the program.

Both the tone and the content of the communication are important. The tone should be serious, reflecting the importance that the program will have to many people's lives. It should be realistic, neither overly optimistic nor overly pessimistic, but reflecting the probability of success. It should acknowledge ignorance and uncertainty where they exist but state in a positive way how knowledge will be acquired and concepts tested.

The tone of the initial communication should reflect the idea that "we are all in this together." It should not imply blame for anyone (even former employees) for the current situation, and it should not single out any group for praise either. It should not have any of the characteristics of a pep rally or a sales pitch. If the company's culture includes periodic communication channels (e.g., meetings or newsletters), it might make sense to adopt their format. On the other hand, if transformation is likely to change the culture, for example, to a more participative form, then the format should so reflect. The idea is to give the employees a preview of what the culture will be at the end of the transformation.

The initial communication (and all subsequent change management activities) should follow the precept: Speak as if your audience is convinced, act as if they are skeptical. The content of the initial communication and the subsequent work of the project should reflect another precept: Say what you are going to do, and do what you say. This does not mean that the transformation team needs to be too detailed and specific. It does mean providing as much of the big picture as possible and saying when the pieces will come together. Where possible, the initial communication should include statements of the commitments that management is prepared to make at this point. But these should be firm commitments, not mere hopes.

Encouraging Upward Communication

A common problem with most company communications systems is that they focus almost exclusively on the downward flow of messages and information. But employees begin to mobilize most strongly behind the company's goals only when the upward flow of communication through the business is as easy and as respected as the downward flow.

Active listening is a key part of the upward communication process. That is where the company learns to listen to its own employees about what does not fit with the new culture, about what is wrong, and to their ideas for change and improvement. It can be tough going at first, with seemingly endless nitpicking and faultfinding. But if the company reacts patiently and constructively, soon the positive ideas start to come through, which is when active listening comes into its own. Listening to the legitimate points employees raise, but doing little about them, means employees perceive you as only *hearing* what they say. They do not reckon you are actively *listening* until you do something positive about what they say. It is at that point they begin to think that what they say is actually worth listening to. In fact, it does not need to be something major, just something visible.

Fostering Cross-Company Communication

Lack of communication *between departments* can often be one of the biggest blockages to implementing effective change.[4] So introducing specific mechanisms to stimulate cross-company interaction becomes an important element in the process. One of the effective ways of doing this is to structure situations where this kind of communication becomes virtually unavoidable.

For example, as part of the company's process redesign, each department head can be given the task of establishing who exactly are the department's "internal customers," that is, those departments to whom they supply information, materials, or finished work. They are then required to meet with these department heads within a specific time frame to determine (just as they would with a customer) their specific requirements, particularly in the context of the company's new goals. Their discussion needs to establish clearly:

- The customer department's top three priority requirements.
- What they "contract" to do on each of these.
- How the supplier department will measure their success on each.
- Regular dates when they will meet together to review progress.

This kind of exercise takes time to complete, of course, but when department heads all over the business become engaged in the process, it certainly gets more cross-company communication going than ever before. It will also improve the quality of the company's process design. Getting the new culture and attitudes to grow throughout the organization can be a long and sometimes slow job, but this exercise, in a "what can I do better for you" context, certainly accelerates the process.

Channels of Communication

No one communication channel can ensure that the right messages are getting across consistently to every employee. Just as educators and psychologists have identified different types of learners, people receive messages in different ways. Some may respond to a general company communique like a newsletter while others need a personal letter or a seminar. To ensure reaching everyone, you have to be willing to use a variety of communication channels. Three very important communication channels were discussed in the section on implementing culture: large group (kick-off) meetings, cascading, and project teams. These will not be discussed further here. Some additional communication channels for keeping employees informed and involved with the transformation process are discussed in the following section.[5]

Newsletters. Newsletters can be one of the most cost-effective methods of consistently communicating the transformation message to your employees. Too often, organizational newsletters are boring and seldom read by employees. You can avoid this if you follow two important rules:

- Maximize the number of employee names listed in the newsletter.
- Maximize the number of employee photographs.

Visual Communication. Banners, posters, and special mottoes are all ways of making the transformation process visible. Be careful not to overuse them, since they can give the impression that transformation is a short-term campaign rather than a continuing effort.

Employee Bulletin Boards. Keep the bulletin board new, fresh, and filled with ideas and information; employees will see it as another message that quality is important to you and to the organization.

Fax and Photocopiers. The fax can be used as an effective means of communicating between plants that are physically separated. Received fax can readily be photocopied and widely distributed.

Letters from the President. In addition to supporting management forums, letters from the president can also be used at any time to provide special recognition. They can also announce an upcoming event or provide instruction and guidance about an activity occurring in the organization.

Computer Screen Messages. In organizations in which employees log onto a mainframe computer or a computer network, it's easy to insert messages that appear on the screen as employees enter the system.

Brown Bag Lunches. Company-funded informal lunches enable the president to share his ideas and views and to answer questions. Even more important, they allow employees to express their ideas and suggestions.

Payroll Stuffers. Payroll stuffers can be used for special announcements or special recognition for employees who have made significant accomplishments. Overusing this communication channel can quickly render it ineffective.

OTHER CHANGE METHODS

Role Modeling

Role modeling, or the setting of an example through one's actions, is a powerful method for shaping behavior. Many of the guidelines for implementing cultural change discusssed previously are examples of role modeling. The challenge of using role modeling in transformational change lies in finding role models who can model the new behavior and still be acceptable to those in the old culture. Role models must be acceptable to the old culture, but must be forward-looking enough to believe in the new vision and creed of the company.

Role modeling operates on two levels. The first has to do with the *learning of specific behaviors*, such as driving a car or learning to swim. For example, employees who attend meetings observe the leadership of those meetings well before being asked to conduct one themselves. The second level has to do with the *process of identification* with someone whose values or way of life are attractive. Some would say that a person's maturity can be measured in part by the nature of the role models with whom he or she has identified.

Role modeling is particularly effective when it is performed by the very high-level or highly visible members of the company. The CEO is probably the most effective role model, especially for cultural change. However, many other influential people in the company can also be very effective.

Coercion

Coercion is any form of influence that plays on the fears of others at moments when their freedom to reject the influence is seen by them as being severely curtailed for one reason or another. More specifically, coercion is any instance of attempted influence that meets the following criteria:

- Use of force, which may range from mild rules to legal or moral pressures to actual physical force.
- Expectation by people that they may be punished if they do not conform, which would cause such feelings as guilt, fear of failure, rejection, and a sense of the loss of something valued.
- Belief by those being coerced that they cannot exit the situation.

In almost every case of transforming an organization from a traditional, authoritarian management structure and system to a more fluid, flexible, knowledge-based, collaborative structure and system, the process of transformation appears to have been initiated with some form of coercion. Use of coercion in this context serves to capture the attention of employees and to heighten their awareness of the problems and possible solutions.

The appropriate and effective use of coercion depends on the presence of several conditions:

It is one step in a process. If the coercion is not disrespectful and if methods other than coercion are clearly being used, people are far less likely to have a lasting negative reaction to any specific act of coercion.

There is prior consideration of the consequences. Since coercion can frequently leave a bad taste in the mouth, it is important to think through and prepare for the range of responses it can generate. This is especially important in the context of how the coercion will impact the cultural change in process.

Those who use coercion pay close attention to the reactions of others. In a transformational context, listening to, taking in, and being willing to talk over the feelings and thoughts of those being coerced is key to successful use. This surfaces in multiple realities, a process that in and of itself creates a beginning level of positive engagement.

It is used sparingly. People can live with the occasional use of coercion without adverse reactions, especially when it is used to correct serious problems. However, if it is used too frequently, it can result in people leaving the organization at the first opportunity.

Those who use it do so with a sense of humility. By this we mean that the use of coercion is a last choice solution to a problem, as none other exists.[6]

Used according to these principles, coercion can be constructive rather than destructive. However, the use of coercion has some serious drawbacks that must be considered:

- Coercion can serve as a vehicle for the neurotic expression of narcissistic, histrionic, or paranoid behavior and as a means of satisfying an individual's inappropriate dysfunctional needs for dominance.
- As a means for getting people to do things they would not otherwise do, coercion works in the short term—but not in the long term.
- Excessive use of coercion will destroy the particapative culture required for the 21st century.

NOTES

1. Burt Nanus, *Visionary Leadership* (Jossey-Bass, 1992).

2. Howard W. Oden, *Managing Corporate Culture, Innovation, and Intrapreneurship* (Quorum, 1997), p. 61.

3. Edward Deevy, *Creating the Resilient Organization* (Prentice-Hall, 1995), pp. 124–126.

4. David Drennan, *Transforming Company Culture* (McGraw-Hill, 1992), p. 105.

5. Roger Tunks, *Fast Track to Quality* (McGraw-Hill, 1992), pp. 213–222.

6. Edwin C. Nevis, Joan Lancourt, and Helen G. Vassallo, *Intentional Revolutions* (Jossey-Bass, 1996), p. 244.

CHAPTER 11

Broad Social Redesign
of the Organization

INTRODUCTION

The purpose of this chapter is to determine the broad organizational characteristics of the future enterprise. To accomplish this we will first document and analyze the current organization. To design the future organization, we will first ascertain the needs of the future enterprise and then develop an organization concept that will satisfy these needs. The Social Management Group (SMG) will be primarily responsible for accomplishing the tasks in this chapter.

DOCUMENT THE EXISTING ORGANIZATION STRUCTURE

Before defining the broad organizational structure of the new organization, it is prudent to document the existing organization and perhaps conduct a partial survey of it. The survey is primarily intended to fill holes in our knowledge of the existing organization and is not intended to be a detailed analysis of the organization. To document the organization we will take a four-pronged approach.

- Gather and update the organization charts and organization manuals of the enterprise and prepare an Organization Map.

- Obtain and study the Enterprise Process Map from the Technical Redesign effort.

- Conduct a partial survey of the existing organization, if needed.

• Compare Organization Map with the Enterprise Process Map, reconcile differences, and revise Organization Map.

Gather and Update Organization Charts and Manuals

Most enterprises will have some form of organization charts and organization manuals that we will call the Organization Map. The degree of completeness and the degree of accuracy will vary greatly among organizations. We want the organization charts and manuals to be as accurate as possible, since they are one of the primary means of ensuring the accuracy of the Enterprise Process Map. However, we should not spend a lot of time and money updating them, since the goal of transformation is to shift to a process organization, in which case the current organization charts and manuals will be useless.

Obtain and Study the Enterprise Process Map

The Enterprise Process Map, as described in Chapter 7, is developed by the Technical Management Group (TMG) to provide the basis for the technical redesign of the enterprise. As such, it should be the most accurate record available of the existing organization. The SMG should act as the design review activity for the TMG to ensure that the Enterprise Process Map is correct. The primary purpose of the Partial Survey in the next section is to investigate areas where the organization charts and the process map differ.

Conduct a Partial Survey of Existing Social Structure

The purpose of this step is to survey a portion of the organization to obtain needed information. To most effectively utilize scarce resources, we will normally survey only in those areas where the organization charts and the process map differ or where we have no information. We will look at typical decision-making patterns, informal group structures, and how work normally gets done.

Where Are Decisions Currently Made?

The formal organization chart can be the starting point for an analysis of decision-making patterns. List the decisions that occur at each block on the chart—not in theory, but in actual practice. Distinguishing between the decisions you would like to have made at a particular level in the organization and those that actually are made there is very important at this point. Often, because the organization is designed to have decisions made at a certain level, we assume that those decisions occur there, when in fact they do not.

An example is the decisions made by a first-level supervisor, particularly in a production facility. We usually ascribe to that person decisions about administering discipline, while first-level supervisors often feel that they have little control over these decisions because they must clear them with their managers, as well as with the personnel department. When decisions require approval by higher levels, you must question whether they are being made by those who originate them or by those who approve them.

Sometimes, decisions that seem logically to be made in one area are actually made by default somewhere else. For example, in the absence of a strong marketing presence, a clerk on the loading dock may be deciding which customers' orders are shipped and when.

Informal Group Structures

Just as decisions are not always made as the organization chart suggests, so the informal organization chart does not always look like its formal counterpart. We want to identify that informal organization.

In most traditional organizations, there is a certain amount of interdependence between departments or functions. Manufacturing relies on engineering for drawings; engineering needs feedback from manufacturing about producibility—the feasibility of manufacturing a particular design. Marketing needs output from manufacturing, and manufacturing needs orders from marketing. Because these functions rely on each other to various extents, people normally develop some relationships across functional lines. Informal task groups may spring up to get work done. Certain people are identified as those to turn to for information about their particular functions. As a result, these people gain informal power within the organization. Networks develop around them. You will even find informal structures within formal divisions. Natural leaders spring up.

Frequently, these informal structures and methods of operation can be described fairly accurately. Simply asking people how they get things done and to whom they talk may uncover this information. First-line supervisors may possess more of this data than anyone else, because they have become masters at getting work done through the informal channels. They generally know who has the information they need and how they can go about getting it. The secret to getting good information in this area is the guarantee of impunity. You may not like what you learn, but you must not punish those who inform you. This information will be invaluable later when you are designing teams for the new organization.

How Does Work Normally Get Done?

The description of how work actually gets done in your organization may be the most eye-opening piece of data that you collect. In fact, how far the actual process diverges from the prescribed process is some indication of the need for a new organization structure. If you discover that work is getting done exactly as you would expect it to be done based on the written policies and the formal organization chart, your structure may be in fairly good shape. But if you find that what actually happens bears only remote resemblance to what should happen, then you can be certain that your decision to redesign your organization is sound.

The data will also give you some idea of what it takes to make things happen in your organization. You should pay special attention to the informal relationships revealed by this information: Who talks to whom to get things done? Which departments constantly must check with each other? How much time is spent in this double-checking? The informal organization will become legitimized only if it can work efficiently and effectively. Effective informal processes can be an important input to developing future formal work processes.

Compare Organization Map with Enterprise Process Map

In comparing the Organization Map with the Enterprise Process Map, we should realize that we are documenting the same organization using two different charting techniques; the organization map uses traditional organization charts while the process map uses IDEF0 or similar flow-charting technique. Regardless of the techniques, the organization is the same and the two charting techniques should tell us so. If there is a difference between the two, we should analyze the difference, conduct a partial survey if warranted, find which technique is in error, and correct the error. We are much more interested in finding and correcting the errors in the process map than we are in the organization charts. The process map will be the basis for all future technical and social redesign, while the organization charts will soon be discarded.

The partial survey should provide the most accurate indication of the existing organization. The survey should especially be conducted in those areas where the organization charts and process map differ.

ANALYZE THE EXISTING ORGANIZATION STRUCTURE

The Functional or Vertical Organization

Under industrialization, bureaucracy was the dominant form of organization. The factory was designed to produce standardized products; the bureaucracy, to produce standardized decisions. Most major corporations developed in an industrial society, based on a bureaucratic model of machine-like division of function, routine activity, permanence, and a very long vertical hierarchy. It was a world of mass markets, uniform goods and services, and long production runs.

Unfortunately, the vertical organization, a fixture of the Industrial Revolution and the hallmark of many of the world's largest businesses, is still the most prevalent type of management structure for medium- and large-scale organizations. The vertical organization is characterized by extensive hierarchies, approval committees, and often snail's-pace decision making. Long response times are required to send information up line and back down line in order to make even basic decisions.

The vertical organization also exhibits resistance to change due to the inherent justification process necessary for investment and to the political strife caused by the isolation of hierarchical structures. The management theorist Peter Drucker refers to these many layers of management in a vertical organization as "boosters, amplifying the very faint signals that come up and down through the organization."

Hierarchies are the best way to segregate people within functions and ultimately to create distrust and isolation. Worst of all, hierarchies close the door to new experiences and evolution by reducing the opportunity for process mutation. If you lock the process up within a confined ecosystem, it will never keep pace with the shifting market climates it inhabits.

Problems with the Traditional Functional Organization

Functional Structure Over-Emphasizes Vertical Relationships. The functional structure promotes the idea that one's boss is the prime customer to be satisfied. Each manager is more interested in satisfying the next-level manager than the real customer. Managers in functional organizations are usually rewarded for satisfying functional goals, such as meeting design deadlines and limiting manufacturing costs, rather than for providing value to customers. This emphasis on vertical reporting relationships to the exclusion of horizontal coordination has led many authors to refer to departments in functional organizations as "chimneys" or "silos."

Functional Structure Separates Employees from Customers. Few employees in the functional organization have direct contact with the customers or even a clear idea of how their work combines with the work of others to satisfy customers. The functional structure tends to insulate employees from learning about customer expectations and their degree of satisfaction with the service or product the firm is providing. Being insulated from customers encourages workers to hold a narrow conception of their responsibilities.

Functional Structure Inhibits Process Improvement. No organizational unit has control over a whole process, although many processes involve a large number of functions. This is because the breakup of the organization into functions is usually unrelated to the processes used to deliver a product to the customer. This structure is likely to create complex wasteful processes, as people do things in one area that must be redone or undone in another. This deficiency is especially important, since the product development process is one of the major processes of an innovative organization.

The Functional Structure Hinders Creativity and Innovation. The functional structure not only hinders an organization's innovativeness but also has a strong negative effect on the creativity and innovativeness of the individual. People feel they cannot change their environment and thus never seek the information and ideas that might change it.

Specific Deficiencies of Your Organization

The preceding two sections discussed the general problems facing most organizations today. However, your organization has undoubtedly experienced specific problems in addition to those listed. They should be documented here to ensure they are corrected in the future design. Following are some areas that should be investigated for possible organizational problems:

- Units with poor results in benchmarking, as conducted in Chapter 7
- Areas with low performance/productivity
- Areas with high conflict
- Areas resistant to change
- Areas with low morale
- Areas with high turnover

DIAGNOSE FUTURE ORGANIZATION NEEDS

Sources of Future Needs

Expressions of need for the future organization structure come primarily from four sources: the company vision, the company's mission and strategies, the company's cultural ideology, and the technical redesign effort—particularly the enterprise concept. The enterprise concept is the most important source of requirements. The SMG must design an organization structure that is capable of managing the process work structure developed by the TMG in their Enterprise Concept. The cultural ideology defines what kind of organization is desired in the future. This will greatly influence the organization structure and the structure of jobs. The company's vision and strategies will have some effect on the organization structure but not nearly as much as the Enterprise Concept or the company's ideology.

The Future Requires Process Organization

The primary purpose of the technical effort is to redesign the company's work processes so that work is accomplished effectively in the future. Concurrently we must redesign the management organization structure so that it can effectively manage the work processes.

Process management has a common overriding purpose: to produce a product for the customer. This purpose is the key to weaving a process horizontally across the firm so that all parts work in unison and not at cross-purposes. Process management and organization is a horizontal technique and structure that operates across vertical functional boundaries to achieve corporate-wide goals and objectives. It provides an approach to implementing important boundary-spanning solutions to meet organization-wide needs.

In process management, the stress on process, or how to align all the operations of the company in order to best produce a product for the customer, is far different from the emphasis of functional management. The customer-focused company has no choice; it must look at itself from the customer's perspective and then reorganize itself by process to best satisfy the customer's requirements.

For process management ideas to flourish, several rules need to be widely understood by managers and workers. The first rule is that product and service requirements are customer focused. Doing only what the producer thinks best is no longer viable in markets crowded with competitors. The second rule is continuous process improvement or the steady monitoring and correction of problems as they occur. Standing still is not a competitive strategy. The third rule is collaboration, concurrency, and integration in the management of work activities across the entire process. This leads not only to improved horizontal communications, but also to shorter development cycle time and to greater quality of work.

These new rules of the game—customer focus, continuous improvement, collaboration, concurrency, and integration—are forcing a new management style upon us. Central to it is the joining of managers and workers horizontally in process teams across their companies. To do this, more and more firms are turning to process management as the principal method for making improvements and stimulating innovative solutions.

A process management team's responsibility is to optimize information flows across departmental barriers. This runs against decades of corporate (and broad cultural) development that actively encouraged specialization and compartmentalization as desirable ends. Greater and greater specialization of activities breeds withdrawal into smaller and smaller social units more and more insulated from one another. The counterpoint to this trend is the belief of process management that the goal should be to maximize the opportunity for human interaction, rather than limit contact. Since one purpose of human interaction is to exchange information, a corollary could be that the purpose of the process organization is, also, to maximize the opportunity for information exchange.

It must be emphasized that process management is not the conventional two-boss matrix management with the vertical functions on one axis and project managers on the other. Neither is it a patchwork of disciplines brought together as an ad hoc team. It is a deliberate effort to build a structure and a process that enables communication and action to occur horizontally across the organization. The ability to undertake coordinated horizontal action and communication is crucial.

The Future Requires Team-Based Organization

Will Future Organizations Require Individuals or Groups as Building Blocks?

In building organizations we can use either individuals or groups as the primary building block. Following are some of the key characteristics that define the two sets of building blocks.[1] When individuals are rewarded for individual performance, informal groups work to go around the system and team playing is only rhetoric; the building blocks are individuals. In organizations where individuals are rewarded for their contribution to a group, where "being a team player" is an actual condition of employment, and where formal groups are used to get the work done, the building blocks are groups.

The building blocks selected will determine many characteristics of the organization. For example, how are salaries and wages determined? Are people paid for their individual performance or for overall group results and their contributions to those results? What sort of behavior is rewarded? Are people encouraged to pitch in and solve problems to get results, or are they rewarded for individual behavior that is not related to results? Are exhortations such as "be a team player" indicative of a real condition of employment? Or are they merely rhetoric?

J. Richard Hackman has described four situations in which group-based designs are probably more appropriate than individually based structures.[2] First he believes that groups are more appropriate when a high degree of interdependence is required to get work done. Hackman adds three other conditions. Groups, he says, are more appropriate as building blocks when meaningful individual work is not possible, when individuals have strong social needs, and when the motivating potential is higher in a group. All three of these conditions are closely related to the issue of motivation.

Many jobs, especially short jobs in sequential relationships, lose their meaning. If I tighten a few bolts and pass the work on to you and if you do the same, neither of us will find much meaning in our jobs. Often, a group design will allow people to work together to build an entire product or perform a complete service, solve problems as they go, and see the results of their work in the finished product or satisfied customer.

In the redesigned organization, the building block will be primarily the group, as discussed in Chapter 12. Understanding what building blocks are used in the existing organization will facilitate the transition to the new organization.

Advantages of Team-Based Organization

What are the advantages of a team-based organization as compared to the more conventional organization based on individual building blocks? In the following paragraphs we will find that organizations institute teams because they expect higher quality, productivity, and profits, greater flexibility and responsiveness to change, and better ability to hire and keep highly qualified employees.

Higher Quality, Productivity, and Profits. To establish and maintain a competitive edge in the quality of their goods and services, organizations should continually make improvements. These incremental improvements to products and processes will most likely be made when employees at all levels are directly involved in the quality effort, as in the case of teamwork. Employees on teams also tend to deliver high quality because their involvement and authority make them highly committed. Frito Lay, for example, has reported significant improvement in quality and cost since it introduced the use of work teams.

Teams improve productivity in the same way they improve quality; that is, they give employees a means by which they can make continuous improvements in work processes. These improvements should improve employees' efficiency as well as the quality of their outputs. When quality and productivity rise, so do profits. Teamwork also raises profitability by reducing costs. For organizations that seek to cut costs by eliminating layers of management, decision making is transferred to employees further down the hierarchy. Teams are a structure within which such decision making can take place successfully.

Greater Flexibility. Successful organizations excel by meeting the specialized needs of their customers. They tailor their products and delivery schedules to each customer's requirements. As a result, organizations today must be flexible. For manufacturers, this means producing small batches on short schedules.

Teams can improve flexibility because team members' broad skills and job descriptions enable them to adapt quickly. Switching to a different order or addressing new customer needs is routine for such a team. Team members have the skills, information, and authority to direct their expertise and commitment toward satisfying those needs.

Greater Responsiveness to Change. Not only must the organization be responsive to variations in customer demand, but it must be able to respond to broader environmental changes. Thanks largely to global competition and technological advances, today's environment is more turbulent. Furthermore, the drive to efficiency has closely integrated the organization's operations. A change affecting one area of the organization quickly has a major impact on other areas. For the organization to respond rapidly, the employees involved in implementing strategies must also be involved in planning those strategies. A logical way to create the necessary involvement is to use teams.

The rapid pace of change in today's environment also means that many organizations are finding they can operate most efficiently by assigning people—employees or contractors—to work on specific projects, then disbanding the team when the project is completed. In other words, these organizations use project teams.

Better Ability to Attract and Retain Good Employees. Effective use of teamwork can make an organization more attractive to current and potential employees. Teamwork offers a chance to meet social needs and enjoy a sense of involvement and achievement. It can make work more interesting, is a good fit with the high value modern employees place on participation in decision making, and provides an opportunity to do something meaningful.

When teamwork makes an organization a more attractive employer, it enables the organization to hire and keep the best people. Also, employees will be reluctant to leave such an organization. While they are with the organization, they can use their participation on a team as a means to contribute in many ways to realizing the organization's objectives.

The Future Requires Networked Organizations

The alternative to corporate bureaucracy is not merely training managers to behave in an empowering way within a bureaucratic structure; it is developing a system of freedoms and institutions analogous to free enterprise, a system of organization that we will call the free *intraprise* network. Free *intraprise* empowers ordinary employees to start a "business" (or intraprise) within the organization if they can find the customers and the capital to do so.

When employees create an intraprise, the form of control changes from dependence on the hierarchy to interdependence with customers and suppliers. Customers, not bureaucrats, are the basic controllers of the free enterprise and free intraprise systems alike. Rather than having a bureaucrat decide, free choices by buyers and sellers throughout the network determine what is needed, what is cost-effective, and what creates the most value. Because there are many different potential customers, an intraprise no longer rises or falls on the opinion of one bureaucrat.

The overall pattern of a 21st-century organization is a network of interdependent intraprises and their associated internal and external customers and suppliers. Some intraprises focus on serving external customers directly, such as the product order and delivery system. Others focus on serving internal customers. Internal intraprises created to serve internal customers can do so more efficiently than bureaucratic departments ever could. Large businesses can consist of relatively small numbers of externally focused intraprises served by a network of internal intraprises.

Within these fluid structures, employees work in self-managing teams, functioning with great autonomy as long as their work is compatible with the mission, values, and objectives of the organization. Some teams are more or less fixed, working together over long spans of time. Others form spontaneously—across functions and levels, even across organizational boundaries—to solve problems and produce innovations, then disband once they have achieved their goals. The product development team is one of the more important of these temporary teams that form and function long enough to achieve its purpose and then disband.

We see the organizational structure of the future as some form of network in which employees are free to move in any direction, even across boundaries of function and level, to link up with anyone to accomplish a task. However, we should not fall into the trap of thinking that a transformed organization will assume only one form. The same organization may adopt many different forms over time, and many different structures may emerge within a single organization as it attempts to accommodate continuous change. It is probably more true to say that networking will be the glue that holds the organization together than to suggest that a particular network structure will be the primary form of organization.

The network organization has the advantage that it can achieve business focus, responsiveness, and, at the same time, reasonable economies of scale. Externally-oriented intraprises have a choice among external and internal suppliers which goes a long way toward ensuring responsiveness. Because of the flexibility of the network, technology and market information moves easily among the intraprises and among various parts of the organization.

A **virtual** organization is an expanded form of the network organization. The virtual organization is simply a network organization that extends beyond the enterprise's legal boundaries. According to William Davidow and Michael S. Malone, authors of *The Virtual Corporation*, the hallmarks of the virtual organization are:

• formerly well defined structures begin to lose their edges;
• seemingly permanent things start to change continuously; and
• products and services adapt to match consumers' desires.[3]

The primary benefit of virtuality is the reduction of organizational response time. The liability is the cultural impediment created whenever an enterprise adopts any structure, namely, that markets change faster than the ability of most enterprise cultures to respond. Many managers and workers misconstrue the virtual corporation, believing that it has no structure and everyone has access to everyone else. It's a wonderful vision, but it's not reality. There has to be some structure.

DEVELOP THE FUTURE ORGANIZATION CONCEPT

Introduction

Early in the transformation effort the SMG should develop the framework for future organization structure. A broad outline of the new organization is needed to provide guidance to (1) the process redesign teams, (2) the teams developing team and individual role descriptions, (3) the human resources planning effort, and (4) the teams working on people support processes.

Sufficient information is not available to develop a detailed organization structure. However, the information available from the Strategic Plan, the Cultural Plan, and the Enterprise Concept developed by the TMG should be sufficient to permit developing an *organization concept*. The detail of the organization concept is midway between a vision and a design. It provides a "who does what" overview of the new process-led enterprise, showing how work is allocated across different processes and teams. Like the enterprise concept, it is very much a creative exercise, seeking to develop the most appropriate organization on a "clean sheet."

In the course of developing the enterprise concept and the organization concept, the TMG and the SMG should work closely with each other since their efforts are so interdependent. They will essentially serve as design review activities for each other. Concentration on a single project for a long period of time can result in "tunnel vision" where the project team can no longer see objectively. Design reviews solve this problem by bringing in a second team that provides a fresh look.

Guidelines for Developing the Future Organization Concept

To provide assistance in developing your organization concept, some organization design guidelines are offered in the following section. These guidelines are based on the experience of a number of companies. They should not be considered all-inclusive and should not be considered as mandatory—they are simply guidelines based on the experience of others. These guidelines will cover the following general areas:

- Build the structure around processes, not functions.
- Use teams as the basic building block of the organization.

- Use networking as the basic organization approach.
- Consider that organizational boundaries are permeable.

Build the Structure Around Processes, Not Functions

Companies must do away with the traditional vertical structures that solidify power bases and management control while creating obstacles for employees who need access to one another to complete the process. Instead, they must create new, flatter, less hierarchical structures based on the goal of getting the right information in the hands of the right people at the right time. Because work teams will serve as the building blocks for this new, flatter structure it is important to remember that the organization should be such that work teams receive the information and support necessary to complete their process in the most effective manner.

During technical redesign, the TMG will completely redesign the core processes of the enterprise. At the time the SMG should change the structure of the management organization to facilitate work teams delivering value to their customers without the hindrance of functional and hierarchical structures.

The new structure, therefore, must be one that is built by using the core processes and work teams as the foundation. You may add support layers, pools of experts, or management positions to the organizational structure only if these additions provide value in added services to the teams and hence to customers. Layers of management, groups, or individuals that do not provide value should not become part of the structure. This only increases your costs and will lead you to a common problem in organizations today, information overload. By designing the structure from the bottom up, rather than from the top down, you can eliminate the unwanted accumulation of data and information that flows down through the structure. This will then free the work teams to focus on the information they need to get the job done.

In the transformed organization, however, there should be a single manager both responsible and accountable for each process: the process owner. The process owner is the lowest-level manager responsible for the entire process. This does not necessarily mean that all of the people involved in the process report to the process owner. What this does mean is that one manager is responsible and accountable for the process; that manager's performance evaluation and incentive compensation depend on the success of the process. Although the number of organizational boundaries traversed by the reengineered process will be reduced, the process may still cross into other managerial domains. The process owner is expected to negotiate with and coordinate with the managers whose domain the process crosses.

There are many advantages to having a single process owner responsible for each process.[4] The greater the scope of ownership the teams have and the greater the reliance on information technology systems, the less hierarchy is needed to link together the activities of these teams. With this new, flatter hierarchy in place it will become clearer how the activities of each support group are linked together and how they are delivering increasing value to their customers.

Given the increasing costs and complexity associated with information technology systems, organizations cannot afford to create structures that serve as obstacles that employees must navigate around to accomplish their work. Instead, organizations should be investing their financial resources to build structures developed by the teams that open communication channels and increase interaction between employees who need to share ideas, information, and best practices.

Use Teams as the Basic Element of the Organization

Modern organizations should use teams as the basic building blocks at all levels.[5] Rather than a rigid formal structure, the organization will be more organic, adapting to changing conditions and the current workload. Most productive work will be accomplished by small teams assisted by technology support. Many teams will have full-time and part-time members who live and work remote from the team's home base, but extensive communication systems will make this completely practical. Ubiquitous electronic communications will allow the organization to be reshaped as the work requires. Which distribution lists one is on and to which data files one has access will be more important than to whom one reports. In fact, a much more accurate picture of the "real" organization will be obtained by analyzing its electronic mail traffic than its organization chart.

Sub-units and teams should be relatively autonomous in comparison to previous organizational eras. Rather than providing traditional supervision, managers will coach, assist with problem solving, and provide linkage to top management, to other organizational units, or to other organizations as required. Teams will have much more latitude to solve problems and much greater access to resources than in the past. Specialized resources, if necessary, will be assigned to teams (rather than to their managers). Because of the reduction of traditional supervisory responsibilities, organizations will tend to be flat, with few middle managers overall.

With large numbers of autonomous teams doing the work, norms and values rather than rules and direct supervision will furnish the cohesion necessary to provide direction and achieve coordination. Leaders will thus spend an increasing amount of time and energy shaping the vision and values of the organization. In addition, organizational leaders will spend a significant amount of time focusing on the development of people, particularly in selecting team leaders and managers. In the more diffused organization, the principal means of control will be a strongly held culture and a network of individuals who use their own leadership skills to build the organization consistent with an overall vision.

An often-used approach is to create small teams of multitalented people with the authority to take action. The idea is to fill the corporation's knowledge reservoir by tapping underground springs of entrepreneurial creativity. It is not necessary to pile up resources to ensure the success of entrepreneurial teams, for they rely on innovation more than resources to reach project goals. Each team can rely on knowledge as its greatest asset and build its own business case as it progresses. If the team is to survive and be successful, it ultimately must pay its own way. Having a healthy sense of independence, self-reliance, and self-responsibility is the mark of a good team.

Use Networking as the Basic Organization Approach

While independence is a virtue for the work teams, connectedness is the goal. The role of the future organization is to provide points of connectivity by redefining roles and responsibilities, driving communication, rewarding achievements, and allowing penalty free failures. As more and more teams start succeeding and as team leaders continue building connectors across the teams, networks start to emerge. Those networks become the very core of the renewed organization and the basis of the future organizational growth.

They must cooperate with each other to survive in an increasingly competitive marketplace. Instead of the traditional firm containing all of the needed capabilities, future organizations will make various alliances to develop, produce, and market goods and services. More companies will evolve into a combination of wholly owned operations, alliances, joint ventures, spinouts, and acquired subsidiaries. They will be linked together in organizational networks that share values, people, information, and operating styles.

Organizations should make arrangements with all links in the value chain, including customers for intermediate products and finished goods and suppliers of raw materials, production technology, capital, and financial services. The need for arrangements will encourage lifelong competitors to collaborate, and, driven by arrangements, historical allies may occasionally find themselves positioned as competitive adversaries. Experimentation will be the rule, with successful innovation the objective. As in any period of active experimentation, however, we can expect many failures.

An increasing number of companies will find they cannot go it alone. They recognize the need to focus their talents, particular strengths, and resources on those areas in which they have a competitive advantage and let others perform functions that can be done better elsewhere. This will lead to the establishment of virtual organizations with alliances and joint ventures that can capitalize on and leverage the particular strengths of the individual partners. Virtual organizations with alliances and joint ventures will become a normal, accepted feature of organizational design.

Those companies that become particularly adept at shaping themselves to face uncertainty will evolve into a combination of wholly owned operations, alliances, joint ventures, spinouts, and acquired subsidiaries. They will not be holding companies, but will be linked together in organizational networks through shared values, people, technology, financial resources, and operating styles. Examples of such organizational networks are Benetton in Europe and Corning in the United States.

Consider That Organization Boundaries Are Permeable

Behavior patterns that today are constrained and blocked by long-standing boundaries between organizational levels and functions, between suppliers and customers, and between geographic locations will be replaced by patterns of free movement across these boundaries. No longer will organizations use boundaries to separate people, tasks, processes, and places; instead the focus will be on how to permeate those boundaries to quickly move ideas, information, decisions, talent, rewards, and actions to where they are most needed.[6] It is this freedom that will create and re-create the organization of the future.

This does not mean that an organization will not have boundaries. On the contrary, boundaries are necessary to separate people, processes, and production; to keep things focused and distinct; and to give the organization shape. However, instead of the relatively rigid boundaries that exist in most organizations today, the organization of the future will have permeable boundaries, like the flexible, movable membranes in a living, evolving organism. The enterprise needs to be fast and flexible, able to change directions quickly and nimbly and to innovate continuously. To do this, four types of boundaries need to be made more permeable and flexible:

Vertical—the Boundaries between Levels and Ranks of People. When vertical boundaries are made more permeable, position is less relevant than competence. This usually leads to faster and better decisions that are made closer to the action and more access to ideas from people anywhere in the organization.

Horizontal—the Boundaries between Functions and Disciplines. By increasing the permeability of horizontal boundaries, battles over turf and territory are replaced by a focus on how to meet customer needs. The collaboration across horizontal boundaries results in streamlined procedures and services for customers, leading to integrated approaches, simplified application procedures, and more effective total response.

External—the Boundaries between the Company and Its Suppliers, Customers, and Regulators. Traditionally, organizations form "we-they" relationships with external constituents and do business through negotiating, haggling, using pressure tactics, withholding information, and playing off customers or suppliers against one another. When this food chain mentality is replaced by a focus on the "value chain," tremendous efficiencies and innovations can be introduced into the entire product or service supply system.

Geographic—the Boundaries between Locations, Cultures, and Markets. Often stemming from national pride, cultural differences, market peculiarities, or worldwide logistics, these boundaries may isolate innovative ideas and lead to competition between headquarters and the field. When geographic boundaries are made more permeable, companies can more rapidly leverage global successes.

Finalizing the Organization Concept

In this section we will finalize the organization concept by specifying how the three main elements of management (leadership, work management, and personnel development) will be accomplished and by specifying the format of the organization concept. Leadership is necessary to get people to work and pull together in the same direction. Work management is necessary to ensure that the right work is done by the right people in the right time frame in the right way. Personnel development is necessary to obtain the skills, knowledge, and orientation of employees to ensure the supply of qualified employees.

Leadership, Work Management, and Personnel Development

In the transformed organization, there is a single manager both responsible and accountable for the process: the process owner. The process owner is the lowest-level manager responsible for the entire process. This does not necessarily mean that all of the people involved in the process report to the process owner. What this does mean is that one manager is responsible and accountable for the process; that manager's performance evaluation and incentive compensation depend on the success of the process. The process owner is expected to negotiate with and coordinate with the managers whose domain the process crosses. Normally the process owner is also the team leader, except when the process is large enough to require two or more teams.

Our task is to identify the process owners and team leaders and their responsibilities for work management and personnel development, to define team leadership, and to assess the need for supervisory management above the process owner. In most companies, there is an informal organizational structure that informally assigns management responsibilities to those individuals better able to perform them than those officially recognized in the formal organizational structure. If we structure the new organization correctly, the differences between the formal and informal organizations ought to vanish.

Transformation usually designs organizations that are "flatter" than they were before. That is, they contain fewer management levels. Since all employees are empowered, more of them are responsible for managing their own work or are part of self-managed teams, so their managers have less responsibility for work management. As a result, each manager can supervise more people. In a transformed organization, it is not uncommon to see managers with ten to twenty direct reports, as compared with the three to seven common in traditional organizations.

We should design the organizational structure to ensure that each team resides within a single organization and to reduce the number of organizational boundaries traversed by the process. The work teams defined to perform the redesigned processes are essentially different from project teams selected to redesign processes. The project design teams are assembled for specific purposes for a specific period of time and then return to their home organizations.

The work teams, by contrast, are permanent features of the process (at least of the current version of the process). They are usually designed to perform activities, sub-processes, or the entire process, that is, repetitive work, rather than a project. Because of the team's durability and the repetitive nature of its work, the members of the team must be located within the same organization, have the same leadership, and ideally, have their personnel development provided from the same source. Some organizations have attempted to use process teams whose members continued to reside in their former functional areas, but this has all of the disadvantages and ambiguities of other forms of "matrix management."

Format of the Organization Concept

The organization concept should contain the following information:

- Identify the time and place where new teams will be formed. This information should be available from the enterprise concept.
- Estimate the number and required skills of team members, team leaders, and process owners.
- Draw the management network that is above process owners and team leaders.
- Estimate the number and qualifications of managers in the management network.
- Indicate how the new process organization will interface with the existing organization.

The organization concept should be sufficiently detailed that (1) top-level management can understand and evaluate it, (2) operating personnel can understand how they would work in the organization, and (3) human resource planners can plan for the human resources to actuate the concept.

DIAGNOSE HUMAN RESOURCE REQUIREMENTS

The organization concept is of little use if we have no people to fill the positions. In this section we will discuss the process to obtain the necessary people. The diagnosis of human resource requirements systematically reviews human resource requirements in detail to ensure that the required number of employees, with the required skills, are available when they are needed. It is the process of matching the internal and external supply of people with job openings anticipated in the organization over a specified period of time. Strategic planning, cultural planning, technical redesign, and organization concept development precede the diagnosis of human resources.

Forecasting human resource requirements involves determining the number and type of employees needed, by skill level and location. These projections will reflect various factors, such as production plans and changes in organization. When employee requirements and availability have been analyzed, the firm can determine whether it will have a surplus or shortage of employees. Ways must be found to reduce the number of employees if a surplus is projected. Some of these methods include restricted hiring, reduced hours, early retirements, and layoffs. If a shortage is forecast, the firm must obtain the proper quantity and quality of workers outside the organization. External recruitment and selection is required.

Steps in Diagnosing Human Resource Requirements

1. *Determine Current Staffing Status.* What are the present skills available, performance adequacies and deficiencies, selection needs, and retention problems? This description should include general problem-solving and interpersonal competencies in addition to specific technical needs.

2. *Identify Present Needs.* What are the current human resource demands? What skills are currently in demand? What are the usual sources of supply for required skills (internal/external)? Are they adequate? Can skills be developed in current employees? Can skill use be improved?

3. *Forecast Future Needs.* What numbers and skills will be needed in the future? Combine information from step 2 (present needs) and the future needs. The primary source of future needs is the organization concept discussed earlier in this chapter. Additional information on future needs can be obtained from the Enterprise Concept, Cultural Plan, and Strategic Plan.

4. *Forecast Future Supply.* In order to forecast availability, the human

resource manager looks to both internal sources (presently employed employees) and external sources (the labor market).

5. *Analyze Gap between Future Needs and Future Supply.* Will the traditional sources be adequate for future needs? Should basic sources be changed? Can the organization develop what it now recruits? Should it recruit what it now develops? What changes might affect our implementation of a strategic human resource plan?

6. *Design and Implement Programs to Close Gap.* Programs will be needed in areas such as recruitment, training, and promotion to enable the organization to satisfy its human resource needs.

In this chapter, we will be primarily concerned with the last four steps, particularly as they involve the enterprise concept and the organization concept. We will assume that the Human Resources Department has already accomplished steps 1 and 2 in a competent manner.

Forecasting Future Needs

The most important and most detailed source of personnel requirements is the organization concept. This document should spell out what kinds of personnel are required where and when. This is the prime requirements document that personnel planners will use in conducting their diagnosis. The second most important requirements document is the enterprise concept that describes the future work structure of the company. The strategic plan that outlines the company's long-range strategic plan for developing value propositions and competencies can be of some help in the long-range requirements.

The development of team and job roles in Chapter 12 will provide much more accurate information regarding the number and qualifications of team members. However, we cannot wait until then to commence our forecasting. We need to start our forecasting now with the information we have, and then update our forecast when more accurate information becomes available.

Forecasting Human Resource Supplies

Although supply forecasts can be derived from both internal and external sources of information, internal information is generally most crucial and more readily available. Once made, the supply forecast can be compared with its demand counterpart to help determine action programming for identifying human resource talent and balancing supply and demand forecasts.

Two judgmental techniques used by organizations to make supply forecasts are *replacement* and *succession* planning. Replacement planning develops replacement charts to show the names of the current occupants of positions in the organization and the names of likely replacements. These charts make it readily apparent where potential vacancies exist and what types of positions most urgently need to be filled. Such a listing can provide the organization with a good estimate of what jobs are likely to become vacant and who will be ready to fill them. In the case of transformation, there will be a number of positions that have never been filled before. These we can treat as vacant positions, giving them the highest priority in the replacement planning system. Succession planning is similar to replacement planning except that it is usually longer term and more developmental and offers greater flexibility.

Analyzing Gap between Future Needs and Future Supply

The first task is to determine the quantity and direction of the gap each year. If the supply is greater than the need in a particular year, that means a program must be initiated to reduce the number of personnel. On the other hand, if the need is greater than the supply, which it normally is, there must be some program to acquire additional personnel. The gap must be stated in terms of skills as well as numbers. We might have an excess of personnel overall but be horribly short in computer engineers. When the gap has been fully defined, it becomes our *Human Resources Requirements* document.

If we have a need for personnel, the question arises as to whether we can recruit them from the labor market or will have to train them in house. If they are not available from the open market, we have no choice. Even if they are available from the labor market, we may elect to train and promote our own people to better motivate the workforce, if the time is available to do the training.

Human Resource Programs

After assessing an organization's human resource needs, action programming must be developed to serve these needs. Such programs may be designed to increase the supply of the right employees in the organization (if forecasts show that demand exceeds supply) or to decrease the number of current employees (if the forecasts show that supply exceeds demand). Although many alternative programs could be proposed and evaluated to address these purposes, only one is presented here, a downsizing program.

Athough the goal of transformation is not to reduce the labor force, the technical redesign often results in lowered labor requirements. With the need for massive layoffs in the past few years (because of economic or technological conditions), organizations have become increasingly sensitive in dealing with the effects of layoffs on employees and are trying to either minimize these effects or eliminate the necessity for layoffs. Attempts to minimize these effects are reflected in redundancy planning. Redundancy planning is essentially personnel planning associated with the process of laying off employees who are no longer needed (that is, they are redundant). Involved in this planning may be outplacement counseling, buyouts, job skill retraining opportunities, and job transfer opportunities. Although redundancy planning has been limited to companies in a few industries, some suggest that the increasing level of international competition will require that this be done in all industries.

NOTES

1. Emily E. Schultheiss, *Optimizing the Organization: How to Link People and Technology* (Ballinger, 1989).

2. J. Richard Hackman, "Work Design," in J. Richard Hackman, Edward W. Lawler III, and Lyman Porter (eds.), *Perspectives on Behavior in Organizations* (McGraw-Hill, 1977), pp. 242–256.

3. William Davidow and Michael S. Malone, *The Virtual Corporation* (HarperBusiness, 1992).

4. Christopher W. Head, *Beyond Corporate Transformation* (Productivity Press, 1997).

5. Francis J. Gouillart and James H. Kelly, *Transforming the Organization: Reframing, Restructuring, Revitalizing, and Renewing* (McGraw-Hill, 1995).

6. Ron Ashkenas et al., *The Boundaryless Organization: Breaking the Chains of Organizational Structure* (Jossey-Bass, 1995).

CHAPTER 12

Detailed Social Redesign
of the Organization

INTRODUCTION

In Chapter 11, we performed a broad design of the organization that resulted in the Organizational Concept. In this chapter we expand upon the Organizational Concept and develop a detailed design. We do this primarily by using the results of the Detailed Technical Process Designs of Chapter 8 in conjunction with the Organizational Concept. The result is a team-based organization that will optimally accomplish the organization's processes while providing the basis for a learning organization.

PREPARING FOR THE TEAM-BASED ORGANIZATION

When workers have been working in the traditional hierarchical organization for some time, they are not prepared to operate in the more democratic team-based network organization. They are not accustomed to working autonomously and making their own decisions. To ensure the success of the team-based organization we need to prepare all employees for operating in it before we implement it.

This can best be done by implementing employee involvement and employee empowerment before implementing the team-based organization. In employee involvement the transition to the new way of operating can be accomplished more gradually in order to reduce the stress and resistance to change of the worker. *Employee involvement is worthwhile in its own right, but it is absolutely essential if you hope to successfully change to a team-based organization.*

Employee Involvement and Empowerment

Employee involvement is a way of engaging employees at all levels in the thinking processes of an organization. It's the recognition that many decisions made in an organization can be made better by soliciting the input of those who may be affected by the decision. It's an understanding that people at all levels of an organization possess unique talents, skills, and creativity that can be of significant value if allowed to be expressed.

Employee empowerment is employee involvement that matters. It's the difference between just having an input and having an input that is heard, seriously considered, and followed up on whether it is accepted or not. The objective of empowerment is to tap the creative and intellectual energy of everybody in the company, not just those in the executive suite, and to provide everyone with the responsibility and the resources to display real leadership within their own individual spheres of competence. In summary, empowerment is *the capability to make a difference in the attainment of individual, team, and organizational goals.*

Most employee involvement systems fail within the first year. The reason is simple; they involve but do not empower employees. Without empowerment, involvement is just another management tool that does not work. For empowerment to occur, companies must undertake two initiatives: (1) identify and change organizational conditions that make people powerless and (2) increase people's confidence that their efforts to accomplish something important will be successful. The need to do both implies that organizational systems often create powerless employees and that these systems must be changed first.

Systems especially needing change are those that specify who can (and cannot) make certain types of decisions. Even when systems are changed to permit empowerment, some individuals who have lived under the old system for a long time are not readily able to operate in an empowered manner. All employees need to be convinced that they can really make a difference and should therefore fully utilize their empowerment.

Empowerment is important primarily because it improves organizational performance. Everyone in an organization is an asset, albeit an asset whose value is not automatically realized. If money is put into a closet instead of a bank, it will not produce results (interest). Similarly, if employees are locked into an organizational closet by restrictive rules that make them powerless, they cannot produce creative and productive results.

Every employee should be empowered with the right and the responsibility to take daily and consistent action to enhance and improve the quality of products and service provided. "Every employee" means just that—everyone from the newest hire to the oldest veteran, from the highest manager to the lowest employees. The idea is that all employees will take the initiative to consistently examine their own work to ensure that it is being produced or provided defect free on a regular basis.

The Essence of Empowerment

Empowerment has two major aspects: direction and capability.[1] These are the two essentials of power; if we lack either one, power disappears. If we know what we are trying to accomplish (that is, we have direction) but lack capability, we will not accomplish our goal. For example, if a software design team has the goal of completing a fully compatible systems architecture in three months but does not have the necessary programming skills, it will not be able to accomplish its goal. Similarly, if a software team has state-of-the art programming skills but no clearly agreed-upon product definition, it will not be able to successfully execute its design task. We will discuss both direction and capability in the pages that follow.

Direction

Having a clear organizational direction is empowering for two major reasons. *First*, it focuses attention and energy. People know where they are supposed to be going, and they can work with others to get there. If there is no direction or if the direction is unclear, collective energy gets so dissipated that coordinated action cannot occur. Second, having a clear organizational direction provides an opportunity for individuals to relate their personal objectives to organizational objectives. Individuals can derive personal meaning from their interpretation of organization objectives; they can fulfill their own aspirations in the process of working to meet business objectives.

Capability

Teams are empowered when they have the following:

*The **knowledge** and **skills** (technical, business, interpersonal, and organizational) required to contribute to team and business-unit performance.* Members of teams need to have the technical competence to do their part of the collective task and the willingness to continually learn so that they do not become obsolete.

***Information** from various sources: organization, business unit, and team.* Information is needed about competitors, customer requirements, resource availability, and upcoming technology and organization changes.

*The **material resources,** including space, time, and equipment, required to perform work well.* Without access to the appropriate resources, people cannot perform well. Adequate resources are an important component of capability.

*The **authority to make decisions** about how the team does its work and to impact decisions made elsewhere that affect the team's work.* Decision-

Figure 12-1
Employee Involvement Methods

Information Sharing Methods
- Information Sharing
- Education and Training
- Survey Feedback

       Idea Generation Methods
       - Suggestion Systems
       - Idea-Generation Groups

              Group Problem Solving Methods
              - Ad Hoc Task Teams
              - Quality Circles

                     Work Redesign Methods
                     - Process Management
                     - Autonomous Networked Teams

making should take place where the expertise resides. This is generally as close as possible to where services and products are produced and often involves multiple interdependencies.

Methods of Employee Involvement

Employee involvement should be viewed as an organizational culture change effort, which must be supported by a strong management commitment, a long-term perspective, and reinforcing organizational systems. Although we should never assume that merely using involvement methods will result in employee involvement, involvement methods do play an important part. Methods provide us with mechanisms that enable employees to become involved in a structured way. Ultimately, we would like to reach a state where employees are involved in problem solving and decision making informally on a day-to-day basis. Until we get there, we must facilitate involvement through organized, structured mechanisms so that the organization can gain some experience and skills in employee involvement.

Because involvement methods are vital elements in our cultural change strategy, it is important that we utilize them intelligently. There are a wide variety of involvement methods, and they vary greatly in terms of their sophistication, organizational support requirements, and effectiveness in supporting change. Given the wide variety of employee involvement methods, it is useful to organize them along a continuum from *information sharing* to *work redesign* as indicated in Figure 12-1.

At the upper left of the continuum are those methods that are relatively simple that can be implemented without a major commitment of management time and resources and can reasonably be effective in a traditional hierarchical organization. The work redesign methods at the lower right of the continuum represent the state of the art in employee involvement—they truly represent *employee empowerment*. They are highly sophisticated, and because they represent a radical departure from traditional management practices, they require extremely high levels of management commitment. They should not even be considered by an organization that is a novice in employee involvement.

Our goal is to educate and train workers so they can work effectively in the area shown in the lower right corner in *autonomous networked teams*, which are the building blocks of the team-based organization.

DESIGNING WORK TEAMS

The end result of the work team design process is somewhat different from that of the technical design process.[2] Technical design results in a tangible object—a software application or a computer system. Work team designs exist primarily on paper, that is, they will consist largely of plans and proposals to be implemented as actual working arrangements and structures in the final organization. Work teams are responsible for producing products or providing services. Unlike the *design* teams, they perform regular, ongoing work. The continuing, predictable, and well-defined nature of their work is their most important characteristic and the one that most strongly influences their design.

Determining the composition and selecting the leaders and members of the *social design teams* that will design new work teams is a highly important responsibility of the Social Management Group. The procedures for team formation outlined in Chapter 5, including having a virtual team to assist the core team, should be followed. The team should be composed of primarily Human Resources and User type people with an Information Technology member if the work team will be using IT.

For best results it is recommended that the social team and the technical team for a specific process be integrated into one team responsible for both the technical design and social design of the process. This approach will achieve better results with fewer people and less time. However, if an integrated project team is not feasible for some reason, it is recommended that the social project team designing the work team should work alongside and in parallel with the technical project team redesigning the process. For those processes for which the technical process redesign has been completed, the technical redesign will be the primary source of information for designing the work team.

Inputs to Work Team Design

The primary inputs available to social project teams designing Work Teams are:

- Inputs directly from the Technical Process Redesign Team during redesign
- The Technical Process Redesign, if already completed
- The Enterprise Concept
- The Organization Concept
- Human Resources Requirements

Composition of Work Teams

Work team members should possess not only the skills they need to fill their assigned roles on the team but also some of the skills of other members so that they can cover for other members when they are absent or can help them when they are overloaded. Team members need cognitive skills as well, for problem solving, troubleshooting, and equipment repair. These cognitive skills will also come in handy as they tinker with and modify their new technology to fit their tasks and modify their tasks to take advantage of the unanticipated opportunities offered by the technology.

Because of the ongoing nature of the team's work, membership is usually fixed and permanent. The size of the team should be limited to the smallest number required to do the work effectively. Depending on the nature of the tasks and purpose, team members may be full- or part-time, working in the same location at approximately the same time (co-located) or not. For example, production team members typically need to be co-located, full-time members of the team.

Leadership

As work teams become more self-managed, the role of the immediate supervisor can change dramatically. In some cases it may be eliminated entirely, with the team reporting directly to the next level of management. Within the team, the supervisor is replaced by the team leader, a position that can be permanently assigned to a particular team member or rotated among some or all. Leadership can also be shared by several team members, with each providing leadership for different aspects of a team's work—technical, administrative, and so forth.

The leader of a self-managed team has a role very different from that of an immediate supervisor. The leader does not tell members what to do or how to do it and does not look over their shoulders to make sure they are doing it right. But self-management does not mean that the leader abdicates responsibility entirely. The appropriate position and approach lies somewhere in between. Leaders of self-managed teams should neither direct nor withdraw; they need to facilitate. Team leaders can foster self-management in three ways:

- *Task management* helps team members determine how they will complete their tasks; the leader provides coaching, consultation, and resources as needed.
- *Boundary management* helps members identify who they need to coordinate and communicate with outside the team; the leader acts as a liaison when necessary.
- *Performance Management* ensures that the team is involved in goal setting and that the goals are aligned with overall business objectives. The leader also sees that the team monitors its performance and steps in when it does not.

Whatever he or she does, the person serving in the team leader role should not perform traditional supervisory functions that can be handled by the team. This would defeat the purpose of the self-managed team and offset one of its most reliable benefits—helping reduce layers of management and supervision. In many cases, special training will be needed to help team leaders adjust to their new roles as coaches, facilitators, and liaisons.

External Connections

The external connections that are critical to work teams are those with others immediately "upstream" and "downstream" from them in the overall work process, whether they work for the same organization or not. This connection means more than receiving materials, subassemblies, or reports from their "suppliers," transforming or otherwise adding value to what they receive and sending it on to their "customers." It also means information about the work in progress—where it is in the process, scheduled completion, and so on—so that the team can coordinate activities and collaborate to solve problems. Work teams also need to maintain connections with those who support their work, such as technical people who fix their equipment, statistical experts who help them analyze data, graphic designers who help them prepare reports, human resources personnel who help them hire new team members, and others with specialized expertise and knowledge.

Information Resources

The more self-managed a team is, the more information and information tools it needs. Self-managed work teams require information about:

- task requirements and constraints;

- general and specific knowledge relevant to the nature and domain of their work (for instance, production cost breakdowns for different products); performance standards, and customer requirements;

- the responsibilities of each team member for certain tasks, the status of the work on each task, and the ways in which variances will effect other tasks;

- the strategic context of their work (for example, where their work fits into the overall process, business forecasts, information about their competitors); and

- experts and other resources that may be available to them—both inside and outside the organization.[3]

Information systems can also include tools for analyzing data and solving problems and a means of online feedback so that individual team members can monitor their individual performance and the performance of the team. New information systems can serve other team needs as well, including communicating with team members and linking the team with customers, suppliers, and those with needed expertise. Applications can also be developed to simulate the consequences of different strategies and actions so that they can make better-informed decisions about their work. All of this added capability can push decision making down or out to all members of the team, ultimately enabling the team to manage itself.

Implementing Work Teams

Simply putting a group of employees together to serve a customer will not create a work team. It certainly won't guarantee high-level performance. Unlike Frederick W. Taylor's scientific management, which broke down work activities into simplified and standardized pieces so management could oversee and control every aspect of employee work, work teams are designed to give employees *ownership* of a complete or large part of a process. This team-based work environment ensures that teams of employees throughout the organization are given direct responsibility for delivering value to customers.

This structure has two unique benefits. First, it pushes decision making downward to the employees who are closest to the customers. This utilizes the talent and skills of employees throughout the company and when combined with a system of process changes, almost always leads to increases in customer satisfaction. Equally important, this structure frees up management to focus on the longer-term strategic issues that are often delayed when management becomes too involved in running the day-to-day operations of the business.

What is needed for these teams to grow and prosper in your organization is the support of a *team management system*. Without a fully aligned and linked management system that continuously supports these natural work teams, the team structure will unravel and all but disappear. To survive and prosper, natural work teams need to have in place the following eight team management system elements:

1. Senior management support
2. Effective team leaders
3. Coaches to support the team leaders
4. Team training
5. Specific performance targets
6. Clearly defined responsibilities for ownership
7. Access to necessary information
8. Ongoing team performance evaluation

Two additional aspects of your organization need to change if you are to deliver the highest value to your customers. They are (1) designing a new performance measurement system and (2) linking compensation and rewards to team performance. These are discussed in greater detail in Chapter 13.

THE NETWORKED ORGANIZATION

Definitions

Many organizations are taking the opportunity to review what actual business they wish to be in, focus on core activity, and manage those elements that are non-core by contracting work to a network of suppliers, both first and second tier. This process is made more practical in many situations by powerful communication links. It also leads to the development of a complex web of relationships that can be described as the *networked organization*.

The networked organization is like a federation or a constellation of business units that are typically interdependent, relying on one another for critical expertise and know-how and having a peer relationship with the center. The center of the network provides the broad strategic vision, a shared organizational and administrative infrastructure, and a unity of mission and purpose. However, each business will see itself as the center of its own unique network within its own value chain.

The networked organization contrasts sharply with the traditional hierarchy. It also contrasts sharply with the concept of the vertically integrated supply chain that many organizations have striven to achieve as their strategy for reducing uncertainty in the supply market. The latter strategy is based on financial domination and control of key elements in the supply chain. Conversely, a network organization is a much more fluid set of arrangements between companies within a network of trading arrangements. The hub company may well at any time be competing with a particular company in some areas while at the same time cooperating in others. Some suppliers will be closely tied into the network, but others will be on the fringe with much looser relationships with the hub.

Electronic communication is making possible speedy dialog across the network in any direction as well as facilitating broadcast messages from any point to all members, opening up the possibility of interactions between all actors within the network. As we saw earlier, this is fast becoming a reality as the result of a number of converging forces—the confluence of two economic trends, the declining cost of computing and of long-distance communication, further compounded by the intensification of global competition and the desire for greater employee empowerment. The hub, even if it ever did have the ability, certainly can no longer control the lines of communication tightly within the network.[4]

External Networking and Alliances

Networking implies both internal and external communication linkages. *Internal networking* occurs within the organization among individuals, teams, and other groups that are part of the organization. *External networking*, on the other hand, occurs between the organization and other organizations or groups in the external environment. Normally an organization will practice both external and internal networking.

If there is anything to be learned from the past decades of change, it is that close alliances between suppliers and their customers are preferable to the distant, adversarial relations that used to be the norm. We have also learned that benchmarking is better than being secretive and aloof. We also accept the idea of working in teams with other firms.

Networking and alliances are essential in global competition. The terms *networking* and *allying* are not identical in meaning but have similar goals and outcomes. *Networking* implies that various organizations have mutually agreed to share information to solve problems and interests they have in common. Central to an *alliance* is sharing information, understanding the goals and mission of each player, and making a long-term commitment to a strategic partnership. More and more firms are forming strategic alliances and/or networks with their vendors and suppliers. They are looking to ally with their suppliers, transportation service providers, and others to create fully integrated flows of material, product, and service to the end customer.

Steps in Networking

There are three basic steps to networking: (1) communicating the strategic improvement plan (internal or external), (2) sharing experiences and expectations, and (3) extending and interfacing.[5]

Step One: Communicate Strategic Improvement Plan

One of the first steps in networking is to communicate your strategic improvement plan to external organizations. Invite suppliers, subcontractors, customers, and others to see and understand your improvement plan. Some may not understand how your principles can improve the quality of their products or services. Others will be eager to learn, share their expertise, and participate in your improvement efforts.

Step Two: Share Experiences and Expectations

The second step is to share experiences and expectations. Many organizations include external organizations in training plans. It should be made clear that commitment to principles of continuous improvement is important to continued networking relationships. Many companies will insist that suppliers be "certified" or "qualified," meaning that the provider has undergone an inspection and audit by the potential purchaser.

Step Three: Extend and Interface

The third step may include a visit to external organization facilities. This can help extend the networking linkage and establish long-lasting relationships. It can also be used to make a systematic evaluation of a supplier's ability to ensure quality products or services.

Some organizations may want to guard or protect proprietary information. When appropriate, require employees to sign a patent agreement, a secrecy agreement, or a no-competition contract. Make employees aware that they are not to divulge company or customer information.

Protect sensitive or secret procedures by placing them in special rooms or enclosures. Do not allow tours, and exclude students, reporters, and curious friends from seeing or hearing about the secret procedures. When employees depart, discuss the importance of ethics, company loyalty, and keeping confidential information secret.

Network Operations

Most organizations are operating in a network whether they know it, like it, or want it. One obvious indicator is the proliferation of connections with other organizations. They take many names—"strategic alliances," "joint ventures," "outsourcing partnerships," and "flexible business networks," to name a few—linking customers, suppliers, and competitors. When executive, staff, and line colleagues form multiple overlapping teams, they too are exploding in numberless cross-functional projects, horizontal corporations, and virtual enterprises. We discuss here some of the features of operating in a networked world.[6]

Networks Cross, but Do Not Smash, Boundaries. In networks, people work closely with clients, customers, vendors, suppliers, and even competitors. They know how to maintain boundaries without being immobilized by them, how to hold joint allegiances, how to balance conflicting interests, and how to tap resources beyond their own four walls, creating situations where everyone wins. Boundaries are the basis for self-identity and diversity, and even the Big Three auto makers are crossing them. Together, they have a dozen consortia underway, investigating everything from the electric car to better crash dummies.

Networks Promote Co-opetition. Networks allow you to cooperate and compete at the same time. Without both competition and cooperation, you cannot succeed in turbulent times that require flexibility, nimbleness, and learning, regardless of the size of your enterprise. "Co-opetition" puts these two apparent opposites into a dynamic dance.

A Network of Teams Is the Most Effective Network. To work across boundaries, people form local teams that bridge time and distance in networks. A team from Massachusetts General Hospital works with its counterpart at Brigham and Women's Hospital as Boston's two health-care giants work through the details of their merger. Little teams make up big networks.

Transitioning to the Networked Organization

Following are a number of changes that must be made for an organization to transition from a traditional hierarchical organization to an innovative networked organization.

Chain of Command to Networking

Networking is an ongoing process of reaching out and getting in touch with others to get tasks done. As we become nodes in a network—knowledge resources—we tap into this available knowledge and our effectiveness increases. Instead of being confined by the chain of command, we can go directly to the sources of knowledge, whether they are inside or outside the enterprise. When a worker joined a certain large innovative organization, he was told a good news–bad news story. The good news was that he had 120,000 people working for him. The bad news was that they do not know it. It was up to him to determine how he could best network himself and build working alliances.

Power of Position to Power of Knowledge

In traditional hierarchical organizations, position and power are defined by boxes and lines: The higher up the position, the more powerful it is. The prerogatives of position legitimize an arbitrary attitude toward subordinates. Superiors need not listen; they merely monitor and control subordinates.

The power of knowledge is fast becoming more important for success. This is not knowledge doled out in tiny bits like pennies, but knowledge that is available to all. As traditional hierarchies are replaced by multiple teams, the individual's knowledge becomes both more important and more accessible, and a lack of knowledge can no longer be hidden behind the walls of organizational boxes. People quickly learn who has knowledge and who will share it. They are the ones who become key players on teams.

Vertical Communication to Horizontal Communication

The shift to horizontal communication should be an obvious one, especially as we see people not as turf owners but as knowledge resources within the network. There will still be vertical communication, of course, but the predominant communication will be horizontal in nature as the core teams leverage knowledge wherever it may be in the enterprise.

Horizontal communication in a networked environment is freer and more fluid, with few bureaucratic barriers. It also facilitates serendipity, where key patterns may be unexpectedly discovered. Perhaps a request from one team to another will provide a clue to the pattern the other team is trying to discern. If we see our work as information processing, we will stay open to discovery, observe the interplay of multiple patterns, and achieve our visions.

The emphasis on horizontal work processes in the innovative organization results in an emphasis on horizontal communication also. Work cannot become more horizontal unless communication also becomes more horizontal.

Distrust and Compliance to Trust and Integrity

The fragmented structure of traditional hierarchies breeds distrust among functions. It is common to hear people complain of how another department throws information over the wall. In the knowledge era, trust and integrity are critical. When people work closely together as resources in a network and as members of teams, it quickly becomes obvious who can be trusted and who cannot.

EDUCATION AND TRAINING

In this section we discuss the education and training policies and procedures of a 21st-century company. In the first part of the section we look at the tangible aspects of education and training. In the latter part we look at the more intangible aspects—creating a learning organization. The Social Management Group is responsible for assembling a social project team that will conduct the Education and Training Analysis.

Determining Education and Training Needs

In this section, we focus on the assessment phase and develop the Education and Training Analysis, which consists of the analysis of the organization's needs, the job's needs, and the person's needs. This section is a follow-on to the Diagnosis of Human Resources in Chapter 11 and the work team design earlier in this chapter.

Inputs to the Education and Training Analysis (ETA)

The following documents should be used as sources in developing the Education and Training Analysis:

- The primary input to the ETA is the work team design conducted earlier in this chapter. It provides the detailed requirements for each new job.
- The Diagnosis of Human Resources described in Chapter 11 is an important input that will provide additional information concerning quantity of future requirements.
- The technical detailed design conducted in accordance with Chapter 8 will also provide technical details.
- The Organization Concept as described in Chapter 11 should be referred to for guidance concerning the form of the overall organization.
- The organization's vision, mission, creed, strategy, and ideology should provide overall guidance.

Organizational Needs Analysis

Human resources diagnosis and work team design translate the organizational concept into specific demands for human resources, skills, and programs for supplying them. Training and development programs play a vital role in matching the supply of human resources and skills with organizational demands.

An organizational analysis of efficiency provides information on the current efficiency of work groups and the organization. The analysis of the organizational climate describes the quality of the organization, how the employees feel about it, and how effective they are. Like the analysis of efficiency, it can help identify where training and development programs may be needed.

These aspects of the organizational needs analysis present only a broad definition of the organization's need for training and development. Nevertheless, they are extremely important in identifying where the training and development programs should be focused and in providing criteria for evaluating the effectiveness of the programs. Many organizations fail to do this analysis, preferring to jump in and train simply because everyone else is doing it.

Job Needs Analysis

Because the organizational needs analysis is too broad to provide detailed training and development needs for specific jobs, it is also necessary to conduct a **job needs analysis**. Essentially, this analysis provides information on the tasks to be performed on each job and the skills necessary to perform those tasks. This information comes primarily from the work team design and the detailed technical process designs.

Person Needs Analysis

The **person needs analysis** can be accomplished by comparing an evaluation of employee proficiency on each required skill dimension with the proficiency level required by the job.

Identifying Critical Skills and Designing an Education Strategy

Project assignments and mentoring are the most effective methods of individual learning, but they can reach only a limited number of individuals. The next best thing is an education strategy involving less customization but more employees.

What distinguishes good educational programs from bad ones is not so much the level of resources committed or the quality of the facilities, but their relevance to the business. Most training dollars spent today are wasted on the ill-focused development of generic skills. A skills or competency model needs to be defined first; only then can skill and competency training be focused and meaningful. Building a skills model involves striking a balance between two extremes. On the one hand, having no skills model is clearly not the answer. At the opposite extreme, building the world's most *thorough* model is equally dangerous.

A Strategy for Training

Most of the successful organizations have built their training strategies on the five training elements listed here. These five elements represent the requirements upon which sound, strategic educational programs can be based.

1. A structured and disciplined training process, cascaded through the organization from the top as the best way to demonstrate senior management's commitment and provide role models.
2. A front-end kick-off session for all employees to orient them to the meaning of transformation, to create an awareness of the need for change, and to describe the organization's transformation plan.
3. A curriculum plan that includes both classroom training and on-the-job training covering the concept and practice of all new and changed processes.
4. Early integration of all the new or revised processes with existing processes in the organization.
5. A curriculum that emphasizes teamwork, trust, openness, and collaborative skills.

TOWARD CONTINUOUS INDIVIDUAL LEARNING

Building Individual Learning

Most corporate reward systems are designed to award people for doing what they were asked to do. As a result, they constitute the weakest form of motivation. Money, banners, trophies, and other symbols are held out as carrots to stimulate motivation in the pursuit of specifically defined goals. Employees and managers learn to expect certain returns for behaviors, each of them operating in their assigned slot. The model remains predominantly paternal, authoritarian, and reactive in that top management "provides" and the firm's personnel receive the various forms of compensation made available. The problem is that the clearly defined rewards produce expected results, not the creative, unexpected, and dramatic outcomes that comprise the very heart of transformation.

Individual learning represents a more advanced stage of renewal. It builds the individual's sense of self-esteem by enhancing his or her store of knowledge, thus promoting an increased level of competence in approaching work-related problems. More important, it creates the opportunity for people to experience perhaps the most fulfilling of all rewards, a sense of *self-actualization*—the pride of recognizing the output of one's mind in the external reality of the workplace and the sense of purpose, productivity, and participation that comes with such achievement.

By promoting individual learning, the corporation recognizes the individual's responsibility for his or her own personal and professional development while accepting its responsibility to create an environment of opportunity in which all can thrive. As greater numbers of individuals with high self-esteem unleash their creativity, they reshape the contours of the firm. The corporation comes alive as employees continuously adapt and improve the way they do their work and constantly redefine their roles and interactions. Rather than dealing with a machine-like firm, leaders become conductors of the bio-corporate symphony, orchestrating the organic growth of the firm as the cells and organs of the corporate body adapt, change, and reproduce.

Creating Individual Learning Opportunities

The organization needs to generate a large number of learning opportunities, generalize this learning beyond a few individuals, do so more swiftly than competitors, and build in the desire and opportunity to learn from others. Learning from failure is not possible if the actions that resulted in the failure were not well planned and based on an explicit model of the organization's functioning. Careful review and planned response can complete the learning cycle described earlier for those individuals involved. Dialogue and sharing can lead to the modification of mental maps. However, the learning is of limited value unless it then has impact on the ways of working such that it adds value to the business over the longer term.

Benchmarking can enable comparisons in performance and produce the setting of targets for future improvement. It can give clear focus for organizational objectives and measured improvement offers an indirect means for assessing the extent to which the organization is achieving this learning state. Examination of best practice both within and outside the organization can assist in the process of developing mental models. Centers of excellence within the organization can be useful in assisting people to develop insights and build their personal models. Laboratories and simulated exercises make it possible for individuals and groups to experiment and time-compress experiences, thus resulting in concentrated learning.

Integrating Individual Learning into the Wider Organization

Organizations ultimately learn via their individual members. However, individuals within organizations often get into a mind-set and stop challenging the assumptions underpinning organization functioning. This may be the result of commonly shared views about "how we do things around here," it might be fear of crossing a strong manager, it might be an unwillingness to be seen as a deviant, or the organization might have well-articulated standard operating procedures.

Organization learning comes about when there is a transfer of knowledge between individuals and an exchange of individual and shared mental models. This requires individuals to make explicit their mental models. Learning is seen to have taken place where there is an increase in the organization's capacity to take effective action in response to changing stimuli. The new mental models will make it possible for the organization to introduce discontinuous steps of improvement that require radically different approaches to tackling issues and solving problems. The extent which this sharing can take place will be influenced by both organizational structure and management style.

The aim of the organization with regard to learning is to share the learning that takes place from each and every interaction with a customer/client, vendor, supplier, employee, and competitor. The challenge for management is to create a climate that encourages this open sharing and particularly the practice of learning from mistakes. This process has to be encouraged across hierarchical levels and organizational boundaries. It also has to transcend time and geographic boundaries as well as the external boundaries of the organization. A learning culture encourages responsible risk taking on the part of individuals and groups; it fosters reflection, open discussion, and debate about experience; and it is willing to acknowledge mistakes—but at the same time individuals are prepared to learn from them. Managers at all levels have to be seen to be practicing the principles and themselves facilitating open dialogue and discussion. Information flows are a major support in developing the learning organization. Timely, accurate, available, and relevant information that is presented in a form usable by those who need it is a prerequisite for the learning organization. Reward systems must recognize and reinforce desired behaviors.

THE LEARNING ORGANIZATION

Knowledge is the key strategic resource of the postindustrial organization. Consequently learning will be the competitive advantage for organizations of the future. Learning is the basis for effective organizational change. Organizations need to know what works and what doesn't work as they try to adapt to a world that seems far more threatening, turbulent, and interconnected than ever before. They must be able to learn from their failures as well as from their successes. They must be able to disseminate and share their knowledge with everyone internal and external to their (increasingly permeable) boundaries—anyone who can help them achieve their goals. They must be able to act on what they know, to carry out in practice the principles that often sound deceptively simple: "we must work together as a team," "we should involve users in systems development," "we need to take risks and learn from our mistakes," and so on.

Toward the Learning Organization

Given its critical role in organizational change, it is not difficult to see why the subject of organizational learning, or its corporeal counterpart, the learning organization, is so popular today and so important for the transformation effort. The learning organization has the capacity to gain insight from its own experience and the experience of others and to modify the way it functions according to such insight. While organizations ultimately learn from their individual members, organizational learning is more than the sum of its parts, more than the accumulated learnings of the individuals within the organization. As Mohrman and Mohrman argue:

The training and development of individuals with new skills, knowledge bases, theories and frameworks does not constitute organizational learning unless such individual learning is translated into altered organizational practices, policies or design features. Individual learning is necessary but not sufficient for organizational learning. It may enable an individual to more effectively enact a role in the organization, but it will not lead to fundamentally altered patterns of behavior.[7]

Teams enabled by new information technology can be one of the most effective mechanisms for organizational learning. With these tools, team members can experiment with and analyze work processes, then disseminate their knowledge throughout the organization. The constraints on learning will dissolve. The key is to provide technology-empowered teams with mechanisms for capturing, organizing, and storing the unstructured electronic communications that are so critical to this kind of analysis and learning. They also need time to explore and reflect, the authority to act on their knowledge, and the motivation to share their learning with others. Knowledge can then grow and spread, unrestrained by unnecessary boundaries, creating a learning organization in every sense of the expression.

Creating Global Learning

Size still matters a lot to businesses, but not as it used to. Economies of scale are disappearing, being replaced by the *economies of global learning*. Everything that a company does has both operational and learning aspects. Unfortunately, the learning aspect is usually ignored or regarded as incidental. At the core of the philosophy of *transformation* is recognizing that learning as vital.

We already have seen in chapters 7 and 8 how a new, more fruitful approach to the reengineering of processes involves mapping the flow of knowledge rather than the chronology of operational steps to generate improvements. We also detailed how creative companies build wider and wider learning loops, in essence transporting knowledge across the entire corporation, bringing to bear the full firepower of the firm at all times rather than just the limited shelling ability of its farthest outposts.

When managed in an integrated way, learning loops form an integrated network, making the corporation a *learning organization.* A learning organization usually consists of at least three major elements:

1. *A knowledge architecture.* The knowledge architecture is the conceptual framework for generating an ever-growing body of systematic knowledge, as well as the structure for matching knowledge to skill requirements. The knowledge architecture should act as the road map for knowledge acquisition, career planning, and training.

2. *A knowledge management process.* The knowledge management process provides the formal methodology for collecting, integrating, and disseminating knowledge. Formal debriefing sessions, organized learning programs attended and supported by senior managers and executives, and recognition and reward systems are the key ingredients of an effective knowledge management process.

3. *A technical architecture.* The technical architecture, destined to become computer-based in virtually every organization, allows every individual to gain access to knowledge wherever and whenever it is needed. It ensures rapid dissemination of knowledge to the people who need it, increasingly through groupware and other network-based software.[8]

A desire to keep pace with technology is driving many companies to invest massively in the creation of global electronic networks that connect their entire global employee population. As was the case with the frenzy of activity at the beginning of the IT wave, much of this activity is destined to fail, which will lead to disappointment and a poor return on some very large investments. *Content*, not technology, should drive the process. Many companies already are discovering that the most sophisticated learning system is of little help if users won't log on. They will log on only if the information available will help them in their individual jobs. Building the electronic superhighway may be aesthetically pleasing, but ultimately it is the quality of the cars riding on it that will make the journey worthwhile.

Everyone Wins in a Continuously Learning Culture

An organizational transformation is never truly complete. Rather, it is a series of large-scale changes—to the culture, processes, structure, and so on—over the course of a given time period, approximately one to three years, followed by continuous learning and ongoing improvement by all employees. Eventually, despite improvement efforts, industry conditions and/or technological developments will necessitate another transformation in the years ahead.

To maximize the effectiveness and prolong the gains realized from the transformation, organizations must make learning available to all employees. Without ongoing learning, employees and the organization become stagnant, and the need for a large-scale upheaval quickly becomes a reality once again. This wastes company resources and creates an environment with little stability and few opportunities to learn new skills. Work teams are responsible for redesigning systems to support or enhance the core processes of the organization.

By installing a formal learning system, employees can continually learn. Only when employees continually learn can they continually improve. But for a continuous improvement culture to become a reality, they need a performance-based compensation system to motivate and reward them. For companies that establish such a culture, everyone wins. Customers receive more value through lower prices, higher-quality products and services, and faster turnaround times. Employees and management will share a percentage of the higher profits they helped achieve and secure their employment as the organization's market share increases. Last, shareholders will realize greater returns as the company increases its overall net worth and as greater numbers of investors try to buy into the company's current and predicted future success.

NOTES

1. Susan Albers Mohrman, Susan G. Cohen, and Allan Mohrman, Jr., *Designing Team-Based Organizations* (Jossey-Bass, 1995), p. 279.

2. Don Mankin, Susan G. Cohen, and Tora K. Bikson, *Teams and Technology: Fulfilling the Promise of the New Organization* (Harvard Business School Press, 1996), p. 269.

3. Ibid., p. 172.

4. David Birchall and Laurence Lyons, *Creating Tomorrow's Organization* (Pitman Publishing, 1995), p. 72.

5. Terry L. Richardson, *Total Quality Management* (AMACOM, 1997), p. 203.

6. Jesson L. Lipnack and Jeffrey Stamps, *The Age of the Network* (Omneo, 1994), p. 17.

7. Mohrman et al., *Designing Team-Based Organizations*, p. 302.

8. Francis J. Gouillart and James H. Kelly, *Transforming the Organization: Reframing, Restructuring, Revitalizing, and Renewing* (McGraw-Hill, 1995), p. 302.

CHAPTER 13

Redesigning Human Resource Processes

INTRODUCTION

At some point the human resource support organization must be changed so that it can better nurture and support the redesigned work processes and work teams. Without such high-level change, the impact of individual work team efforts will remain limited and local. The ultimate goal is not team effectiveness but organizational effectiveness via teams. Therefore, organizations should implement macro-level changes to complement the micro-level changes made in Chapter 12. This chapter is about how organizations can take this last important step.

In this chapter our principal focus is on team redesign of human resource processes. We will first look at the new role of human resources in the new environment and then discuss the changes required in the following processes to enable them to properly support a networked team-based organization.

- Recruiting and Selection
- Performance Measurement and Assessment
- Recognition and Reward
- Career Planning and Development

Each process will have to adapt to a networked team-based organization and evolve into new roles. Ultimately, the very organization itself—its structure, form, and culture—must adapt to, reinforce, and become one with the changes transpiring within and across its boundaries.

For each of these processes we recommend that a social design team be formed following the procedures outlined in Chapter 5. The design teams would have the responsibility of investigating their assigned service process and developing ideas for changing and improving it. The teams should be composed of HR and IT professionals plus users of the service. The redesign methods for the technical redesign teams outlined in chapters 6 and 8 are applicable to the social redesign team.

It is suggested that an organization **not** restrict their team redesign efforts to the four processes just listed. With limited space, we covered only those areas that were most important and for which we could provide the most assistance. However, there are a number of additional areas worthy of investigation. Some of them are listed in Chapter 10, pp. 212–213.

A NEW ROLE FOR HUMAN RESOURCES

The team-based networked organization has a number of features that help break down formal, well-defined specializations and personnel categories. At the very least, they make the boundaries that separate them less relevant. By increasing interdependence and collaboration, one team member's tasks become inseparable from another's. The same holds for technology: access by some users to information and tools previously available only to others blurs the boundaries between specializations and changes professional identities. New reward systems separate pay from formal job categories and attach it instead to performance, skill, and knowledge. Lateral careers reduce the barriers of job, process, and hierarchy. Together, they add up to a new logic for work and organizations.

The essence of this new logic—which argues for flexibility, permeable boundaries, and uncertainty—has significant implications for human resource practice.[1] Over the years, the HR function has been the antithesis of this new logic. The very tasks and tools of the trade (affirmative action plans, the *Dictionary of Occupational Titles*, functional job analysis, compensation packages, etc.) reflect the largely formal, specialized, reactive, and hierarchical nature of traditional human resource work. Like many staff professionals, HR practitioners are rooted in their functional specialties and resist change. The result often is that the very people who think of themselves as agents of change may act as inhibitors of change because of the way in which they ply their trade.

But new kinds of organizations require new ways of working for human resource professionals as well as for those they typically support. The dynamic and ambiguous nature of team-based, technology-enabled organizations means that HR professionals will be working under very different and potentially unsettling circumstances. As if that were not enough, the issues they will address—information technology and organization design—are largely unfamiliar and go well beyond their traditional scope.

Fortunately, they will not be alone in navigating, adapting, and shaping this unfamiliar territory.

The Changing Environment for Human Resources

Job design is rapidly evolving. The traditional obsession with measuring employee fit is giving way to a focus on employee growth. The once stable, well-defined jobs of years past are now continually evolving, with the overall purpose of making the organization more adaptable in changing markets. Creativity, resourcefulness, flexibility, innovation, and adaptability are becoming much more important than the ability to perform a precisely specified job.

The increased complexity of our environment is transforming HR by overturning the traditional view of how to motivate employees. This new view mandates that all HR efforts be directed toward increasing performance, including investment in training and career development. The premise is that if we coordinate the levers of employee motivation and performance with a well-defined set of performance outcomes, we will get the highest level of motivation and performance. The employee's incentive to reach defined goals is pay—in part individual, in part focused on the team, in part linked to organizational performance.

The HR control function (payroll, labor negotiations, legal procedure governing employment) is no longer the heart of the matter. All the rest is what's important, and it revolves around service delivery: helping managers hire the best people, retain them, train them effectively, compensate them fairly, consult and communicate with them, accommodate them, discipline and fire them, manage their absenteeism, and the like. In a few—far too few—organizations, HR professionals are stepping up to this role with initiative, a sense of urgency, and an understanding of what adds value to the business.

Revised Human Resources Practices

If the networked organization is to be effective, the systems and processes put in place must be staffed by highly qualified people. People must be regarded as critical system elements that must be managed with quality and consistency. In traditional organizations, human resource managers identify, prepare, direct, and reward employees for following rather narrow objectives. In networked organizations, human resources managers develop policies and procedures to assure that employees can perform multiple roles, improvise when necessary, and direct themselves toward continuous improvement of both products and processes. *Human resources has evolved from a support function to a leadership function.* This requires not only a significant adjustment on the part or human resources professionals, but line managers as well.

For a networked organization to operate effectively, human resource professionals must recruit, develop motivate, and retain its most valuable resource—creative people. In order to carry out this important responsibility, human resource managers have developed a number of new policies and practices. We will explore some of these policies and practices.

They integrate all their human resource plans and policies into a coherent design that supports the corporate vision, mission, and creed. Human resource plans must follow and support the highest-level direction of the company, the vision, and the mission. Long-term plans concentrate on developing the continuous-learning environment and developing new systems for empowering and developing employees. The cascade meetings, discussed in Chapter 10, provide a means for ensuring that human resource plans are aligned with the company's vision, mission, and creed.

They develop a comprehensive and concerted effort for hiring creative people. They develop such a reputation for being a creative, exciting place to work that the line forms outside their door. To keep up the talent flow, they encourage and reward employees for recommending new hires. They continue to recruit from colleges and universities, but they also consider work-study programs and making contact with potential hires in high school, then following the outstanding students through college before hiring them permanently.

They continually improve key personnel management processes such as recruitment, hiring, training, performance evaluation, and recognition. A key approach to improving human resource practices is the use of employee surveys and measurement of key indicators. Employees also participate in focus groups to identify causes and work toward solutions.

They hire individuals to make a lifetime contribution, not to fill a specific position. Many of the better companies, such as Hewlett-Packard, look for a specific set of skills, for instance, electrical engineering, math ability, or experience in dealing with the public. But the criteria that really matter to them are personal attributes and abilities that will contribute to the company for years, not just for weeks or months.

They train constantly and integrate the training into ongoing operations. Training can solve a multitude of ills, but only if it is related to the present and future activities of the person being trained. Even when the training is designed to develop employees (management, leadership, etc.), it's built around how work is actually performed.

They make the challenge and worth of the work itself the most important motivator for high performance—for everyone. Effective performers should earn well, but should never think of pay as the primary motivator. Everyone, from the most junior clerk to the CEO, should view his or her job as an intriguing challenge. Everyone should want to and be expected to contribute in the fullest way from the very first day.

They do not motivate by money, but they ensure their compensation system is congruent with the emphasis on creativity. Creativity cannot be motivated by money alone. However, money rewards must be consistent with individual and team contributions, or they will act as powerful de-motivators. Actually, in an innovative organization, money can cause more problems than it solves. A company should start with a challenge. If the employees rise to the challenge—pay them for it.

RECRUITING AND SELECTING PERSONNEL

To be sure, dimensions such as technology, strategy, global alliances, and innovation are all critical components that will affect competitive advantage in the future. However, each of these areas is still dependent on and driven by human talent. Therefore, we believe that future economic and strategic advantage will rest with the organizations that can most effectively *attract, develop*, and *retain* a diverse group of the best and the brightest human talent in the marketplace. With this premise in mind, this section will expand on these three core processes as well as provide some final thoughts on building the organization of the future.

Attracting the Best

Although we have separated the three core organizational processes, we have done so only for purposes of explanation and clarification. We fundamentally believe that organizations whose environment fosters continuous human development will simultaneously attract and retain their human capital.

Attracting the best begins with an organization's ability to understand the psychological predisposition of those entering the workforce. This, by the way, is no simple task. A *Time* magazine cover story on the 20-something generation stated that they have only a "hazy sense" of their own identity. In interviews, respondents struggled with trying to define themselves and their generation. Complicating the matter is the fact that they are not about to let the older generation define and clarify for them who they are and what they want.

Current research would suggest, however, that some trends are beginning to emerge. It is becoming clear that although employees no longer expect lifelong employment, they do expect employability, an experience that allows them to develop their portfolio of transferable skills. It is also apparent that top talents will have far better understanding of their own market value and will thus be quite demanding concerning their rewards (tangible and psychic) and compensation (money and opportunity). Unlike past generations, they will operate from a quid pro quo perspective in which they will demand value received for value given. Finally, we believe that employees in the future will expect comprehensive disclosure from their prospective employers.

Now, while these absolute demands, desires, and expectations seem obvious as well as consistent with today's workforce, we believe that, in the future, the relative degree of skill development, recognition, and disclosure required will greatly increase as will the intensity and vibrato of the demands. Let us expand on each of these points, beginning with what we call corporate candor, followed by recognition and compensation, and ending with employability.

Importance of Human Capital

Any of the organizational variables we have described here has the potential of becoming a core building block of the organization of the future. Perhaps the only safe claim we can make is that human capital, above and beyond all other variables, will be the core building block for the organization of the future.[2] Organizations of today would be wise to critically evaluate their human resource systems and specifically their practices for attracting, developing, and retaining human capital.

In attracting the best, keep in mind that top talent comes in all shapes, sizes, colors, and ages. Diversity must be understood and embraced if organizations are to attract the best. EQ (emotional and social intelligence) will be as relevant, if not more relevant, than IQ when considering top talent. Be prepared to work hard at attracting the best, because they will attract many others like themselves. Like a lead engine in a train, they are attached to and bring with them valuable cargo outside of themselves.

In developing the best, the organization of the future must have a strategic human resource function. We believe that top human resources departments will have two distinct functions in the future: human resource administration, involving salary administration, labor relations, legal affairs, and compliance, and human resource strategy, involving strategic systems and approaches for attracting (recruiting), developing, and retaining human capital. If human capital is presumptively the core building block, the function that is responsible must be strategic in nature and must therefore be elevated to where finance, marketing, and operations are today.

Finally, in retaining the best, organizations must be perceived as credible. And because credibility is a perceived phenomenon, organizations must periodically survey their talent base to determine the appropriate course of action for maintaining and building credibility.

Selection

Who selects people and what criteria they use are two areas that may need attention in the restructured organization. While this book does not pretend to offer a complete guide to selection and hiring, a brief discussion of each of these practices is in order.

Who Makes the Selection?

In a number of organizations that are built around teams, the personnel department performs only an initial screening of job applicants. Final selection for employment is left up to the teams themselves. There are both benefits and drawbacks to this approach.

One benefit is that the teams retain more control over the input to their processes. Teams' ability to control their input is an important feature of a social-technical systems design. If the principle applies to the selection of their own members, they will probably work more diligently to bring newcomers up to speed and make them an integral part of the team. Group cohesion in a high-performance team can be valuable to the organization.

A drawback, however, is that cliques can develop if teams are allowed to choose every new member. Particularly in untrained teams, this can lead to the selection of people based on idiosyncratic criteria. Teams can develop an internal homogeneity that may hamper their creativity and limit their collective point of view.

Criteria for Selection

You may want to modify your selection process to include some skills or abilities that you have not sought before. For example, you will want people who can work with others. Among the interpersonal aptitudes that you might seek is the ability to listen and to communicate. You also will want people who have the ability to learn new skills, so you may want to add flexibility and problem solving to the criteria that you use in your initial selection procedures. While most of these skills can be taught to some extent and while you may have to teach them to your existing workforce, you may decide that you could save some training time if you select new employees who already have some of these skills and abilities.

One of the most important things to remember is that a change in the rules of your organization may change the skills and abilities that you need. Your challenge will be to apply the new criteria equally to all applicants and to be sure that your criteria do not eliminate unfairly any particular group or class of people. One way to develop the new criteria may be to involve your steering group or a special task force of team members who have acquired some experience with the new structure.

PERFORMANCE MEASUREMENT AND ASSESSMENT

Despite the intrinsic link between them, the process for changing assessment procedures differs in important ways from the process for changing reward systems. New assessment procedures can often be implemented at the level of individual teams, while new reward systems require changing the formal human resource policies for an entire business unit or organization. The former can happen without the latter, but not vice versa. Consequently, team-based performance assessment should precede the implementation of team-based reward systems. The following section reflects this temporal and functional logic. We first discuss the team-based assessment procedures that can be implemented by individual teams and managers; then we turn to new reward systems that can be implemented only by the larger organizations of which they are a part.

The Traditional Performance Measurement System

Traditional measurement systems, solely focused on functional outcomes and overall financial performance, fail to provide work teams with the necessary feedback they need to improve their performance. To sustain a competitive advantage you must have continual improvement throughout the company. Consequently, it is important to design a new performance measurement system that continuously measures team progress and team performance in addition to the overall financial performance of the company. This is the only way teams can continuously succeed in delivering increased value to their customers and the only way management can track the return provided to stakeholders.

In the traditional organization the measurement system was developed with three main principles in mind:

1. To measure functional outcomes
2. To measure overall financial performance
3. To control the workforce

Under the traditional system, the company gathered information and sent it upward through the managerial layers to inform top management of the activities of each functional area. Top management then analyzed the information and sent directives down to the functional directors to increase market share, lower product costs, cut the marketing budget, or improve quality, depending on the functional area being controlled. The functional directors then issued the same directives down to the middle managers under their command, who in turn passed these orders down to area supervisors, who at last delivered the message to employees.

The central problem with this system is that it failed to give the frontline employees specific information on how they should go about improving their performance or where they needed to focus their improvement efforts. In a sense, employees were being asked to play the game, but they were not allowed to track their performance or keep score. Management controlled the information and would sometimes let employees know the score at some point in the future, often weeks or months away. More often than not the score was announced to them in the form of a threat to improve performance or face dismissal. Under this system employees throughout the company did not know whether they were doing well, nor did they know what they needed to change in order to improve their performance.

Individuals and teams need the responsibility for keeping score, otherwise they will lose interest in their work—motivation and morale suffer. In the absence of specific feedback concerning their performance, employees could not, nor did they have the desire to, proactively make process improvements, improvements that would ultimately benefit the company. It is no wonder that many companies operating under the traditional organizational model fell victim to competitors who early on realized the value of providing their employees with performance feedback and empowering them to make ongoing improvements to their work.

Changing Assessment Practices at the Team Level

A critical first step in moving from competition between individual performers to collaboration among team members is to change performance assessment practices. The very process of assessing team performance, even in the absence of rewards tied to that performance, can have a significant impact. Indeed, recent research suggests that once team goals have been defined and performance assessed, rewards in and of themselves will result in only a small additional improvement in performance.

What this means in terms of immediate practice is that teams and their managers should:

- Identify and define team goals as well as methods for measuring progress toward these goals;

- Add criteria to performance appraisals for individual team members that are related to their contribution to team performance;

- Discard evaluation procedures that put individual team members in competition with each other—by ranking team members, for example, or making comparisons between them; and

- Assess team performance and individual contributions to team performance systematically when possible. These assessments should incorporate input from managers, team members, and customers as well as other teams and individuals with whom the team collaborates to produce its goods or services.[3]

Developing a Performance-Based Measurement System

Developing a new performance measurement system is not difficult if an organization has properly designed and established new processes and work teams. This is because the measurement system needs only to measure the results of the teams. It is when the processes are complicated and the teams are lacking structure or ownership of a large part of the process that you run into difficulties. Additionally, a new performance measurement system can become difficult to implement if employees view the new measurement system as a means by which top management can better monitor and control their behavior.

Under the new performance measurement system, companies have their newly established work teams gather the feedback required to help them continually improve their performance. The new measurement system also empowers teams to measure, manage, and improve their piece of the process. An organization can develop a new system by incorporating the following five principles:

1. Let teams take the lead in designing the new system.
2. Create process measures, not functional measures.
3. Use only a few key measurements.
4. Ensure that management does not use the new system to punish or control teams.
5. Integrate long-term and short-term performance measures.[4]

Let Teams Take the Lead in Designing the New System

The work teams in the organization must play the lead role in developing the new performance measurement system. Since they are the ones doing the work, they are most capable of determining the type of measures they need to gauge their performance. This enables the teams to measure, manage, and improve their piece of the process without being dependent on management to point out areas that need improvement. A win-win situation is created as management saves time and work teams gain more control and ownership over their work.

To create an effective performance measurement system, an organization must use a joint development process. By using work team members as lead designers, individual teams can develop measures that will build in the feedback necessary for them to gauge their progress and improve their performance. From management's perspective, the measurement system should provide information on a few key measures that identify the performance of the company as a whole. By tracking a balanced set of key measures, management can assess the current financial state of the company as well as ensure that progress is being made throughout the company to maintain its competitive advantage.

Create Process Measures, Not Functional Measures

Because your work teams are designed to operate the core processes of the organization, you are ready to create a new measurement system based on process outcomes, not functional outcomes. In fact, if you designed your new organizational structure according to the recommendations in chapters 11 and 12, there are no longer any functional silos in place, for you have created a team-based organization.

Process measures enable work teams to gauge their progress when the measures constantly indicate to the teams how well they are delivering value to their customers and adding to the bottom line of the organization. The measures must be specific so that the team members can receive feedback that clearly shows them what aspects of their work are improving and where they need to focus their improvement efforts. Direct and immediate feedback from customers, both internal and external, is the best means by which team members can understand if they are truly delivering value to their customers. Immediate feedback is necessary because it allows team members to correct problems before the costs increase significantly and, more important, before the customers end up with the product or service containing the problem.

Use Only a Few Key Measurements

Too large a number of measurements will shift a work team's focus from the customer, where it should be, to collecting data and monitoring activities. A handful of measurements can suffice in most situations, as a few measurements usually can give work teams enough feedback to determine their performance levels and track their progress. Work teams can use the following general guidelines to help them select measures that provide them with the necessary feedback without spending too much time gathering and analyzing information.

- Select four or five performance measures that will be customer-focused outcomes, not activities.
- Each key area should have a measure.
- Periodically review measures to determine if they need to be replaced by other, more useful ones.
- Share measures with other teams; when similar measures are identified, the separate teams should consider becoming one larger team.
- Measure only those outcomes that are controlled by the team.

If teams need help creating measures for their work, they should first try to meet with other teams that have successfully established effective performance measures. If you need to turn to management for help, you need to ensure that the measures remain focused on improving team performance. Used for any other purpose, measures become punitive.

Ensure That Management Does Not Use Measurement System to Control Teams

By having the work teams be the lead developers of the new measurement system, you can usually prohibit management from installing measurements that can be used to control the teams. However, over time some "old school" managers, who have the old mentality of mistrusting employees, may manipulate the measurement system back to constantly monitoring the team's every move.

To truly empower the work teams throughout the organization, management must trust each and every one of its employees. Otherwise, management will eventually use the measurement system to control and monitor the activities of its employees, regressing to the old school thinking and undermining their organizational transformation effort.

Integrate Long-Term and Short-Term Performance Measures

Just as work teams must receive the information and feedback they need to improve their performance, management needs long-term, strategic measures that reflect current performance and help predict future performance across the entire organization. By aligning and creating what is commonly called a balanced scorecard, companies establish for all employees a link between their team activities and the company's overall performance. This has two primary benefits. One, by developing a system that links the performance of every team in the organization, senior management is able to quickly pull together all scores to accurately assess the company's overall business performance.

With the balanced scorecard, companies can measure their performance along four dimensions: (1) financial, (2) customer satisfaction, (3) internal business processes, and (4) learning and growth.[5] This has many benefits. First, by focusing on more than just the financial aspect of the business the company can focus on the activities that will drive future performance, that is, customer satisfaction and learning and growth. Additionally, by linking together the performance of all of the work teams in the organization, senior management is able to quickly pull together all scores to accurately assess the company's current business performance.

With an aligned, linked, and balanced system, everyone is focused on their work team objectives and the company's strategic goals. When a shift in strategic direction is deemed necessary, the already established measurement system serves as a communication pathway that aids in the development of new team objectives and performance targets, targets that are in line with the new or modified strategy.

In the absence of a clearly established method for keeping a balanced score throughout the company, organizations struggle with communicating and educating their employees on the performance and learning goals in place at all levels of the company. Also, if work teams do not know what numbers determine a win, they will have difficulty assessing their performance. This leads to confusion, especially when you ask teams to undertake performance improvement efforts. They simply will not know what to improve first or how to allocate their time or resources.

RECOGNITION AND REWARD SYSTEM

Recognition is the act of acknowledging, approving, or appreciating an activity or service. Recognition is an ongoing activity that doesn't focus only on one particular achievement and that is not given only at award ceremonies. It is directed at an individual's self-esteem and social needs. It is an intangible acknowledgment of a person's or team's accomplishments—the sincere "thank you," the feeling of involvement when an employee is asked for input, the realization and demonstration of appreciation for each person's unique contributions to the business. In short, recognition is ongoing appreciation and concern for people and as such it is central to reward-giving behavior. The forms of acknowledgment most commonly used in recognition are praise, personal "thank you's," letters, mementos, and special lunches or dinners.

Reward is the direct delivery of money or something of financial value. In contrast to recognition, rewards should punctuate appropriate achievements and serve as manifestations of ongoing recognition. While recognition is an intangible expression of worth, rewards are concrete expressions of appreciation that are meaningful to the receiver. Recognition is always powerful, but reward without recognition is weak. Unfortunately, too often we express appreciation with a plaque or cash award without demonstrating a sincere appreciation of an employee's contributions. When rewards displace recognition, they are a waste of an opportunity and resource. Typical rewards are pay promotional increases, bonuses, benefits, company cars, profit sharing, and trips.

Traditional Recognition and Reward Systems

Traditional compensation systems were built for traditional organizations, compensating employees for individual work and rewarding managers for movement up the career ladder. As organizations transform into team-based organizations, it is no wonder they find that the compensation systems of the past do not sufficiently recognize, reward, and retain employees for the future.

One of the main reasons why traditional compensation systems fail to align with newly transformed organizations is that they do not reward and recognize teamwork. In fact, traditional compensation systems commonly discourage teamwork, because yearly raises and bonuses usually come from a fixed sum of money that is divided among the organization's members. Under this system individuals are forced to compete against each other, rather than help each other, to increase their yearly salary. Traditional compensation reinforces lone-ranger behaviors and grandstanding as opposed to teamwork.

Develop a Performance-Based Recognition and Reward System

Unlike traditional, bureaucratic organizations, where jobs were purposely narrow and tasks relatively simple and repetitive, in newly transformed organizations employees are responsible for managing their performance, improving their work, working with customers, learning new skills, and developing new capabilities. With these new-found responsibilities there must follow a performance-based reward system that motivates and compensates performance across all of these areas—a system that recognizes, rewards, and retains employees.

Developing a new recognition and reward system is a significant undertaking, but it is a necessary step in completing the transformation of an organization. It is this step that provides all employees with the motivation to continuously learn, improve, and perform to their fullest potential. An organization that has been undergoing a transformation but then suddenly stops short by failing to redesign the reward system is like a marathon runner quitting at the 25th mile.

The new system should be simple and easy to understand and administer. It should reinforce the goals of the organization and be economically and legally sound. Most importantly, compensation should be linked to individual, team, and company performance. The following six principles should be followed in creating this type of system:

1. Allow people to develop their own rewards.

2. Foster alignment of rewards with the goals and measures of the organization.

3. Create a proper mix of individual, team, and business unit performance measures.

4. Share results to motivate and reward teams that deliver value to their customers.

5. Extend reward system beyond corporate boundaries.

6. Disperse recognition and non-monetary recognition frequently.

Allow People to Develop Their Own Rewards

A corporation cannot avoid expressing a view of human life through the rewards it offers to its people. The emerging view of life in successful companies recognizes the sanctity of the individual as prerequisite to corporate success. Consequently, formerly rigid and hierarchical reward systems are moving way to systems that provide structure but flexibility, such that individuals can discover their own motivations and create their own development path within the corporation. The most effective systems offer tangible rewards—involving formal recognition and financial incentives for achievement—as well as intangible rewards, such as letting people follow through on the ideas they generate. Above all, they promote learning and knowledge sharing, not just for the organization but for the individual as well.

To establish a proper mix of individual, team, and business unit performance measures for the new compensation system, you should form a compensation team made up of a cross-section of organizational members. Similar to project teams redesigning processes and the organizational structure, a compensation team can readily develop a performance-based compensation system that aligns and links with the systems and structures already in place within the organization.

Compensation teams are successful when management and employees work together to develop a system that is both economically and legally sound and that motivates and rewards all employees. Neither management nor employees working in isolation could develop a system that meets these requirements. Management needs information from employees regarding what provides motivation, while employees need help with economic and legal considerations.

Foster Alignment of Rewards with the Goals and Measures of the Organization

A corporation's goals and measures are inextricably connected; rewards are the glue that binds them. In most companies achieving this linkage is a major challenge, for their reward systems rely predominantly on financial incentives indexed to the company's financial performance. In reality, financial performance is only one of many drivers of success, which is why many forward-looking companies are developing reward systems based upon a balanced perspective of goals and measures.

The Balanced Scorecard provides a helpful framework for building and aligning measurement and reward systems. Just as corporations use the four broad categories of measures of the Balanced Scorecard (financial, customer, operational, learning) to build their measurement system, so they can use the same categories to build their reward system. In both measurement and reward systems, the key is to connect the measures and rewards to an integrated "story" about how the corporation intends to transform itself. The role of leaders is to foster the aligning of measures and rewards and to maintain the integrity of the interrelationship between them.

Most leaders agree that the most difficult challenges of transformation emerge around cultural conflicts. Ninety percent of what people call cultural conflicts exist because of conflicts in measures and rewards. The implication is obvious: Align measures and rewards, and you have solved some, if not most, of your most significant transformational problems.

Create a Proper Mix of Individual, Team, and Business Unit Performance Measures

A new compensation system must account for the individuals in the organization. Too much emphasis on work teams or company performance can overshadow the work done by the individuals inside the teams and throughout the organization. There is no standard (or perfect) formula you can use to determine the individual, team, and company performance results ratio. An appropriate mix is usually determined by the degree of interdependency existing between the individual team members and the different teams in the organization.

As a rule, when there is a high degree of interdependency between members of the teams and among the teams themselves, then team and company performance should determine a large percentage of the bonuses that are paid out. Conversely, when teams are mostly autonomous and team members have other responsibilities outside of their immediate team, compensation should be based mostly on a mixture of individual and team performance. In all cases some percentage of compensation should be based in all three areas. Even if the percentage of compensation reflected from company or business unit performance is a token amount or results in no money being distributed, a three-prong compensation system helps employees to stay focused on the overall goals and objectives of the company.

Share Results to Motivate and Reward Teams That Deliver Value to Their Customers

The central aspect of the new compensation system must be to reward those work teams that deliver value to their customers. Whether it concerns internal or external customers, you can measure delivered value by determining the degree by which the various teams accomplished or exceeded their performance objectives. Rewarding those teams that deliver added value to their customers benefits everyone in the organization.

When you are designing a new compensation system, you can create a win-win situation for all organizational members by having the organization reward work teams only when they deliver a certain level (or greater) of value to their customers. By designing the system this way, the organization ensures itself that any financial reward payouts are only a percentage of the extra profit the teams bring in. Increasing the value delivered to the customers, the profit received by the company, and the rewards distributed to the team members are certainly compelling reasons why top management should give teams financial incentives.

Extend Reward System beyond Corporate Boundaries

As companies extend their networking outward to their allies, customers and suppliers, the rewards system must adapt accordingly. The logic of aligning rewards to the measurement system applies equally to customers, suppliers, and alliance partners.[6] External members of the supply chain may be viewed as employees of a different type. Like employees, they provide products and services for a price, based on varying sources of motivation. Like employees, they may be more or less motivated as a function of how they are treated. And like employees, they usually want more out of the relationship than just financial security.

But unlike relations with employees, it is difficult to extend other than financial rewards to them directly. Within the firm the reward system is quite transparent, taking the form of a paycheck, a direct compliment or thank you, or a promotion. The communication of a reward to a customer or a supplier is by definition more subtle, more indirect. It may take the form of a price reduction or inclusion in a meeting or celebration, among many possible gestures.

Disperse Rewards and Non-monetary Recognition Frequently

Effective reward or recognition systems link high levels of performance with immediate financial payouts as often as possible. A reward system can pay out a high percentage to the teams coupled with other types of positive reinforcement, but without frequent distribution of rewards, the compensation system may not be motivating to the teams. Teams must see how changing their behavior can influence their near-term and long-term financial situation in a positive way.

In general, you should distribute bonuses to employees or teams soon after they meet their desired performance objectives. The frequency of the payouts will depend on the nature of the organization designing the new compensation system. If product completion or service delivery is complex and requires several months, organizations may be forced to pay out bonuses semiannually or even yearly. To link performance with compensation more closely, organizations in these situations might consider adopting a plan that allows team members to see how much they are increasing their bonus, on a monthly or quarterly basis, but then saves the actual financial payout for when the product is completed or the service delivered.

It is important for individuals and work teams to understand up front how frequently the organization will be distributing rewards or recognition. To aid in this understanding, some organizations have created recognition charts that show how often rewards and recognition will occur.

CAREER PATHS AND DEVELOPMENT

Traditional Career Path

The traditional career path is one wherein an employee progresses vertically upward in the organization from one specific job to the next. The assumption is that each job is essential preparation for the next, higher-level job. Therefore, an employee must move, step by step, from one job to the next to gain needed experience and preparation. This type of career path is most likely to be found in clerical and production operations.

One of the biggest advantages of the traditional career path is that it is straightforward. The path is clearly laid out, and the employee knows the specific sequence of jobs through which he or she must progress. However, it fails to recognize that other jobs may provide equivalent or better experience that could enable an employee to advance without performing certain jobs in the established sequence. Another potentially serious disadvantage of the traditional career path is that of blockage; that long-term employee at one level who is not capable of being promoted to the next level may block the progress of other employees in lower positions. Perhaps the greatest challenge to the traditional career path is the new mode of international competition, which has drastically changed the way the game is played. The certainties of yesterday's business methods and growth have vanished in many industries, and neither organizations nor individuals can be assured of ever regaining them.

Network Career Path and Career Development

No longer can skillful, smart, conscientious, hardworking employees count on fast progress up the traditional career ladder. After years of downsizing, not much remains of the traditional management hierarchy. What little has survived cannot accommodate the bulge of aging baby boomers trying to squeeze through a promotion bottleneck that grows narrower each year. Only a few will make it through and move into management careers. As a result, what may well be the most important reward system of all, career advancement, is no longer available in its traditional form. New, network models of career progression are needed to give these ambitious, highly educated employees opportunities for growth and new challenges to strive for. Team-based, technology-enabled organizations will have to aim their human resource policies in a new direction.

What Are Network Career Paths?

The network career path contains both a vertical sequence of jobs and a series of horizontal opportunities. The network career path recognizes the interchangeability of experience at certain levels and the need to broaden experience at one level before promotion to a higher level. This approach more realistically represents opportunities for employee development in network organizations than does the traditional career path. The vertical and horizontal options lessen the probability of blockage. One disadvantage of this type of career path is that explaining to employees the specific route the career may take for a given line of work is more difficult.

Network career moves can take place in two ways: team to team and job to job within a team. In these cases, the individuals themselves do not necessarily move from one job to another. What does move, to a higher level in this case, are their skills and the complexity of the tasks they perform. For example, secretaries now operate and maintain computers and other office equipment, manage information flows, and create databases.

Lateral moves from team to team can also serve multiple interests. Employees acquire valuable experience and skills from each team they work on or each unit they rotate through. The teams, the units, and the overall organization also gain from the experience, skills, and perspectives employees acquire as they move from one assignment to the next. These days, both companies and employees are healthier if employees have multiple skills, if they can move easily across functional boundaries, if they are comfortable switching back and forth between regular duties and special projects, and if they feel comfortable moving on when the right fit within one company can no longer be found.

Policies and Programs that Foster Network Career Development

Individuals and organizations can do a number of things to foster network career paths. For example, to cultivate the kind of people who can "bridge the cultural gap" between the information technology department and the business teams it serves, Keen says that "firms must make crossing the 'cultural divide' a requirement for advancement."[7] He proposes assigning selected individuals from information technology to a business department or team for periods ranging from six months to two years. Similar transfers would occur in the opposite direction as well. For example, local gurus could take a temporary assignment in information technology to develop their contacts and skills.

Eventually, these employees return to their original departments or units with the broadened perspectives and lateral skills they acquired during their transfer assignments. They are now well positioned to facilitate collaboration between historically separate parts of the organization. The applicability of this policy extends beyond information technology. It can be used to build other bridges, cross other boundaries, and develop other skills. Lateral career moves from one team, project, or department to another should be encouraged, regardless of the cultures or functions involved.

Other formal policies, programs, and systems can also support lateral career movement. Human resource information systems that track people skill levels, current job assignments, and job opportunities are good examples. Either on their own or with the help of career counselors, employees can use these systems to search for work assignments that match their experience, training, and interests. Similarly, teams can scan for potential new members who meet the skill and other requirements of the team.

Designing Network Career Paths

This section provides a solution to one of the vexing problems of transformation.[8] In transformed processes, job distinctions based on hierarchical position and reporting relationships tend to be replaced by distinctions based on knowledge and skill. But since most jobs are enriched, they are multidimensional, so it is difficult to compare them directly.

We first assign measures of the skill, knowledge, and orientation required for each job. This will give us a rough measure of the worth of each job. We next measure the difficulty of making a transition from one job to the next. This transition measure turns out to be a more discriminatory measure and allows us to rank all jobs from least difficult to most difficult. This ranking of jobs can then be used to develop career paths.

NOTES

1. Don Mankin, Susan G. Cohen, and Tora K. Bikson, *Teams and Technology: Fulfilling the Promise of the New Organization* (Harvard Business School Press, 1996), p. 230.

2. Anthony F. Smith and Tim Kelly, "Human Capital in the Digital Economy," in Frances Hesselbein, Marshall Goldsmith, and Richard Beckhard (eds.), *The Organization of the Future* (Jossey-Bass, 1997), p. 210.

3. Mankin et al.,*Teams and Technology*, p. 220.

4. Christopher W. Head, *Beyond Corporate Transformation* (Productivity Press, 1997), p. 170.

5. Robert S. Kaplan and David P. Norton, *The Balanced Scorecard: Translating Strategy into Action* (Harvard Business School Press, 1996).

6. Francis J. Gouillart and James H. Kelly, *Transforming the Organization: Reframing, Restructuring, Revitalizing, and Renewing* (McGraw-Hill, 1995), p. 249.

7. Peter G. W. Keen, *The Process Edge* (Harvard Business School Press, 1997), p. 184.

8. Raymond L. Manganelli and Mark M. Klein, *The Reengineering Handbook: A Step-by-Step Guide to Business Transformation* (AMACOM, 1994), p. 176.

PART IV

Completing
the Transformation

Evaluating and Incorporating Redesigned Systems

In Chapter 7 we broke down the enterprise system into a number of processes so that the task of redesigning each process and ultimately the enterprise would be feasible. In chapters 8 through 13 we redesigned and optimized each of these processes from a work, IT, and HR standpoint. And now comes the time to reunite these redesigned processes with their parent enterprise. We use the term *incorporate* for this reuniting process. By incorporate we mean: to unite or work into something already existent so as to form an indistinguishable whole, to blend or combine thoroughly, and to unite as one body. Other authors have used the words implement, integrate, and install for this phase, but we consider that *incorporate* more accurately conveys the meaning of what we are doing.

Incorporation is an important aspect of transformation. Far more transformation efforts fail for lack of effective incorporation management than because their technical or social designs are flawed. Throughout this chapter we will assume that we are incorporating a single process to simplify the discussion.

DIAGNOSE PERFORMANCE OF REDESIGNED PROTOTYPE

Before incorporating the redesigned process into the enterprise system, we must make sure that the process is operating properly and is ready to be incorporated. We will do so in this section.

Conduct Trial Run and Evaluate Performance of Prototype

Conducting a trial run will determine whether or not your process improvements have reduced or eliminated the root cause(s) of your identified process problem areas and have achieved performance goals as stated in the project plan. Also, the trial run will help you determine whether your improvements have satisfied your customers' requirements. Truly assessing the impact of process improvements requires that you:

- Solicit customer feedback during your trial-run period.
- Review data related to your process improvement.
- Determine if the root cause of process problem areas has been reduced or eliminated.
- Verify that your improvements in process performance have been sustained.

Solicit Customer Feedback During Your Trial-run Period. The goal of process improvement is to better satisfy the customer and to ensure that processes meet or exceed customer requirements. Give your improvement effort the acid test: Ask your customers! You may feel that your effort is successful, but if your customers feel otherwise, you have not succeeded.

You may not have all the deficiencies ironed out during the trial-run period, but you should still see results. If not, you may have to go back to the drawing board. If customers sense improvement, then you are on the right track. You may still have to double your efforts, but at least you can see the light at the end of the tunnel.

Reviewing, Determining, and Verifying. Here's where you put to work the data you gathered in the previous phase. Data does not lie or cheat. Study it to determine whether your improvements have actually accomplished what you had hoped. There are two prime criteria for process assessment: effectiveness and efficiency. In process operations, effectiveness refers to how well the output meets customer requirements—a measure of actual against intended output. Efficiency is a measure of how well the internal operations are performed in terms of output and resources required to achieve the output. Process assessment must take into account both effectiveness and efficiency.

Next, determine if the root cause of your process problem areas has been reduced or eliminated. If one of your process problem areas is poor communication, and your work group found that the root cause was lack of communication skills, has your improvement effort taken care of that problem? Have communication skills improved? After you have reviewed the data and determined if the root cause has been reduced or eliminated, verify that your improvements to process performance have been sustained.

Prototypes and Prototyping

A *prototype* is defined as an approximation of the process along one or more dimensions of interest. Under this definition, any entity that exhibits some aspect of the process that is of interest to the design team can be viewed as a prototype. This definition is purposely broad and includes prototypes ranging from concept sketches to fully functional artifacts. *Prototyping* is the process of developing such approximations to a process.

Need for Prototypes and Prototyping

Increasing global competition has imposed severe demands on transformation. Companies who want to lead the way must get up to full speed quickly and cannot afford any missteps. Improved processes must be designed properly in minimum time. In order to compete in this manner, a design team has to learn rapidly. Many design efforts involve the integration of many functions. In these integrated efforts, prototypes are the key to increased learning, reduced mistakes, and increased system integrity.

Prototypes are one of the most powerful tools a design team can use to resolve important questions quickly and unambiguously. In addition, they provide a common understanding and integrating force for all members of the team, regardless of the members' differences in function and culture. Yet, far too often, companies do not create enough prototypes, nor do they create them early enough to resolve important uncertainties. Furthermore, those that are made are often inadequate to prove out performance in production, compounding rather than solving problems. *The traditional approach to prototyping is not effective.*

A new approach must be taken. Prototyping is no longer done only to answer questions at final review time; *it is done to allow the team to progress swiftly and intelligently through the incremental steps of design.* Prototypes are no longer the exclusive domain of the engineer. They are the common language that knits together the design team, the company that supports the team, and the team's eventual customers.

Using Prototypes to Reduce Cost, Time, and Risk

Early learning decreases uncertainty; thus the effectiveness of prototyping depends on the *timing* of prototypes throughout the design program. Effective early prototyping reduces the cost of processes, reduces the design time, and reduces the design risk.

Minimizing Cost by Minimizing Late Design Changes. The process of design is by its nature a process of change. But when extensive design changes are introduced late in the design cycle they can undermine even the best of project plans. Late design changes invariably upset the optimum balance between the features, cost, and quality required of the process. In the long term, the negative consequences of late changes can only lead to costly, inferior processes and can permanently pervade a company by creating a demoralized work force, poor productivity, and severely delayed schedules.

An effective approach to design changes is one in which early prototyping is used to flush out problems. The approach emphasizes quick turn-around—which requires early prototypes to check out important ideas quickly to avoid problems in the later stages that would necessitate a re-design. Early problem detection is achieved by early and frequent analyt-ical and physical prototypes that are characterized by a reasonably high authenticity of the parts and processes. The intent of such early prototyp-ing is not to seek perfection but to gain essential knowledge.

To make early prototyping possible, design teams must be fully inte-grated from the beginning. Especially, manufacturing people should be integrated so that the earliest prototypes will reflect the realities of pro-duction procedures. Early prototyping will require that management invest more money up front. To implement this strategy, the team must enjoy priority access to prototyping resources such as simulation software, an extensive database, and shop facilities.

The Timing of Prototypes. Time plays an absolutely critical role in the design of a new process. The design latitude essential to creating the best balance between the fundamental cost of a process, its competitive fea-tures, and its quality is only attainable in the early stages of design. The real window of opportunity is the period prior to the completion of the preliminary design. After that decision point, the changes that are possible can only have a marginal effect on the basic process. Most process design managers will agree that about 85 percent of the ultimate cost of the process is determined during the first 15 percent of the design time. Hence rapid learning and the ability to make critical decisions early are essential for process success. Early prototypes provide one of the most effective means for achieving the learning essential to sound decisions.

Because substantial learning accompanies each prototype stage, it fol-lows that early prototyping with subsequent updates at important junc-tures can provide several major benefits. These include a reduction in total design time, a reduction in the risk introduced by innovation, and the early detection of problems, which leads to the avoidance of expensive late de-sign changes.

Limiting Risk with Early Prototypes. In competitive process lines, sig-nificant innovation is vital and must be achieved with very tight time schedules. Innovation runs the risk of extended design time or even fail-ure, which always come with ventures into unfamiliar territory. Because of time pressures and reduced design flexibility, problems that crop up late in the design cycles have serious consequences. Ferreting out problems early, with a strategy of early prototyping, allows for corrections at the time of greatest design adaptability, thereby reducing risk.

Using Prototypes to Improve Quality. Even if early prototyping is used to get the project off to a strong start, the use of system prototypes near the end of the design cycle is critical. There is a strong relationship be-tween the quality of the full system prototype and the final quality of the end process. The number of problems that can be solved between the system prototype and production is very limited. The greater the number of problems remaining in the final system prototype, the greater the likelihood that problems will persist when production begins. Even with a frantic effort at the end, products that require major design changes after final systems prototyping will probably be significantly deficient at process incorporation.

Very often, the most effective way to obtain the array of design information needed is to use a spectrum of prototypes. The precise nature of the prototype varies widely according to the questions it is intended to answer. The best results are achieved when design teams use prototypes that are best suited for a particular stage of design.

All prototypes play important, but different, roles in the resolution of crucial design questions. Most early prototypes are fashioned as models, mockups, or computer simulations and are useful in scoping out basic process characteristics in the early stages, even though their completeness is low. As the design proceeds, subsystems and configuration prototypes that more closely represent the process are used in the Preliminary Design Stage. As production ramp-up approaches, the full-system prototypes and the production prototypes are called into action as a final check of systems integration.

Selecting Redesigned Processes for Incorporation

Evaluating the Potential Costs and Benefits of Each Alternative. The purpose of this step is to estimate the cost and benefit of the various processes to provide the basis for deciding which processes to incorporate. For the most part, this task uses standard cost-benefit analysis. Since most managers have lived with these studies throughout their careers, we will assume that our readers have considerable knowledge in performing and using these studies. The following discussion will be directed to considerations that we wish to highlight or that apply especially to transformation.

The first task in defining both costs and benefits is to calculate the changes resulting from the redesigned process. This evaluation is essentially a review of the process and interface lists to make certain that all changes are considered. Following this check, the complete extent of the changes that the new design will cause should be documented. Each change to a work flow, business function, process, job, or support must be considered. The degree and nature of each change will be the basis for costing that change. As the individual changes are aggregated into higher-level arrangements, the costs will be grouped for presentation.

Two different types of costs are associated with each new process: the one-time cost of incorporation and the continuing cost of operation afterward. The cost of incorporation, added to the cost of the redesigning project, will be the investment that the company will make in the new process.

In transformation, it is often the intangibles that provide the most compelling reason to incorporate a new operational design. In the long run, improving process reliability and customer satisfaction will provide the highest benefit—certainly more than cutting a cost or eliminating positions from the payroll. For "bottom-line" managers, this concept is foreign; accepting this category of benefit as valid represents a paradigm shift for these individuals.

Selecting the Best Processes. The approach used to select the best alternatives will vary in each company. The differences will be related primarily to corporate culture: Regardless of the selection approach, the selection of the best alternative will be related to benefit and cost—selecting the process with the greatest benefit, the least impact, and smallest cost.

The selectors will change with respect to the scope of the effort. With large high-impact efforts, the Executive Steering Board will be the final selection authority. For department-oriented change, process improvement, and often problem-resolution-oriented change, the management groups will probably make the final decision. For efforts that remain internal to a department, the department manager may select the alternative.

The selection review opens the alternative designs to comment and potentially to change. As managers become more familiar with the design, they may notice opportunities for improvement that have been overlooked. The managers will provide a different perspective and offer different backgrounds from which to evaluate the design. Any required changes must be put through all appropriate impact analysis and design method tasks. As these changes may significantly modify the costs and/or the benefits, the cost-benefit analysis must be reviewed and updated where necessary.

PREPARE FOR INCORPORATION

Developing the Incorporation Plan

Having designed and tested a prototype and selected a process, an organization faces the considerable challenge of migrating from the current process environment to the radically new design. Study and design should encompass the entire organization so that relationships and work flow can be seen clearly. You need to study how all the pieces fit together in order to identify the relationships and find the optimum design. If you are incorporating more than one process at a time, you must also take into account the interactions among the processes.

But you need not *incorporate* all the changes at once. You can change your entire organization all at once or gradually, piece by piece. A full "cutover" may be difficult or impossible. If the new process involves customers, revenues, or valued employees or if the process change will be highly visible internally or externally (and for what important process are these conditions not true?), the firm may not want to risk a full, abrupt transition. Alternatives to full cutover include using a pilot, phased introduction or creating an entirely new business unit.

Should We Use a Pilot?

A *pilot* is a smaller scale, but fully operational, implementation of a new process in a relatively small unit of the organization based on a particular geography, product, or set of customers. Although pilots are often viewed as a means of testing a new process (or other type of intervention), the goal should be to achieve success rather than merely test. Thus, the unit selected should be the one most capable of achieving successful change.

Scope of the Change

One factor that may influence your decision is the scope of the change you are introducing, in terms of both the degree of difference between the old and the new and the size of your organization.

Difference between Old and New. If the new units and relationships are very different from the old ones, it will be more difficult to make changes in one part of the organization at a time. You cannot simply isolate an existing section and begin changing the way it operates; you must form new sections, taking people from existing sections to do so. If this is your situation, you may want to incorporate incrementally across the board, moving to some interim structure. Sometimes, you can move people into their new positions but introduce them gradually to new ways of operating. Another option is to move a few people into the new structure and let them begin working in new ways and then extend the changes to the rest of the organization.

Size of the Organization. In a small organization with fewer than 100 people, there is probably little need to incorporate structural changes bit by bit. In large organizations of more than 500 people, incorporating the changes all at once will be more difficult and may prove to be impossible. Between these extremes, the area is gray. Here, the nature of the change may be your guide.

Other Considerations

If you are moving from an organization that uses individuals as the critical unit to a structure with teams or groups as the key unit, as we propose, many supporting changes must be made throughout the organization. New ways of managing, new ways of thinking about training, and new ways of solving problems, perhaps even new ways of selecting people,

Figure 14-1
Checklist for Locating a Pilot Area

Good Choice	Poor Choice
*People involved are interested in change.	*Many people in the pilot believe that the new structure will limit or reduce the power or influence they hold currently.
*People involved are motivated to make the organization successful.	
*Process involved is sound.	*Process involved is at or near the end of its life cycle.
*Customers involved are solid.	
*Pilot is visible to the rest of the organization.	*Customers involved are on the brink of taking their business elsewhere.
*Pilot area is relatively independent from the rest of the organization.	*Pilot group is dependent on other areas in order to do its work successfully.

are also necessary. These changes are the subjects of chapters 12 and 13. They need not all be incorporated at once, but the organization must know that you are aware of the need for the changes and that you and your steering group or staff will ensure that the new structure receives all supporting changes necessary to make it a successful, competitive organization.

Starting with a Pilot

An airplane pilot steers the airplane to its destination, making course adjustments to account for variances in wind and weather. The role of a pilot effort in process incorporation is similar.

Advantages of a Pilot. Perhaps the greatest advantage of a pilot incorporation is that mistakes can be contained, examined, and learned from. By working first with a small piece of your organization, you can use the results there to make adjustments in subsequent segments. Given that the pace of change is forced by pressures of competition, cost, and customer need, frequently the business just cannot wait until all parts of the process are complete before rolling it out.

The second advantage is that early incorporation can be used to create a demand for the new processes. By incorporating the process in part, it should be possible to deliver at least a subset of the benefits of the new ways of working. By doing so, it is possible to create a taste for the benefits and improvements that will ultimately accrue. This, managed correctly, is an incredibly powerful lever for change. People begin to see the new ways of working as desirable, rather than an imposition, once they have seen what a partial incorporation can provide. It turns one of the biggest problems of organizational change on its head—the difficulties raised by imposing solutions upon people are replaced by a demand for the new ways of working.

Choosing a Pilot Group. You should choose your pilot area carefully, with an eye toward maximum success. If the pilot is highly successful, this will facilitate incorporating the remainder of the processes. Figure 14-1 provides a convenient checklist for the characteristics that distinguish a potentially successful pilot from an unsuccessful one.[1]

Other Incorporation Strategies

One migration approach is to begin with a *pilot* and follow with a *phased introduction*. A firm might, for example, incorporate new systems capabilities and skills as they become available. A phased approach may be the most economically feasible, in that companies can derive some financial benefit from the process change earlier than might otherwise be possible, but it is not necessarily less disruptive than a full cutover. In fact, the sense of constant change and instability may be difficult for some employees to handle.

To be effective, the incorporation plan must address every action to build the new operational environment and then move from the present operation to the new one. This plan is thus very detailed. Each person's role must be considered and all tasks assigned. Control over the process is provided through the coordination of personnel, task relationships, and technology acquisition.

Developing the Test Plan

This plan contains the methods to be used for system validation, that is, it determines how to verify the correctness and quality of the process. The two main tools of verification are *standards* and *independent review*. Standards are important for several reasons. First, they provide direction to the developers; second, they provide a benchmark for the reviewers; and third, they help to condition the expectations of the clients. Independent review means that people other than the developers review the process. "Review" may include system, stress, parallel or pilot testing, inspection or observation, walk throughs, and demonstrations.

The plan also covers the methods to be used for incorporation and develops a time-phased deployment plan. Several issues are involved in incorporation. First, the new system may be replacing (partially or completely) an existing system. The plan must identify existing system roles and interfaces in the process and determine how these will change. It must also decide how to dispose of the existing data: Will it be converted, allowed to "run off," or be ignored? How will the new system results be reconciled with the existing system results? The transformation team must assess and document incorporation requirements. The time and resources involved in incorporation can be substantial and are often underestimated.

There are also several issues involved in the deployment, or *fielding*, of the system, particularly in a geographically dispersed organization. The personnel who will be involved in fielding the system "on site" should be involved in planning. The deployment plan should address such issues as: What training will be required at each site? What documentation? How will each site get help with their problems? How can the impact of the new system on each site be coordinated with that site's business cycle?

Finally, the task assesses the impacts of the new system and defines fallback and contingency plans. These are especially important in view of Murphy's law: If anything can go wrong, it will. The last thing we want to have happen is to discover that the new system doesn't work and we have no way to revert to the old system.

Prepare and Implement Plan for "Selling" Process

The word "selling" appears in quotations here because its interpretation at this point differs from the usual meaning.[2] First, "selling" refers to obtaining organization-wide acceptance of a solution that could not possibly have involved everyone in the project effort. A second meaning concerns transferring a solution found effective in one part of an organization to other departments or locations. Some examples include a good inventory control and accounting system in one warehouse to the other fourteen in the company. This meaning is often called *institutionalizing* the solution or system as soon as it has been proven successful.

By this point, there is a small constituency that favors the solution. Links to the various support services are mostly in place. This step seeks to organize the larger constituency and its resources to secure the *continuing* sanction of all those who can influence the incorporation.

This plan begins with identification of the stakeholders and their likely issues. Some stakeholders are jobs that many people hold. The people usually have common interests so the job can be treated as one stakeholder. Other stakeholders (typically managers) hold unique jobs, so the stakeholder is the individual. When the program is executed, however, each person must be treated as an individual, regardless of his or her job.

While the employees are an obvious class of stakeholder, there are many others. Depending on the organization, these may include distributors and sales representatives, suppliers, shareholders, regulators, and directors. For each stakeholder, this plan also identifies their expected avenues of resistance and defines measures of the level of resistance or buy-in. It then plans a communications program, a program to assess buy-in and intervene, if necessary, and a general education and training program for all personnel.

The plan that results from this step will most likely contain a list of whom you should meet with regularly, who is responsible in the other departments, what is to be covered, who is to be responsible for actual changes, what monitoring methods are to be used, and so on.

UPDATE DESIGN OF EXISTING ENTERPRISE SYSTEM

This design is concerned with updating the existing core system so it can support the redesigned process(es). This design is particularly important when the IT aspects of the process has changed. The existing information system is required to enable all the newly designed processes to operate properly. It includes modeling sub-processes, modeling data, defining applications, and designing dialogs and screens. Alternatively, this task could involve the selection of a commercially available application package and the external design of any modifications. The updating of the existing core system should be initiated in chapters 8 and 9 and must be completed in this stage to enable the installation of the redesigned processes.

The design and development of automated application systems is an enterprise fraught with risk and difficulty. Notwithstanding the fact that larger organizations have been building such systems for 30 years or more, the success rate is considerably lower than for other similar organizational undertakings. The primary cause of this unsatisfactory performance is that most organizations have not reengineered their process for systems design. The design of customized application systems to implement the technical design of a reengineered process should be avoided if at all possible. Such design not only increases the risk of failure, it invariably lengthens the time for incorporation.

Fortunately, there is now a rich variety of off-the-shelf application packages available for most business applications.[3] Many packages contain built-in options that permit different organizations to customize the application to their needs. One of the most useful of such packages is SAP, which supports more than 800 processes. Even when a single application package lacks all of the required features and functions, an organization still has several options for using the package. One option is to *modify* the package, that is, to change some of the package vendor's code. This option is the least desirable because it increases both the risk and the difficulty of maintaining the system. A second option is to *extend* the package, that is, to leave the vendor's code unchanged but to write additional code that works with the package. This option of extending the package is less risky than the first. A third option is to *integrate* the package, that is, to make the package work with another package or custom program by using the integration features of the operating environment. Especially with microcomputer operating environments such as Microsoft Windows or UNIX, the integration capabilities are extensive. This option is the least risky of the three.

Perform Platform Design

In this section we are concerned with the design of the subsystem (commonly referred to as the "platform") that will immediately support the redesigned process. For packages, this task is performed by the vendor. We first select the platform or platforms on which the application system will be mounted. For information systems, we are primarily talking about selecting the computers on which the applications programs will run. For both information systems and physical systems, the platform consists of hardware and software. The primary difference is in the terminal devices. Information systems terminals provide human interface. Physical systems terminals provide interfaces with both humans and things.

The platform selection decision should be driven by the needs and availability of the application software. All other things being equal, a redesign team should first select the most suitable software application package and then select the platform that package best runs on. That is why we place the selection of the package in Chapter 9. But often a redesign team will not have a completely free choice in the selection of the platform. Sometimes, the system must interact with other systems; the best way is to mount the new system on the same platform as the old. Other times, the organization has made a strategic decision to mount all new design on the same platform.

Once the platform has been selected, the remaining work of the task depends on whether the application will be based on a package or will be custom developed. If the application is based on a package, the next step involves selecting the package options to be used and/or designing extensions or modifications to the package or to the interfaces between the package and other systems. If the application is custom developed, the next step is to design the physical data structure. This means mapping the attributes of an entry into data fields, deciding which data fields should reside in which records or tables, and specifying how the relationships among entities should be represented. It also means specifying the media on which the data will reside and the methods of assessing the data. The choices here are limited by the capabilities of the data management subsystem of the selected platform.

Place and Train Personnel

Place Personnel

Placement involves the evaluation and matching of employee skills, knowledge, abilities, and aptitude with job demands. In Chapter 11 (pp. 241–243) we planned for the long-range recruiting and selection of personnel. In Chapter 12 (pp. 249–252) we discussed the general characteristics of work team members. In this task we look at specific work teams and select specific people to fill the specific jobs on that team.

The assessment of potential ability is very important, because determination of the disposition of each person should be based on potential ability and not on the job they now hold. Some people are underqualified for their jobs. Other people are overqualified. And some people possess skills, knowledge, and orientation unrelated to their present job but very desirable in another job. The assessment of each person is then matched against the job requirements of specific work teams, and people are assigned where they can best contribute.

Looking at the larger picture, transformation usually improves the efficiency and effectiveness of a process and the productivity of the people involved in the process. It is usually true that fewer people can handle the same amount of work. This means that, all else being equal, there will be too many people for the amount of work. The question then becomes what to do with those people.

The answer to this question depends to a great extent on the company's business strategy and culture. If the strategy is to retrench, downsize, surrender market share, and exit certain businesses, then it may well be appropriate to reduce staff. On the other hand, if the strategy is expansive, to grow, enter new markets, and expand market share, then it is possibly inappropriate to reduce staff. Even if it appears more profitable in the short term to shed certain employees while hiring others, this may be an anomaly of our accounting systems.

In spite of all these tactics, it is often necessary to reduce staff; the question then becomes which staff to retain. The first criterion should be the person's aptitude for the new job. The second criterion should be the person's buy-in to the change, whether they approach it with enthusiasm or fear. Once we know who will staff the redesigned process and how their current skills, knowledge, and orientation compare with the job requirements, we can prescribe the training needs of each person. The training needs from this task are then used to finalize the components of the education and training curriculum and to assign individuals to specific courses, as discussed in the next section.

Train Personnel

This task provides training in the operation, administration, and maintenance of the new process, *just in time* for the staff to assume their new responsibilities. It also includes coaching as they assume those responsibilities. We want to train personnel just in time because too early means that they will forget what they've been taught and too late means that they are unprepared for their responsibilities.

Sometimes we train personnel to work with the system while it is still being tested. This gives the staff additional time to develop their comfort and proficiency with the system before they have to use it "live," and it gives the system developers additional and unplanned test cases to evaluate. But the system should be in a reasonably good state before we allow people to work with it, or we run the risk of alienating them.

Members of the work team rarely possess all of the skills they need at the time the team is formed. They almost always require some training. This can include:

- training in the skills team members need to perform their tasks;
- training in problem-solving group interaction and conflict management to help members work more effectively in groups;
- cross-training to provide members with the variety of skills required for team flexibility;
- training in quality analysis or statistical process control to help teams monitor and improve their performance; and
- business and economic education to help teams understand their activities in the context of overall business goals and strategy.

Prepare and Provide Operational Support

While we cannot specify the required operational resources for every process (since each process is unique), we can offer two important generalizations. First, people must have the skills, abilities, and knowledge to implement and operate the process. Second, all of the materials, equipment, information, and personnel necessary to operate the redesigned process must be ready before it is incorporated.

The following suggestions for operational support are only *partial* in number and *suggestive* in scope:

- *Inputs.* Introduce customers/clients/users to new ordering/ information/monetary requirements, order new forms, get new material specifications and quality levels, set up bills of material, establish continuing attitude survey of users and customers, and establish line of credit for operating funds.
- *Outputs.* Set up financial accountability methods, measure quality of product/ service in users' perceptions, get regulatory clearances for services/products, and organize distributors for new advertising campaign.
- *Environment.* Change to new organizational structure, develop the political support for continued operation, set up departmental operating rules, prepare for letters "smoothing" the way, and arrange for new organizational design.
- *Personnel.* Train personnel for new assignment(s), transfer/hire new personnel, set up job descriptions, establish and evaluate performance requirements, train troubleshooters to handle difficulties, and obtain needed professional services.
- *Material.* Order new equipment, arrange for refurbishing of tooling, and obtain comparisons of equipment specifications.
- *Information Aids.* Update maintenance manuals, establish regulations, set up incorporation guides, re-program software for monitoring activities.[4]

INCORPORATE REDESIGNED PROCESS

Conduct Final Test of Redesigned Process

This task produces an operations-ready version of the new process. When the process is based on a custom-designed system, this task includes design and testing of databases, design and testing of systems and procedures, and documentation. When the process is based on a package, this task includes installation and modification or extension of the package and its testing. In either case, the task also includes conversion of data.

This task puts the incorporation schedule into operation. It starts the transition to real-world modes of operating. Installation is influenced by many of the same dynamic events that affect the other steps. Some of the events that can be expected are timing delays, timing speedups, branching to a new phase, cycling within one or between two phases, environmentally caused interruptions, scheduling delays, and failure recycles.

Testing is usually a multi-step, multilevel procedure, proceeding from the testing of the smallest system units, through larger and larger aggregates of system units, until the entire system is tested as a unit. Even then, additional testing is usually performed to determine the behavior of the system under stress, to compare the results of the new system with that of the old, and to develop client comfort with the system.

All of the activities included in this task should have been planned and included in the test section of the incorporation plan. A pilot that operates the redesigned process in a limited area only may be used to identify problems and make needed corrections before full deployment.

Incorporate Redesigned Process and Monitor

With the final design and test of the redesigned process completed, it is now time to incorporate the process into its parent system and monitor its operation. Because it is impossible to plan for every contingency when incorporating a process, the best preparation is to build in a *monitoring* function to look for and solve problems. Initially monitoring should be viewed as a learning experience rather than a matter of strict adherence to a set of system specifications and an installation schedule. A *redesigned process is not a videocassette that can just be inserted and expected to perform.*

In addition to time and cost per "unit," other performance data provide good monitoring indices: efficiency, productivity, budgetary control ratings, excess direct labor cost ratio, equipment utilization ratio, cumulative failures or failure rate, number of breakdowns, and so on. One point at which it may be desirable, and often profitable, to discontinue follow-up and debugging efforts occurs when the learning curve reaches a plateau or when reliability or other factors reach the desired level and stay relatively constant for awhile.

Most people expect an immediate improvement in performance when a new process is incorporated. However, there is usually an initial downturn in performance, and the increase in performance comes much later than anticipated. New systems and equipment do not immediately perform as expected, and adaptation, debugging, retraining, reorienting departments and clarifying information channels are needed—all adding to the costs and deterioration of performance.

Evaluate Performance of Redesigned Process

When the flaws detected during the monitoring phase are corrected, it is then time to evaluate the performance of the redesigned process. Performance measurements for the whole process or its components are contained in the test section of the incorporation plan. They are expressed in various units: time per output unit, time per element, time per work component, output units per minute (or hour), number of people served per week, dollars per transaction, percentage of machine utilization, per capita complaints, productivity index, percentage of material utilization, hours of direct labor, cost per unit, and so on.

A performance measure should be expressed as an expected value (mean, mode, minimum, etc.), with its associated variability and confidence levels. Variability limits are psychologically desirable for operators and managers who already know that each performance cycle will not take an exactly identical time. All parts of the performance measure need updating periodically as part of normal operating activities. A performance measure must be associated with a well-defined activity, artifact, or outcome. The measure attains greater accuracy and precision (less variability) the greater the specificity of the real-world phenomenon to which it refers.

The work team should periodically assess just how well the process's purposes, objectives, and overall goals are being attained. This goes beyond daily or weekly performance reports that an organization would normally have prepared. Goals, objectives, values, and purposes were agreed upon for each process, and a solution was selected to achieve them. How well are they being accomplished, now that a period of time (a year or so) has elapsed? In addition to providing an audit and review function, this evaluation may signify that further improvement of a process should be initiated.

Critical to the evaluation are the perceptions of operating personnel and clients. These people need to feel comfortable with the solution and perceive its advantages. Clients and managers need to know that benefits are accruing through the changed "behavior" of the organizational personnel. Customers in particular should perceive the benefits and pleasures of a better-quality or lower-priced product or service.

Refine Process and Continue Operating

By now, your initial improvement efforts have been successful or you have refined them so that you can reach your goals. But it's not over yet.

You need to make sure that your improved process will not revert to the old way of doing things once it is installed in the operational system. To keep your process in top form, you have to standardize it and monitor its ongoing improvement. Only then will the incorporation in the operational system be successful.

Gather and Utilize Ongoing Customer and Supplier Feedback

It is feedback that fuels the effectiveness of any process changes. Gathering customer feedback allows you to gauge how you are doing and whether your changes are targeted correctly. You will not be making decisions in a vacuum.

Gathering feedback from your suppliers is also critical. They can let you know if your demands are within reason. Providing feedback to your suppliers also allows them to make additional changes to please you *(if your feedback suggests correction)* or gives them the motivation to work harder for you *(if your feedback is positive)*.

Hone and Continually Improve Process Performance Gains

Standardizing your process and monitoring its ongoing improvement will keep you in close touch with your process. That's the only way you will be able to reach your goal of performing your process in the best way possible. By now you have established intermediate goals that serve as *"performance milestones"* along the way to achieving your objectives. You should continually strive to reach the next milestone until you attain your ultimate goal.

FOLLOW-UP ACTIONS

Celebrate!

We are expecting, and rightly so, major increases in performance as the result of the transformation. However, the reality is that these large improvements may not be achieved in a short time. So welcome the small improvements as they occur, as long as the incorporation process continues.

The people involved in developing and incorporating the redesigned processes deserve an opportunity to celebrate their successes. Small improvements should have small celebrations, while the incorporation of a major process should be a more notable event. Chapter 13 discussed several ways in which recognition and reward can be given for achieving results. Informal arrangements may be appropriate for people directly involved with a process—a lunch or dinner, a picnic, a movie, a round of drinks after work, or a party. There should be more formal mechanisms for the whole organization.

Provide for Continuous Improvement

Transformation is too difficult and painful a process to engage in without good reason. If an organization correctly identifies its business objectives and its business processes, correctly assesses the impact of each process on the business objectives, and realizes a vision for breakthrough performance of the process, the only thing left for it to do is to build continuous improvement into the process. Then the organization should not have to transform unless it again encounters a change in its business strategy or environment.

For continuous process improvement to take place, three requirements must be met:

- Process personnel must be given clear performance goals, measures of goal attainment and information on the current and past values of those measures.
- Process personnel must be given the tools necessary to effect changes in performance.
- Process personnel must be given the responsibility, authority, and incentives for improving performance.[5]

Transformation provides the technical and social context for continuous improvement. On the social side, it provides empowered and motivated employees with the ability to contribute in a meaningful and self-rewarding manner. On the technical side, it provides the information and tools to assess current performance and improve upon it.

NOTES

1. Emily E. Schultheiss, *Optimizing the Organization: How to Link People and Technology* (Ballinger, 1989), p. 117.
2. Glen D. Hoffhor, John W. Moran, and Gerald Nadler, *Breakthrough Thinking in TQM* (Prentice-Hall, 1994), p. 320.
3. Raymond L. Manganelli and Mark M. Klein, *The Reengineering Handbook: A Step-by-Step Guide to Business Transformation* (AMACOM, 1994), p. 197.
4. Hoffhor et al., *Breakthrough Thinking in TQM*, p. 322.
5. Manganelli and Klein, *The Reengineering Handbook*, p. 207.

CHAPTER 15

Integrating the Transformation

INTRODUCTION

The Concept of Integration

Integration means to form, coordinate, or blend all components into a smooth function or unified whole, thus causing all the parts to work together in a manner that will make the whole process most productive. Each organization as a whole displays a relatively high or low degree of overall integration. Other things being equal, the greater the total degree of integration or fit among the various components, the more effective the organization will be. Put another way, the degree to which the strategy, work, people, structure, and culture are smoothly aligned will determine the organization's ability to compete and succeed.

The basic dynamic of integration sees the organization as most effective when its pieces fit together. If we also consider strategy, this view expands to include the fit between the organization and its larger environment. An organization is most effective when its strategy is consistent with its environment (in light of organizational resources and history) and when the organizational components fit the tasks necessary to implement that strategy.

Achieving integration requires describing the system, identifying problems, and determining the sources of poor fit. Various components can be configured in different ways and still achieve some degree of desired output. Therefore, the question becomes that of determining combinations of components that will lead to the greatest degree of integration and not a question of finding the one best way of managing. Another way to think about integration is to consider it in terms of the total organization. In that case it involves three essential elements:

- The *hardware*—the computers, monitors, keyboards, modems, disk drives, servers, cables, printers, scanners, and other physical pieces of equipment that make up a computer system
- The *software*—the encoded sets of instructions that allow hardware components to function, both individually and collectively, as a system or network
- The *peopleware*—the human interface—the people who actually select and use the software that make the hardware perform its assigned functions

Clearly, the effectiveness of each component is dependent on how well it meshes with the rest of the system. Neither hardware, nor software, nor people are of any use whatsoever in the absence of the other two. Some hardware and software are simply incompatible; together, they are useless. Beyond that, there are all kinds of software that will run on all kinds of hardware—but some combinations work much more smoothly than others. And even if you've found the optimal combination of hardware and software, it will not do any good unless the people using it understand how to use the software and the equipment. They've got to have a clear idea of the work they're supposed to perform, and they must be motivated to do it in a swift and conscientious way.

The Need for Integration

Transformation is a large endeavor involving many people. The actions of all these people must be well integrated if transformation is to be successful. In the transformation process we are primarily concerned with two types of integration: cross-function integration and cross-stage integration.

Cross-function integration is concerned with improving how the major functions in transformation (work redesign, IT redesign, and social redesign) work together to achieve optimum results. A functionally integrated process is characterized by joint, proactive decision making among all redesign teams. Joint decision making means that experts from each function work as contributors of disciplinary expertise and not as defenders of their own function's agenda or their boss's orders. An integrated process also causes team members to anticipate and manage problems and actively exploit opportunities for progress that exist at the interfaces between different technologies.

Cross-stage integration is concerned with improving the coordination of effort *across the stages of the transformation process*. Because transformation is a long and complex process, we wisely divide it into stages so we can better perform and manage it. However, we must ensure that information is passed along the process, particularly from the earlier stages

Figure 15-1
Major Tasks and Outputs of the Transformation Process

<u>REDESIGN EFFORTS</u>

Stage	Work Redesign	IT Redesign	Social Redesign
Diagnose System	Diagnose Existing and Future Enterprise *(pp. 134-140)* **Output = Process Map**	Diagnose Process Maps to Obtain Data Model *(pp. 180-182)* **Output = Data Model**	Diagnose Existing and Future Organizations *(pp. 223-230)* **Output = Organization Map**
Broad System Design	Develop Enterprise Concept *(pp. 140-143)* **Output = Enterprise Concept**	Develop Enterprise IT Architecture *(pp. 182-183)* **Output = Enterprise IT Architecture**	Develop Organization Concept *(pp. 234-240)* **Output = Organization Concept**
Diagnose Process	Determine Customer Requirements for Process *(pp. 159-160)* **Output = Customer Requirements**	Define IT Requirements for Process *(pp. 184-185)* **Output = IT Requirements**	Diagnose Human Resources Requirements *(pp. 241-244)* **Output = Human Resources Requirements**
Detailed Process Design	Conduct Detailed Analysis and Redesign *(pp. 169-176)* **Output = Work Design**	Detailed IT Design of Individual Process *(pp. 185-191)* **Output = Information Design**	Complete Design of the Work Team *(pp. 249-252)* **Output = Social Design**

to later stages, so that work will proceed efficiently from one stage to the next. We can consider cross-function integration to be integration across *technologies*, while cross-stage integration is integration across *time*.

The two types of integration can be better understood by referring to Figure 15-1, where we have plotted four stages of the transformation process versus the three types of redesign efforts. For each of the twelve intersections a specific major *task* and the *output* of that major task are provided. There are many more than twelve tasks, but if we integrate the twelve major tasks shown in Figure 15-1, we will be able to integrate all other tasks, since they are controlled by the twelve major tasks. The page numbers in each block provide the location in the book where the task and output are described more completely. Cross-stage integration is required among the four stages of Diagnose System, Broad System Design, Diagnose Process, and Detailed Process Design. Cross-functional integration is required between the three redesign efforts of: Work Redesign, IT Redesign, and Social Redesign.

We expect the need for cross-stage integration to be much less than the need for cross-functional integration. Normally the design and the diagnosis stages are performed by the same team for both the system and the process. So there would be little need for additional integration for these two hand-offs. The biggest cross-stage problem is the hand-off from system design to process diagnosis. In this case two entirely different groups are involved. For example, the Technical Management Group would hand-off to a Technical Project Team that had just been formed. To solve this problem, we have developed a detailed procedure in Chapter 5 for developing a comprehensive project plan that will handle this hand-off.

The Transformation process proceeds from the top to the bottom of Figure 15-1, that is, from the *Diagnose System* stage to the *Detailed Process Design* stage. In general, transformation proceeds from left to right, starting with *Work Redesign* and ending with *Social Redesign*. For example, in the Diagnose System stage, the Work Design team (TMG) will first develop a Process Map using IDEF0, or a similar process mapping method. Using the Process Map as an input, the IT Design team will develop the Data Model, using IDEF1 or a similar data modeling method. And last, the Social Design team (SMG), with the Process Map and perhaps the Data Model as inputs, will develop the Organization Map, using IDEF3 or a similar procedure. In some stages, particularly the detailed process design stage, the three design efforts are often carried out simultaneously, since they are often performed by the same team.

Achieving Cross-Functional Integration

A critical element of the interaction between cross-functional groups is the pattern of communications.[1] The quality and effectiveness of the communications pattern is primarily determined by four characteristics: richness, frequency, direction, and timing. It is desirable to have communications that are (1) direct face-to-face and rich in content; (2) high frequency, intense, and on-line; (3) two-way; and (4) early in the process. Poor communications are characterized by those that are (1) sparse, (2) infrequent, (3) one-way, and (4) late.

A more important characteristic pertains to how groups link up. They can link up in **series**, in **parallel**, or **in between**. The *serial* linkup that has no cross-functional integration is the classic relationship in which the later group waits to begin its work until the earlier group has completely finished its work. For example, IT redesign would not start until a final fullblown process map is received from work redesign, and social redesign would not start until the final data model is received from IT redesign. Not only is this serial method of operating very slow, but the later group does not get any of the background on how the earlier group arrived at their decisions.

In contrast is the *parallel* or full cross-functional integration method of linking up. In this method, members of the later group not only participate in a preliminary and ongoing dialog with their earlier counterparts, but they use that information and insight to get a flying start on their own work. This changes the content of the later work in the early phases of effort and is also likely to change fundamentally the content and manner of communication between the two groups. Feedback will reflect actual practice in attempting to use the output of the earlier group. The parallel mode of linking up will foster face-to-face discussion, direct observations, and interactions that are needed for joint problem solving.

The ultimate version of the parallel linkup is to have all people on the same team. To reduce the need for cross-functional integration, all functions should be included on *one team*. However, this is not always feasible for a number of reasons, so we should be prepared to provide the required integration in other ways. In the following pages we investigate a number of additional methods for achieving integration.

INTEGRATION THROUGH ENLIGHTENED DIRECTION SETTING

Introduction

The traditional hierarchy relied on autocratic direction setting that cascaded through the various chains of command of the organization. Each chain translated corporate direction into direction for that part of the organization, its specificity increasing as the direction was passed down. Thus the direction received by the technical core of the organization was both narrow and specific. Indeed, it was not uncommon to talk to highly skilled and experienced individuals who were uninformed about organizational direction beyond their immediate job assignment. In several organizations in the early stages of the transition to teams, we saw "team" members who were unaware of even each other's goals and assignments. Little wonder that cross-functional integration in these traditional organizations was the purview of managers, often those relatively high in the organizational hierarchy. Little wonder, too, that direction was often fuzzy: Managers could get away with not giving clear direction because they could count on being able to resolve ambiguous issues themselves.

Rather than use cascaded hierarchical direction, team-based organizations must rely on developing extremely clear direction that is well known and well understood. People must work with the same rich understanding of the direction of the organization if:

- Issues are to be resolved laterally—that is, within and between teams

- Cross-functional teams are to be able to make complex trade-offs on issues that cannot be easily handled from the perspective of a single discipline or function.

If members of teams are to work together effectively, they must be provided integrated direction. What can an organization do to establish and communicate clear direction? Let us turn now to that question.

Importance of Vision, Strategy, and Culture in Direction Setting

A company's **vision** is a picture of the company sometime in the future. It promotes a shared mental framework that provides mental focus and a sense of purpose. Visions are usually short and graphically stated so they can be easily remembered and visualized. Visions can be considered a shorthand version of strategy and planned culture combined. A company's **strategy** is an expression of what it intends to *do*, or *achieve*, in the *external* environment. Strategy is primarily concerned with products, customers, competitors, and other elements of the *external* environment. A company's ideology or planned **culture** is an expression of what the company intends to *be*, or *become*, and pertains to the *internal* environment of the company. It is primarily concerned with employees, values, principles, beliefs, and other elements of the *internal* environment.

If an organization is to be successful, these three important expressions of corporate direction (vision, strategy, and planned culture) must be well matched and supportive, that is, their development and implementation must be integrated. The proper alignment between culture and strategy is of great importance. A close culture-strategy alignment promotes a smooth-running successful company; a mismatch poses real obstacles. The better the fit between culture and strategy, the less managers have to depend on policies, rules, procedures, and supervision to invoke what people should and should not do; rather, cultural norms are so well-known and accepted that they automatically guide behavior. A forward-looking company does not seek a mere balance between the vision, culture, and strategy; it seeks to develop all to their highest level at the same time, all the time.

The organizational culture supports organizational strategy by providing a base of continuity around which an innovative company can evolve, experiment, and change. By being clear about what are the core values and beliefs (and therefore relatively fixed), a company can more easily seek strategic change and movement in all that is not core. The strategy supports the culture, for without continual change and forward movement, the company—the carrier of the core—will fall behind in an ever-changing world and cease to be strong, or perhaps even to exist.

A tight culture-strategy alignment is a powerful lever for channeling behavior and helping employees do their jobs in a more strategy-supportive manner:

- Culturally approved behavior thrives, while culturally disapproved behavior gets squashed and often penalized. In a company where strategy and culture are misaligned, ingrained values and operating philosophies don't cultivate strategy-supportive work habits. Often the very kinds of behavior needed to execute strategy successfully run afoul of the culture and attract negative recognition rather than praise and reward.

- A strong strategy-supportive culture nurtures and motivates people to do their best; it provides structure, standards, and a value system in which to operate; and it promotes strong company identification among employees.

Importance and Difficulty of Matching Culture with Strategy

Aligning culture to strategy is particularly relevant today since the old approaches to doing business do not create sustainable competitive advantages. No longer can businesses focus on one strategic goal, such as cost leadership or differentiation in quality, customization, or innovation. Instead, they must pursue strategies focused on several goals, such as cost leadership and quality differentiation or cost leadership and customization. These multiple strategies require capabilities that combine aspects of stable and flexible cultures.[2] How to create a culture that develops and maintains these contrary capabilities adds a level of complexity to the design of effective culture/strategy fits, while accelerating competitive conditions makes it even more essential to discover the most effective match.

When executives set about the arduous task of forging an ideal alloy from a brilliant strategy and a strong culture, they begin by carefully analyzing two important groups: *customers* and *employees*. While strategic thinking aims at getting and keeping customers, culture building attracts, develops, motivates, and unifies the right kind of employees. When the organization's strategy to get and keep customers requires employees to act and think in unaccustomed ways, employees may respond poorly or even feel resentful. On the other hand, no matter how strongly an organization's culture motivates and develops employees, if customers do not perceive better products and services as a result, the culture has been wasted.

Additional Guidelines for Integration Through Direction Setting

Although an integrated strategy and planned culture are extremely important, there are other, lesser actions in direction setting that can have a significant effect on integration.

Align Goals Vertically and Laterally. Strategy gets translated into goals. In an organization that is a system of teams, the goals are for performing units (for example, individuals, teams, or product lines) nested within each

other as well as for the organization as a whole. These unit goals, in combination, must add up to the business goals. This raises issues of fit in two
areas: (1) between systemic levels (the goals of a lower-level unit, such as
an individual or a team, must fit with the goals of the higher-level business
unit in which that individual or team is embedded) and (2) between units
at the same level within a larger unit. The goals of all the teams in a
business unit must fit with each other, and the goals of all the individuals
within a team must fit with each other. This means that the goal-setting
process must be both vertically and laterally conducted.

Choose Goals That are Measurable. The data indicates very clearly that
having measurable team goals is related to team and business-unit effectiveness. These goals include performance targets, such as cost, quality,
schedule, revenue, and profit. They also include such goals as reusing a
certain amount of software code, earning a particular percentage of revenue from new products or new customers, and achieving an order of a
certain magnitude from a particular new customer.

Assign Rewards in Accordance with Organizational Goals. The reward
system is a direction-setting element of the organization because it influences the course of organizational effort. We are using the term *rewards*
very broadly here to refer to desired outcomes such as increased compensation, acknowledgment and recognition, and career advancement and
growth opportunities that accrue to organizational members as a result of
certain behaviors or performances.

Do Not Assume That Direction Precludes Empowerment. The issue of
direction has been particularly troublesome in organizations that see themselves as moving toward self-managed or empowered teams. Managers are
often reluctant to provide much direction, for fear of violating the spirit
of empowerment. Our research suggests, however, that providing direction
is critical to the empowerment process. In fact, not providing direction is
disempowering. However, the sort of direction required is different from
the traditional notion captured in the phrase "directive management"—a
practice in which managers tell subordinates what to do and how to do it
and monitor very closely the daily work activities. The direction that is
key in team-based organizations is based on broad knowledge of where
the organization is headed, its strategy for getting there, and the criteria
and priorities that result; and it is the translation of that broad direction
into local goals that aligns the various performing units of the organization
and the individuals within teams.

Plan Collectively. Team member involvement in the planning process is
related to team effectiveness. Ineffective teams in the companies we studied tended to have managers who developed and "kept" the plans, allowing little team input or influence.

Plans, regular updates and reviews of progress against plans, and determination of steps needed to address discrepancies are part of the process

of effective teams and underlie their ability to become more effective over time. This planning and review cycle is a team responsibility and a core team process. The role of management in the planning process is to

- Ensure that it is happening in a systematic manner,
- Ensure that the plans fit with the organization's needs for team performance (which may require an approval process),
- Periodically review with the team its progress against plans, and
- Be available to help the team problem-solve when obstacles arise.

THE INTEGRATED SOCIAL-TECHNICAL APPROACH

Origins of the Integrated Social-Technical Approach

Researchers from the Tavistock Institute, studying the introduction of new technology in British coal mines (and later in the weaving industry in India), discovered that technological innovation alone could not explain differences in performance. In fact, certain technological changes that were intended to increase performance resulted instead in performance declines. Research revealed that high performance resulted when the design of the technical system and the design of the social system of work were integrated.

Building on group dynamics and general systems theory, the Tavistock researchers demonstrated that high performance required that the needs of the organization's social system and the needs of the technical system be considered equally and simultaneously in the design process. They argued that a set of design principles different from the classical "one man/one job" approach be used to construct work systems. Rather than fitting jobs (and thus people) to the optimum technical system, the joint optimization of both the social and technical systems would be required.

Research over subsequent years led to the development of the *integrated social-technical* approach to work design, often called the *sociotechnical* approach. At the core of the integrated social-technical approach are the two elements—social and technical—designed deliberately to fit each other. Where a high degree of fit was achieved, performance increased. By the late 1960s, a large amount of experience (largely outside of the United States) had begun to accrue so that the principles of integrated social-technical work design could be articulated. At the core of the approach are five principles:

1. Although rules and work processes critical to overall success should be identified, no more rules should be specified than are absolutely essential.
2. Variances, or deviations, from the ideal process should be controlled at the point of origin.

3. Each member of the system should be skilled in more than one function so that the work system is flexible and adaptive.

4. Roles that are interdependent should be within the same departmental boundaries.

5. Information systems should be designed primarily to provide information to the point of action and problem solving.

In practice, integrated social-technical design also led to the heavy use of teams to manage interdependent work, with those teams empowered to manage their own work processes and flows. This approach therefore became known as "autonomous work teams" and was prevalent in Europe during the 1970s. During the 1960s and 1970s, an additional element was added. A number of designers pointed out that most of the integrated social-technical design work had been done with an internal focus. They argued that effective work system design needed to start with an external or "open systems" perspective, starting with the external stakeholders (customers, suppliers, competitors). Work system design would thus start with an understanding of environmental requirements, demands, and opportunities.

Optimization of Social-Technical System Design

Social-technical systems theorists have long recognized the need for changes in the way work systems are designed. The traditional design strategy employed by industrial engineers in manufacturing plants, for example, is to design the assembly line for maximum throughput and then to determine what kinds of jobs are required to run the line. This approach maximizes one performance criterion (throughput) while perhaps also considering a few additional performance criteria (e.g., labor cost) as constraints, at the expense of social system criteria, such as job quality. Instead, social-technical systems theorists have argued, work system designers should adopt the principle of "joint optimization," in which the social-technical system is designed to achieve both technical and social system goals simultaneously. Applied to information systems, the concept of joint optimization refers to the "strategic triangle" of business strategy, IT strategy, and organization strategy.[3] Applied to Business Process Reengineering, the principle of joint optimization implies that strategy, process, jobs, management structures and systems, and information and information technology should all be co-designed.

The principle of joint-optimization, while conceptually quite simple, is very difficult to achieve in practice. In the first place, design itself is a difficult skill to teach and learn. Design involves synthetic reasoning that is much more difficult to "program" than is analysis. Consequently, while we have many methodologies for job and business process analysis, we have almost no methodologies for job and process design.

Second, it is hard to structure a design process in which two or more quite different dimensions are considered simultaneously and given equal weight. Most social-technical systems design approaches do not address this problem well. For instance, the traditional social-technical systems approach starts with an analysis of unit processes and variances in the technical system.[4] The technical system analysis is followed by a description of social system needs and the roles that are required to cope with the production variances. This approach does not consider (as BPR experts would advocate) the possibility of a completely different role system performing a completely different technological process for accomplishing the same task.

An alternative social-technical systems approach provides more scope for radically different social systems by creating two separate design teams—one for the technical system, one for the social system—that operate in parallel. Once the teams have independently enumerated social and technical alternatives, the teams meet jointly to match them up. Alternatives that do not match are rejected, and the matched pairs are ranked. While this approach avoids some of the limitations of the traditional technical system, it ignores potential synergies between the social and technical realms. Thus, the designers who use it might have a tendency to overlook social system designs that are only possible given a radically new technology.

Recursive-Sequential Social-Technical Design Process

Given the difficulty of achieving a jointly optimized design, even the very best social-technical designers seem to have adopted a design approach that is predominantly sequential, but employs some recursion. In this approach, one design dimension implicitly dominates the others. The dominant dimension usually reflects the designer's primary expertise or specialty; individual designers do not usually vary the dominant dimension on different design projects. The dominant dimension is designed first, becoming the "fixed" or center point around which all other elements are designed; the other dimensions are tailored to match it. Recursion comes in when the form of the dominant element is designed or selected. Here, the best designers consider non-dominant elements as constraints on the form of the dominant member.

The recursive-sequential design approach is certainly an improvement over designs in which a single criterion is optimized. However, it still falls short of the joint optimization ideal. More important (since the ideal may be impossible to realize in practice), the recursive-sequential design approach opens the door to conflicts of philosophy and technique among organizational improvement specialists who adopt *different dominant dimensions* as the starting point for design.

INTEGRATION THROUGH TECHNOLOGY

The goal in technical integration is to avoid creating "technology islands"—systems that cannot directly communicate with each other. For example, to get information from users on one "island" to users on another may require printing out a copy and sending it via another, less efficient channel—by fax, mail, or courier. A similar problem may also occur at the level of individual systems or workstations. Applications that are not integrated—"application islands"—require users to execute extra time-consuming steps, which also increase the possibility of errors. For example, to create reports and documents users often need to key in data from formatted text files into spreadsheets, and vice versa.

The information technology design selected should enable users of one system to communicate and work with users of other systems—directly, seamlessly, and transparently. Ideally, individuals and teams should:

- Have access to and be able to work with information resources, people, and other units throughout the organization and beyond;
- Be able to integrate their own data and tools with each other as well as to integrate them with those of the people with whom they work.
- Be free of constraints on communication by virtue of their location or the location of the resources and people they work with, the particular hardware and software they use, or the vendors that produced them.

Ideally, technology should pose no limits on who those users (individuals or teams) work with, what they work on, or what information and tools they use. Instead, the limits should be policy based and managerial, reflecting such considerations as work needs and tasks, data integrity, security, and efficiency. The closer systems are to this ideal, the easier it is for users to collaborate.

The key to technical integration is open, nonproprietary standards. *Standards* are defined as "agreements on formats, procedures, and interfaces that permit designers of hardware, software, data bases, and telecommunications facilities to develop products and systems independent of one another with the assurance that they will be compatible with any other product or system that adheres to the same standards." According to Keen, the author of this definition, nonproprietary, or open, standards are the single most important element in achieving integration of the corporate information and communications resource.[5] To support effective, technology-enabled, boundary-spanning collaboration and teams, these cannot be just corporate or industry standards. Rather, the agreements noted above must be widely shared and, ultimately, international in their reach.

A number of standards now compete for dominance. The Open Systems Interconnection (OSI) reference model is perhaps the most promising source for these standards. The goal of the OSI movement is to replace manufacturers' proprietary standards with "open" interfaces, architectures, and protocols. The objective is to facilitate integration between different organizations and between different parts of the same organization, even if the organizations or their parts have different information technologies.

INTEGRATION THROUGH TEAMS

In regard to integrating through teams, we have two different types of teams to consider. Design teams, described in Chapter 5, are temporary, with the responsibility of *redesigning* a process, and are composed of IT, HR, and User members. Work teams, described in Chapter 12, are permanent, with the responsibility of *performing* a certain process. The following remarks will apply to both types of teams unless indicated otherwise.

The creation of redesign and work teams encourages individuals to coordinate by increasing the ease of integration and the motivation to integrate. Individuals on teams are accessible to one another and are held mutually accountable for the overall outcomes. However, the creation of teams does not address two kinds of additional integration.[6] First, in complex settings involving non-routine work, it is highly unlikely that all of the interdependencies will be housed within one team. Second, strategic integration may be required across several or all of the teams that constitute the business unit. For example, total cost targets for a product may be achieved by dynamically managing cost overruns and under runs across multiple teams. One client team with a potential large, long-term client may sell an initial system with a lower margin while another client team is in a cash-cow stage because of high-margin follow-up business. An integrating team may create common direction and facilitate such trade-offs across the work teams.

The next section will first deal with mechanisms to integrate *among* teams—that is, mechanisms that enable teams whose work is interdependent to integrate with one another. The second section will deal with mechanisms to integrate *across* a business unit that involves many different performing units whose work has to achieve common purpose and be conducted within a common direction.

Integration across Teams That Are Interdependent

There are different kinds of interdependencies between teams. In some cases, the work of individuals in multiple teams has to technically fit with the work of others. In these cases, the individuals can establish an informal connection, integrating as needed. If an engineer in one team is designing a device that has to fit into an environment being designed by an engineer in another team, for example, these two engineers can coordinate through specifications and through mutual problem solving.

In other cases, because the work of an entire team is affected by work that is going on in another team, the ongoing work of the two teams has to fit together. In these cases, there are several ways in which the work can be integrated:

Liaison Roles. These integrating mechanisms are generally taken on by trusted and respected individuals, in addition to their normal duties. This is a fairly informal method of making sure associated groups regularly share appropriate information. It may be sufficient to appoint a member of a third team as the liaison between two teams. For example, the relationship between each product, the line marketing team, and the corresponding product design teams is handled through a liaison from the marketing team. That individual attends product design team meetings with the purpose of sharing marketing information that would be useful in the design process and gleaning information about the emerging design to inform the development of marketing materials. The liaison is a member of the marketing team, not the design team, but deals with design team members extensively and informally.

Overlapping Membership. Overlapping membership is chosen by many companies as a mechanism for achieving close alignment. For example, an IT person and an HR person can be members of two design teams. They work with one design team when their expertise is needed and with the second team when it needs their expertise. They share the experience gained from one team with the other team.

Cross-team Integrating Teams. Cross-team integrating teams serve as an integrating link between two or more teams. For instance, a cross-team software integrating team would consist of representatives and systems engineers from both work teams. This team deals with the systemic decisions and trade-offs that emerge and takes responsibility for making sure that changes are documented and communicated between teams in a timely manner.

Integration across Multiple Teams and Components of a Business Unit

Liaison roles, overlapping membership, and cross-teams are ways of integrating the operational interdependencies *between* work teams. Other mechanisms are necessary to perform integration that transcends particular teams and to deal with deliberations or perform technical tasks at a broader scope—deliberations and tasks that create the context in which the teams operate.[7]

These integrating mechanisms—management teams and ad hoc integrating teams—address broader-scope issues in the system than the work teams do. Consequently, in a systems sense, they are at a higher hierarchical level. But that does not mean that the individuals who compose them are at a higher hierarchical rank in the organization. It merely means that larger scope teams or individuals have the authority to make decisions within which smaller-scope teams must operate.

Management Teams. In most companies, a cross-functional management team is formed to manage the business unit. The work teams report as collective units to the cross-functional management team that forges strategy and direction for the constellation of teams in the business unit. They also make resource trade-offs between the different teams based on the strategy and the needs of the teams and manages the performance of the various teams that report to them.

Ad Hoc Integrating Teams. Many organizations use a variety of non-management integrating teams to further integrate the work teams and to deal with other tasks and deliberations that have to occur in the organization. Although these mechanisms are representative in nature, they have authority for issues at a broader scope in the organization.

Further Actions to Improve Integration

Although the methods discussed are the most powerful means for enhancing the integration of teams, there are additional actions for improving integration.[8] We group these actions under the following four headings: co-location of team members, cross-training of team members, development of interpersonal communications skills, and prototyping and simulation.

Co-location

One of the first actions after creating a redesign team is to locate its members in one place and to locate it near other redesign teams. Co-location has many benefits: It enables frequent interaction, quick feedback, bonding between members, mutual education, the substitution of an auditing mentality with cooperation, and an enhanced ability to conduct concurrent engineering.

Cross-Functional Training

Even if a team can eliminate physical barriers, co-location will only lead to improved communication and integration if team members can understand and appreciate the needs and challenges of each other's work. This requires cross-training. Serving on cross-functional teams is itself one way to achieve some degree of cross-training; rotating assignments between functional areas is another. In addition to being cross-trained, it is helpful to have experienced cross-functional team members and even better if team members have worked together previously.

Team Building and Interpersonal Skills

Another action that leads to strong integration is deliberate development of team-building skills. All team members on a redesign team perform important roles as information providers, knowledge consultants, problem-solvers, energizers, and ambassadors who articulate the constraints and capabilities of their respective functions. But to bring about integration, the contribution of team members must go beyond simply providing inputs; each person must constructively convert these inputs into operating parameters for the project as a whole. To do so, they must learn the languages of different functions, build relationships with other team members, receive feedback openly, and engage in give-and-take negotiations.

Prototyping and Simulation

In the Detailed Process Design stage, one of the most important communications tools is using prototypes to facilitate discussions across functional differences. By focusing the team's communications on the physical reality of what they are doing, cross-functional integration is enhanced. Communications and problem solving can also be enhanced by visiting other facilities to benchmark ideas, and by using graphs and models to demonstrate the concepts being discussed.

Summary of Integration Through Teams

Fully integrated transformation processes are characterized by joint decision making by all team members from the start of the project. Early and late groups operate in parallel and jointly choose the constraints under which they will operate. The team's focus is anchored by the desired technical and economic performance of the end process. Parallel processes enable teams to be more aggressive in exploiting opportunities at the interfaces between technical groups—for example, in trade-offs between information technology and human resources. While integrated processes do utilize formal coordination mechanisms, they also benefit extensively from the real-time, spontaneous, informal interactions made possible by co-location of team members and other strategies. More important, these interactions help build a shared language, common experiences, and trust that enable system integration issues to be addressed simultaneously with the development of functional policies.

NOTES

1. Adapted from Steven C. Wheelwright and Kim B. Clark, *Revolutionizing Product Development* (Free Press, 1992), pp. 175–184.

2. Jerry N. Luftman (ed.), *Competing in the Information Age* (Oxford University Press, 1996), p. 308.

3. Richard E. Walton, *Up and Running: Integrating Information Technology and the Organization* (Harvard Business School Press, 1989), p. 132.

4. J. C. Taylor and D. F. Felton, *Performance by Design: Sociotechnical Systems in North America* (Prentice-Hall, 1993), p. 108.

5. P. G. W. Keen, *Every Manager's Guide to Information Technology: A Glossary of Concepts for Today's Business Leaders* (Harvard Business School Press, 1991), p. 120.

6. Susan Albers Mohrman, Susan G. Cohen, and Allan Mohrman, Jr., *Designing Team-Based Organizations* (Jossey-Bass, 1995), p. 114.

7. Ibid., p. 120.

8. Adapted from H. Kent Bowen, Kim B. Clark, Charles A. Holloway, and Steven C. Wheelwright (eds.), *The Perpetual Enterprise Machine* (Oxford University Press, 1994).

Selected Bibliography

PART I: INITIATING TRANSFORMATION

The Situation Facing Today's Organizations

Crawford, Richard. *In the Era of Human Capital.* HarperBusiness, 1991.

Dertouzos, Michael. *What Will Be.* HarperEdge, 1997.

Drucker, Peter F. *Managing for the Future: The 1990s and Beyond.* Dutton, 1992.

Drucker, Peter F. *Post-Capitalist Society.* HarperBusiness, 1993.

Feather, Frank. *The Future Consumer.* Warwick, 1994.

Gates, Bill. *The Road Ahead*, Viking, 1995.

Gilder, George. *The Quantum Revolution in Economics and Technology.* Simon & Schuster, 1989.

Hope, Jeremy, and Tony Hope. *Competing in the Third Wave: The Ten Key Management Issues of the Information Age.* Harvard Business School Press, 1997.

Linstone, Harold A. *The Challenge of the 21st Century: Managing Technology and Ourselves in a Shrinking World.* State University of New York Press, 1994.

Luftman, Jerry M. (ed.). *Competing in the Information Age.* Oxford University Press, 1996.

Meadows, Donella H., Dennis L. Meadows, and Jorgen Randers. *Beyond the Limits: Confronting Global Collapse.* Chelsea Green, 1992.

Naisbitt, John. *Megatrends: Ten New Directions Transforming Our Lives.* Warner Books, 1984.

Naisbitt, John, and Patricia Aburdene. *Megatrends 2000.* William Morrow, 1990.

Popcorn, Faith. *The Popcorn Report: On the Future of Your Company, Your World, and Your Life.* HarperBusiness, 1991.

Reich, Robert B. *Tales of a New America.* Random House, 1987.

Reich, Robert B. *The Work of Nations: Preparing Ourselves for 21st Century Capitalism.* Knopf, 1991.

Toffler, Alvin. *Power Shift: Knowledge, Wealth, and Violence at the Edge of the 21st Century*. Bantam Books, 1990.

Toffler, Alvin. *The Third Wave*. William Morrow, 1980.

Toffler, Alvin, and Heidi Toffler. *Creating a New Civilization*. Turner Publishing, 1994.

The Transformation Process

Bainbridge, Colin. *Designing for Change: A Practical Guide to Business Transformation*. Wiley, 1996.

Fletcher, Beverly. *Organizational Transformation Theory and Practice: A Practitioner's Profiles and Themes*. Praeger, 1990.

Gouillart, Francis J., and James H. Kelly. *Transforming the Organization: Reframing, Restructuring, Revitalizing, and Renewing*. McGraw-Hill, 1995.

Halal, William E. *The New Management: Democratic and Entrepreneurial Managers Are Transforming Organizations*. Berrett-Koehler, 1996.

Hambrick, Donald C., Michael L. Tushmand, and David A. Nadler. *Navigating Change: How CEOs, Top Teams and Boards Steer Transformation*. Harvard Business School Press, 1997.

Head, Christopher W. *Beyond Corporate Transformation*. Productivity Press, 1997.

Kilmann, Ralph H., and T. R. Covin. *Corporate Transformation: Revitalizing Organizations for the Competitive World*. Jossey-Bass, 1988.

Kochan, Thomas A., and Michael Useem (eds.). *Transforming Organizations*. Oxford University Press, 1992.

Levy, Ames, and Uri Merry. *Organizational Transformation: Approaches, Strategies, and Theories*. Praeger, 1986.

Miles, Robert H. *Corporate Comeback: The Story of Renewal and Transformation at National Semiconductor*. Jossey-Bass, 1996.

Miles, Robert H. *Leading Corporate Transformation: A Blueprint for Corporate Renewal*. Jossey-Bass, 1997.

Morton, Michael, Lester C. Thurow, and Morton Scott. *The Corporation of the 1990s: Information Technology and Organizational Transformation*. Oxford University Press, 1991.

Nadler, David A. *Discontinuous Change: Leading Organizational Transformation*. Jossey-Bass, 1995.

Naisbitt, John, and Patricia Aburdene. *Re-inventing the Corporation*. Warner Books, 1985.

Quinn, Robert E. *Paradox and Transformation: Toward a Theory of Change in Organization and Management*. Ballinger, 1988.

Vollmann, Thomas E. *The Transformation Imperative: Achieving Market Dominance through Radical Change*. Harvard Business School Press, 1996.

Whitsett, David A., and Irving R. Burling. *Achieving Successful Organizational Transformation*. Quorum, 1996.

Transformational Leadership

Albrecht, Karl. *The Northbound Train: Finding the Purpose, Setting the Direction, and Shaping the Destiny of Your Organization*. AMACOM, 1994.

Bennis, Warren. *Why Leaders Can't Lead*. Jossey-Bass, 1990.

Block, Peter. *The Empowered Manager*. Jossey-Bass, 1987.

Block, Peter. *Stewardship*. Berret-Koehler, 1996.

Conger, Jay A. *The Charismatic Leader*. Jossey-Bass, 1989.

Covey, Stephen R. *Principle-Centered Leadership*. Simon & Schuster, 1992.

Hesselbein, Frances, Marshall Goldsmith, and Richard Beckhard (eds.). *The Leader of the Future: New Visions, Strategies, and Practices for the Next Era*. Jossey-Bass, 1996.

Koesterbaum, Peter. *Leadership: A Philosophy for Leaders*. Jossey-Bass, 1991.

Kotter, John P. *A Force for Change: How Leadership Is Different from Management*. Free Press, 1990.

Kotter, John P. *The Leadership Factor*. Free Press, 1988.

Kotter, John P. *Leading Change*. Harvard Business School Press, 1996.

Kouzes, James M., and Barry Z. Posner. *Credibility: How Leaders Gain and Lose It, Why People Demand It*. Jossey-Bass, 1995.

Kouzes, James M., and Barry Z. Posner. *The Leadership Challenge*. Jossey-Bass, 1995.

Leavitt, Harold J. *Corporate Pathfinders: Building Vision and Values into Organizations*. Penguin, 1987.

Nadler, David A., and Mark B. Nadler. *Champions of Change: How CEOs Are Mastering the Skills of Radical Change*. Jossey-Bass, 1998.

Nanus, Burt. *Visionary Leadership: Creating a Compelling Sense of Direction for Your Company*. Jossey-Bass, 1992.

Quinn, Robert E. *Deep Change: Discovering the Leader Within*. Jossey-Bass, 1996.

Tichy, Noel M., and Mary Anne Devanna. *The Transformational Leader*. Wiley, 1990.

Vaill, Peter B. *Managing as a Performing Art: New Ideas for a World of Chaotic Change*. Jossey-Bass, 1991.

Wheatley, Margaret. *Leadership and the New Science: Learning about Organizations from an Orderly Universe*. Berret-Koehler, 1994.

Strategic Planning for Transformation

Andrews, Kenneth R. *The Concept of Corporate Strategy*. Irwin, 1980.

Ansoff, H. Igor. *The New Corporate Strategy*. Wiley, 1988.

Blackburn, Joseph D. *Time-Based Competition*. Business One Irwin, 1991.

Hamel, Gary, and C. K. Prahalad. *Competing for the Future*. Harvard Business School Press, 1996.

Kanter, Rosabeth Moss. *World Class: Thriving Locally in the Global Economy*. Simon & Schuster, 1995.

Kaplan, Robert S., and David P. Norton. *The Balanced Scorecard: Translating Strategy into Action*. Harvard Business School Press, 1996.

Keen, Peter G. W. *Competing in Time: Using Telecommunications for Competitive Advantage*. Ballinger, 1988.

Magaziner, Ira, and Mark Patinkin. *The Silent War: Inside the Global Business Battles Shaping America's Future*. Random House, 1989.

Ohmae, Kenichi. *The Borderless World: Power and Strategy in the Interlinked Economy*. HarperCollins, 1991.

Porter, Michael E. *Competitive Advantage: Creating and Sustaining Superior Per-formance*. Free Press, 1985.

Porter, Michael E. *The Competitive Advantage of Nations*. Free Press, 1990.

Porter, Michael E. *Competitive Strategy: Techniques for Analyzing Industries and Competitors*. Free Press, 1980.

Rumelt, Richard P., et al. *Fundamental Issues in Strategy: A Research Agenda*. McGraw-Hill, 1994.

Stalk, George, Jr., and Thomas M. Hout. *Competing against Time*. Free Press, 1990.

Starr, Martin K. *Global Corporate Alliances and the Competitive Edge*. Quorum, 1991.

Tomasko, Robert M. *Rethinking the Corporation: The Architecture of Change*. AMACOM, 1993.

Transforming the Organizational Culture

Bolman, Lee G., and Terrence E. Deal. *Reframing Organizations*, 2nd ed. Jossey-Bass, 1997.

Collins, James C., and Jerry I. Porras. *Built to Last*. HarperBusiness, 1994.

Deal, Terence E., and Allan A. Kennedy. *Corporate Cultures: The Rites and Rit-uals of Corporate Life*. Addison-Wesley, 1982.

Deal, Terence E., and Allan Kennedy. *Managing the Hidden Organization*. War-ner, 1994.

Deevy, Edward. *Creating the Resilient Organization*. Prentice-Hall, 1995.

Drennan, David. *Transforming Company Culture*. McGraw-Hill, 1992.

Fishman, Daniel B., and Cary Cherniss (eds.). *The Human Side of Corporate Com-petitiveness*. Sage, 1990.

Harris, Phillip R. *Management in Transition: Transforming Managerial Practices and Organizational Strategies for a New Work Culture*. Jossey-Bass, 1987.

Kotter, John P., and James L. Heskett. *Corporate Culture and Performance*. Free Press, 1992.

Makower, Joel. *Beyond the Bottom Line: Putting Social Responsibility to Work for Your Business and the World*. Simon & Schuster, 1994.

Marshall, Edward M. *Transforming the Way We Work: Power of the Collaborative Workplace*. AMACOM, 1995.

Oden, Howard W. *Managing Corporate Culture, Innovation, and Intrapreneurship*. Quorum, 1997.

Peters, Tom. *Liberation Management: Necessary Disorganization for the Nanosec-ond Nineties*. Knopf, 1992.

Peters, Tom. *Thriving on Chaos: Handbook for a Management Revolution*. Knopf, 1987.

Peters, Tom, and Robert H. Waterman, Jr. *In Search of Excellence*. Harper and Row, 1982.

Schein, Edgar H. *Organizational Culture and Leadership*, 2nd ed. Jossey-Bass, 1992.

Schneider, William E. *The Reengineering Alternative*. Irwin, 1994.

Shenkman, Michael. *The Strategic Heart: Using the New Science to Lead Growing Organizations*. Quorum, 1996.

PART II: TECHNICALLY REDESIGNING THE ORGANIZATION

Process Mapping

Hunt, V. Daniel. *Process Mapping*. Wiley, 1996.

Mayer, Richard J. (ed.). *IDEF1 Modeling: A Reconstruction of the Original Air Force Report*. Knowledge Based Systems, Inc., 1992.

National Institute of Standards and Technology. *Integration Definition for Function Modeling (IDEF0)*. FIPS PUB 183. Secretary of Commerce, December 1993.

National Institute of Standards and Technology. *Integration Definition for Information Modeling (IDEF1X)*. FIPS PUB 184. Secretary of Commerce, December 1993.

Process Improvement

Burton, Terence T., and John W. Moran. *The Future Focused Organization*. Prentice-Hall, 1995.

Chang, Richard Y. *Continuous Process Improvement*. Richard Chang Associates, 1994.

Denton, D. Keith. *Horizontal Management*. Lexington, 1991.

Dimancescu, Dan. *The Seamless Enterprise*. Omneo, 1992.

Flannigan, Eileen, and Jon Scott. *Process Improvement*. Crisp, 1995.

Harrington, H. James. *The Improvement Process: How America's Leading Companies Improve Quality*. ASQC Press, 1987

Joiner, Brian L. *Fourth Generation Management*. McGraw-Hill, 1994.

Melan, Eugene H. *Process Management: Methods for Improving Products and Service*. ASQC Press, 1993.

Oden, Howard W. *Maximizing Manufacturing Performance*. Engineering and Management Press, 1999.

Robson, George D. *Continuous Process Improvement: Simplifying Work Flow Systems*. Free Press, 1991.

Rummler, Geary A., and A. P. Brache. *Improving Performance: How to Manage White Space on the Organization Chart*. Jossey-Bass, 1995.

Business Process Reengineering

Carr, David K. *Best Practices in Reengineering: What Works and What Doesn't in the Engineering Process*. McGraw-Hill, 1995.

Champy, James. *Reengineering Management*. HarperBusiness, 1995.

Crego, Edwin T., Jr., and Peter D. Schiffrin. *Customer Centered Reengineering*. Irwin, 1995.

Cross, Kelvin F., John J. Feather, and Richard L. Lynch. *Corporate Renaissance: The Art of Reengineering*. Blackwell, 1994.

Darnton, Geoffrey, and Moksha Darnton. *Business Process Analysis*. International Business Press, 1997.

Davenport, Thomas H. *Process Innovation*. Harvard Business School Press, 1993.

Fried, Louis. *Managing Information Technology in Turbulent Times*. Wiley, 1995.

Graham, Morris A., and Melvin J. Lebaron. *The Horizontal Revolution: Reengineering Your Organization through Teams*. Jossey-Bass, 1994.

Grover, Varun, and William J. Kettinger. *Business Process Change: Reengineering Concepts, Methods, and Technologies*. Idea Group, 1995.

Hammer, Michael, and James Champy. *Reengineering the Corporation: A Manifesto for Business Revolution*. HarperCollins, 1993.

Hammer, Michael, and Steven A. Stanton. *The Reengineering Revolution*. HarperBusiness, 1995.

Keen, Peter G. W. *The Process Edge*. Harvard Business School Press, 1997.

Kouloupoulous, Thomas M. *Smart Companies, Smart Tools: Transforming Business Process into Business Assets*. Van Nostrand Reinhold, 1997.

Manganelli, Raymond L., and Mark M. Klein. *The Reengineering Handbook: A Step-by-Step Guide to Business Transformation*. AMACOM, 1994.

Morris, Daniel, and Joel Brandon. *Reengineering Your Business*. McGraw-Hill, 1993.

Nolan, Richard L., et al. *Reengineering the Organization*. Harvard Business School Press, 1995.

Detailed Technical Process Design

Boxwell, Robert J., Jr. *Benchmarking for Competitive Advantage*. McGraw-Hill, 1994.

Camp, Robert C. *Benchmarking:The Search for Industry Best Practices that Lead to Superior Performance*. Quality Press/Quality Resources, 1989.

Groover, Mikell P. *Automation, Production Systems, and Computer Integrated Manufacturing*. Prentice-Hall, 1987.

Harrington, Joseph. *Computer Integrated Manufacturing*. Industrial Press, 1973.

Leibfried, Kathleen H. J., and C. J McNair. *Benchmarking: A Tool for Continuous Improvement*. Omneo, 1992.

Osborn, Alex F. *Applied Imagination*. Charles Scribner's Sons, 1957.

Shrenkser, Warren L. *CIM: A Working Definition*. SME, 1990.

Singe, Nanui. *Systems Approach to Completing Integrated Design and Manufacturing*. Wiley, 1996.

Spendolini, Michael J. *The Benchmarking Book*. APICS, 1992.

Vajpayee, S. Kant. *Principles of Computer-Integrated Manufacturing*. Prentice-Hall, 1995.

Information Analysis and Redesign

Cortada, James W. *Best Practices in Information Technology: How Corporations Get the Most Value from Exploiting Their Digital Investments*. Prentice Hall PTR, 1997.

Donovan, John J. *Business Re-engineering with Information Technology*. Prentice Hall PTR, 1994.

Fried, Louis. *Managing Information Technology in Turbulent Times*. Wiley, 1995.

Keen, Peter G. W. *Every Manager's Guide to Information Technology: A Glossary of Concepts for Today's Business Leaders.* Harvard Business School Press, 1991.

Keen, Peter G. W. *Shaping the Future: Business Design through Information Technology.* Harvard Business School Press, 1991.

McKenney, James L., with Richard O. Mason and Duncan G. Copeland. *Waves of Change: Business Evolution through Information Technology.* Harvard Business School Press, 1995.

Scott Morton, Michael (ed.). *The Corporation of the 1990s: Information Technology and Organizational Transformation.* Oxford University Press, 1991.

Tapscott, Don. *The Digital Economy: Promise and Peril in the Age of Networked Intelligence.* McGraw-Hill, 1996.

Tapscott, Don. *Growing Up Digital: The Rise of the Net Generation.* McGraw-Hill, 1997.

Tapscott, Don, and Art Caston. *Paradigm Shift: The New Promise of Information Technology.* McGraw-Hill, 1993.

Walton, Richard E. *Up and Running: Integrating Information Technology and the Organization.* Harvard Business School Press, 1989.

Zuboff, Shoshana. *In the Age of the Smart Machine: The Future of Work and Power.* Basic Books, 1984.

PART III: SOCIALLY REDESIGNING THE ORGANIZATION

Total Quality Management

Berry, Thomas H. *Managing the Total Quality Transformation.* ASQC Press, 1991.

Bounds, Greg, et al. *Beyond Total Quality Management: Toward the Emerging Paradigm.* McGraw-Hill, 1994.

Brocka, Bruce, and M. Suzanne Brocka. *Quality Management: Implementing the Best Ideas of the Masters.* Business One Irwin, 1992.

Deming, W. Edwards. *Out of the Crisis.* MIT Press, 1986.

Feigenbaum, Armand V. *Total Quality Control,* 3rd ed. McGraw-Hill, 1991.

Garwin, David A. *Managing Quality: The Strategic and Competitive Edge.* Free Press, 1988.

George, Stephen. *The Baldrige Quality System: A Way to Transform Your Business.* Wiley, 1992.

George, Stephen. *Uncommon Sense: Creating Business Excellence in Your Organization.* Wiley, 1997.

Goetsch, David L., and Stanley Davis. *Implementing Total Quality.* Prentice-Hall, 1995.

Greene, Richard T. *Global Quality: A Synthesis of the World's Best Management Methods.* ASQC/Irwin, 1993.

Groocock, J. M. *The Chain of Quality: Market Dominance through Product Superiority.* Wiley, 1986.

Hoffhor, Glen D., John W. Moran, and Gerald Nadler. *Breakthrough Thinking in TQM.* Prentice-Hall, 1994.

Lawler, Edward W., Susan Albers Mohrman, and Gerald E. Ledford, Jr. *Creating*

High Performance Organizations: Practice and Results of Employee Involvement and TQM in Fortune 1000 Companies. Jossey-Bass, 1995.

Maramonte, Kevin R. *Building the Invisible Quality Corporation: The Executive Guide to Transcending TQM.* Quorum, 1996.

Richardson, Terry L. *Total Quality Management.* AMACOM, 1997.

Schmidt, Warren H., and Jerome P. Finnigan. *The Race without a Finish Line.* Jossey-Bass, 1992.

Shores, A. Richard. *A TQM Approach to Achieving Manufacturing Excellence.* ASQC Press, 1990.

Spechler, Jay W. *Managing Quality in America's Most Admired Companies: Case Studies.* Berrett-Koehler, 1993.

Townsend, Patrick L. *Commit to Quality.* Wiley, 1986.

Tunks, Roger. *Fast Track to Quality.* McGraw-Hill, 1992.

Organizational Change

Belasco, James A., and Ralph C. Stayer. *Flight of the Buffalo: Soaring to Excellence: Learning to Let Employees Lead.* Warner Books, 1993.

Byham, William C., and Jeff Cox. *Zapp! The Lightning of Empowerment.* Harmony Books, 1990.

Carr, Clay. *The Competitive Power of Constant Creativity.* AMACOM, 1994.

Carr, David K., Kelvin J. Hard, and William J. Trahant. *Managing the Change Process: A Field Book for Change Agents, Consultants, Team Leaders, and Reengineering Managers.* McGraw-Hill, 1996.

Champy, James, and Nitin Nohria. *Fast Forward: The Best Ideas of Managing Business Change.* Harvard Business School Press, 1996.

Garfield, Charles. *Second to None: How Our Smartest Companies Put People First.* Business One Irwin, 1992.

Harkman, J. Richard, et al. *Perspectives on Behavior in Organizations.* McGraw-Hill, 1997.

Hutton, David W. *The Change Agent's Handbook.* ASQC Press, 1994.

Kanter, Rosabeth Moss. *The Changemasters.* Simon & Schuster, 1983.

Kanter, Rosabeth Moss. *When Giants Learn to Dance.* Simon & Schuster, 1989.

Kanter, Rosabeth Moss, Barry A. Stein, and Todd D. Jack. *The Challenge of Organizational Change.* Free Press, 1992.

Lawler, Edward E. *High-Involvement Management: Participative Strategies for Improving Organizational Performance.* Jossey-Bass, 1986.

Nevis, Edwin C., Joan Lancourt, and Helen G. Vassallo. *Intentional Revolutions.* Jossey-Bass, 1996.

Schultheiss, Emily E. *Optimizing the Organization: How to Link People and Technology.* Ballinger, 1989.

Tushman, Michael L., and Charles A. O'Reilly III. *Winning through Innovation: A Practical Guide to Leading Organizational Change and Renewal.* Harvard Business School Press, 1997.

Broad Social Redesign of the Organization

Ackoff, Russell L. *The Democratic Corporation*. Oxford University Press, 1994.

Albrecht, Karl, with Steven A. Albrecht. *The Creative Organization*. Dow Jones Irwin, 1987.

Ashkenas, Ron, et al. *The Boundaryless Organization: Breaking the Chains of Organizational Structure*. Jossey-Bass, 1995.

Benveniste, Guy. *The Twenty-First Century Organization: Analyzing Current Trends, Imagining the Future*. Jossey-Bass, 1994.

Birchall, David, and Laurence Lyons. *Creating Tomorrow's Organization*. Pitman Publishing, 1995.

Davenport, Thomas H., and Laurence Prusak. *Working Knowledge: How Organizations Manage What They Know*. Harvard Business School Press, 1998.

Davidow, William, and Michael S. Malone. *The Virtual Corporation*. HarperBusiness, 1992.

Galbraith, Jay R. *Competing with Flexible Lateral Organization*, 2nd ed. Addison-Wesley, 1994.

Galbraith, Jay R., and Edward E. Lawler III. *Organizing for the Future*. Jossey-Bass, 1993.

Ghoshal, Sumantra, and Christopher A. Bartlett. *The Individualized Corporation: Great Companies Are Defined by Purpose, Process, and People*. HarperBusiness, 1997.

Goldman, Steven L., Roger N. Nagel, and Kenneth Preiss. *Agile Competitors and Virtual Organizations*. Van Nostrand Reinhold, 1995.

Grenier, Raymond, and George Mites. *Going Virtual: Moving Your Organization into the 21st Century*. Prentice-Hall, 1995.

Handy, Charles. *The Age of Paradox*. Harvard Business School Press, 1995.

Handy, Charles. *Understanding Organizations*. Oxford University Press, 1993.

Hesselbein, Frances, Marshall Goldsmith, and Richard Beckard. *The Organization of the Future*. Jossey-Bass, 1997.

Janov, Jill. *The Inventive Organization*. Jossey-Bass, 1994.

Kast, Fremont E., and James E. Rosenweig. *Organization and Management*, 4th ed. McGraw-Hill, 1985.

Lawler, Edward E. III. *Creating High Performance Organizations*. Jossey-Bass, 1994.

Marquardt, Michael. *The Global Learning Organization*. Irwin, 1994.

Miles, Robert H. *Macro Organizational Behavior*. Goodyear, 1980.

Mohrman, Susan Albers. *Managing Complexity in High Tech Organizations*. Oxford University Press, 1990.

Mohrman, Susan Albers. *Self-Designing Organizations: Learning How to Create High Performance*. Addison-Wesley, 1989.

Nadler, David A. *Competing by Design: The Power of Organizational Architecture*. Oxford University Press, 1997.

Nadler, David A., Marc S. Gersten, and Robert B. Shaw. *Organizational Architecture: Design for Changing Organizations*. Jossey-Bass, 1992.

Senge, Peter M. *The Fifth Discipline*. Doubleday/Currency, 1990.

Detailed Social Redesign: Team-Based Networked Organizations

Boyett, Joseph H., and Henry P. Conn. *Workplace 2000*. Plume, 1991.
Hackman, J. Richard (ed.). *Groups That Work (and Those That Don't)*. Jossey-Bass, 1988.
Hackman, J. Richard, and Greg Oldham. *Work Redesign*. Addison-Wesley, 1980.
Katzenbach, Jon R., and Douglas K. Smith. *The Wisdom of Teams*. Harper-Business, 1993.
Lipnack, Jesson L., and Jeffrey Stamps. *The Age of the Network*. Omneo, 1994.
Mankin, Don, Susan G. Cohen, and Tora K. Bikson. *Teams and Technology: Fulfilling the Promise of the New Organization*. Harvard Business School Press, 1996.
Manz, Charles C., and Henry P. Sims. *Business without Bosses*. Wiley, 1993.
Mohrman, Susan Albers, Susan G. Cohen, and Allan Mohrman, Jr. *Designing Team-Based Organizations*. Jossey-Bass, 1995.
Pfeffer, Jeffrey. *Competitive Advantage through People*. Harvard Business School Press, 1994.
Scholtes, Peter R. *The Team Handbook*. ASQC Press, 1988.
Shonk, James H. *Team-Based Organizations: Developing a Successful Team Environment*. Business One Irwin, 1992.

PART IV: COMPLETING THE TRANSFORMATION

Integrating the Transformation

Bowen, H. Kent, Kim B. Clark, Charles A. Holloway, and Steven C. Wheelwright (eds.). *The Perpetual Enterprise Machine*. Oxford University Press, 1994.
Savage, Charles M. *Fifth Generation Management: Integrating Enterprises through Human Networking*. Digital Press, 1990.
Taylor, J. C., and D. F. Felton. *Performance by Design: Sociotechnical Systems in North America*. Prentice-Hall, 1993.
Wallace, Thomas F., and Steven Bennett (eds.). *World Class Manufacturing*. Omneo, 1994.
Wheelwright, Steven C., and Kim B. Clark. *Revolutionizing Product Development*. Free Press, 1992.

Index

A0 or context diagram, 127
All-employee conferences, 208–9
Attribute classes, 197

Benchmark performance, 145
Brainstorming, 142–43
Broad social redesign, 223–30
  analyze existing structure
    functional or vertical?, 226–27
    list specific deficiencies of your or-
      ganization, 228
    problems with the functional or-
      ganization, 227–28
  conduct partial survey of existing
    structure
    compare organization map with
      enterprise process map, 226
    how does work normally get
      done?, 225–26
    investigate informal group struc-
      tures, 225
    where are decisions currently
      made?, 224–25
  diagnose future organization needs,
    228
    sources of future needs, 228
    will future require process organi-
      zation?, 229–30

    will future require team-based or-
      ganization?, 230
  document existing organization, 223–
    24
    analyze existing structure, 226
    conduct a partial survey of exist-
      ing structure, 224
    gather and update organization
      charts, 224
    study enterprise process map, 224
  introduction, 223

Change
  changing our approach to, 9
  growing need for radical, 8
Checklists, using, 143
Clean-sheet approach, 117
Company ideology, 73
Comparison of work and IT develop-
  ment procedures, 181
Competencies, matching with value
  propositions, 61
Constrained precedence links, 130
Core competencies
  building, 143
  finding, 60
Core team member responsibilities
  and qualifications, 97

Core values, 73
Cultural change, 204–20
  cascading, a periodic approach, 211
    cascading process, 210
    making the process successful, 211
    overview, 210
    who should lead the meetings, 210
  communications role, 215–18
    active listening, 217
    encouraging upward communica-
      tions, 217
    fostering cross-company communi-
      cation, 217
    initial communication, 216
    need for communication, 215
    using all channels, 218
  guidelines for implementing, 213
  initial kick-off conferences, 207–8
    all-employee conferences, 208
    high-level managers conference,
      207
    middle managers conference, 207
  introduction to, 204
  middle managers, old and new, 208
  other change methods, 219–20
    coercion, 220
    role modeling, 219
  role of high-level leaders, 205–6
    actions speak louder than words,
      206
    getting ready for kick-off, 205
    involve everyone in implementa-
      tion, 206
  social project team efforts, 211–12
    introduction and definition, 211
    suggested topics for, 212
  summary of implementation efforts,
    213
Cultural creed, 72, 80
Cultural guiding principles, 82
Cultural ideology, 79
Cultural planning, 71–86
  conduct external analysis, 74
    analyze corporate strategy and ex-
      ternal culture, 76
    influence of leader's vision, 75
    influence of mission and external
      environment, 75

conduct internal analysis, 77, 78
  develop company ideology, 79
  develop cultural improvement plans,
    85
  introduction to, 71
  is there an ideal ideology?, 84
  outputs of cultural planning, 72
    company ideology, 73, 79
    core values, 73, 81
    cultural creed, 72, 80
    guiding principles, 72, 82
  process of, 74
  testing and improving the ideology,
    85
Cultural planning council, 35, 73, 92
Cultural values, 81
Culture, 314
  adaptive, 76
  definition, 67
  essence of, 67
  nature of its transformation, 70
  non-adaptive, 76
  observable and hidden levels of, 68
  transforming of, 67
  why is it important?, 69
Customer values, types of
  customer intimacy, 62
  operational excellence, 62
  product leadership, 62

Developing resources, capabilities, and
    competencies
  developing capabilities, 56
  developing competencies, 57
  developing core competencies, 68
  developing resources, 56
  ephemeral nature of core competen-
    cies, 60
  recent emphasis on core competen-
    cies, 58
Diagnose future organization needs
  will future require networked orga-
    nizations?, 232
  will future require team-based or-
    ganization?
    advantages of team-based organi-
      zation, 231

individuals or groups as building
blocks?, 230
Diagnose performance prototype
prototypes and prototyping
minimizing cost by minimizing
late design changes, 293

Employee empowerment, 246
Employee involvement, 246
and empowerment, difference between, 246
Enterprise concept
develop, 140
improving through creative synthesis, 141
brainstorming, 142
Osborn's general checklist, 143
using checklists, 143
Entity class, 195
Entity class diagrams, 195
Evaluate and incorporate redesigned
process, 291–95
conduct trial run of prototype, 291
diagnose performance of prototype
prototypes and prototyping, 292
need for prototypes and prototyping, 293
new approach must be taken,
293
selecting redesigned processes for
incorporation, 295
using prototypes to reduce cost,
time and risk, 293
limiting risk with early prototypes, 294
timing of prototypes, 294
using prototypes to improve quality, 294
introduction, 291
Executive Steering Board, 35, 91
Executive summary, 152

Guiding principles, 73

Hamel, Gary, 44
High-level leaders, definition, 19
High-level managers conference, 207
Human resources, 241–86

career paths and development, 284
network career path, 284
designing network career path,
286
programs that foster network
career development, 285
what are network career paths?,
285
traditional career path, 284
human resource processes
changing environment for, 269
introduction, 267
new role for, 268
revised practices for, 269
human resource requirements
human resource requirements
analyzing gap between future
needs and future supply, 243
forecasting future needs, 242
forecasting human resource supplies, 242
human resource programs, 243
steps in diagnosing, 241
performance measurement and assessment
changing assessment practices, 275
developing a performance-based
system, 276
traditional performance measurement system, 274
recognition and reward system
performance-based recognition
and rewards
align rewards with organization's goals, 281
allow people to develop their
own rewards, 281
create proper mix of measures,
282
disperse rewards and recognition frequently, 283
extend reward system beyond
corporate boundaries, 283
reward teams that deliver value
to customers, 282
traditional recognition and reward
systems, 279
recruiting and selecting personnel

attracting the best, 271
importance of human capital, 272
selecting personnel, 273

IDEF0, A0 diagram, 124
See also Process modeling
IDEF1, 193
entity class, 195
See also Process modeling
IDEF3, 132
links in IDEF3, 133
See also Process modeling
Implementing transformation
consolidating gains, 39
high-level leaders' role, 35
actions speak louder than words,
37
approach transformation as a
campaign, 36
involve everyone in implementation, 37
short-term wins
role of, 37
role of management in, 37
Incorporate redesigned process
conduct final test of redesigned
process, 304
evaluate performance of redesigned
process, 308
follow-up actions
celebrate!, 307
provide for continuous improvement, 308
incorporate redesigned process and
monitor, 305
refine process and continue operating
continually improve process performance, 307
utilize ongoing feedback, 307
Information redesign of processes
change in the role of IT department,
179
design teams and IT
connecting team with the IT department, 192
sources of expertise, 191

information technology architecture,
182
information technology development
process, 180
collect information for IT design,
181
comparison of work and IT development procedures, 181
define detailed IT requirements,
184
detailed IT design, 185–91
business-to-business networks,
190
integration of internal business
operations, 189
localized process improvements,
185
performing new tasks, 188
redefining the business, 191
develop enterprise IT architecture, 182
developing new IT capability, 180
introduction, 179
Information technology, detailed design, 185
Information technology, detailed requirements, 184
Integration
cross-function, 310
cross-stage, 310

Kick-off conferences, 206
Kotter and Heskett study, 74–75

Leadership, transformational, 19
Learning organization
creating global learning, 263
everyone wins in, 264
introduction, 262
more than sum of individual learning, 262

Measurement system, 38
cause and effect feature of the, 39
developing the, 38
Middle managers conference, 207–8

Networked organization, 253–57
  definition, 253–54
  external networking and alliances, 254
  network operations, 255–56
  steps in networking, 255
    step one: communicate strategic improvement plan, 255
    step two: share experiences and expectations, 255
    step three: extend and interface, 255
  transitioning to the networked organization, 256
  chain of command to networking, 256
  distrust and compliance to trust and integrity, 257
  power of position to power of knowledge, 257
  vertical communications to horizontal communications, 257

Organization
  functional, 113
  process, 113
Organization and management plan of project plan, 153
Organization concept
  finalizing, 239
    format of the organization concept, 240
    identify the process owners and team leaders, 239
  guidelines for developing organization concept, 234
    build the structure around processes, 235
    consider boundaries are permeable, 238
    use networking as the basic approach, 237
    use teams as the basic element, 236
  introduction, 234
Organization for transformation, 91–95
  consultants and facilitators, 95
  Cultural Planning Council, 92

Executive Steering Board, 91
  line management, 94
  rationale for the, 95
  Social Management Group, 93
  Social Project Team, 94
  Strategic Planning Council, 91
  Technical Management Group, 93
  Technical Project Team, 94
Organization for transformation, block diagram, 34, 90
Organization transformation process, flow diagram of, 16
Organizational change
  four responses to, 11
    adaptation, 12
    conversion, 12
    reclamation, 12
    tuning, 11
  scope of, 10
  timing of, 11
    proactive, or anticipatory, 11
    reactive, 11
Organizational change, scope of
  incremental, or continuous, 10
  radical, or discontinuous, 10
Organizational culture
  Kotter and Heskett study, 70
  Osborn's general checklist, 143

Performance measurement and assessment
  developing a performance-based system
    create process, not functional measures, 277
    do not use measurement system to control teams, 278
    integrate long- and short-term measures, 278
    let teams take the lead, 276
    use only a few key measurements, 277
  traditional performance measurement system, 274
Personnel
  place, 303
  train, 304
Platform design, 301

Prahalad, C. K., 44
Preparations for transformation, 20
  Executive Steering Board
    building a critical mass of support
      for, 26
    desired characteristics of mem-
      bers, 24
    developing an, 23
    educating the, 25
    forming the, 24
    why do we need?, 23
  heighten commitment to change
    achieving commitment for trans-
      formation, 22
    create dissatisfaction with current
      state, 20
    creating a sense of urgency, 20
    increasing the commitment to
      change, 21
    role of crises, 21
Prepare for incorporation, 296
  develop incorporation plan, 296
    should we use a pilot?, 297
    starting with a pilot, 298
  perform platform design, 301
  place and train personnel, 302
    place personnel, 302
    train personnel, 303
  prepare and provide operational
    support, 304
  prepare plan for "selling" process,
    300
  update design of existing enterprise
    system, 300
    developing the test plan, 299
    other incorporation strategies, 299
Preparing for the team-based organi-
    zation
  employee involvement and empow-
    erment, 246
  employee involvement methods, 248
    group problem solving methods,
      248
    idea generation methods, 248
    information sharing methods, 248
    work redesign methods, 248
  essence of empowerment, direction
    and capability, 246

Process architecture
  compatible with organization con-
    cept?, 164
  definition, 164
  process breakdown, 165
  smoothing process flow, 166–68
    analyze flows for redundancies,
      167
    construct the ideal flow, 168
    eliminate buffers, 166
    identify bottlenecks and balance
      the flow, 168
    maximize process throughput rate,
      168
    search for and correct discontinui-
      ties, 167
  structured, top-down design, 170
Process concept, 152
  process attributes, 152
  process objectives, 152
Process mapping
  definition, 119
  relationship to process design, 120
Process modeling
  basics of, 120
  IDEF (Icam) (DEFinition), 121
  IDEF0, functional modeling method,
    122
    A0 or context diagram, 127
    decomposition structure, 123
    main path, 126
    node index, 125
    preparing a process map, 127
    process diagram reading steps,
      125
    process map, 125
    process map organization, 122
  IDEF1, information modeling
    method, 193
    entity class, 195
    entity class diagrams, 195
    entity diagram, 197
    multiphase development, 194
    phase one: define entity classes,
      194–95
    phase two: define relation classes,
      195–96

phase three: identify key classes, 196–97
phase four: identify non-key attribute classes, 197
relation matrix, 196
IDEF1X, data modeling system, 198
IDEF3, process description capture method, 132
constrained precedence links in, 134
introduction to, 132
role of links in, 133
simple precedence links in, 133
IDEF4, object-oriented design system, 204
Process organization, need for, 114
Process redesign
basics of, 114
clean-sheet approach, 117
definition of terms, 111
function, 111
processes, 111
evolution of
business process reengineering (BPR), 114
computer-integrated manufacturing (CIM), 114
continuous process improvement (CPI), 114
just-in-time (JIT), 114
total quality management (TQM), 114
major decisions in, 117
need for, 114
Process redesign, cautions
design for the future, 118
overemphasis on large radical improvements, 119
overemphasis on processes, 119
Process redesign, creative, 160
breaking the rules, 161
from ideas to designs, 161
fundamentals of, 160
guidelines for, 163
iteration of designs, 162
Process redesign, detailed, 169
evaluate and redesign sub-processes, 160

modularize and decentralize, 174
relocate and retime controls, 173
utilize performance enablers, 174
constraints of IT and HR enablers, 176
information technology enablers, 174
organization enablers, 175
Processes, types of
core value-adding, 116
management, 117
non-core value-adding, 116
non–value-adding, 116
superfluous, 117
support, 117
value-adding, 116
Processes to be redesigned
allocate to project team for implementation
develop individual process concept, 151
prepare a project plan, 152
select for redesign
evaluate the potential costs and benefits, 148
final selection, 150
identify number of processes, 145
prioritize processes, 149
qualitative ranking of ideas, 146
screening methods for selecting, 146
selecting the method for screening, 148
weighted multi-criteria matrix, 147
Project definition, 153
Project plan, elements of, 152–53
enterprise concept, 153
enterprise process map, 153
executive summary, 152
organization and management plan, 153
process concept, 152
project definition, 153
risk management plan, 153
Project redesign team
jump starting the, 156
must understand process plan, 156
training and preparations, 157

Project team planning, 102
  stage 1: formulate the project, 102
  stage 2: charter and training, 102
  stage 3: data collection and research, 102
  stage 4: process mapping, 102
  stage 5: benchmarking, 104
  stage 6: developing integration plan, 104
Project teams
  assembling the, 98
  composition of, 96
  core team, 96
  managing, 96
  role in transformation, 96
  virtual team, 96
Prototypes and prototyping, 292

Qualitative ranking of process ideas, 146

Recruiting and selecting personnel
  selecting personnel
    criteria for selection, 273
    who makes the selection?, 273
Relation matrix, 195
Risk management plan, 153

Screening, selecting the method for, 148
Screening methods for selecting processes, 146
Simple precedence links, 129
Small's general checklist, 143
Social change
  cultural (intangible aspects), 204
  much different from technical change, 203
  nature of, 203
  tangible aspects, 203
Social management group, 35, 93
Social project team, 94
Social-technical approach
  introduction to, 15
  rationale for, 15
Strategic planning, 43
Strategic planning council, 35, 91
  role of, 45

Strategic planning process, 46–55
  conduct external analysis, 49
  conduct internal analysis, 55
  define the mission statement, 47
  define strategic intent, 48
  determining how to satisfy customers' needs, 51
  determining what needs to satisfy, 52
  determining which customers to serve, 52
  focusing on the customer, 49
  importance of internal analysis, 55
  outline of, 46
  relationship between mission and strategic intent, 49
  resources, capabilities, and competencies, 56
Strategy
  changing nature of in the 21st century, 44
  communicate new strategic direction, 65
  definition, 43
  dependence upon mission and strategic intent, 64
  evaluate results, 65
  lessons learned from the past, 44
    good strategy evolves continuously, 44
    managers must keep learning, 44
    need for cultural planning, 44
  nature of, 64
System types
  closed, 14
  open, 14
Systems approach, 14

Team-based organization
  education and training, 258
    designing an education strategy, 259
    determining education and training needs, 258
    education and training analysis (ETA), 258
    identifying critical skills, 259
    job needs analysis, 259

organizational needs analysis, 258–59
person needs analysis, 259
strategy for training, 259–60
individual learning, continuous
building individual learning, 260
creating individual learning opportunities, 261
integrating individual learning into the wider organization, 261–62
Team-based organization, detailed design
introduction, 245
preparing for the team-based organization, 245
Technical management group, 35, 93, 155
Technical project team, 94, 155
Technical redesign, 134–43
collect and analyze information, 134
collect information on future processes, 136
determine future customer requirements, 138
customer requirements feedback, 139
develop interview survey questions, 139
identify customers' future requirements, 138
identify your future customers, 142
interview/survey your customer, 143
develop enterprise process map, 134
enterprise concept, develop, 140
identify existing external customers, 134
Technical redesign of work process
determine future customer requirements, 159
document and analyze existing process, 157
identify your customers' future requirements, 160
interview your customers, 160
introduction, 155

Technobabble, 32
Transformation, integrating the, 309–19
achieving cross-functional integration, 312
integrated social-technical approach optimization of, 318
origins of the, 317–18
recursive-sequential, 319
integration through direction setting
additional guidelines for integration through direction setting, 315
importance of matching culture with strategy, 315
importance of vision, strategy and culture, 314
introduction, 313
integration through teams, 321–24
across multiple components of a business, 323
ad hoc integrating teams, 323
management teams, 323
across teams that are interdependent, 322
cross-team integrating teams, 322
liaison roles, 322
overlapping membership, 322
further actions to improve integration, 323
co-location, 323
cross-functional training, 324
prototyping and simulation, 324
team building and interpersonal skills, 324
integration through technology, 320
introduction, 309
need for integration, 310
cross-function, 311
cross-stage, 311
Transformation plan
content and structure of, 100
developing a, 99
key success factors of, 101
Transformation planning dilemmas
balance between control and empowerment, 104

plan or experiment, 105
Transformation process
  introducing the, 3
  situation facing today's organiza-
      tions, 3
    business process reengineering, 7
    convergence of products and ser-
        vices, 5
    education of the workforce, 6
    global production networks, 5
    information technology, 6
    market fragmentation, 4
    production in arbitrary lot sizes, 4
    shrinking product lifetimes, 5
    simultaneous competition and co-
        operation, 6
    societal turbulence, 4
    total quality management, 7
    workplace diversity and mobility,
        7
Transformational change
  characteristics of, 12
  implementing, 17
  nature of, 10

Value delivery system
  definition, 53
  designing a, 53
Value propositions
  choosing the right one, 62
  definition, 51
  developing, 52

matching with competencies, 61
segmenting the customer base by
    benefits, 54
Virtual organization, 233
Vision, 314
Vision, communication of
  communicate by example, 33
  interactive two-way communication,
      33
  keep it simple, 32
  repeat, repeat, repeat, 33
  use many different forums, 32
  use metaphor, analogy, and exam-
      ple, 32
Vision, enterprise
  creating the vision, 29
  developing an, 28
  nature of an effective vision, 29
  relationship to other company plans,
      31
  testing and improving, 30
  vision, communication of, 31
  why vision is essential, 28

Weighted multi-criteria matrix, 147
Work teams design, 249
  composition of work teams, 250
  external connections, 251
  implementing work teams, 252
  information resources, 251
  inputs to, 250
  team leadership, 250

About the Author

HOWARD W. ODEN is a consultant and Associate Professor of Management at Nichols College, Dudley, Massachusetts, specializing in entrepreneurship, innovation, and the management of organizational change. He has published more than 40 technical papers and four books, including *Managing Corporate Culture, Innovation, and Entrepreneurship* (Quorum, 1997).

ISBN 1-56720-226-8

9 781567 202267

HARDCOVER BAR CODE